Knights for the Blind
in the
Battle against Darkness

Volume One

The Esoteric Helen Keller

Animation, Eloquence, Mystery

Doug Baldwin

ISBN: 978-1-7369953-0-3

*Cover art & illustrations by Terry LeBarr, Swanton, OH
(gonefishn@yahoo.com)*
The great cover illustrations and the artwork throughout all my books were designed and brought to life by my friend Terry LeBarr in Swanton, Ohio. I am delighted by Terry's drawings and I am proud of Terry's important contribution to the Helen Keller story and to the important themes in this book. The cover for this book is especially wonderful. There is something splendid in the quiet eloquence of Helen standing motionless beside a stone wall, framed by a beautiful tree. Helen's daily walks often took her to a stone wall that ran through her property. She loved to be outside in nature.

*Book design by Sarah E. Holroyd
(https://sleepingcatbooks.com)*
The cover and interior layout of this book were designed by Sarah Holroyd. Sarah's work is excellent (wonderful), I appreciate her many talents, and I am proud of our longstanding professional relationship. Sarah is the owner of Sleeping Cat Books, an author services company which provides copyediting, proofreading, and print/ebook services to independent authors. Sarah also runs Sleeping Cat Press, which releases bilingual English-French editions and multi-author anthologies.

Contents

INTRODUCTION

The very fact that we are still here carrying on the contest against the hosts of annihilation proves that on the whole the battle has gone for humanity. ~ *Out of the Dark*, by Helen Keller, 1913.

Who is this book for?

Something benevolent called me to write this book—that was my end of an unseen bargain, to let intuitive energy guide my words. I do not know why synchronicity brought *you* to the book. I imagine that you have a spiritual guardian in charge of your reading list. Whether you believe in spiritual guardians or not, there you are, here I am—let us get on with the mutual task at hand. Welcome to the journey.

As I wrote this book, seeking answers to human cognition through a study of Helen Keller's mind, I realized that I was not alone on my quest. I sense that this book is for people like you who never stop seeking to understand themselves. I like to think that Helen Keller guided both of us to this place.

There are many like-minded individuals who track Helen Keller books. I am one of those creatures; I have a small Helen Keller library, which slowly expanded the more I researched her fascinating and unusual life. Welcome to those readers who also admire and appreciate Helen Keller and Annie Sullivan. This book is unique; no other book in your collection is like this volume.

This is my fifth book; the last four books were essentially explorations into the evolution of human consciousness. There is a growing population of people, all over the planet, who are becoming obsessed with comprehending consciousness. How does the human mind work, they wonder? How *should* a human mind develop? How might a deaf-blind wunderkind like Helen Keller help with our efforts to understand understanding? Helen Keller was determined that human beings evolve their consciousness—for Helen, this meant the evolution of spirituality, a collective effort to become a kinder species. Therefore, this book is for individuals seeking to understand their own minds, people who are working to create a kinder world.

Helen and I, and quite probably you, agree that human beings cannot go on killing each other and trashing the planet—something must change, and that change must occur in the minds of human beings. A cognitive evolution must occur; we must become the agents of our own transformation. As I said in my science fiction book (*A Martyr for Mandelbrot*), "It is no longer okay to be stupid." Fortunately, it is possible for each of us, in our own fashion, to grow out of being stupid and unkind. Helen Keller holds many clues to how we can collectively become a kinder and more reasonable species.

I also wrote this book because, as a special education teacher, I taught blind kids for over thirty years and felt a responsibility to share what I had discovered from the challenges of teaching. I owe my former students and their parents for all the love sent in my direction. I was blessed to have my job and now I am called upon to give some love back. Therefore, this book is for people who are blind, or deaf, or deaf-blind and, as well, for their families, friends, and teachers.

I often imagine talking with graduate students studying in my field (Orientation and Mobility). For thirty years, I taught blind and severely visually impaired students to independently navigate. I wish I could have professionally helped Helen Keller and Anne Sullivan; there is much Helen did not know despite her magnificent mind. Therefore, this book is also for graduate students, their professors, and for the experts in the field of Blind Rehabilitation—especially Orientation and Mobility Specialists.

A common theme in my books has been that the profession of Orientation and Mobility (O&M) needs to change its primary focus. I have argued that O&M specialists need to work with people who have navigational disabilities, not just with blind people. Therefore, this book makes a plea for change in my chosen profession, suggesting a road to transformation. Consequently, this book is for the high-level thinkers in my field who are open to dialogue about alternative futures for our profession.

Finally, this book is for my immediate and extended family and for my good friends; they are the ones in my life who are consistent, who politely care about my Egoic obsessions—as I care deeply about their well-being and their passions.

The Heartbeat of the Book: Helen Keller's Mind

You would not be reading these words if Helen Keller had not called to you, as she has been calling to me for decades now. I invite you to join me on a voyage of discovery, a fresh look at the mind of Helen Keller.

Most of us first encounter Helen's story in elementary school; she is a favorite subject in children's literature. Helen's story is considered a classic tale, a hero's journey. She was deaf and blind and yet she carved out a fascinating life. She could not see, and she could not hear, but she set out to make the world a better place—and she succeeded. The heroine won out over disability and against impossible odds.

Maybe, as you got older you saw the classic black and white movie *The Miracle Worker* with that unforgettable scene at the breakfast table—that epic battle between two extraordinary females; Helen was six (almost seven) and Anne Sullivan was twenty-one when that memorable "food fight" broke out and shocked audiences.

Maybe you saw the stage play and watched in awe, tears running down your face, as Helen Keller stood suddenly very still, stunned, as water flowed over her fingers at the famous water pump scene and then, suddenly—like lightning striking—Helen realized that there was a way for a deaf-blind girl to communicate with others and a way to learn about the world. Your heart just about stops when moments later you watch Helen tenderly ask Anne Sullivan's name and Sullivan spells T-E-A-C-H-E-R on the palm of Helen's hand. As a teacher myself, that image sends chills of gladness through my soul.

I suspect you know about the miracle and the miracle worker; you arrived at this moment already knowledgeable.[1] Therefore, you are right to ask if this book is different from all that came before. The answer is yes, this is a fresh approach. It will take a few chapters to lay out the new perspectives, but I can give you some important beginning hints in this introduction.

My journey with Helen Keller did not end after I read about her in elementary school and after I saw the black and white classic movie when I was a teenager. I did not see, as a young college student studying visual science, that my career would be in special education teaching blind children. I did not know that Anne Sullivan would be a role model for teachers like me who work every day with severely impaired children—thirty years, in my case.[2] The journey of Helen Keller and Anne Sullivan felt deeply personal to me. As I worked on this book, I began to feel an attachment to the two women, and that attachment slowly turned into love, awe, appreciation, and thankfulness.

As I grew older, Helen Keller felt like a friendly shadow; her story, her struggles and triumphs were in the background as I moved through my career. One event stood out for me. I married my wife Katherine in the afternoon of Saturday June 1, 1968. As I was saying "I do," to Katherine, Helen Keller was saying "Goodbye" to the world. Helen died in the afternoon of June 1, 1968 at her home (Arcan Ridge 2) near Westport, Connecticut. She died peacefully, "drifting off in her sleep," just a few weeks before her 88th birthday. I was 23 and Katherine was 22 on that first day of June when we married in the Episcopal church in downtown Flint, Michigan.

I am curious about synchronicities—like the coincidence of marriage and death—and I enjoy imagining that life is magical; I sense that serendipity arrives mysteriously, seemingly without reason. I am a self-ordained romantic optimist, walking around happily in a Shakespeare-like play where *all the world is a stage*. This playful perspective is a product of my senior years—I was not always so optimistic. I suspect my consciousness evolved because of my life journey.

Maybe, you feel something similar; maybe you also feel like your life is a stage play and you have the leading role. When we envision ourselves in this personal stage play, we also envision magic energy following us around, protecting us, guiding us. It seems we should occasionally put aside the hardnosed science that is rightfully suspicious of synchronicity and "magic." We should, I think, strut proudly around on the stage that is our life and be okay with feeling an aura of magic engulfing our bodies. Which brings me to the purpose for this book, to that which is fresh, fascinating, and magically inspired.

As you see from the title, this is Volume One of a book series called *Knights for the Blind in the Battle against Darkness*. This first volume is called *The Esoteric Helen Keller*. Basically, the term "esoteric" means *hidden*—however, keep in mind that there are many nuances and layers to the concept of *hiddenness*. Think of an archeological excavation. As we dig deeper and deeper in an exploratory trench, we encounter earlier and earlier cultures. The same applies when we dig deeper and deeper into the evolutionary history of the human mind; as we explore human consciousness, we find ever more insights that were previously hidden. The evolution of human consciousness plays a central role in this review of Helen Keller's mind.

There is magic afoot, synchronicity, serendipity, the opening act of a stage play about a mysterious woman who was deaf and blind, an unusual woman, remarkable and lovable. However, we do not gain much by just studying the outward appearances of Helen Keller's life, and, anyway, that has been done numerous times and does not need to be repeated. We love a good story, especially a hero's journey, but just laying down a person's history is insufficient; lovely "secrets" are missed when we just skim the surface of a life.

The deepest mysteries of life are hidden, clouded over by our primary senses, vision, and hearing. When we examine Helen's life, we can do so without clouds of vision and clouds of hearing obstructing our view—we can more clearly perceive Helen's soul when the clouds of attention clear. Our own souls also come into sharper focus when we stop paying so much attention to hearing and vision. In other words, Helen helps us envision our own souls, which lie hidden behind visual and auditory appearances. I suggest to you that Helen Keller's life is a portal, a window we can peer into that will inform us about our own spiritual development.

But now I am sailing toward the fringes of things and I do not want to lose your interest. Trust me, it is worth your time to peer into Helen Keller's mind. Maybe, as we explore *levels of consciousness* together you might sense that something is hidden inside of you. Perhaps that which is hidden is your soul, the "eyes of the heart," looking around and within at hidden worlds. Helen Keller is the beginning of our journey to locate that which is hidden within us.

Most of our lives are quite busy, with spouses, children, jobs, births and deaths, good times, and bad times. We do not have much opportunity in our younger years for speculating about souls and spirits and the meaning of life. However, after retirement, especially when we reach our senior years, as I have, we can turn our attention to spirituality. We can ask how we got here on this planet. What was our purpose in the few decades that we visited the earth? Many of us, as is true for me, ask if we might still make a few contributions before we must exit life.

I retired in 2010 and was enjoying the last decades of my life when I got an urge to write books. I had always wanted to write, but career and family joys had kept my focus on my kids, my wife, and on my profession. However, when my seventies arrived and the kids and grandkids were living in other states, and Katherine had died from ovarian cancer after a long battle, I was suddenly alone in Saginaw, Michigan (just me and Napoleon, my daughter Annie's cat who came to visit about ten years ago and, thankfully, never left). Writing books gave me a purpose and a way to contribute—a late-in-life mission, for which I am deeply grateful.

I spent a career, over thirty years, teaching blind kids how to navigate their environment; I have been blessed by the experience of being a special education teacher.[3] I felt deeply that I should give something back before my life ran out. I had learned a few things and I was determined not to die before I got it down on paper and shared what I had discovered. Having a mission in our elder years is an important choice that aids in mental well-being.

As I said above, I wrote four books before this one; two are textbook-like tomes about the evolution of consciousness and the last was science fiction, also about the evolution of consciousness. The first book, *Bugs, Blindness, and the Pursuit of Happiness* (2016), was a successful experiment in self-publishing. All the books had the same focus: I had found a connection between navigation and the evolution of consciousness; a *new slant* I called it because I did not want to imply that I had ultimate answers to how human minds work. I just wanted to make a small contribution alongside the professionals who struggle daily to figure out how human cognition works. I figured it was okay if my profession, Orientation and Mobility, offered a small contribution to the vast, global effort to understand consciousness.

You will understand, I hope, that because of my career and passions I could not write about Helen Keller without trying to understand her unique deaf-blind mind in a larger context, around the evolution of cognition. I am quite sure Helen is okay with my speculations. She spent her life in the service of others; *the foundation of Helen Keller's philosophy of life is Love.* My long cognitive journey to comprehend human consciousness arrives at a similar Philosophy of Love.[4]

When I started writing this book, my main concern was professional. Knowing how human beings navigate, I was able to ask how a deaf-blind person could continue to navigate after the sudden loss of vision and hearing. My background gave me license to speculate on Helen's cognitive strengths and weaknesses. I could dip into neuroscience and speculate on how a brain rewires itself after severe sensory loss. However, as I did the research and as I speculated, other questions besides navigational ability arose.

For example, how did Helen Keller develop such a profound ability to remember; why was her memory so unusually astute? How did Helen's mind become so articulate and so sophisticated (so early) compared to others in her culture? Why did her level of consciousness move so quickly beyond her culture? Why did Helen's remarkable mind guide her in a humanitarian direction? Why did Love and Service arise as prime motivators for her? Why did Helen become a socialist, a suffragette, an author with a profound mastery of language? And are these questions related? Is there a common denominator? Does a rewired brain hold the key to all these queries? This complex book, about the evolution of Helen Keller's mind, quickly took on parallel and, at times, overlapping themes. I soon realized that I was using different lenses to peer into Helen's development.

～

I get up every morning and stagger sleepy-eyed, coffee in hand, to my computer. On some mornings, I awake with insights that beg to be added to the book. This morning, for example, was such a morning. I thrashed about in a dream state for what seemed hours. I had experienced a dream about the violence that would visit the human species if occupants of Planet Earth did not take the next decade of brain/mind research exceedingly seriously.

We are entering a critical time in history. We are learning, very rapidly, how to alter the human brain. In effect, altering the neocortex of the brain alters worldviews—what we think, how we react emotionally, and how we behave depends on how reality appears to us. Helen Keller had a neocortex crafted by deaf-blindness; her worldview, which she stated clearly and often, was that Love should create humanity's reality. Helen felt that Love should create the future. Where there is no Love, there is a vacuum, a nothingness. That vacuum sucks ill-will and violence into the world. At the moment, there is no universal, international agreement that Love should create humanity's future.

Helen Keller felt that human minds should be crafted to become kind, empathetic, peace-loving, and tolerant—above all else, compassion should guide our decisions. Our goal, as we deliberately alter human brains (alter our very DNA), should not just be about intellectual excellence, or athletic prowess, or physical beauty. These are secondary to loving-kindness. Helen Keller is an example of "right thinking and right feeling;" she is a role model for how we should direct the evolution of the human mind.

A few scientists are re-engineering the human brain as if it were a supercomputer sitting on a lab desk, as if the search for greater intelligence was our goal—essentially, ignoring the evolution of compassion. Science is giving us the power to control our own cognitive evolution at a very primitive time in human history, when wars still rage, pandemics still outmatch medicine, the climate still spins out of control, and leadership is polarized to the point of paralysis.

It is also true that we do not know how minds work and how they should evolve. Each generation seems to believe that it has, more or less, reached the pinnacle of understanding, as if no more surprises—like neuroplasticity, synesthesia, and epigenetics—remain to be discovered. Prescription mind-altering drugs and various illegal hallucinogens suggest that we are just at the beginning of our ability to alter the mind. It seems quite clear that there are surprises ahead—there are technologies of consciousness (mind control, mind expansion, esoteric serendipities) we cannot yet even conceive—yet we march exponentially forward to build robots and AI systems that alter worldviews and behaviors. We do not have a plan and we do not have international oversight. Helen Keller would keep asking, "Where is compassion, tolerance, and Love in this exponential mad dash into the blades of the future?"

On the other hand, Helen Keller would salute the march of science as it endeavors to understand consciousness, even though playing God is obviously quite dangerous. Ethics and global cooperation must rise to the surface of the debate. Modern minds that are as sophisticated as Helen Keller's mind need to lead the effort to keep kindness at the forefront of the dialogue as we craft the future of consciousness.

This exploration into Helen Keller's consciousness is an opportunity for you to examine the evolution of *your own* consciousness. I cannot shake the esoteric notion that you are meant to be on this road trip—the right people seem to arrive at the right time to begin a shared journey. The world is much stranger and more wonderful than we have so far discovered. Take a seat, the Esoteric Express is pulling out of the station.

Outline of the Book

The central theme of this book is Helen Keller's mind. Each chapter looks at her cognitive development through a different lens, including esotericism and the evolution of consciousness. I am building a cognitive gestalt from many different puzzle pieces.

There are two immediate responsibilities that need to be addressed as we begin this book. I already told you that this is the first volume in a series, and I told you that esotericism—the exploration of Helen Keller's "hidden" mind—is an important theme. Therefore, my first task in **Chapter One** is to discuss *Knights for the Blind*, the authors I chose to celebrate in these volumes. There are common themes that run through the books in this series, and I need to make those themes clear to you from the beginning. I call Chapter One Knights for the Blind in the Battle against Darkness.

Not many admirers of Helen Keller and Anne Sullivan would also be esoteric scholars. Clearly, I had to explain what this field of study was about and why I felt it was relevant to Helen Keller's cognitive development. This is fascinating stuff, handed down through the ages by our ancestors. I hope you enjoy these ancient, but still highly significant concepts. I call **Chapter Two** *The Esoteric Helen Keller.*

It was also my task to look at Helen's history. You might have arrived here with little awareness of Helen's life. Others know a lot about Helen Keller's story but have missed important insights. In the interest of filling in gaps in the dialogue about Helen Keller and Anne Sullivan, I wrote a companion book to this text that follows Helen's life in a chronological sequence. The companion book is called *Helen Keller: A Timeline of Her Life.* Initially, the timeline was a chapter for this book, but it grew so large it became its own volume. If you need or want background information before diving into the complex study of Helen's mental evolution, have a look at the companion book.

Chapter Three is called The Evolution of Helen Keller's Mind. This is the *emotional heart* of my efforts. I developed a theory about the evolution of consciousness in my earlier books and I applied that complex theory to Helen Keller's mind in this book. I hope you find the discussion of levels of consciousness as fascinating as I do. This chapter is also a template for how I will peer into other complex minds in the volumes after this book.

Exploring levels of consciousness is delicate business; the potential for misunderstanding and alarm is great. I found myself dancing on the edges of things one moment and then plunging into the deep end the next moment. This chapter is a tool for self-study as well as a tool for cautiously considering the worldviews of others.

Chapter Four is a philosophical and scientific exploration of navigation and consciousness—this chapter is the *intellectual heart* of my efforts. There is a reason why Helen Keller was able to move around on her own without sights and sounds to guide her, and there are reasons why she developed such a complex and awe-inspiring mind.

This academic section is perhaps most relevant to cognitive scientists and philosophers; however, this erudite discussion is a new way to look at human cognition—well worth everyone's effort, in my opinion. Scholars who are interested in the evolution of consciousness will incorporate my viewpoint into their own—accepting or rejecting my perspective based on their own knowledge base. Hopefully, something good will come of that future blending of minds and I will have made a small contribution to the dialogue about the evolution of human consciousness. Chapter Four is called *Our Strange Duet*.

Chapter Four explores current brain science blended with cognitive philosophy. It is a deep dive into the biology and architecture of the brain and mind; the chapter soars well beyond Helen Keller. I followed my instincts and passions as I crafted this discussion, knowing full well that it was beyond the purview of most Helen Keller enthusiasts.

Chapter Five draws on the research and philosophies of others who contributed to the cognitive philosophy I call Navigational Consciousness; this chapter was added to support the evolutionary perspective discussed in Chapter Four. I looked first at two philosophers, Søren Kierkegaard and Rudolf Steiner and compared their worldviews with Helen Keller. I then looked briefly at the professional (neuroscience) perspective of three remarkable men: Cambridge professor Simon Baron-Cohen, Jeff Hawkins, creator of the neuroscience center Numenta, and futurist Ray Kurzweil. I added three final sections on navigation: Quantum Navigation; Expanding the Concept of Navigation; and Why Navigational Consciousness Matters.

When I finished writing Chapters Four and Five, I realized that I had just embedded an entire cognitive philosophy into the middle of a book about Helen Keller. I instinctively realized that there was no way to explain a miracle like Helen Keller without addressing the miracle of consciousness.

Chapter Six is called *A Wonderful Child*. Anne Sullivan insisted that no one was going to turn her student into a child prodigy, so I entered this chapter with trepidation, even though I felt it necessary to go against Sullivan's wishes. The Egoic mind likes to label, categorize, and make judgments, so it is easy for the Ego to call Helen Keller a prodigy. However, the Self (the Soul) is not sure that labeling is a good idea in a world that is always in flux; truth seems always paradoxical and many-layered.

Clearly, Helen was proficient with language in a way that is extraordinary for a deaf-blind individual; it is her language facility that suggests she was a child prodigy. Language was key to the evolution of Helen Keller's remarkable mind. In Chapter Six, I explored the controversial idea that Helen became a linguistic prodigy. I also came to a rather obvious conclusion, as I ended Chapter Six, that Helen Keller could justifiably be referred to as a Spiritual Prodigy.

As I edited Chapter Six (repeatedly), I could see that I had spiraled into a morass of caveats. The whole arena of labeling is a mine field. I felt very self-conscious as I contrived to weave magic into Helen's quite normal life. Indeed, she and everyone around her insisted that her accomplishments were just extraordinary adaptions. She was not an alien with superhuman abilities. She was a lovely human being with strong moral values and deep compassion.

In **Chapter Seven**, I asked the question *What if Helen Keller had been trained by my colleague Daniel Kish and his Visioneering Team?* What if Helen Keller had studied spatial layouts, used a long cane and modern technology, and been trained by an Orientation and Mobility specialist to use Egocentric and Allocentric processing? What if she had a guide dog (which she probably would have, given her love of dogs)? In other words, if Helen Heller had been born today, what new tools and strategies could she have used to acquire deeper insights about the world? How might her mind have evolved differently?

Chapter Seven is also a great introduction to my friend and colleague Daniel Kish. As a blind pioneer, famous for using active echolocation for navigation, Daniel is an intellectual phenomenon himself and he is the subject of volume two in this series.[5] Daniel stands on the shoulders of Helen Keller and Anne Sullivan (he is a combination of both their souls).[6] Daniel's mission, his passion, and his stubborn determination complement the work and spiritual mission of both the miracle Helen Keller and the miracle worker Anne Sullivan. In this chapter, Helen passes the torch to Daniel Kish and his *Visioneering* team. This chapter is called *Passing the Torch to the Visionaries.*

CHAPTER ONE: KNIGHTS FOR THE BLIND

The Seven Knightly Virtues: Courage, Justice, Mercy, Generosity, Faith, Nobility, Hope.

Cultural Warriors

This book series is about Knights for the Blind, cultural warriors who fought against ignorance and neglect, human beings who made the decision to be of service to others—these are the Blind Knights who went into battle to win basic human rights for others like them. Each of these Knights went into battle without being able to see, yet Helen Keller is the most famous of them because she fought the demons with neither light nor sound to guide her. She was a champion for human rights long before that idea was culturally acceptable.

There are five overlapping themes that weave through the lives of the extraordinary blind individuals featured in this book series. I will reiterate these themes in each volume of the series.

One: *Knights for the Blind are foremost champions for social justice, not only for blind and disabled people, but for everyone.* Helen Keller stands above all others because she had a broad human rights agenda, speaking not just for the blind, or the deaf, or the deaf-blind, or women, or the poor, but for all suffering humanity, a group that includes you and me.

I like author Georgina Kleege's comment—about herself as a blind woman—toward the end of her book about Helen Keller called *Blind*

Rage (2006). It is a good message for the naysayers (the "Normals," as Professor Kleege calls us):

> I don't enjoy feeling like we exist to offer illuminating insights to the Normals. But in my more generous moments (few and far between as they are), I feel it's something worth doing. They need a lot of help. [7]

I think Helen Keller, Daniel Kish, and Jacques Lusseyran—authors featured in this book series—would agree with Professor Kleege: *the sighted need a lot of help* with their worldviews and attitudes. It is ironic that a deaf-blind girl, after examining her own fate, found a way to profoundly help the perceptually deaf-blind Normals. By the time she was a teenager, Helen Keller had already proclaimed that her task in life, her passion, would be to address universal suffering. She developed a Christ-like consciousness and the heart of a Buddha. She also carried through with her teenage dedication. She put her proclamations into action; she made a difference in her time, and she continues to impact lives to this day.

Two: *Each author, in their own way, saw blindness **not** as a tragic life-ending disaster but as a challenging gift.* Helen Keller *saw life as a gift*—in all its many imperfect forms. She did not see herself as a mythological superhero, even though history has insisted on holding her high above the rest of us. Helen Keller was radiant and eloquent; we listen to her with respect and awe. We stare at Helen's sweet smile, like we stare at the Mona Lisa, with her enigmatic grin, and we wonder what is going on in that deaf-blind universe. Here Helen is speaking to the sighted population:

> We differ, blind and seeing, not in the nature of our handicap, but in the understanding and idealism we put into the art of living. It is only when we put imagination and feeling behind the senses that they attain their full value. [8]

Helen Keller is telling us that all humanity has a common bond: here we stand, shoulder-to-shoulder on this planet. Suffering is inherent in our dimension. What seems to set us apart—regardless of physical characteristics—is how we master the art of living, how we deal with suffering. Knights for the Blind tell us that we can determine our individual response to suffering. We can forge an attitude about life; we can choose to see life as a gift, or we can dwell in boredom or depression.

Three: *Each of the authors discovered that their perceptions were different from the sighted in fundamental ways.* Consequently, many blind authors pondered how the mind works, and they considered how a blind-mind functioned compared to a sighted-mind. Several blind authors explored what it means to be conscious.

Helen Keller said on more than one occasion—echoing the sentiments of her good friend Mark Twain—that human beings, the Normals, were deaf-blind creatures. This was a dig at the level of consciousness of most humans who sleepwalk through their days. Perhaps she also meant that many of the common folk were not very empathetic or creative. They might go to church for the requisite hours on Sunday, for example, but they were not very Christian in their daily actions—they served nobody except themselves. However, I think there is a deeper meaning to her statement that most of humanity is perceptually deaf and blind.

When Helen was a Phantom (her self-definition), alone in her dark silence before Anne Sullivan arrived, she was deaf-blind to the wonders and horrors that sight and sound reveal. Helen Keller asks suffering humanity: What if there is more than eyes and ears reveal? What if the Normals are deaf-blind to a greater spirituality, to additional senses, to esoteric hidden worlds that reside behind physical appearances? We know about the spaces and forms that sight reveals, and we know the sound of events in our auditory landscape. But suppose there is a spiritual realm, an esoteric reality, that cannot be seen or heard with these senses—or perhaps can only be perceived using whole-body vibratory sensing. Helen Keller was connected to such a vibratory universe. Her life suggests that the Normals are missing something deeply fundamental and supremely important.

Perhaps we all need an Anne Sullivan who can lead us to a mythological water pump to reveal a different kind of language and new sensory modalities. We will stay perceptually and spiritually deaf-blind until we learn to perceive in new and powerful ways.

Four: *There is also a spiritual core that weaves through each author's life. Something about blindness offers a different perspective or understanding of spirituality.*

Besides being a warrior for human rights, there is something else equally powerful to remember: There is a *spiritual defiance* in Helen Keller that smolders below the surface. Outwardly, she is mild-mannered, she greets the world with that sweet smile on her face, she offers her open palm to each visitor, but she has a power, a little frightening, that transcends silence and darkness. There seems to be a well of creativity in the universe that comes through a portal that is dark and silent; Helen was closer to this well of creativity, closer to the Source than the rest of us. She got the message, through this portal, long before most of the Normals did, that human consciousness needed to evolve.

Helen Keller gave her entire life to her religious creed: *care about and serve others*, take care of your own self, care about the Earth, and care about all the creatures that dwell alongside humanity—bring love to the effort. In other words, dedicate your life to making the world a kinder place. There is suffering all around the globe, generation after generation is born into an imperfect world, and no one escapes the grief and angst of existence. Instead of complaining about our lives, instead of feeling sorry for ourselves, instead of churning in a sea of angst, *we should be actively working* to make things better, moment-to-moment, one sentient creature at a time, one problem at a time. *A deaf-blind girl did it.* Sit with that powerful image for a moment. That deaf-blind girl is our role model.

I believe, as did Helen Keller, that there is an evolutionary trend toward compassion and wisdom; a light is driving out the darkness of ignorance and cruelty. Helen Keller found this message in her religion; she learned to sense spiritual (vibratory) energy, and, as she did so, she modeled what humanity ought to be doing. She showed us by the example of her life how our consciousness ought to be evolving.

Five: Understanding navigation is a common thread that appears in the writings of most blind authors. Every blind or visually impaired individual is faced with the challenge of safe and efficient movement—purposeful movement is severely impacted by blindness; adaptations are necessary.

There is little in the literature about Helen's ability to navigate on her own—there seemed always to be a friend nearby to guide her movements, or a wall to follow, or a rope to guide the way. Almost always someone had her in their sights as she explored the world. She did not use a cane and she received no navigational training—there were no mobility specialists available in her youth. However, she *could* get around her own living spaces without guidance, and she quickly learned new spaces as she encountered them. When Anne Sullivan first encountered Helen in Tuscumbia, Alabama, Helen was racing around the house as if she could see and hear. How could this be?

It is hard enough for the lay population to understand how anyone who is blind could learn to navigate independently. Add deafness to the equation, and then self-motivated, efficient navigation seems even more outside the realm of possibility. However, as Orientation and Mobility specialists know, blind individuals can easily navigate environments using the remaining senses. It is much more difficult to teach navigation to the deaf-blind, but it is possible—Helen Keller learned her way around her house even without formal training.

There is something profound waiting to walk onto the stage of human awareness. There is an aha! moment waiting to happen. Many astute blind individuals become aware of a hidden profundity, even if they are not able to explain their intuition. Simply put, *human navigation holds a secret to the evolution of human consciousness.* The blind authors in this book series knew intuitively that this was true, because they could feel their own consciousness struggle when faced with diminished ease of movement. They knew that their very core was affected when animation was restricted, and they wrote about their angst. My study of these blind experts helped me visualize a dual-process theory of consciousness based on the evolution of navigation, which I will tell you about as our journey continues.

Astute Blind Authors

> My Darkness had been filled with the light of intelligence, and behold, the outer day-lit world was stumbling and groping in social blindness! [9]

Astute blind authors often write about the challenges they face that are in addition to the day-to-day issues arising from physical blindness. These extra challenges arise from ignorance and false assumptions held by members of their cultures. Therefore, blind authors often confront (and write about) pervasive *social* and *perceptual* ignorance; they perceive a universal cultural blindness that negatively impacts their lives. As many blind authors point out, most sighted individuals are not aware of *their own* perceptual limitations. Here is how Helen Keller expressed her feelings in a speech to the Twentieth Century Club in 1922:

> It is easier to teach the blind to see the beauty of the universe than to teach ignorance to think and insensitivity to feel. Many people with perfect ears are emotionally deaf, and many with splendid eyes are blind in their perceptions.

That quote is a brilliant summation of the challenges faced by blind people, both historically and existing to this day. Most sighted people have not examined their own essence; therefore, most sighted people have varieties of mind-blindness. Ironically, most sighted people are unaware of their own cognitive blindness—they have not followed the famous dictum of Socrates: *Know thyself.*

The saying *Know thyself* is a principle of esotericism, which I will address in the next chapter. It is easy to misinterpret this gem of wisdom, so I will take a moment to elaborate. The saying does not refer to the Ego; it refers to the Soul (the Self). The saying means to "understand your Soul." Socrates was talking about a kind of knowledge called *Gnosis,* which is the source of wisdom.

The Gnostics, an early sect of Christianity, differentiated Egoic-knowledge from Soul-knowledge. *Know thyself* is a proclamation that human beings have two minds, an Egoic-mind and a Gnostic-mind. To know thyself means to understand cognitive duality and to comprehend the distinction between our two minds. Human beings know about their Egos, but the Self (Soul) has been hidden from them. In a way, "To know thyself" is to understand the source of esotericism, the source of that which is hidden—which is the Soul. This is a complex understanding. I will discuss cognitive duality in detail in Chapter Four.

The adult Helen Keller could sense her soul operating beneath her Egoic mind. She understood that human beings had dual minds, even though she never said this directly in her writings. Helen's powerful Faith came from her Soul; she had *intuitive knowing* as well as *intellectual understanding.*

Helen Keller teaches us that you do not have to see or hear to perceive ignorance and cruelty. She also taught us that a deaf-blind voice can be just as powerful, articulate, and impactful as a sighted voice. Like Helen Keller, the other blind authors featured in this book series were powerful and articulate. Knights for the Blind came to know that *all of humanity is* navigating through darkness and silence.

The universe that is your mind cannot be understood by me or by anyone else on the planet. You are alone, encased inside a mental miracle, or so it feels to our Egoic Mind. However, beneath the surface of everyday reality, beneath the turbulent waves of everyday challenges, we sense an undercurrent; we feel a connection to other minds. We begin to wonder (to challenge) if it is true—as the Ego insists—that we are alone in our conscious world.

We can try to communicate with others with our unique Egoic Minds, but if we become convinced that we can completely understand another's mind, we are fooling ourselves. One cognitive galaxy cannot completely understand another cognitive galaxy; consciousness is too complex. Therefore, an innate *social blindness is a fundamental property of humanity.* We are trying to communicate through a social darkness, hoping to relate to others in our everyday world, but we always fall short; misunderstandings and false assumptions *inevitably* color human interactions.

We are also *perceptually* blind creatures. What we personally sense in the environment is not the same as what others are sensing. But we assume that our sensations and perceptions are identical to others because things get done in a cooperative way; something works *well enough.* Dig below the surface, however, and the truth unravels into chaos. *Perceptual blindness is pervasive and is another fundamental property of humanity*—our ability to pay *attention* and our ability to be *aware* (two distinct abilities) are fleeting and flawed. We are navigating through darkness, hoping to arrive happy and safe at some distant location where we can exist peacefully alongside others.

Physically blind individuals must contend with *both* the perceptual blindness and the social blindness inherent in their cultures, *as well as* the challenges of actual blindness. Ironically, physically blind individuals often find the attitudes, the intolerance and insensitivity of their fellow (sighted) humans to be a far greater challenge than physical blindness. As we explore blindness in the pages (and books) ahead, keep in mind the pervasive social and perceptual blindness inherent in the human condition; it is a theme that arises repeatedly in the writings of blind authors.

Helen Keller was fiercely strong-willed. From a young age she insisted on doing things her own way. She had little patience for those who tried to impose their worldviews on her. She knew that mind-blindness was pervasive in her culture and she had little patience for people who had not examined their own cognition. In her journal, (written shortly after the death of Anne Sullivan) Helen reflects on her own independent spirit:

> A gust of irritability is blowing through me just now because there has been a recurrence of a tendency in some people to try to run my affairs. This seems all the stranger to me because since I was seventeen, I have arranged my own life. At the age of twenty-two I began working very hard for whatever money I have earned during the past thirty-four years. Of my own accord I have undertaken public responsibilities in America and other lands. After Teacher's health broke down, I worked very much alone with Polly's hand to furnish information and her voice to reinforce my halting speech. Yet there are still those who appear to think it is incumbent upon them to alter my life course according to their own ideas! There was some excuse when I was young and bewildered in the search of something worth doing. But mother and Teacher knew me better than anybody else ever did, and they never dictated the course of action I should follow . . . Unless I keep on my guard against uncalled-for though well-meant interference, they cannot help me any more than they can help any other person who weakly surrenders his will to another. [10]

In the above paragraph, Helen admits what we see clearly in retrospect; it was primarily her mother, Kate Adams Keller, and her teacher, Anne Sullivan Macy who gave Helen emotional stability as she slowly evolved her own confidence and talent. After both their deaths, Helen carried on remarkably well and with great conviction and eloquence. It was Polly Thomson who assumed the roles left unattended when Kate Keller and then Anne Sullivan died. Whatever healthy, loving support she got during her lifetime, Helen Keller was her own woman, an utterly amazing human being.

Astounded as I am at Helen's remarkable life, I felt mildly uncomfortable as I read the above quote. For I have gone ahead and put words in Helen's mouth at times in this book and I have assigned an esoteric label to her complex life. I hope she is looking down at my efforts with approval, although I am sure she would also feel occasional irritation at the assumption that anyone could know her mind, her vivid emotions, or her spiritual complexity.

Reluctantly Having to Choose

For those who are deaf or deaf-blind who come to these words, I apologize for my emphasis on blindness. Blind rehabilitation was my profession, what I know, and where I feel confident to expound. There is another universe of knowledge and experience in the arena of deafness and again in the arena of deaf-blindness. I will sometimes speak of these arenas, but with much less authority. There are sophisticated deaf and deaf-blind cultures within which highly capable writers and artists could explore the life of Helen Keller if that was their desire. I leave it to others more qualified than I am to explore Helen Keller's deafness and her deaf-blindness.

Helen Keller also felt this conflict—to serve two missions—however, she ended up reluctantly having to choose. Here are her own words on the subject:

> Lack of hearing has always been a heavier handicap to me than blindness. Sealed ears render more difficult every path to knowledge. The deaf are as hungry for a word as the blind are for a book under their fingers, yet it is harder to find people who will talk with the deaf than people who will supply the sightless with embossed books. That has not been my individual experience, I am glad to say. Sympathy has sweetened my days within society; religion and philosophy have assuaged my sorrows; but I remain unsatisfied, thinking how many deaf persons are immured and lonely through others' neglect or impatience. Regretfully I perceive the impossibility of working for both the blind and the deaf as I have often longed to do. The effort to alleviate misfortune more than fills a lifetime; and besides these tasks are redoubled by the endeavor to safeguard human eyes and ears against disease, accident, ignorance. Reluctantly, therefore, I have confined my activities almost exclusively to the dwellers in the Dark Land. [11]

It is important to emphasize that Helen Keller gave her energy, her heart, the voice of her fiery soul to the challenges facing *all* of mankind. She was a champion for all humanity, not just the blind, the deaf, and the deaf-blind. And *she did* attend to the needs of the deaf and deaf-blind as often as time and circumstances allowed in her busy life. She was drawn into her role as spokesperson for the blind community because her daily income (her financial survival) was tied to the American Foundation for the Blind.

The discussion of consciousness and navigation, of course, is relevant to deaf and deaf-blind individuals, as are the philosophies and strategies of the profession of Orientation and Mobility. Likewise, the study of esotericism is relevant to all humanity.

Navigating through the dark is the fate *of all* sentient creatures. There are levels of perceptual blindness—levels of consciousness, degrees of spiritual unfolding—that we must *all* traverse during our sojourn on earth. We are still cognitively evolving as a species, and we are each individually evolving on a spiritual journey; some people, because of age and opportunity, are more sophisticated than others. Helen Keller was exceptionally sophisticated; she was extraordinarily loving, tolerant, determined, and awake—and she was also stubborn, a fierce debater, an impassioned humanitarian, and a vocal change-agent; she fought for what she believed in.

Helen's wakefulness and her kindness together constituted her animation, her combative spirit. She was sensing the world all around using her whole body. She could read an environment vibrationally and she could read another human being the same way. When she did read other human beings—their spirituality and compassion—she had some astute observations. When we look at another human being, we do not see their minds operating. We can guess (if we are not blind) from eye movements and body language what others are thinking and feeling but we can never be sure what is happening inside another dynamic mind. The eyes see appearances but not essence—that is what Helen tells us repeatedly.

Helen Keller spent her entire life in the presence of silence and darkness. She was in direct contact with the subtle energy we call *spiritual*. Remarkably, Helen could turn sacred energy into fruitful action for the good of others. Helen Keller knew how to use the invisible and silent elements at work beneath everyday reality.

I said above that the deaf and deaf-blind have their own cultures. This is also true of blind communities; blind individuals have common interests and common goals and so have evolved a sophisticated culture of their own. I am painfully aware that being a sighted male, part of the sighted culture, is a disadvantage in this context. I remember being enthusiastically supportive of my wife Katherine's involvement in the women's rights movement in the 1960s. However, no matter how supportive and vocal I was, I was still an outsider. The same applies here; there is no way I can avoid the "outsider" label.

My friend and colleague Daniel Kish has often said that he resents it when the sighted purport to speak for the blindness community. This "outsider" realization hung over me as I wrote this book. I came to the topic, and decided to write the book, because of my career in the blindness field, my friendship with Daniel, and because of my fascination with the evolution of human consciousness. I believe that consciousness is the bridge that connects all our cultures and all our common challenges.

Chapter Two: The Esoteric Helen Keller

The material eye, be it ever so keen, fails to penetrate the world of spiritual will, where the elements at work are invisible and silent. [12]

Magic Wands and the Cold Logic of Artificial Intelligence

More men like you are needed with a magic wand to break the fetters of routine and conjure back the fairies to hedge and wall and workshop. [13]

We assume that normal eyes and ears can perceive a universe that poor deaf-blind Helen Keller could never know. Helen agrees that her limitations are severe, but also warns us that our own perceptions fail to see the esoteric (hidden) realms:

I admit that there are innumerable marvels in the visible universe unguessed by me. Likewise, O confident critic, there are myriad sensations perceived by me of which you do not dream. [14]

What are these myriad sensations that the sighted and hearing cannot perceive? *Why* can't we easily perceive what Helen Keller could detect?

Why do we need to conjure back the fairies? Surely fairies are not real. Surely magic wands only work in Disney movies. Surely this is imagination playing with words. Was Helen just being poetic, using metaphor, was she being whimsical, playing with language, or is there a more serious message embedded in the quote above?

There is something intuitive, empathic, and ethereal about Helen Keller. She used her articulate empathy to confront waves of discontent and danger in her time on earth (1880 to 1968). Magic is still in her words; her messages still have healing power. And we *still* need to listen to Helen Keller; her wisdom needs to be restated, especially in our own discontented and dangerous time.

Humanity in our era is facing unprecedented challenges as technological changes outpace the evolution of the human mind. Intellect alone will not save us from climate change, viral pandemics, the rise of the surveillance state, unfettered genetic experiments, synthetic biology, slaughter bots, drone warfare, uneducated masses who would vote again for Fascism, and endless patriarchal wars. We need to open the portals and let the life-affirming elves back in—that was Helen Keller's message to us; we need the magic powers of esotericism to balance the cold logic of artificial intelligence.

Most people who come to a book such as this, with fascination and curiosity about Helen Keller, would not know about esotericism. Therefore, I will spend several pages clarifying this academic domain, explaining what it has to do with Helen Keller. The reader will also find themselves very soon faced with more academic abstractions, including the evolution of consciousness and a field called dual-process theory. *Do not panic*; absorb what you can and let the dialogue slowly draw your interest. I will address the questions raised above as you move through the chapters of this book.

Bright She Was

What secret power, I wonder, caused this blossoming miracle? What mysterious force guided the seedling from the dark earth up to the light, through leaf and stem and bud, to glorious fulfillment in the perfect flower? Who could have dreamed that such beauty lurked in the dark earth, was latent in the tiny seed we planted? Beautiful flower, you have taught me to see a little way into the hidden heart of things. Now I understand that the darkness everywhere may hold possibilities better even than my hopes. [15]

In the quote above, Helen Keller is inadvertently giving us a picture of her own life—she is the flower, a blossoming miracle that came from a latent seed hidden in darkness and silence. Who could have dreamed that such beauty lay hidden in the quiet shadows? Now, in hindsight, we can see how this perfect flower evolved—we have pictures and supporting documents, we can watch Helen Keller grow from a seed to a flowering beauty. The fragrance from this rare flower still saturates the modern world, long after the flower has returned to the earth.

The rare flower that was Helen Keller is now a universal memory; she is a role model for the rest of us, especially on the days when we are complaining about our lot in life. Whatever energy flowed through her—whatever we choose to call this mystery that brought forth the flower—it was positive energy, life-affirming, hopeful, and loving; it was also the source of Helen's unshakable Faith, a well-spring of inexplicable, intuitive energy that radiated from her essence. Somehow, the energy that entered her could also be radiated outward—almost everyone she met commented on her radiance.

~

I awoke this morning with a smile, thinking to myself (whimsically), "Maybe Yoda knew Helen Keller." I could hear the Star Wars sage Yoda telling us: *Bright she was.* If we conjure back the fairies to hedge and wall and workshop, we also conjure Yoda—and we know the wonderment and hope that Yoda brought to world culture. Helen Keller knew the power of the Force. It is no accident that the first book she wrote, in her final year at college, was called *Optimism* (1903)—she was riding the waves of the Force when she wrote *Optimism*. Helen was quoted in a Harrisburg, Pennsylvania newspaper article saying:

"Keep your face to the sunshine, and you cannot see the shadows."

This is a common bit of American wisdom that numerous authors have quoted (Walt Whitman, for example). One of America's most treasured

Country songs also encourages us to "Live on the Sunnyside, always on the Sunnyside." Helen tells us that *if we keep our face toward the sunshine, shadows will disappear—the dark side will not bother us if our worldview is optimistic.* In other words, optimism is embedded in the Force; both Helen and Yoda knew this secret. Of course, Helen Keller did not avoid the darker regions of life, but her positive mental attitude was informed by a force called Faith; she knew that an inner radiance could penetrate and overpower the dark side.

In the quote below, Helen says she loves certain writers because they are optimistic, but they are not simplistic; they are not bullied by the forces of pessimism and negativity:

> I love all writers whose minds . . . bubble up in the sunshine of optimism . . . [such optimistic minds are] fountains of joy and good will, with occasionally a splash of anger and here and there a healing spray of sympathy and pity. [16]

Helen Keller never stopped being optimistic her entire life. When she encountered minds like her own, she was grateful and said so. When faced with tragedy—like the horrors of war—Helen fell back on her Faith and her positive nature. She spent many hours with newly blinded soldiers in both the First and Second World Wars. Many of the soldiers were angry at their fate, many were deeply depressed, many more were confused and felt hopeless. Helen comforted these men by her very presence—if a deaf-blind woman could be cheerful, dedicated, active, and optimistic then so could they. I like this quote by Helen from the book *The Three Lives of Helen Keller* (1962):

> Long ago I determined not to complain. The mortally wounded must strive to live out their days cheerfully for the sake of others. That is what religion is for—to keep the hearts brave to fight it out to the end with a smiling face.

Helen followed her own advice to the soldiers; her eyes and ears were "mortally wounded," but she ignored her impairments—she found religion and used Love and Service to guide her for a lifetime. I smile every time I read her phrase, "Fight it out to the end with a smiling face." We each know illness is coming as we approach old age. We know tragedy can strike any moment, unexpectedly. We know that one day—

not long from now, perhaps—we will die. We might as well smile into the darkness and silence and defiantly soldier on.

As we survey the whole of Helen Keller's life, we see that she was determined, curious, gregarious, full of intense energy, and most of the time she was optimistic and hopeful. She was also a prolific communicator. She wrote several books, many magazine articles, and she left us numerous letters, essays, and speeches; she has been a favorite subject of biographers for decades. This book takes its place alongside a library full of rich information about Helen Keller's long and very full life.

I sense that it is Helen's esoteric power—her mysterious sensual essence—that magnetically draws seekers to her story. Bright she was, and we are attracted to her light. We are fascinated and puzzled by her radiance; where, we wonder, is this energy coming from, how is it radiated outward, and how can this mysterious energy be affecting us even now, long after Helen has passed? I am fascinated by this mysterious energy and, perhaps like you, I am on a hunt to find some clues about its origin and its purpose.

Undetected energy is constantly entering and leaving the human body, affecting our mind in subtle ways. I sense that this esoteric (hidden) energy must somehow be related to the functioning of the mind and to the evolution of human consciousness. How do human minds work? What is consciousness and how did it arise? We must attempt to answer these difficult questions if we are to understand the esoteric Helen Keller.

Many of our greatest thinkers took on the puzzle of consciousness. Some, like psychoanalyst Carl Jung, spent an entire lifetime exploring human cognition. As I was reading Jung's *Red Book* (2009), I learned that he had spent years introspecting about his *own* mind—how did *his* mind work, he wondered? Jung famously asked: What are dreams? What is imagination? What are thoughts? Modern scientists are still asking these same basic questions.

Early in his career, Jung became fascinated with the study of esotericism and wrote extensively about Alchemy and Hermeticism. Jung felt that many ancient scholars had asked the same question: *How do minds work?* Jung concluded that these early esoteric thinkers knew something was hidden from the common man—hidden from men who presumably were not cognitively evolved enough to understand. Jung also saw that esotericism was about cognitive evolution, about the dawn of consciousness and stages of mental growth. Ancient alchemical insights were in harmony with Jung's psychoanalytical speculations.

After several decades of introspection and alchemical research, Jung started to speak of an unconsciousness mind. Then he said something chilling. He said that *he could feel* "something alive down there." Jung felt that he was the host of something that was not him, not who he thought he was.

Jung was a scientist, a very practical man, so he would not say that this "hidden host" had no material explanation, although in his time, much less was known in the sciences. We are still puzzled by the notion of the unconsciousness, especially a collective unconsciousness that connects all of humanity, like the entwined underground roots in a forest. Helen Keller's esoteric energy seemed to position her closer to the unconscious mind and she seemed to be within reach of the collective unconscious. Here are Helen's words:

> It seems to me that there is in each of us a capacity to comprehend the impressions and emotions which have been experienced by mankind from the beginning. Each individual has a subconscious memory of the green earth and murmuring waters, and blindness and deafness cannot rob him of this gift from past generations. This inherited capacity is a sort of sixth sense—a soul-sense which sees, hears, feels, all in one. [17]

That is a remarkable quote, coming as it does from a woman born in 1880. Helen seems to anticipate epigenetics, the passing down of experience (whole behaviors) from one generation to the next. In Chapter Four, I will discuss the sixth sense, although my definition will vary from what Helen is referring to in her quote. From my perspective, Helen had a highly evolved sixth sense, which naturally developed and compensated for her deafness and blindness.

Helen Keller might also have been a child prodigy—I will address that possibility in Chapter Five. When we look at savants and prodigies, we do not discover any plausible scientific explanations for their abilities. Savants and prodigies are born knowing things they never learned or practiced—they just show up at birth, for example, with the ability to compose music or play the piano. If the collective unconscious is a material reality, it might explain savants and prodigies. For now, the human mind is still a deep mystery. Helen Keller is a gateway through which we can explore this mystery. Was she drawing on a collective unconscious? If so, how?

The masters of mind-exploration were the Buddhists. After thousands of years of meditation, Buddhist monks (and Hindu gurus) enigmatically told us: *You are That.* When Jung looked deeply inside his mind, he saw something looking back. He could have said "I am that." He could have said, "I am that something which feels like it is not me." How very strange this sensation is, and not a little frightening, especially when first detected.

Helen Keller was closer to this esoteric mystery—closer to "that"— because her vision and her hearing did not blur her inner vision. She *felt* the mystery looking at her from deep within her mind, and she felt this subtle energy even as a young girl.

I will offer a (speculative) scientific explanation for *You are That* and for Jung's concept of the unconscious in Chapter Four. However, I must add that spiritual people, like Helen Keller, would generally not allow reductionist science—theories and hypotheses—to cloud inner vision or denigrate Faith. Helen Keller would have challenged purely scientific explanations as the final say in spiritual matters.

As a writer, I confess that I am straddling a mental fence. I am deeply moved, in awe, and yet puzzled by Helen's Faith—I do not have her gifts. I seem to be standing in the gap between Faith and Intellect, trying my best to define the two polarities as equal but mutually exclusive (more about that perspective later). Because of my dilemma, I need to amend this nascent esoteric journey with a strong caveat.

In no way am I suggesting that we abandon the methodology of science. I am also not denigrating our powerful Egoic consciousness, nor am I suggesting that esotericism cannot be probed and—to various degrees—explained by scientific knowledge and the powers of reasoning. Indeed, I am suggesting that *there is a science and logic to esotericism,* even a logic to Faith. I suggest that the mystical perspective, with the fairies and magic wands, is scientifically valid, supremely important, and needs to be explored—to humanity's benefit. In other words, I agree with Helen Keller, it is time to "conjure back the fairies to hedge and wall and workshop."

Physicist and author Richard Feynman, a man of science with a drawer full of magic wands, defended the Ego's reductionist technique (using the scientific method). For Feynman, as we dissect the flower (or look deeply within using a microscope), we discover layer after layer of mystery and beauty. At all scales of observation, we find the fairies (mysteries) at work. Feynman was in awe of creativity and mystery. He was playful, musical, and jolly; he was an example of an evolved Soul even as he defended reason and scientific experimentation.

Richard Feynman is loved and deeply respected because he saw a wholeness at every scale of observation and he playfully and carefully explained his passion for science. Life for this wonderfully creative scientist was everywhere a fascinating puzzle to be solved and appreciated. Life was fun because it never ran out of puzzles and surprises. I suggest we look at consciousness as Feynman might have, as a deep, fun, mysterious conundrum that holds ever more amazing complexity for us to explore and appreciate.

Richard Feynman, Carl Jung, Yoda, and Helen Keller would have been good friends had they been contemporaries (bright they were). Helen's good friend William James, another bright star, warned humanity repeatedly not to be too sure about the nature of reality, he insisted that we keep ourselves open to further discoveries. The esoteric realms, James suggested, "forbid a premature closing of our accounts with reality." In other words, do not be cocky about the "reality" that informs your worldview; the odds that you remain cognitively and spiritually unevolved are about 100%.

Our current obsessive fascination with the evolution of consciousness has arrived at a critical time in human history. We need to understand how minds evolve because our complex technologies must be used for benevolence, not for destructiveness. In every country, there still exist clan minds that have not evolved enough to grasp the power and eloquence of science. These medieval minds fail to appreciate or employ science and reason and they have no grasp of Faith (as opposed to belief, which they have in abundance). The Covid-19 pandemic sweeping over America (as I write this) is a case in point, as is the climate crisis. Too many ignorant and harmful decisions are being made by minds incapable of higher-order thinking skills, minds that seem also to be disconnected from spirituality. This simply cannot continue to happen—the future of the human species depends on a knowledgeable, empathetic public, and on sophisticated leadership. I will pick this thread up again when I discuss levels of consciousness in Chapter Three.

Every New Generation Discovers the Miracle

When my childhood friend Ron Waxell and I visited Ivy Green, Helen Keller's Tuscumbia, Alabama birthplace, now on the National Register of Historic Places, I asked the volunteer guide who showed us the Keller family home if there was anything left to say about Helen Keller. Were there any stones left unturned, I wondered, anything remaining to explore and report about Helen Keller's life? I asked this, of course, because I was working on this book.

Apologetically and sincerely the guide said, rather emphatically, "No." Evidently, Helen Keller's life has been thoroughly researched and dissected; all anyone can do now is rehash and reflect about earlier commentaries. In no way do I fault this gracious guide for her heartfelt opinion because she was mirroring what most people feel: we have dissected Helen Keller's life enough—leave history alone, they say, stop rehashing.

I was not bothered by the tour guide's well-meaning observation that there is nothing more to say about Helen Keller's life, for two reasons. First, every new generation discovers the miracle and the miracle worker. The Keller-Sullivan story has become a global mythology—it is now the property of humanity at large. Therefore, it is okay—expected and embraced—for every new generation to express awe and reflect anew. Every year, a new group of writers, historians, scientists, educators, poets, philosophers, film makers, sculptors, and painters rediscover the mythology and reinterpret the miracle in contemporary language or images.

It is also true that each new generation has exponentially more knowledge to draw on compared to the last generation. For example, as I crafted this book, I had access to scientific research data that did not exist ten years ago. I could also draw on newly formed Helen Keller Digital Archives at The American Foundation for the Blind, at the Perkins School for the Blind, and through multiple scholarly search engines. I could discuss synesthesia, dual-process theory, and the mirroring and projection systems innate to human consciousness— these are arenas of study that only appeared in the last few decades. The field of consciousness research has exploded—it will not be long before this new frontier reveals much more about how human cognition works. Using all these new tools, I applied the science of navigation and the science of consciousness to the Helen Keller story—that has never been done before.

Second, I felt that I did, indeed, have a new perspective on Helen Keller and Anne Sullivan that resulted from my life experiences, especially my professional education and my interest in the evolution of human consciousness and esotericism. Let me take a moment to explain this fresh perspective.

My education was unique. I started my career with a degree in visual science, eventually receiving a doctorate in optometry. After the doctorate, I got a master's degree in blind rehabilitation. My master's degree in blind rehabilitation focused on a field called Orientation and Mobility, the study of human navigation with an emphasis on teaching blind and visually impaired people to independently travel. In 1980, I was hired by the Saginaw Public School System in Michigan as their sole Orientation and Mobility specialist. The Millet Learning Center, where my office was located, is a special education facility charged with educating about 300 of the most severely impaired children in the region. I stayed at Millet for over 30 years, working with sighted as well as visually impaired students.

Because of my education as an optometrist and my teaching experience with sighted children in special education, I became quite knowledgeable about the science of *visually-guided navigation*, which sighted people use to get around. In addition, because of my education in blind rehabilitation and my teaching experience with blind children, I became aware of the science of *non-visually-guided navigation*, which blind and deaf-blind people use to negotiate environments. Consequently, my initial perspective on Helen Keller *revolved around her ability to navigate* without hearing and vision. If you pause to reflect, you will realize just how amazing it is for a deaf-blind person to navigate *at all*.

Imagine yourself in an auditorium filled with people watching a movie. Now you lose your vision. Now you lose your hearing. Now you need to go to the bathroom. How will you navigate without vision or hearing? I was educated in a profession that can answer that question; the profession of Orientation and Mobility contains skill sets and philosophies that are used to teach navigation to people who have navigational disabilities. In other words, there are ways to teach blind individuals to navigate quite efficiently. It is harder to teach navigation skills to deaf-blind people, but it is still possible.

As a young deaf-blind child, Helen Keller locked her mother in a pantry, threw away the key, and then sat on the porch at Ivy Green and giggled—so the story goes (according to Helen). Her ability to pull off this childhood prank means she had an extraordinarily complex understanding of spatial layout; she had learned at a young age to navigate through her familiar world without using vision or hearing. How did she do that? How did Helen Keller's deaf-blind brain rewire itself to enable Helen to function in her environment?

I was able to consider that question—how her brain rewired—at least in part, because of a long career working with the navigation problems of children in special education, mostly blind and severely visually impaired children. I spent my career thinking about navigation.

After I retired, I made a logical connection between navigation and the evolution of consciousness—a rather remarkable revelation that amazes me still. I published two books about the evolution of consciousness (in 2017 and 2018), in which I argued that the evolution of navigation, as it occurred in bilateral creatures, gave rise to a strange dual cognition. My hypothesis that navigation is related to the evolution of consciousness is an esoteric philosophy; it is outside-the-box thinking, coming from blind rehabilitation and not from "accepted brain-based disciplines" like neuroscience or cognitive psychology. [18]

My *Navigational Consciousness hypothesis,* as I call my set of ideas, establishes an avenue that explains popular memes like left-brain versus right-brain and fast-brain versus slow-brain. As I said in my early textbooks, we are still using scientific memes that emerged from less sophisticated times in history. Terminology like *objective/subjective, conscious/ unconscious,* and *right-brain/left-brain*—to list three scientific memes— are relatively outdated and tend to block or redirect fresh thinking about the evolution of cognition. We still use these terms (I will too), but we need to realize that these concepts are losing their value as we go forward.

It is also germane to realize that the hypothesis of Navigational Consciousness goes beyond this summary-look at Helen Keller's remarkable mind; there are profound implications for society that are embedded in this discussion of the evolution of consciousness. We cannot make the important decisions that face us in this technological wildfire, which we are now experiencing, unless we get a handle on human cognitive evolution. We must immensely increase our understanding of human cognition, especially the evolution of spirituality, emotion, and compassion (with our magic wands and Fairy Lords helping) if we are to beat back the forces of ignorance, stupidity, and the aggressive ill-will currently sweeping over our fragile planet.

More than Meets the Eye

For over 30 years during my career, I taught blind and visually impaired students to navigate safely and efficiently through our world—through an environment built by and for a sighted population. I also set up two non-profit agencies, a vision clinic for handicapped children [19] and an institute to explore sophisticated navigational technologies for blind and visually impaired students.[20] I eventually realized that I had become knowledgeable not only about *blind navigation*, but *human navigation*. I also realized, after teaching for three decades, that every child with a severe disability (blindness, deafness, autism, physical and emotional impairments, etc.) also had (to various degrees) a *navigational disability*—a term that I defined. I will briefly explore the concept of navigational disability later in the text.

As I stated above, after retirement, I made a connection between the evolution of navigation and the evolution of human consciousness. My two textbooks explored a perspective called *dual-process theory*, which I (and many others before me) contend is the basis for humanity's curious dual cognition. Therefore, I write from the perspective of someone who has an overview of both sighted and blind navigation as well as a perspective on the evolution of humanity's dual cognition. This is a complex perspective—a confluence of theories and hypotheses— that I will explore in this volume. Dialogue about the evolution of consciousness weaves throughout the lives of all the Knights for the Blind discussed in this series—it is a theme I will repeatedly return to in the volumes that follow this book.

It is important to understand the distinction between a hypothesis and a theory. A theory is a tested and well-accepted (peer-reviewed) scientific explanation for phenomena. A hypothesis is a *suggested explanation* for a phenomenon, or a prediction of possible correlations among phenomena. I have often mixed the two terms in my writing because dual-process theory has a long history and is well-respected as a plausible explanation for cognitive functioning; therefore, to call dual-process a theory is acceptable. However, my own thought-process, which expanded dual-process theory to fit my profession, is a hypothesis. I am writing about a perspective—Navigational Consciousness—that is little known and, therefore, untested, it cannot be called a theory. This is an important distinction. As I look back over my earlier books, I see places where I used the term *theory* when I should have used *hypothesis*.

I want to also underline that I write from a moment in time and from within a masculine sight-based mindset; I am aware (or strive to be aware) of my own mind-blindness and I am, therefore, hesitant to make definitive statements, as if I had final answers (I do not). On the other hand, I will write boldly and with conviction (as Helen Keller would have) but understand that I feel humbled by the scope of this discussion and I am quite aware of the potential for unintended errors in judgement or reasoning.

Writing about consciousness, navigation, esotericism, and human evolution is like writing about existence itself; I am swimming in infinity, trying to describe the experience. And while I am dogpaddling through this sea of abstractions, I am also telling the Helen Keller story from an esoteric perspective. I have a lot of explaining to do in the pages ahead, about esotericism, navigation, consciousness, and evolution; please stay with me as I explore some unfamiliar and, at times, complex ideas.

I write fiction as well as non-fiction, so I am not afraid to allow my own beliefs and emotions to bubble over onto a page. I am also in harmony with Helen Keller's spiritual energy. I agree in many ways with her political views, and like Helen, I am okay with strong words bundled with strong emotions. I hold close to my heart Helen Keller's passionate in-your-face way of confronting social evils. When I am talking about the hidden and rebellious Helen Keller, my own voice joins in the chorus. In other words, this is not a textbook or a summary of history. I do not find it true or helpful to reduce the fiery Helen Keller to dry prose and dead facts. This is an exploration of the esoteric Helen Keller, where passion and strong convictions sit at the same table with imagination and mystery.

Helen is our guide to this journey:

> The blind are not supposed to be the best of guides. Still, though I cannot warrant not to lose you, I promise that you shall not be led to fire or water or fall into a deep pit. If you will follow me patiently, you will find that "there's a sound so fine, nothing lives twixt it and silence," and that there is more meant in things than meets the eye. [21]

Helen is echoing Shakespeare in the quote above. She and the Bard are channeling the same muse. The fairy with the magic wand whispers:

"There are more things in Heaven and Earth, Horatio, than are dreamt of in your science." (~ *Hamlet*, by William Shakespeare).

Western Esotericism

> Western esotericism has been a pervasive presence in Western culture from late antiquity to the present day, but until recently it was largely ignored by scholars and surrounded by misconceptions and prejudice. [22]

Because of my interest in the evolution of consciousness, I began to explore the field of esotericism. This led me to review the ideas of two remarkable men, William James, and Carl Jung. Both William James (the Father of American Psychology) and Psychoanalyst Carl Jung noticed the same cognitive mysteries that I am exploring in this book. James and Jung had no fear probing the fringes of science; both these intellectual giants were comfortable with fairies hanging out in their workshops.[23] I will have more to say about Jung and James later in the book.

Esotericism is now a well-respected academic discipline with study programs in universities around the world. However, esotericism is not a justification for superstition, nor does it embrace New Age fringe thinking, although some "fringe thinking" is not to be dismissed out-of-hand.[24] The core principles of esotericism were initially trampled (buried) in the rush to bring rational thinking to humanity during the Age of Enlightenment (late 1600s to 1700s). A more sophisticated and cautious science has now turned its penetrating vision back into history and is currently embracing the study of esoteric thought.

Esotericism has several related definitions, but, overall, it is the study of topics that are outside the mainstream of current thought, often outside social acceptance or outside the norms of current scientific belief. That is one reason esoteric ideas were often hidden—some things are better left unsaid in a public forum.

My hypothesis that navigation and consciousness are inextricably linked has implications that reach deep inside the psyche of our culture—there is much in the hypothesis that is outside the mainstream of current thought. For example, a primary principle of Navigational Consciousness is that we have two minds that are mutually exclusive—

when one mind operates the other mind is hidden. This presents us with a mysterious conundrum: our species is inherently and consistently (and understandably) confused. Much of esotericism deals with this innate confusion, with the conundrum of oscillating (alternating) "hidden minds."

Helen Keller is suggesting that one of our minds has been denied long enough—this hidden mind is the silent soul-sister calmly abiding in the shadows behind her boisterous twin brother, the Ego. The Soul-mind that can imagine fairies and magic wands has been in hiding ever since Enlightenment thinkers exiled such "unreasonable superstitions." Here is how English neuropsychologist Nicholas Humphrey summarized the perspective of the Enlightenment period:

> [We will find in science] a sufficient explanation for everything that is or might be. Not only should there be no need to postulate an interventionist deity, but there should also be no need to introduce any other messy hypothesis . . . No need for a life-force, or élan vital, to explain the difference between dead and living matter; no need for a human soul to explain the difference between consciousness and unconsciousness; no need, still less, for magic powers of action or perception at a distance to explain the co-called miracles that superstitious people still made claims for . . . As Julien de La Mettrie had written in *L'Homme-machine*: "The soul is, then, an empty symbol . . . animate bodies will possess all they need in order to move, sense, think, repeat, and behave, in a word, all they want of the physical; and of the mental, too, which depends thereon." [25]

What is so remarkable for me, as I ponder this powerful quotation, is that it is possible to agree with the above observation and, yet, to know that the statement is also false. In other words, one of our two minds can use the scientific method to benefit mankind, while our second mind can dwell in Faith without a shred of need for rational thinking. Human beings are a curious paradox, a mysterious conundrum. Esotericism is about this conundrum. Earlier sages discovered humanity's dual cognition and so, also, did the great minds in philosophy, religion, and psychology; every field of study eventually came face-to-face with our cognitive paradox.

Science has truly given us miracles, and these gifts continue to flow. The scientific method may well be the most important materialistic invention ever created by the human mind. But something was wrong with the proclamations of the Enlightenment; the creative community knew this intuitively. There has been fierce resistance to the Enlightenment ever since it emerged. I love this paragraph by Nicholas Humphrey:

> Science, with its chainsaws and bulldozers of reason, has felled the tropical rain forests of spirituality. It has wreaked ecological destruction on fairyland. It has extinguished the leprechauns, the elves, and goblins. It has caused a global change in the weather of imagination. It has made a dustbowl of our Eden and created an inner drought. And all this, not to bring greater peace or happiness, but to satisfy people's hunger for the Big Macs of technology. [26]

Evidently, Nicholas Humphrey was channeling the same muse as Helen Keller when he wrote that eloquent paragraph. He and Helen could see the need to bring the fairies back. Humanity has raced forward with a new ability to reason using the scientific method, however, peace and happiness have gotten inadvertently trampled in our eagerness to wolf down *dustbowl technologies*. We are now satiated with scientific brilliance, but we are starving to death spiritually. Our Egoic minds have overheated while our Allocentric Soul-minds have withered. Helen Keller and Nicholas Humphrey tell us (each in their own way) that "it is time to bring back the fairies."

I should pause here to stress that Nicholas Humphrey was a neuropsychologist, an astute cognitive philosopher who won the Nobel Prize in medicine in 1981. In his 2011 book *Soul Dust: The Magic of Consciousness*, Humphrey argued that consciousness was "a magical-mystery show that we stage inside our own heads—a show that paves the way for spirituality and allows us to reap the rewards, and anxieties, of living in a "soul niche." Because of his balancing the spiritual with the scientific, Humphrey has been described as a Romantic Scientist. My point is that Humphrey was a cautious scientist who might resist being labeled as a lover of fairylands. However, he knew that the "soul niche" was an essential characteristic of the human mind.

From my perspective, great thinkers like Nicholas Humphrey end up straddling the fence between reason and spirituality because human beings have dual minds; we feel uneasy when we deny one mind or the other. Navigational Consciousness contends that each of our minds is deaf-blind to the other. How amazing, appropriate, and timely that such a proclamation should show up in a book about deaf-blind Helen Keller—many forces came together to make this happen; I am as surprised as anyone else that this flow of diverse energies converged. The hypothesis of Navigational Consciousness will become clearer as you work your way through the book, but especially as you read Chapter Four.

Aristotle defined *esoteric* as "something that was learned long before it was understood." Therefore, Aristotle knew that the human mind had to be dual; if we could *know something* and *not know* (the very same) *something* (at the same time), then two minds must be at work. The Allocentric mind (where the fairies live) knows things long before information trickles into the Egocentric mind.

This dialogue about navigation and consciousness is relevant to Helen Keller because Helen's mind was highly evolved, a model, in my opinion, for the direction human cognition ought to evolve. Helen Keller's mind showcases the evolution of spirituality—the primacy of Love and the importance of Service-to-Others. Many unevolved minds in her era rejected her "Love and Service" worldview as pollyannaish nonsense. Helen's worldview was esoteric; it was too strange for many of her contemporaries who lived in their Egoic minds and who were unaware of their Esoteric (hidden) souls.

Esotericism is sometimes called *the study of rejected knowledge,* knowledge not for the masses. For example, when I came across Helen Keller's passion for Swedenborgian theology, with Emanuel Swedenborg's belief in out-of-body experiences and spiritual evolution, I felt right at home. I did not reject Helen's spiritual understanding; I embraced her faith-based perspective with great interest. However, a materialistic mind would reject Swedenborg's insights quickly, seeing superstition and unreasonable conclusions, rather than esoteric food-for-thought. I will discuss Emanuel Swedenborg's influence on Helen Keller in Chapter Three.

"The masses" have become more sophisticated over time, so what would have been rejected in the Middle Ages is now accepted with little fuss. However, in our time, esotericism is still toying with the fringes of reality and is occasionally looked on with skepticism in some academic silos.

I have been a member of an esoteric study group at Saginaw Valley State University in Saginaw, Michigan for over ten years. My friend

Wayne O'Brien created the group and moderates the discussions. Wayne, who was a professor at Arizona State University, helped me craft the central theme of this book: *that Helen Keller is a portal into the esoteric domain.* Wayne O'Brien has a background in developmental psychology, in cognitive evolution, and he has vast knowledge of esoteric thought, including the ideas of Rudolf Steiner, Edgar Cayce, and many other mystical thinkers. My own views have been heavily influenced by Wayne O'Brien, including the idea of exploring the esoteric Helen Keller.

The basic text we use for the interest group is *The Western Esoteric Traditions: A Historical Introduction* (2008) by Nicholas Goodrick-Clarke. In that book, Goodrick-Clarke lists six fundamental concepts underpinning esoteric thought, using an outline set forth by Antoine Faivre. Dr. Faivre is emeritus professor of esoteric and mystical currents at the Ecole Pratique des Hautes Etudes at the Sorbonne in France. Faivre's outline serves as a simple overview. Although other scholars have debated the merits of Faivre's taxonomy, I find his perspective clear and quite helpful.

It is my intention in this book to display Helen Keller's life on an esoteric loom. Helen lived in esoteric realms; to portray her as otherwise misses the fundamental core of her personality. The loom is a good metaphor because the threads of a weaving dive deep and then resurface—a cycle that repeats between that which can be perceived and that which is hidden. From individual threads, which initially seem to have no magic or beauty, come colorful and memorable patterns. In other words, sometimes the threads of a life can be observed clearly, while at other times, threads are hidden from view. *That which is hidden holds the secrets of esotericism.*

Here are the six principles upon which esoteric thought is founded (according to Professor Faivre), along with some insights about Helen Keller's life that relate to esotericism:

One: Correspondences

The ancient perspective called *Correspondence* dates back at least 5,000 years, but probably goes back much further in pre-history. The Egyptian God Thoth is said to have brought this revelation to mankind. The Greeks turned the God Thoth into Hermes Trismegistus, the

God of Wisdom, who was "three times great." Hermes Trismegistus is credited with the birth of Alchemy and with most (if not all) of the esoteric traditions that have appeared on the fringes of societies for centuries, including Alchemy, Rosicrucianism, Gnosticism, Occultism, Hermeticism, Neoplatonism, Theosophy, Spiritualism, Kabbalah, American Transcendentalism, and Freemasonry, to name a few of the better-known esoteric disciplines. Emanuel Swedenborg is part of this legacy, which also places Helen Keller in this ancient, mysterious glow.

There is a meme, which first appeared in a document called The Emerald Tablet between the 6th and 8th centuries, which captures the concept of Esoteric Correspondence; here is the meme: *As Above, So Below.* Christians and Muslims took this ancient principle and said: *On Earth, as it is in Heaven.* What this meme implies is that everything was created using the same set of fundamental (fractal) patterns, the same algorithm is used repeatedly by nature to design its creations. What we find at one layer of observation, we also find at larger and at smaller scales. For example, if we discover that atoms combine to form molecules, we can then speculate that something had combined earlier to form atoms and that molecules will join in novel ways to create something new. Once you understand this concept, it helps address diverse problems in many fields of study. As I reflect on my writing, I see that I employed Correspondence throughout this book, but especially as I crafted the cognitive philosophy explained in Chapter Four. You will see the magic phrase *As Above, So Below* often as you journey through the book.

Using the meme *as above so below*, human beings looked around them and saw goodness and evil existing side-by-side on earth. The reasoning that followed from this observation was that—in realms above this earthly domain—there had to be a Heaven where goodness mirrored earthly kindness, but there also had to be a Hell where cruelty on earth was mirrored by a greater universal hatefulness. Goodness and evil were experienced in space and in time; therefore, human beings projected Heaven and Hell to be physical locations where space and time continued for human beings after they died.

In the paragraphs below, I interpreted the ideas of Emanuel Swedenborg and Helen Keller in contemporary language—colored, perhaps, by my own professional perspective. Swedenborg's and Helen Keller's belief structure may very well have held that Heaven and Hell were actual locations. In other words, in Swedenborg's and Helen

Keller's books the concepts of Heaven and Hell are more concrete than what I am summarizing here.

Swedenborg taught that the Bible was allegorical and that, like other spiritual books, it was the study of the evolution of spirituality—the study (or the evidence) of the evolution of consciousness. In other words, Heaven and Hell are descriptions of the human mind undergoing cognitive evolution. An unevolved mind can be hateful, intolerant, and Hellish. In contrast, an evolved mind can be compassionate, tolerant, and Heavenly. The location of Heaven and the location of Hell are— from some spiritual and neuroscience perspectives—constructs of the human imagination (the Kingdom Within).

Whether you believe that or not, the evolution toward a more spiritual world was a core faith that Helen Keller accepted her entire life. For Helen Keller, Heaven may be an actual destination after death, *but it was also a state of mind* where love and kindness prevailed; the role of humanity was, therefore, to make the earth (and the human mind) as much as possible in the image of Loving-Kindness. I find the following quote by Canadian psychiatrist Maurice Burke to be a nice summary of the kind of internal spiritual life Helen was striving to attain:

> Religion will not depend on tradition. It will not be believed and disbelieved. It will not be a part of life, belonging to certain hours, times, occasions. It will not be in sacred books nor in the mouths of priests. It will not dwell in churches and meetings and forms and days. Its life will not be in prayers, hymns nor discourses. It will not depend on special revelations, on the words of gods who came down to teach, nor on any bible or bibles. It will have no mission to save men from their sins or to secure them entrance to heaven. It will not teach a future immortality nor future glories, for immortality and all glory will exist in the here and now. The evidence of immortality will live in every heart as sight in every eye. ~ Cosmic Consciousness: A Study in the Evolution of the Human Mind, by Maurice Burke, 1901.

Spirituality is a state of mind, a worldview that is enough within itself. Nothing need come from external sources because the Kingdom of consciousness is whole and within—loving-kindness is a condition of being. There are portals the mind can pass through to enrich itself. For

Helen Keller, the Christian bible and the books of Emanuel Swedenborg were the portals through which she enriched her highly evolved mind.

Helen Keller and Emanuel Swedenborg felt that a God of Goodness could not be a punishing God. There was nothing vindictive, aggressive, or hateful in a Loving God. This benevolent Power would never create the Hell depicted in many Christian interpretations. Here is Helen expressing her feelings about the Devil:

> There are moments when I feel that the Shylocks, the Judases, and even the Devil, are broken spokes in the great wheel of good which shall in due time be made whole. [27]

Of course, Helen Keller (and Swedenborg) faced a philosophical dilemma: Why so much evil in the world? Why didn't a Great and Good God build a kinder universe in the first place? This dilemma has been debated since human beings learned to think. Cruelty and evil exist in our earthly domain alongside the loving kindness of saints. There are still human beings who lack empathy, who are hateful, who aggressively embrace intolerance, and there are human beings who are empathetic, kind, and who fight against intolerance. Helen Keller knew that *it was not okay* to let evil rage unchecked; we must have our Justice Warriors— our Helen Kellers—to fight against the forces of evil. The way Helen decided to fight evil was by using the energy generated by her Faith to propagate waves of Love:

> It is wonderful how much time good people spend fighting the devil. If they would only expend the same amount of energy loving their fellow men, the devil would die in his own tracks of ennui. [28]

I would change her word "wonderful" in the quote above to "bewildering," or "tragic." I do enjoy her image of the devil dying from ennui; the poor devil is listless and bored because he has nothing to do in the land of kindness.

∾

There is an important assumption embedded in the meme *As Above so Below*. This is the assumption of connectedness. Everything is networked, otherwise there could be no influence between levels: the above could not influence the below, nor could the below influence the above unless the two were somehow connected. In other words, there are threads that weave through the whole fabric of our lives, through the universe, in every cell, in every quark. For example, human beings are land-based creatures who live in an atmosphere, embedded in a material world, surrounded by other life forms. There is no way science can honestly study a human being outside the physical world they are embedded within; human beings are part of a vast interlocking network.

Helen Keller was also embedded within a time in history. She was affected by that cultural world, by the technology of her time, and by the people around her. This environmental/cultural impact was a two-way flow because Helen Keller also impacted her time; she influenced her friends and her culture—she is still influencing us. Helen Keller favored Democratic and Socialist approaches to governing and economics because she believed they were the most compassionate and spiritually evolved systems. I will discuss her political views later in the book.

∼

The esoteric principle of *Correspondence* was addressed mathematically in the 1800s by English mathematician George Boole. Boole wrote a book in 1854 called *An Investigation of the Laws of Thought* in which he described what today we call Boolean algebra. Boole maintained that there were universal laws of thought that human beings could use to solve problems. From an esoteric perspective, what Boole did was show us that the human mind had evolved to solve "if and then" problems. In other words, the Law of Correspondence enables problem solving: *If* something is true at this scale, *then* it is also true at other scales.

Only human beings have evolved this ability to scale insights up and down: if something is mathematically true on one scale, then it very probably will be mathematically true at other scales of observation. What esoteric thought and Boole's mathematics show us is that the ability to solve if/and/then problems, in a way, defines our humanity— we are the only species that has evolved the ability to use logic to solve problems.

Something happened in the human neocortex about a 100,000 years ago that enabled the mind to discover and manipulate patterns; we became the *pattern-solving species and we learned to invent, to create*. The principle of *Correspondence* predates Boole's equations by thousands of years. At some point in human history, humanity became self-conscious of the ability to solve problems using pattern analysis. Cambridge University Professor Simon Baron-Cohen has an excellent discussion about the evolution of our systemizing mind in his book *The Pattern Seekers: How Autism Drives Human Invention* (2020). I reviewed Baron-Cohen's insights in Chapter Five.

Why and how did human beings evolve the ability to solve if/and/then problems? What happened in evolution that gave us the ability to work with patterns, with logic, with laws and with rules. I will provide a plausible answer to that complex question in Chapter Four using my Navigational Consciousness hypothesis.

Two: Living Nature

This basic esoteric idea (living nature) states that everything in our universe is alive and conscious. However, the degree of aliveness and the degree of wakefulness vary. There is a spiritual (spiral) ladder that can be climbed, starting from little animation (like a rock) to ever greater animation (as in animals); meager consciousness evolves toward enlightenment. In other words, everything in our universe is animated, composed of vibratory energy—this energy varies with levels of consciousness, growing more powerful as we climb the ladder of wakefulness. Modern quantum physics has now caught up with this ancient esoteric understanding; quantum mechanics postulates that the universe is vibratory and energetically networked.

Science has also taught us that our vision system is so powerful it acts as a filter, blocking awareness of vibrational patterns other than from light waves. The same is true of hearing: sound compression patterns overpower awareness of finer vibrations. Helen Keller did not have visual images or sound patterns suppressing her perception of low-threshold vibrations. She was in daily (continuous) contact with the essence of the universe—much more so than the rest of humanity; neither vision nor hearing blocked her perception of the simplest vibrational patterns. Therefore, Helen Keller was in direct contact with a subtler world. She knew that consciousness permeated the universe because she could perceive it, even in the rocks of a stonewall, as one of her books demonstrated (*The Song of the Stone Wall*, 1910).

I am fascinated with the idea that human beings are born with a potential *energetic makeup* that unfolds developmentally so long as ample experiences are made available during a lifespan. In other words, we are born with a genetic pattern that pre-determines our personalities, our animation, and even our strengths and weaknesses. This energetic structure determines what we will obsess about as we grow, where our interests will migrate, what we are predestined to be good at, what our mission in life evolves to become, and how energetically we address life's challenges. We are a river flowing happily within a grooved channel, heading into the future.

If we do not find our groove, if we do not flow within the channel best suited to our energetic pattern, then we struggle. To *get into a zone* means to find the groove (the channel) you were meant to flow through. Getting esoteric help from "fairies with magic wands" is called channeling.

The Enneagram is a geometric system developed from ancient esoteric principles (as well as modern manifestations) to study energetic structures. The Enneagram has two divisions, the Egocentric *Personality-Enneagram,* and the Allocentric *Process-Enneagram.* I am fascinated that such a system was created initially by people long ago (in special schools and monasteries in the East). Ancient scholars were trying to figure out how the human being works, especially the structure and behavior of human minds—both collectively and individually. The Enneagram is a complex tool for studying energetic structures. All I can do in this context is suggest further research if you have an interest.

Later, in Chapter Six, I will address the conundrum of prodigies and savants, individuals who are born with almost inexplicable energetic structures. Somehow, epigenetically, individuals are born with (almost) fully formed energetic structures. From a retrospective viewpoint, Helen Keller seems to have been born with a remarkably optimistic, trusting, faith-based personality that was predestined to become spiritually vivid. The ancient esoteric principles discussed here easily flowed through her because the natural inhibiting structures built into vision and hearing were absent.

Energetic structures come into being, exist for a while, and then completely dissipate. This is the esoteric understanding called *impermanence.* Nothing stays in the same form; everything is part of an ever-changing flow—evolution rolls on and on. Each of us is born and then we go through our life cycle, and then we disappear. All the books we wrote, films we made, inventions we created, houses, cities, countries we lived in, our great and small contributions are (sadly, I suppose) erased. We are soon forgotten and all that we worked so hard to accomplish in our brief sojourn on the planet is forgotten. Look back at recorded history and witness what has dissipated; notice how fast change washed over all that seemed permanent and dependable. History, too, will someday be erased.

Impermanence need not be depressing. It puts the Ego in perspective. Our hoarding and arrogance, our power trips, our clinging to form, and our Egoic beliefs are invalidated by change. The Ego becomes a temporary but useful tool that we can use to extend and enrich our changing form. A sense of peace arises when we accept unceasing flow as a universal law; we are happier if we simply ride the waves of impermanence.

However, all life forms struggle against impermanence. The goal of *life* is to survive as long as possible in a healthy, purposeful state. We strive to cure diseases and extend the human life span. We stubbornly record what came before and we try hard to learn from the past. Our minds are memory machines; we are built to fight impermanence. We create worldviews and desperately cling to them so that our beliefs are not washed away with each tidal change. Life is the organic order that struggles to balance universal chaos.

My two books about Helen Keller are an effort to preserve and honor Helen's time on earth. I am trying to keep the memory of Helen alive. But even as I do so, there are minds on social media suggesting she never existed. There was a movement, not long ago, to take the study of Helen Keller out of the public-school curriculum ostensibly because she was no longer relevant to modern times, but probably because her Swedenborgian Christianity clashed with regional orthodoxy. The Nazis burned her books to erase Helen Keller from history; she stood for loving-kindness and life; the Nazis stood for hatefulness and death.

Impermanence is chipping away at Helen Keller's legacy. The life-affirming energy that flows through my energetic structure resists the forces of annihilation. I offer two Helen Keller books this year to slow the tide of impermanence and forgetfulness.

Three: Imagination

Human beings are not just composed of intellect, emotions, and bodies. Human beings also have a uniquely created *sense of imagination*: the ability to dream, to daydream, to muse about the future, to reflect on the past, to live in the everyday world as if they were the star of a cosmic stage play. Other creatures have bodies, cognitive abilities, and emotions, but only human beings (as far as we know) have the power of imagination. Therefore, imagination is considered uniquely important within esoteric thought. Out of imagination came our historic myths, rituals, symbolism, archetypes, and ethereal realms filled with unseen entities, such as angels, fairies, spirits, gods, and demons.

Within esotericism, imagination is understood to be a tool for "going-out-of-body" to explore realms beyond vision and hearing, beyond appearances, beyond our current worldviews. Journeys "out-of-body" are on a bell curve, from momentary daydreams, through Jung's *active imagination*, to remote viewing, to allegedly leaving the corporal realm to visit other locations. In esotericism, something wonderfully strange is envisioned to be all around us as we go about the mundane tasks of a day. Most levels of reality, from an esoteric perspective, exist beyond our immediate perception; only our imaginary powers can allow us to travel to these foreign realms.

Esoteric thought envisions imagination as a connection between the macro-world and the micro-world (at many scales), a bridge between "as above" and "so below." It is as if macro worlds and micro worlds cannot directly communicate with each other because of an intermediary fog between them. Imagination can penetrate this fog and can travel back and forth between the macro-world and the micro-world receiving and delivering information. However, this information must be translated. The language of the fog uses serendipity, synchronicity, dreams, energetic imagination, archetypal symbolism, and intuitive feelings to deliver messages from above to below and from below to above. That is why, according to esoteric thought, there are spirit guides of various forms living in the fog; these guides can translate between micro and macro worlds.

We cannot enter higher realms unless we know how to dwell in playful imagination, the kind of playful, enthusiastic, all-encompassing energy that we see when young children spontaneously dance. That is the meaning of the Bible verse "Except ye become as little children, ye cannot enter the Kingdom of Heaven." Playful imagination (joyful flow) comes from the Allocentric mind, never from the Egocentric mind.

The Intellect cannot use imagination as a tool for discovery or communication; Intellect is its own tool (another kind of cognitive tool). In the words of dual-process theory, the Egocentric mind cannot avail itself of the wisdom found through imagination. *Allocentric* and *Egocentric* are the names I give to our two minds, which emerged from the evolution of navigation (explained in Chapter Four). The Egocentric mind uses intelligence, which is different from wisdom—wisdom is experientially based. Only the Allocentric mind can intuit the metaphorical symbolism found in the imagination; only the Allocentric mind can become wiser through imaginary experiences. Intuitive help arrives to the seeker, the scientist, the researcher, and the artist, but only when the Intellect (the Egoic mind) is resting (hidden) and only after we ask for help from the fog (from the unconscious). Asking for help shows that we understand the question. You cannot get an answer to a confused, ill-defined, unevolved question.

Western philosophers have long grappled with the duality of the mind. Many of the first philosophers (Hobbes, Goethe, Steiner, Coleridge, Kant, Fiche, Hegel, etc.) saw imagination as the creative spark that happened when the polarity—the gap (the fog) between intellect and creativity, between science and art, between the Egocentric mind and the Allocentric mind—was suddenly bridged. In other words, *imagination evolved as a mechanism to link mankind's dual cognition.* The Romantic movement in history was founded on the idea that the ability to use imagination as a cognitive tool was a feature of a sophisticated, innovative, and evolving mind.

In harmony with Western philosophical thought, Helen Keller differentiated Faith from Intellect; she saw them both as valuable tools, but she considered Faith the stronger and more important of the two. She had a strong Intellect, but she was also wise beyond her years and culture. She used words like they were magic spells, which could transform the reader; it was as if many of her words and thoughts came directly from the imaginary realm.

Helen Keller is sometimes criticized for using visual and auditory images in her writings. She often spoke eloquently of the world of visual images and sounds as if she could see and hear normally. This was, in part, (we can speculate) her esoteric imaginative skills at play. I also suspect that synesthesia played a role—I will discuss synesthesia in

Chapter Six. Perhaps, Helen Keller could travel through the fog easier than the rest of us; messages effortlessly flowed into her open mind. Gifts came to her from esoteric realms because she was open to subtle energies.

Four: Transmutation

Transmutation means to go from one level of consciousness to a higher level of consciousness. Esoteric thinkers hold this idea to be fundamental for human beings. Transmutation implies that there is a hierarchy of awareness, of wisdom, of intellect, of spirituality. We are narcissistic creatures at birth with no wisdom and little knowledge, but we grow in the direction of empathy, wakefulness, wisdom, tolerance, intellect, and loving-kindness. Some of this transmutation occurs naturally during the developmental growth cycle, but at the higher stages of consciousness, work is required to go beyond our basic trust in a material world.

It is a core esoteric belief that consciousness can be transformed from a primitive state to a more sophisticated state. For example, a mind can be transmuted from a Narcissistic state to an Ethnocentric state through a prescribed process, often a sanctioned rite-of-passage.

Here is another way to think about this: two forces are held in balance by a gap, a force field. The two forces have been called by many different names throughout history: for example, *negative polarity* and *inhibition* are set opposed to *positive polarity* and *excitation* (just words for opposing forces). In other words, there are two poles of equal power held apart by a force-filled gap. In esoteric thought, a catalyst happens (a profound experience, the magic of imagination), and the two poles suddenly, momentarily, and inexplicably collapse into each other and transmute the individual to a higher plane of awareness.

It is as if a wave-form is collapsing in a quantum-like state and the result is a thought, an insight, a transformative particle-like moment. At higher energy scales, a collapsing wave is so powerful that the particle-like emergence results in an individual experiencing a higher state of consciousness.

The idea that human beings can journey through cognitive and spiritual stages goes back thousands of years. Zoroaster held this perspective as early as 1500 BC, and some scholars say the idea dates to the Neolithic age 12,000 years ago with the advent of the domestication of plants and animals. Transmutation is now being scientifically observed and documented, primarily in the work of developmental and cognitive psychologists.

For some reason, Helen Keller evolved quickly through levels of consciousness. She had a very evolved Soul (she was high up on the spiritual ladder of consciousness) by the time she was a teenager. We can only speculate why this might be, but I will offer two possibilities.

First, early trauma to the brain necessitates neural rewiring to circumvent tissue damage. As healing occurs, especially in a rapidly growing young brain, cross-wiring can result. Unusual neural connections can develop between brain regions, connections that do not occur in "normal" brains. Rewired brains can create unusual neural networks that give us our savants, synesthetes, prodigies, and peculiar geniuses. Perhaps, Helen Keller was one such prodigy; certainly, she was neuronally-wired differently than the rest of us (see Chapter Six).

Second, as I stated earlier, vision and hearing are powerful filters; therefore, when optical images and sound-based images are missing, sensory filtering is dramatically reduced. Helen Keller is a rare look at what can happen in the absence of light-wave and sound-wave imaging. Perhaps the ability to move through levels of consciousness is made easier in the absence of the inhibiting powers of vision and hearing.

Five: Concordance

> Theologians may quarrel, but the mystics of the world speak the same language. ~ Meister Eckhart

The esoteric principle of Concordance asserts that *there is a fundamental unifying principle, a Common Source, from which all spiritual practices emerge.* Therefore, we would expect to find that all the world's religious traditions, at their core, are variations of the same set of esoteric doctrines—all were created on the same esoteric loom. In other words, the heart of Christianity is the same heart that beats inside Buddhism, Islam, Judaism, Hinduism, and Sikhism. Likewise, the wisdom found in Alchemy is the same wisdom found in Rosicrucianism. Gnostic wisdom mirrors the wisdom found in Hermeticism. And the principles of Neoplatonism are also seen in Theosophy, the Kabbalah, and Freemasonry. It is the same set of patterns repeating because the Ultimate Source—call it God if you want—is the same. This insight is where the meme "We are all one" comes from; the Source is Oneness, and that singularity includes all that was created by the Source.

Helen Keller had no doubt that all the people of the world were united under a common God. Names changed and traditions varied, but for Helen Keller *The Source* was everywhere the same. This knowledge makes every human being equal to every other human being in the eyes of *The Source* and is why *every* human being is perceived to be worthy of Divine attention and respect.

Traditional religions often contend that they are complete in their worldviews and proclamations; therefore, there is no need within traditional religions for challenges or objections to church doctrine— nothing is hidden in the traditional church, everything is literal in the practices of dogmatism, and nothing can be challenged. Traditional religious practices hold that only church members are the chosen ones in the eyes of the God they worship. Not surprisingly, Helen Keller's views, that *all* people are loved by a single Source, were rejected out-of-hand by orthodoxy.

The field of esotericism (in the West) has documented the struggle between esoteric principles and Christian doctrine—that is one reason that esoteric thought had to be hidden, because it was exceedingly dangerous to expound ideas outside accepted religious circles; many people were murdered in the name of religion. Helen Keller's esotericism points to the mystery at the core of all religions, at hidden forces at work beneath traditional trappings and dogmas. Such claims, that religion contains hidden secrets and esoteric mysteries and that the Source is common to all religions, was immediately rejected by traditional (surface-based) religions. Helen Keller, in her radical years, was criticized and demonized by the preachers of traditional religious dogma.

Six: Transmission

The final esoteric principle is that it is exceedingly difficult, maybe impossible, to reach the highest rung of the spiritual ladder without superhuman help. Indeed, without a spiritual leader like Jesus, Buddha, Muhammad, or Krishna, the final steps of the spiritual transformation cannot be attained. Angels, fairies, and various spirit guides are the esoteric helpers who assist the supreme spiritual leaders at each level of consciousness. The transmission of esoteric teachings requires the guidance of a teacher who can reveal the highest stages of spiritual evolution when a disciple is ready. There is a process of initiation that occurs, usually with the help of spirit guides (like bodhisattvas or angels). The great religious texts contain directions for how to attain spiritual evolution, how to move toward Enlightenment, or Heaven, or Paradise, or Nirvana (all these terms are different names for the same insight).

Helen Keller followed the spiritual leadership of Jesus; but she was an unusual Christian because she was a Swedenborgian. As such, she considered the Bible to be allegorical and mythological, a gift from God to help humanity cognitively and compassionately evolve. According to esoteric thought, in the fog between the macro and the micro worlds, figures like Jesus and Buddha (using their spirit guides) show followers *The Way*. There is a path that spirals upward, a spiritual ladder winds towards higher realms. Heaven was real (as a spiritual goal) for Helen Keller; she had absolutely no doubt that something was divinely hidden behind everyday reality.

I will pause here for a brief aside to note that the words "Faith" and "Belief" are often used interchangeably, as if they were synonyms. This is not how Helen Keller understood the terms. People who *believe* are capable of murder, even in the name of religion. On the other hand, Faith is silent, knowing, accepting, and non-violent. You can debate with a person who holds beliefs, maybe get into a bar fight with someone who does not share your worldview. However, it is useless to try to debate a person who has Faith. They *know;* there is no need for them to discuss anything. They have no need to convince others.

In our dual minds, we contain the processes that give birth to both Belief *and* Faith. Belief resides in the Egocentric mind; Faith resides in the Allocentric mind. Faith and Belief (in dual-process theory) are equally powerful, deaf-blind to each other, and they oscillate—they take turns manifesting.

Using dual-process theory—which I discuss in Chapter Four—human consciousness is a duality. Because of this cognitive split, human beings have created distinctions like belief/faith, attention/awareness, spirit/soul, and ego/self. These concepts are not synonyms, they are mutually exclusive ideas coming from our dual cognition. This is a hypothesis I postulated when I expanded dual-process theory to fit my profession, Orientation and Mobility. It is also an expansion of a theory that has found favor in sociology and economics, but not so much in the hard sciences—where I have taken the discussion.

Look in a full-length mirror. Draw an imaginary line running down the exact center of your body. Notice that you have two mirror-image halves. You may be "all one," but your totality is composed of two duplicate halves. This analogy holds for your entire mental make-up. You have one mind, but that mind is composed of two mirror image minds. Refer to chapters Four and Five for a more in-depth exploration of dual-process theory.

To write this book, I had to stand in the fog and allow imagination to ferry insights into my mind, which I tried to keep open. One thought came to me quite forcefully: the human mind is evolving; that is the essential message of all the esoteric disciplines. Something is changing generation to generation; consciousness is getting ever more sophisticated, complex, and articulate.

Helen Keller is a mirror into which we can look to see the future of human consciousness. She was ahead of her time, smarter than most, more spiritually evolved, and she was more involved in the affairs of human development. Helen Keller could not see or hear, and yet she was astoundingly conscious—that observation leaves us almost speechless.

One tool I used to get in touch with Helen Keller's soul was to go to the places where she once stood and imagine her still alive, still speaking her mind. I started my journey where she was born, in Tuscumbia, Alabama.

Exiled from the Light

When my friend Ron Waxell and I arrived at Ivy Green to stand on the spot where Helen Keller was born, we were greeted with a chorus of bird song, as if the birds were celebrating our visit. A kitten rushed off the porch of the house and raced to greet us—from quite a distance. As I knelt to pet the little kitten, I felt like Helen Keller was greeting Ron and me; Helen was wishing me well as I wrote about her life.

Ron and I were welcomed to Ivy Green; my effort to honor Knights for the Blind felt as if it was being blessed. Ron Waxell has been my friend for over 60 years. We have a brotherly bond based on mutual respect, trust, and good-natured humor. Ron read much of this manuscript and shared his gentle reflections as I considered the impact of my words.

Inside the house, the pictures of Helen with her many dogs stood out for me. Helen knew that dogs are loyal creatures; they do not betray the people they love. For a dog, love is unconditional. Dogs also seem to sense things that human beings cannot. Helen was vibrationally in-tune with her dogs; she could sense the rhythms of nature and the silent language of animals. She seems to have been especially attuned to the emotions of dogs:

> I have had many dog friends—huge mastiffs, soft-eyed spaniels, wood-wise setters, and honest, homely bull terriers . . . my dog friends seem to understand my limitations, and always keep close beside me when I am alone. I love their affectionate ways and the eloquent wag of their tails. [29]

Many people with a Modern Level of Consciousness might denigrate the notion that animalistic spirits and magical living have validity. The voice of the Intellect will not accept what looks like old-fashioned superstition and fanciful dreaming. However, intelligence is just one half of the formula that creates humanity; intellect is wonderful but limited. As I write, I will not shy away from metaphorically walking among the spirit guides. Human imagination is far more mysterious and impactful than the scientific mind has so far discovered. Helen Keller knew this about human imagination; her intuitive abilities were profound, and she had a remarkably sophisticated spirituality.

Few know, in depth, about Helen Keller's fascinating spiritual journey. As I discussed above, Helen followed the teachings of a Swedish Renaissance man named Emanuel Swedenborg (1688–1722), and she became a devout Swedenborgian when she was just a teenager. I also became fascinated with Emanuel Swedenborg's extraordinary method for gathering spiritual information, and I studied his work long before I realized his association with Helen Keller.

Like psychics and mystics before and after him, Swedenborg went on *out-of-body journeys*, including numerous visits to Heaven and Hell where he took notes and came back with a new understanding of Christianity: The Bible was allegorical and metaphorical, according to Swedenborg; the Bible was not meant to be taken literally—that is what Swedenborg was told when he visited Heaven.

Helen left us with one out-of-body musing, documented in the book *Light in my Darkness* (1994):

> I had been sitting quietly in the library for half an hour. I turned to my teacher and said, "Such a strange thing has happened! I have been far away all this time, and I haven't left the room."
>
> "What do you mean, Helen?" she asked, surprised.
>
> "Why," I cried, "I have been in Athens!"
>
> Scarcely were the words out of my mouth when a bright, amazing realization seemed to catch my mind and set it ablaze. I perceived the realness of my soul and its sheer independence of all conditions of place and body. It was clear to me that it was because I was a spirit that I had so vividly "seen" and felt a place thousands of miles away. Space was nothing to spirit![30]

We have no idea what Helen experienced. Clearly, she thought she was out of her body and thousands of miles away. I wish she were here today in our hyper-scientific world, so we could study her experiences using modern technology. For now, we will have to absorb her words and add them to the whole mystery of her life. Skeptics, of course, will not accept Helen's interpretation as a physical journey outside her body; they would call such an event *proprioceptive hallucination*, or daydreaming. On the other hand, psychics and mystics would say *they know* what Helen experienced because they, too, have been out-of-body and have traveled to distant lands. I am somewhere in between these two views— still hanging out in the fog.

Helen Keller was spiritually wide open, actively following the dictates of her religion. She had an out-of-body experience that felt amazing to her, so she shared it with her teacher (and now with us). Helen would not have argued with the skeptics, her personality was fueled by her silent Faith.

The world Helen Keller perceived around her was not a kind or gentle world; she was soon to experience two world wars that together murdered a hundred million human beings—that level of stupid cruelty is beyond comprehension. However, even in the absence of war, injustice and cruelty were everywhere on the planet. If you are called to serve, as Helen Keller saw her mission, and if injustice confronts you and blocks your way, then you fight to make things better. Doing nothing is not an option for a truly spiritual person. And so, Helen Keller sat down at her typewriter and went to work.

Helen Keller also went through her deaf and blind existence with an eagerness to learn. Her breakthrough at the famous water fountain informed all of humanity about what it means to be conscious, and she wrote eloquently about this. She was independent in familiar settings and could navigate these spaces with no danger or difficulty. She existed in a tactual, olfactory, spiritual, and vibrational universe. Her life helps us understand what it means to perceive the world primarily through smell and vibration, although, very importantly, she had a fully functioning internal sensory system. Her vestibular, proprioceptive, and kinesthetic abilities were normal—Helen Keller became an expert at sensing the world using her whole body. That is why she could navigate, because her inner senses were relatively unimpaired. I will pick this theme up later in the book, in chapters Four and Five.

Helen's vibrational and olfactory senses developed to such an extent that she could identify her friends by their characteristic smell and by the vibration of the floor as they approached. The skin on her hands became so sensitive that she could "hear" and "converse" with people solely through fingerspelling. This method is now a common way to communicate with deaf-blind individuals, but it was relatively new in the time when Helen Keller and Anne Sullivan teamed up to converse with the world.

Helen Keller shows us that severe sensory disability does not have to limit intellectual, ethical, political, and spiritual development. Helen's life is dramatic evidence that fighters for social equality, for religious freedom, for the highest moral values, for the evolution of human consciousness, and for spiritual sophistication can prevail despite the loss of sensory capabilities. Apparently, if Helen Keller is the evidence, something wonderful can arise *from* sensory deprivation, something that ignites an inner spiritual light. Remarkably, Helen even felt that her deaf-blindness was a gift:

> As Epictetus was banished from Rome, and [then] *found himself* so I believe *I have been exiled from the light* so that I may help, if ever so little, to demonstrate the power of mind to overcome limitation. [31]

The italics above are mine. My intention is not only to clarify her message but also to highlight her wonderful language: *she has been exiled from the light.* That is a powerful revelation, a stunning insight—

she senses that there is a reason she has been banished from the land of vision. Remarkably, Helen feels that *she has been honored* with silence and darkness. This is the ultimate optimism; her character has reframed her situation. Instead of seeing her life as a great tragedy, her positive nature insists that she has been blessed with an opportunity to serve others as a role model. She feels that she is on earth to show her fellow human beings that affliction and depravation can be overcome, especially since *our mission on earth is to help others.* In other words, everyone needs to find a way to serve others and then, through service, personal afflictions and depravations diminish. Helen often repeated this conviction in her speeches and writing: *deaf-blindness is a gift that comes with grave responsibilities.*

As we look back on her life, we see that Helen Keller lived with Faith, she spoke her mind, she was courageous, and she chose a life full of adventure and boldness. In her 1957 book called *The Open Door*, Helen wrote these often-quoted words:

> Avoiding danger is no safer in the long run than outright exposure. The fearful are caught as often as the bold. Faith alone defends. *Life is either a daring adventure or nothing.*[32]

I added the italics because that sentence is an arrow to the heart. Helen is telling us to live life as if it is a grand adventure, because *it is a grand adventure.* There is another powerful observation in the above quote. Helen says that *the human mind can overcome limitations.* Our minds can feel emotion, make intentions, direct activities to accomplish intentions, and our minds can imagine a future and reimagine (and learn from) the past. The human mind can even (to various degrees) heal its own physical wounds and emotional scars. The human mind can make and use tools and create art. The human mind can build and nurture relationships. And when vision and hearing are lost, the mind not only continues to operate but it becomes stronger. Just as the sense of smell "ups its game" when vision and hearing are lost—something we would expect to happen—the mind itself grows in acuteness; the mind must "up its game" when deaf-blindness strikes. Of course, this uprising of cognitive ability only manifests when the brain itself has not been seriously damaged, as was the situation for Helen Keller.

CHAPTER THREE: THE EVOLUTION OF HELEN KELLER'S MIND

All human beings live both in this natural world and in the spiritual realm at the same time. ~ *My Religion*, by Helen Keller, 1927.

What I Know

After my retirement from teaching, after thirty years working with blind kids, I decided to pursue my lifelong interest in writing. In my generation, the ultimate accomplishment was to write a book. Now, of course, there are many ways to electronically share worldviews, from podcasts to Facebook, Instagram, Snapchat, Twitter, YouTube, Tik Tok, Reddit, Clubhouse, etc. I sense that reading an entire book in this age of short-burst communication is a major chore for younger generations. Things change, generations change; and I am fine with this natural turn of events. I am happy to compile what I know and then leave it for AI (artificial intelligence) to select smart-burst insights from the book and deliver paragraphs as needed.

The joy for me is in the creation. I write because I love to synthesize. I love to report. Like many others, my mission is with words, rather than with musical notes or mathematical symbols—I have found my creative family and I am content. With hindsight, I see that my books are self-reflective and self-conscious, perhaps excessively so, but I am also okay with the "working things out as I create" approach.

As strange as it sounds, I am trepidatious about sharing what I create. I am uncomfortable with discussing my musings or justifying my speculations. I would rather "write it all down, throw the book into the digital pool, and get on with my next book." As for marketing, that seems abhorrent to me—I say this with a good-natured grin. This book, like my others, will sit on the shelf waiting for the right minds to find it. Maybe that is you, since you got this far. I wish you well with your own mission, your own special journey.

Deciding to write books after retirement was the easy part. The hard part was deciding what I should write about. The folklore dictum is "write about what you know." I had seven decades of experiences and education to draw on. So, I made a list of "what I know." Here is the list I created:

1. *I know how the vision system works.* I was trained as an optometrist and I worked for over thirty years in a special education setting with students who had numerous kinds of vision impairments. Of course, science discovers more each day about how our senses work, so my knowledge is always tentative and growing—and nobody completely understands vision, even to this day.

2. *I know about child development.* I worked with children from infants to young adults during my career in special education. The study of human development is complex and ongoing, so my knowledge is also ongoing. Like any parent, I got most of my hands-on understanding of child development by raising three kids—all of whom, I am quite happy to say, are now sophisticated and well-adjusted adults.

3. *I am familiar with the full spectrum of special education labels.* During my thirty years as a special education professional, I worked with children who were blind, visually impaired, deaf, hearing impaired, deaf-blind, autistic, and emotionally, physically, and cognitively impaired. I do not like words like "impaired," or "disabled," because they overlook the soul of the young person; the labels redirect our attention away from everything about a child that is normal. I use these terms because I have no other words—just know that I do not like the negative impact such labels have on students, parents, teachers, and caregivers.

4. *I know the science behind human navigation.* I know how human beings came to navigate through their world and I know what

happens when there are navigational disabilities. I know this because I have been an Orientation and Mobility specialist for over forty years. The science of navigation is complex and what we know expands month by month.

5. *I know a great deal about the human brain, the emerging mind, and the evolution of consciousness.* I became obsessed with consciousness studies as I struggled to understand my students. Figuring out how the human mind works is the new frontier of science; there is an intense focus on consciousness studies going on in universities all over the planet. I will discuss consciousness below.

6. *My study of the human mind slowly combined with my knowledge about human navigation.* Consequently, my focus eventually settled on a discipline called "dual-process theory," which is relevant to the study of human navigation (and to Helen Keller). I eventually expanded dual-process theory and allied my perspective to the evolution of human consciousness. That confluence of specializations is the subject of Chapter Four.

7. *My obsession with the evolution of the human mind led to a fascination with esotericism.* For over ten years, I was part of an esoteric study group at Saginaw Valley State University. Esotericism is deeply related to the study of consciousness—it is (in part) the history (and insights) of pre-scientific thought about the evolution of consciousness.

You know, of course, that to call myself a vision specialist, navigation specialist, or a developmental specialist can only be partially and temporarily true. Knowledge in these subject areas is growing exponentially—there is no way one human being can grasp the whole of any discipline. In the above list, I have identified my interests and the arenas where my professional attention most often landed. Because of my education and professional experience, I know relatively more about these fields than a typical citizen.

As I reviewed the above list, it became clear what my books should be about. My goal as an author was to blend special education (child development), human navigation, blindness, and the evolution of cognition into coherent publications. What happened, of course, is that the seven knowledge domains listed above influenced all my books. Given the complexity of the list, when people ask me, "What is your recent book about?" my initial reaction is slow in coming. My journey has not been simple, and the trek has not been linear. Therefore, this book, like my other books, is a blend of the seven interests listed above. Here are my four previous books:

> *Bugs, Blindness, and the Pursuit of Happiness*, 2016
> *Consciousness: A New Slant on an Old Conundrum*, 2017
> *The Confusion Caused by Being Your Own Twin*, 2018
> *A Martyr for Mandelbrot; Inside the Minds of God*, 2019

I decided that my fifth book would be called *Knights for the Blind in the Battle against Darkness*. The initial idea was that I would feature blind individuals who had written about their blindness. I had a list of remarkable people ready to go. My initial decision was to write just one volume. In a single volume, I would write about Helen Keller, Daniel Kish, Jacques Lusseyran, Zoltan Torey, Russell Targ, Oliver Sacks, Kenneth Jernigan, Mike May, and maybe others. So, I started chapter one about Helen Keller. After that chapter reached two hundred pages, the obvious dawned on me: this had to be a book series and not a single book.

As I did research for this volume, I became deeply fascinated with Helen Keller and Anne Sullivan (the two are inseparable). Many of my interests coalesced around the story of Helen's life. Putting this book together has been a wonderful (and extraordinarily complex) experience.

A Short Survey

Let us now begin the long but fascinating task of analyzing Helen Keller's cognitive development. My goal is to draw you into Helen's mental journey, into the evolution of her deaf-blind mind. I am going to ask you some leading questions as I set up a discussion about Helen's consciousness; think of the questions as a short survey. This is a simple *yes* or *no* survey; you will probably want to elaborate, but let your complex mind rest for a moment; just write *yes* or write *no*:

1. Do you think it is important to be a kind person?
2. Do you think it is important to be an intelligent person?

3. Do you think it is important to be a wise person?
4. Do you think it is important to actively work to promote kindness, intelligence, and wisdom?

Got your answers? Great! Thank you for taking this short survey! Keep your answers in front of you. Now, on a separate piece of paper, write down your definition of *kindness, intelligence, wisdom, evolution, consciousness*, and *action*. Here is where you can elaborate, lay down caveats, cautions, and cite sources. I will get another cup of coffee while you write.

By the way, I love my Keurig coffee maker. I am having a Starbuck's breakfast blend this morning, with way too much cream. How are you coming with those definitions? It is not wise or intelligent to skip over the definition of important concepts, but, of course, you know that. I am going to make some toast while you finish defining the terms—I see that you are still hard at it. I will not add *socialism, communism, capitalism*, and *frustration* to your list, even though they are each relevant to any discussion of Helen Keller's mind. I will be right back with my toast. Take your time. Your worldview matters: indeed, the future of humanity depends on how wise, intelligent, kind, and socially active you and your fellow humans are.

It is my contention that you must have good definitions for these terms, as well as solid answers to this four-question survey, so that you can comprehend Helen Keller's spiritual mind. Helen's values and religious convictions made many people in her culture, mostly males in positions of power, terribly angry. If she had not been deaf and blind (and so deeply loved by so many), she would have ended up in jail alongside suffragettes Susan B. Anthony and Alice Paul.

Okay, times up. Put your name and date at the top of the page and pass your papers to the front. I will give them to my graduate students for grading. Also, quite importantly, we will use your answers to determine *your* level of consciousness. You will then receive a grade on your mastery of kindness, intelligence, wisdom, and social responsibility. After we measure your level of consciousness—based on how you defined the concepts—we will then post on social media how kind, smart, wise, and socially responsible you are, or could be.

As I said, thank you for taking the survey. These are not easy terms to define; abstract concepts require the guidance of Supreme Courts and Emeritus Professors of Thought. But, of course, you know that.

And I was just kidding about posting your ideas on social media (and I do not have any graduate students). There are people on social media who value hatefulness and ignorance and who have little to no sense of responsibility. It has been proven wrong (by social media and history) that humanity has, so far, evolved to be a stable and empathetic species.

I did not expect that you would quickly define these abstract concepts in a way that everyone would agree with; these complex words (concepts) have been the subject of debate throughout history. But that is the point—these terms cannot be nailed down for observation; they are moving targets, swiftly changing clouds. *Of course*, I know that you value kindness, intelligence, wisdom, and action—however, the question we face is this: "*To what degree* do we value these four emotionally-heavy concepts?"

This discussion of levels of consciousness is very much in tune with one of the esoteric themes of this book. The esoteric concept of *Transmutation* is about moving from primitive levels of consciousness to more sophisticated levels. Our more astute ancestors knew about this process of cognitive evolution; however, they carefully hid their discussions from a public perceived to be hostile (even violent) to the dialogue. In my opinion, Helen Keller spoke from a high level of consciousness to a public (an average cultural level of cognition) which had lower cognitive development than she did. Helen quickly found out—as the media responded to her books and articles—why ancient esoteric thinkers kept their insights to themselves.

What is Consciousness?

Consciousness has not been satisfactorily defined. We use the term, just like we do other sophisticated abstractions, as if we know what we are talking about. However, we really do not know what we are talking about; that is why the study of consciousness is the new frontier of science. We want to understand our minds, but a human mind is so complex that the task seems insurmountable—we are asking our mind, which is a process, to explain itself. Hard as it is, modern science has not shied away from the effort to comprehend what consciousness is and how it works.

You are quite aware whether you are awake or sleeping. In a broad sense, to be conscious means you are not asleep. That is easy to understand, but it is not what I am talking about here. In part, I am asking this question: "*How* awake are you during the day?" In the morning, as we stare blurry-eyed and fuzzy-headed at one of our screens, we are arguably less awake than later in the afternoon when we are trying to solve a dilemma of some kind, like a relationship issue or a technology glitch. So, you agree, I hope, that there are degrees of wakefulness. Put another way, there are energetically identifiable *states of consciousness*. Some people "sleepwalk" through their days, while others seem acutely alert and highly functional. *States* of consciousness are not the same as *levels* of consciousness—I will explain this distinction further in the paragraphs that follow.

When Alchemists, Buddhist monks, and modern scientists looked at the mind, they concluded that there are identifiable, predictable *levels (stages) of* consciousness, as well as energetic *states* of consciousness— furthermore, there is a correlation between states and levels. Ancient (esoteric) writing (alongside modern scientific studies of consciousness) found that people who were most awake (in a higher energetic *state*), were also more compassionate, more tolerant, intelligent, wise, and socially concerned (and active) than people who were less awake. Generally, individuals with lower states of wakefulness appeared to be less kind, not as intelligent, not as experienced, and not as socially active compared to more cognitively energetic people. I know this is a rather stark over-generalization, however, it is a good controversial starting point for this complex discussion.

States of consciousness are fleeting and have diurnal rhythms; in contrast, *levels* of consciousness tend to be firmly entrenched—it is difficult to change an individual's level of consciousness, while a cup of coffee might alter that same person's energetic state. As we study *levels* of consciousness, we find that people define reality and hold shared values in accordance with their worldviews—a worldview is what a level of consciousness accepts as true (as reality). As I write this, the United States has a highly polarized population. The reason for the polarization, I contend, has to do with levels of consciousness in conflict. Meaning-making, the sense of what is real, and the feeling of what it means to be awake, varies among cognitive groups.

Very importantly, each level of consciousness discussed below has constructed emotional patterns that characterize the group. In other words, each level of consciousness has an emotional perspective that is backed up by concepts and perceptions; a worldview is as much emotionally defined as it is conceptually defined. I suggest that in America, Narcissistic minds, Tribal minds, and Traditional minds are in conflict with Modern, Post-Modern, and Integral minds. Narcissistic minds, Tribal minds, and Traditional minds cannot comprehend the different worldviews of more sophisticated minds. I will discuss these levels of consciousness below, especially as they relate to Helen Keller's spiritual and cognitive unfolding.

Because every *level* of consciousness defines reality differently, the meaning of abstract concepts and the emotions attached to these concepts varies. For example, religion and politics vary within each worldview. Every level of consciousness defines words like (for example), *God, intelligence, wisdom, freedom,* and *responsibility* differently. These definitions can be so far apart that the meaning of terms can be diametrically opposite when we compare low levels of consciousness with higher levels. The God of a narcissist, for example, is the opposite of the God of a spiritually sophisticated individual. A narcissistic God is selfish, aggressive, mean-spirited, and the spitting image of the mind conjuring the God. Contrary to this narcissistic religious view, the God of a more sophisticated person is generous, gentle, benevolent, and ephemeral.

Abstract thinking varies with levels of consciousness. At lower levels of cognition, there are simpler ideas, vaguely formed. Lower cognition cannot grasp highly abstract, symbol-based concepts. The higher up the tree of consciousness, the more thinking is abstract, tenuous, dynamic, and networked. This is a hierarchical design, a pyramid wherein the base-levels of consciousness enable the higher stories of the pyramid. The brain constructs worldviews on the shoulders of older, less evolved worldviews. In other words, each level of consciousness is an addition to what came before—our ideas and cognitive processing evolve toward greater and greater abstraction.

Each level of consciousness also has characteristic emotional worldviews that define the level. Interestingly, humor—what is funny and what is not funny—varies with levels of consciousness. A narcissistic racist does not find Mark Twain's humor to be funny. We do not find many comedians on the lower rungs of consciousness (or poets, or any of the creative types of humanity). I suggest this is because minds with low levels of consciousness do not have self-reflective abilities; such minds (evidently) cannot consistently grasp irony, nuance, or the non-literal.

From a biological perspective, especially as we look at brain anatomy and physiology, what we find is that the brain builds a model of the environment. The brain then uses this model to understand and act on the domain where it lives. A brain constantly gathers evidence that supports the model of reality that it has created (a built-in confirmation bias). In other words, the human brain is constantly trying to maximize the evidence for its own behaviors. This is a biological imperative; we must create an internal model of the universe if we are to move through, react to, and influence the environment—and influence those who reside near us.

If we challenge a given individual's model of reality, their mind will rebel; a mind will not give up a perfectly functional method for staying alive and for justifying habitual behaviors. And that is the task we face when we suggest that there are different ways to model reality, different ways a mind might build a model of the universe through which it moves. A lower level of consciousness will not abandon what has worked in the past without evidence that it should rebuild its model of reality.

I suggest that Helen Keller quickly evolved to have a high level of consciousness. She did not use the language we use today to discuss levels of consciousness, but her language and actions, her dedication to service and her compassion, place her at the upper regions of cognition. It is my task below to track Helen Keller's mind as it evolved from a low level of consciousness (in her childhood) to higher levels of consciousness, which evolved as she matured. Somehow, Helen's mind continually altered its model of reality. Before we get to that, however, we need to explore a perspective that came from developmental psychology and cognitive science; the idea that there are levels of consciousness came from decades of research into how human beings cognitively and spiritually evolve.

Levels of Cognitive Evolution

Scientists have been studying human development for over a century. They have looked (in amazing detail) at babies (birth to one), toddlers (two and three), preschoolers (four and five), grade-schoolers (six to twelve), teenagers (13 to 19), and young adults (20 to 25). Developmental studies are spread across a wide range of topics, including physical maturation, emotional growth, social interaction, language facility, and cognitive sophistication. Most laymen conclude that human development peaks in the twenties, sails along at a steady level for a few decades, and then declines in the senior years. There is partial truth to this perspective (especially regarding physical maturation); however, a much more sophisticated view has emerged in the last few decades, especially around the issue of cognitive and spiritual development.

Modern developmental scientists now say that human development evolves beyond the twenties; these scientists have created scales of development that purport to show that human beings can gain ever more sophisticated and refined mental skills right up to the point of death. In other words, there is no such thing as a mature and final adult developmental stage; human beings have the potential to continue their cognitive, emotional, spiritual, and social development over a lifetime. The same holds for entire cultures, which are an average of the levels of consciousness of the populous; a culture, just like an individual, can grow in cognitive sophistication—cultures can evolve (or de-evolve).

When I discussed the evolution of consciousness in my previous books, I frequently referenced the developmental theories of Susanne Cook-Greuter;[33] her work is called "The Nine Levels of Increasing Embrace in Ego Development." Cook-Greuter's perspective is aligned with the philosophy of author Ken Wilber at Wilber's Integral Institute[34] where the evolution of consciousness is a primary focus. It is quite significant that Susanne Cook-Greuter used the phrase *increasing embrace*. Her developmental scale is as much about spiritual and emotional development as it is about intellectual (Egoic) development. It is the spiritual (developmental) pathway that I am most concerned with as I examine Helen Keller's cognitive journey. With each leap to a higher level of consciousness, Helen became more loving, more tolerant, and more concerned about the whole of humanity.

In my earlier books, I primarily used the developmental theories of Ken Wilber, Susanne Cook-Greuter, and developmental philosopher Jean Gebser[35] to build a combined scale of developmental perspectives. These popular concepts (of Wilber, Gebser, and Cook-Greuter)—alongside an ever-increasing number of developmental scales—are one tool used in academic circles to discuss the evolution of mind and consciousness.

Developmental theories have also gained political salience when used to compare so called "less-developed minds" with "more evolved minds." Caution is recommended by the developers of these scales, especially when lay populations use developmental scales to label and judge each other. Researchers are quick to point out that their purpose is *not to label and judge individuals*—as Susanne Cook-Greuter's list below makes clear. However, even as I am cautious to not over-generalize, I will not shy away from walking around on this treacherous "labeling and judging" terrain. *In a Democracy, we need a wise, intelligent, compassionate, well-informed, and socially responsible populous; otherwise, unevolved minds will vote for dictators and oligarchs and we will end up undermining our core democratic values.*

There is an underlying assumption hidden within the developmental scales. Carl Jung believed that the different mental layers in a person corresponded to the developmental history of humanity. In other words, it is assumed that the maturational stages which an individual mind goes through during a person's lifetime have been ancestrally passed down through the ages, through what is now called *epigenetics*. Each new generation starts with a baseline (genetic) gift from ancestral minds and then adds to our genetic heritage through current experiences, which are then passed to the next generation. Evidently, human beings have built-in potentials for cognitively evolving our species generation to generation in a patterned (predictable) way. The collective human mind seems to be steadily evolving to be ever more complex, generation to generation.

Below are the general principles of developmental scales that Susanne Cook-Greuter lists in her online paper "Nine Levels of Increasing Embrace in Ego Development: A Full-Spectrum Theory of Vertical Growth and Meaning Making (my commentary is in brackets):"

- *Growth [cognitive, emotional, spiritual] occurs in a logical sequence of stages* from birth to adulthood [birth to death]. The movement is often likened to an ever-widening spiral. [In other words, maturation can be geometrically depicted as a spiral staircase, not a linear ladder—evolution is a circuitous process, as if it were derived from the Golden Ratio (the Fibonacci sequence).]
- *Worldviews evolve from simple to complex*, from static to dynamic, and from egocentric, to socio-centric, to world-centric. [Each level of cognition has a self-sustaining worldview; each level literally "makes meaning." Each level of consciousness defines what is real or not real, and what is true or not true. Each level has religious, political, ethical, and social views which are different

from those above or below on the comparative scale. Abstract concepts like *Love, Kindness, Intelligence, Wisdom, and God* are defined by each level of consciousness to fit the meaning-making of the group. William Blake said, "As a man is, so he sees."]

- *Later stages are reached only by journeying through the earlier stages.* Once a stage has been traversed, it remains a part of the individual's response repertoire. [Moving from one stage to the next depends on experiences. Without meaningful jolts, rites-of-passage, or supreme effort, movement stagnates at a level. There is no guarantee that individuals will reach higher levels of consciousness.]

- *Each level of consciousness includes and transcends the previous ones.* [All the levels attained are embodied within us; we must go through each stage, which then becomes the foundation for evolution to the next higher stage. Our level of consciousness is affected by our health, what we eat and drink, what physical shape we are in, and by the stress of the environment we inhabit. Consequently, there is a level of gravity that defines each level; on some days we seem aware and mentally complex, other days less so. On our down days, we are prone to sink to lesser levels of sophistication. In other words, *A person who has reached a higher level can understand earlier worldviews (because they have been there and done that), but a person at an earlier level cannot understand more sophisticated levels of cognition.*]

- *Each later stage in the sequence is more differentiated, integrated, flexible, and capable* of optimally functioning in a rapidly changing and ever more complex world. [Your compassion, intelligence, wisdom, and sense of social responsibility grow with each movement upward. Each of us needs to cognitively evolve to keep pace with technological disruptions.]

- *A person's stage of development influences what they notice and can become aware of,* and therefore, what they can describe, articulate, cultivate, influence, and change. [As I write this, the phrase "fake news" has become a social meme in America. People who have a low level of consciousness cannot understand more sophisticated individuals, therefore, whatever comes from above—from a more sophisticated mind—is rejected as "fake." In a similar way, when people with higher levels of consciousness look down at others on the spiritual pathway, the worldview of those below appears to be fueled by "fake news," influenced by propaganda and (often) insipid memes. Each level of consciousness is a plateau (bubble) filled with like-minded individuals. This collective of individuals reinforces the worldview that defines the level. Conformation bias leads to what is called homophily, the tendency for like-minded people to gather and support an agreed upon worldview. The result is an echo chamber, a segregated community that is often misinformed due to the design of social media platforms (and human nature) that encourage and solidify echo chambers. There is usually no effort to explore ideas outside the worldview.]

- As healthy development unfolds, *there is an increase in a person's autonomy, freedom, tolerance for differences and ambiguity, flexibility, self-awareness,* and skill in interacting with the environment. [Once we are aware of these levels of consciousness, we feel called upon to follow the pathways that lead to greater and greater mental health.]

- *Defensive posturing decreases as an individual becomes more sophisticated.* [People with low levels of consciousness are reactionary, quick to condemn, and quick with retribution. Their bodies speak a silent language of rejection. The spiritually evolved level of consciousness is cautious, careful to react, emotions are felt and controlled, and tolerance and respect for others is the norm.]

- Derailment in development, lack of integration, trauma, and psychopathology are seen at all levels. Thus, *later stages are not more adjusted or "happier" than earlier stages* [depression, bipolar disorders, existential angst, PTSD, and so on, manifest at all levels of consciousness. In other words, emotional integrity is impacted at any level of cognition.]

- The depth, complexity, and scope of what people notice can expand throughout life. Yet no matter how evolved we become, *our knowledge and understanding are always partial and incomplete.* [Our senses are limited in scope and our powers of attention are dynamic and not always reliable. We are always learning, and we must continue to learn over our entire lifespan.]

- *Development occurs through the interplay between person and environment,* not just by one or the other. Development is a potential; it cannot be guaranteed. [Experiences matter and quality experiences matter most.]

- While vertical development can be invited, and the environment optimally structured towards growth, it cannot be forced. *People have the right to be who they are at any station in life.* [You can choose to reside at lower levels of consciousness. It takes a lot of time and effort (and good fortune) to experience transmutation. It is like exercise and diet, you can be flabby and malnourished, or you can put in the painful effort required to be healthy—the choice is yours to make. To put this in a less accusatory way, if you have a Modern Mind or a Post-Modern Mind (for example) and you are happy with your career, family, and life-trajectory, you need not feel guilty because you have yet to attain Christ Consciousness or Buddhist Enlightenment. "You be you," is a current meme addressing this perspective. However, I am not sure that Jesus or Buddha or Krishna would agree with this "giving up" on spiritual practice.]

- *The later the stage, the more variability for unique self-expression exists*, and the less readily we can determine where a person's center of gravity lies. [There are only a few (million?) people at the higher levels of consciousness and their sophistication is not readily understood by others. The most innovative, creative, and socially active individuals come from these higher levels of cognition.]

- All stage descriptions are idealizations that no human being fits entirely. [Be aware that this is a theoretical discipline. Be careful not to go overboard when applying this perspective to dynamic, complex, evolving human beings—receive one person at a time, threat them with respect, and judge them (if you must judge) with extreme caution.]

I used the above outline when I crafted my own composite developmental scale to describe human cognitive evolution. I added the ideas of philosopher Jean Gebser who had described the structure of human consciousness in a historical context before Cook-Greuter or Wilber developed their perspectives. I also used Ken Wilber's complex perspectives and intricately interwove his theories with Gebser and Cook-Greuter. I was working out the concepts as I began writing my first three books on consciousness—I am sure there are a few naïve and incomplete ideas (mixed with my brand of humor) in the earlier texts, but foundational perspectives still feel sound. I added dual-process theory to the developmental scales, which I will discuss in the next chapter.

The concept of a *worldview* has anatomical and physiological support in the neuroscience community. The biological design that makes human beings smarter than other animals is the relatively large size of our neocortex, which is the most advanced processing region of the brain. Primates may share 99% of our genetic makeup but our neocortex is the size of a table napkin—much larger than any of the primates. Primates have neocortices about the size of a business envelope when spread out.

The primary role of a neocortex is to construct a model of the world—a spatial framework that enables straight-ahead navigation. In other words, *Worldview Creation* is the main reason to have a neocortex. Our behaviors are determined by these hardwired (but malleable) neuronally-derived worldviews. We make predictions moment-to-moment based on these models of reality.

A cortical model (a worldview) gives us our invariants, a stable reality. A neocortical model also allows us to decide almost instantly if an observation—something in the environment—does not fit the model. A worldview model can be updated, based on new knowledge or fresh (especially unique) experiences. Getting "out of a comfort zone" forces the brain to reconsider hardwired representations of reality. To move from one level of consciousness (based on a simple worldview) to a higher level of consciousness (based on an updated and more sophisticated worldview), involves neural rewiring, the creation of a different brain. It is no wonder that we find it so hard to "change a mind."

～

Moving through *levels* of consciousness described above is not (as I stated earlier) the same as moving through *states* of wakefulness—experienced meditators can move at will through states of consciousness; however, it is much harder to move through levels of consciousness. Susanne Cook-Greuter in her outline of cognitive evolution (discussed above) uses the terms "level" and "stage" as synonyms. However, she also makes an important clarification that "states" of consciousness are fleeting relative to levels (or stages).

There are currently seven accepted *states* of consciousness. Here are the seven, from the slowest frequency waves to the highest frequency waves:

1. Epsilon-wave state (.1 to .5 hertz): a state of suspended animation.
2. Delta-wave state (.5 to 4 hertz): deep sleep and dreaming.
3. Theta-wave state (4 to 9 hertz), a waking-dream state. Also the zone where psychic experiences manifest.
4. Alpha-wave state (8 to 12 hertz), a relaxed (reflective, pensive) background state.
5. Beta-wave state (12 to 35 hertz): the busy mind we use for everyday activities—our so-called awake-mind.
6. Gamma-wave state (35 to 100 hertz): present during maximum performance (physical and mental) and during profound concentration (intense periods of study).
7. Lambda-wave state (100 to 200 hertz): believed to be related to transcendence, bliss, and a sense of oneness.

The slow waves, Epsilon, Delta, Theta, and Alpha occur when the eyes are closed. Beta, Gamma, and Lambda waves manifest when the eyes are open. People with higher levels of consciousness often experiment with willfully moving themselves through *states* of consciousness using meditation, tai chi, contemplative prayer, yoga, (etc.) to self-develop. Presumably, the lowest *levels* of consciousness (Narcissistic, Ethnocentric and Traditional minds) are aware of the slower Beta waves but are not aware of higher-frequency waves.

When higher-order thinking is required, the higher frequency waves must be used—high-Beta to high-Gamma. Therefore, lower *levels* and lower *states* of consciousness are both related to less evolved minds, to Narcissistic, Ethnocentric and Traditional minds. Higher levels and higher states of consciousness are related to more evolved minds—Modern, Post-modern, Integral, and Post-integral (discussed below).

It is my contention to show that Helen Keller had a very evolved, highly sophisticated mind. I will argue below that she had an emerging Post-modern mind in a time when most minds were struggling to move into the Modern level of consciousness. Most minds were Traditional or Tribal in Helen's time—her behaviors were beyond the comprehension of these less evolved minds.

We face a conundrum as we begin this investigation of Helen Keller's highly evolved mind: if higher *states* of consciousness are triggered by an eyes-open condition, how did Helen's blind-mind become entrained to Beta, Gamma and Lambda states—in other words, how was she able to concentrate/study/focus with high-frequency intensity without vision?

We are forced to conclude—with Helen Keller as the evidence—that it is possible to reach high levels of consciousness and high states of consciousness without vision and hearing. But how is this accomplished? Perhaps embeddedness is a plausible answer.

All human behavior is accomplished by the whole organism—that is the meaning of embeddedness. The senses never work in isolation—they are a team; each sense is embedded within the team of senses. If the observed behavior is, for example, *concentration on a task* or goal, all the senses are involved (even though one sense may dominate). If we remove a sense, the other senses simply continue with the task. Therefore, states of consciousness and levels of consciousness must be the work of the total organism—the higher frequencies must somehow be attainable without vision.

∾

Below is the developmental outline I used in my earlier textbooks. I will use this list as I suggest the spiritual and cognitive pathway that enabled Helen Keller to develop such an extraordinary mind. As I said, the list below is a distillation of several developmental theories:

- The Infant Mind
- The Archaic Mind
- The Tribal Mind
- The Warrior Mind
- The Traditional Mind
- The Modern Mind
- The Post-Modern Mind
- The Integral Mind
- The Post-Integral Mind

Each of the minds listed above represents a level of consciousness (an echo chamber composed of like-minded individuals). It is understood that the minds of human beings move through these stages, unless, for some reason, they get stuck at a level and fail to cognitively develop further. The discussion of these levels of consciousness is relevant to Helen Keller because she was, in my opinion, more cognitively and spiritually evolved than most of her contemporaries in the early 1900s. It is no accident that she befriended like-minded and highly evolved souls like Harvard Professor William James and American icon Mark Twain. My plan is to look at Helen Keller's lifespan and surmise how and when she moved through stages of cognitive and spiritual growth.

I need to emphasize again that developmental scales are theoretical. They are based on research techniques that then draw tentative hypotheses about how consciousness evolves. I combined several of these theoretical scales and added dual-process theory when I crafted the scale used below. In other words, you might think of what follows as a plausible tool, a reasoned approach for considering how minds evolve and especially how Helen Keller's mind might have evolved. Enjoy the discussion but do not suspend your critical mind—reality is more complex than I am able to depict in this summary.

Before we head out on this journey, however, there is something I want you to know. I am going to compare human souls, one alongside the other, and I am going to imply that some souls are more sophisticated than others. I am going to tell you that the human mind has been evolving through eons. With each passing era, the human brain evolved, and the mind became more and more aware of itself and of other minds. I am going to tell you that even though we speak the same language and travel from birth to death together, and laugh and cry, succeed, and fail, and try again, even though one life looks the same as another, we are quite different individuals—*despite appearances, we are not all alike*. We are on the same spiritual path, but we are at different points on the upward spiral.

Here is what my *inner preacher* must tell you and you must understand: *Your task in this existence is to carry Love forward*. That is as clear as I can say it. Helen Keller said as much, but I am stating it again, because I do not want you to misinterpret what you are about to read. No matter where your level of consciousness on the day when you read this, I am not saying that you do not contain Love, that you do not value Love, or that you do not deserve Love—you do. I am saying that it is necessary for Love to endure from generation to generation, no matter what barriers stand in the way. You have a responsibility to be on the team that moves Love from generation to generation. Another way to say this is that you are part of the evolution of the human species, part of the team (in this era) charged with keeping loving-kindness thriving into the next generation. Our species is on an unknown journey toward an unknown destination—trust that you are not only a miracle, with a cosmic mind unlike any other, but also that you are a member of an evolving species.

A primary reason to discuss levels of consciousness is to request that you take Love seriously, that you, too, like Helen Keller, also become a champion for the continuation of Love, that you hold the treasure within, that you share the treasure while you are living, and when you depart this life, you leave Love behind to grow in others. Helen Keller's message to us is simply that we honor the Christian values of Love and Service—she says it repeatedly in her books and essays. Notice that this message is quite esoteric—it is outside-the-box "thinking." Historically, Love carries only lip-service; it is rarely placed above Egoic intelligence or valued more than patriarchal aggression.

I could not have written this book with integrity without hammering that insight into your mind, over and over. Helen Keller holds the mirror of Love before our face and does not let us look away. She asks humanity to stop being selfish, ignorant, and cruel. Move in the direction of Love.

Consider this question: When did this life force we call *Love* begin for human beings? Was it in the Stone Age when people began to bury their dead, when they began to hold ceremonies honoring the dead, when a deep sense of loss, grief, and bewilderment were first felt—maybe long before Homo Sapiens? Something happened to our ancient ancestors as they became aware of being a creature that was alive, animated, and social. Our ancestors began to feel this thing we call *Love*.

Love wishes to endure long after we are gone. Love has been on a long, long journey and now the preservation and the further evolution of Love rests within you. That means you have inherited a grave responsibility. The survival of humanity, our species, depends upon the outcome of the battle between Love and Indifference (and hatefulness). There is a fundamental seed in the universe that gives rise to the energy we call Love. As evolution flows, Love takes root and expands with the awakening of the mind.

I must tell you this because I want you to know that each of the levels of consciousness discussed below contains people who know what Love is—there are kind people everywhere you go on the planet. There is laughter and sadness at each level and each level has intrinsic value. However, the reason to travel the spiritual path is to develop greater and greater Love, to get better at Loving. Being smart, evolving a powerful Egoic mind is not the only reason to go on this life-journey. As valuable and miraculous as our Egoic minds are, Love is the primary reason why human life (culture) exists and must endure. We are vessels on a voyage—we carry a cargo, a treasure trove called Love.

Also be aware that each level of consciousness discussed below has artists and musicians who feel the spiritual journey and are on their way through developmental levels, reaching for something higher up the mountain that is more sophisticated and compassionate then where they find themselves. When we look at our children growing up, we marvel and feel joyful as they go through their lives. We love then as infants, we love them as toddlers, we love them as preteens and teens, and we love and marvel at our children as young adults. What I am suggesting below, from my perch at the end of the limb, as a man in his late seventies, is that there are other stages that our children go through beyond their twenties, stages that are also marvelous and that should fill us with wonderment and appreciation.

Knowing about these levels of consciousness does not diminish our wonderment and support for our children as they grow. However, there are forces that weigh on our children that might prevent them from becoming more cognitively sophisticated, more emotionally compassionate, or more socially responsible—there are cultural and technological pressures that can cause their moral, spiritual, and mental sophistication to freeze up and stop growing. For example, I suggest that being a narcissist for a lifetime robs an individual from experiencing the spiritual journey.

~

Do Not turn Spirituality into an Egoic obsession. The discussion below will go horribly wrong if you take these levels of consciousness to imply that there ought to be a spiritual ruling elite. We do not want another Eugenics movement championing the idea that only those with sophisticated levels of consciousness are truly worthy of replication. That outcome would be the exact opposite of my intentions. The Ego must be careful with this knowledge.

I have made a distinction between our two minds (Chapter Four) and I have argued that we have two sets of language, one Egoic and the other Allocentric (Soul-driven). The result of this dual-process perspective is that Belief is not the same as Faith, and the Ego is not the same as the Self (Soul). Now I suggest—using dual-process thinking—that *religion* is Egoic while *spirituality* is about the evolution of the Soul. Religion can be clannish, belief-based, and capable (as history clearly shows) of being the work of cruel, self-serving Egos—the Devil often dresses as a Saint. Spirituality, however, is a whole-body awareness of empathy, compassion, and joyful animation; spirituality is silently faith-based, and it arises from within. Spirituality is non-violent, tolerant, and it does not tire out or need a rest—it also does not divide people into categories of worthiness. Spirituality evolves as Love evolves.

Do Not turn this discussion into an excuse to propagate a particular religion. Remember the esoteric principle of concordance: *All* the world's religious traditions, at their core, are variations of the same set of esoteric doctrines—all religions were created on the same esoteric loom. It is Love and Service that links the core of all religions. If we lose that awareness, if we fail to see the differentiation between Egoic religions and spiritual practices, we will drain spirituality from the core of humanity.

Do Not turn this discussion into an excuse to propagate a particular race or ethnic background. Enough madness has occurred around issues of race and ethnicity to last through eternity—we do not need further reasons to justify eugenics and war. Studies of levels of consciousness *are tools* for exploring the evolution of cognition and spirituality—research findings are always in flux, always tentative, always open to challenge, and always done with the intention of bringing humanity together rather than dividing us.

These developmental scales are often referred to as *Ego-development* scales. Only an Ego would conceive of a pathway, a step-by-step journey, or a spiral hierarchy. However, the Self (Soul) is like music or dance that occurs in the moment. The Self flows and plays; it does not have a trajectory. These developmental scales are rational depictions, an attempt to explain cognition using a theoretical (logical) framework. The Ego-scales are, therefore, useful, and important, but they represent only one half of what makes us human beings.

If you are troubled as you explore this comparative approach to understanding cognition, it is probably your Soul rebelling against outside interference with the playful flow of your being. Ironically, as the Egoic rational hierarchy is revealed, the result is a spiritual one, as if the Ego—after careful study—has logically derived, validated, and honored the Soul.

Singer/songwriter Willie Nelson once said that "music cuts through everything." What Willie means, I think, is that human beings can, at any time, disappear into the rhythms and melodies of music. In my terminology, the Soul is entirely about flow, harmony, and compassion; as such, the Soul (the Allocentric mind) is an escape from the labeling obsession of the stressed-out Egoic mind. It does not matter where you and I reside on these developmental scales because we can escape at any time into the Soul-mind where we blend with all other human beings in a harmonic bliss—when lost in the music or the dance, we are all equal.

Helen Keller was stripped bare of visual and auditory sensations at nineteen months of age. However, after her illness, Helen was left with a primal connection to something that transcends everyday human activity. She felt this power at her core, and she eventually discovered that its name was *Love*. Helen became Love's champion as she matured—she became a channel, a voice, a messenger, a translator, a witness for Love. However, she was not born this way (with this grandiose self-proclaimed mission) she had to go through many of the levels of consciousness described below.

Pause for a moment to reflect that Anne Sullivan was able to teach Helen Keller concepts like *love*. It is one thing to describe a noun, a thing, but quite another challenge to get across the essence of a process, of evolution, of inner-connectedness. Sullivan taught Helen the meaning of "to think" by fingerspelling t-h-i-n-k on Helen's forehead. A lesser mind than Sullivan's would have avoided the incredible challenge of teaching concepts. Sullivan was a fiercely determined woman worthy of her legendary title *The Miracle Worker*.

There is one other important insight to consider when we examine these levels of consciousness. Human beings tend to settle into a level of consciousness and stay there for a lifetime, for as long as that life is not rocked by extreme conditions that destroy habitual patterns of behavior. Helen would have been a normal Southern Belle had her body not been assaulted at nineteen months, forging a deaf-blind mind.

It is often necessary to shock an old pattern of consciousness into the next level of cognitive and emotional sophistication. Trauma causes a useful catharsis; we might voluntarily undergo a rite-of-passage designed to deliberately cause a (mild) traumatic experience with the intention of altering a mind. Wars and pandemics often wipe out the habits of individuals, groups, cultures, governing bodies, and global systems. For example, the Black Death (in the year 1347) signaled the end of the Middle Ages and heralded the arrival of the Renaissance. Wars create new technologies that go on to disrupt old ways of socializing, doing business, and communicating. Often the death of a loved one sends the mind spiraling out of control, severely shocking the body, destroying routines and behaviors.

My point is that changes to levels of cognition often come from unexpected external shocks rather than conscious intent. I would also suggest that global trauma like we are experiencing as I write this (the Covid pandemic), can forge positive social and cultural changes that might never have occurred had not disaster visited the planet. Individuals can also find themselves in traumatic circumstances that shred their worldview and cause a reformation of their cognition. The research of developmental psychologists and cognitive scientists suggest that there are developmental stages that can predict where a mind (or set of minds) might go after trauma.

If you are pondering what to do with this complex developmental set of theories, I suggest that you remember to treat everyone you meet with deep respect. In Stuttgart, Germany on October 6, 1922, philosopher Rudolf Steiner, in a lecture to young followers, gave us the guidelines for how we should go forth day-by-day:

> In going through life and meeting individuals we must always have an open heart—an open mind for the individual. Towards each single individual we should be able to unfold a completely new human feeling . . . we do justice to a human being only when we see in the person an entirely new personality . . . if we come with a general idea in our heads, saying that a human being should be like this or like that, we are being unjust . . . with every definition of a human being we really put up a screen to make the human being invisible.

Putting people into categories and judging them based on categorical definitions is a dubious undertaking, an entirely Egocentric process. The Ego development scales that I am about to discuss are valuable and enlightening tools, but they only have complete value when we remember to honor people, one at a time. We do not have the cognitive capacity to accurately judge the cosmically complex minds of individual human beings. Judge (if you must) cautiously, generously, tentatively, and wisely. Ken Wilber was a co-developer of the developmental levels of consciousness discussed below. After decades of work, he posted this on his Integral Website:

> I have one major rule: Everybody is right. More specifically, everybody—Including me—has some important pieces of truth, and all of those pieces need to be honored, cherished, and included in a more gracious, spacious, and compassionate embrace.

Think of each person you encounter as a mind that knows something that you do not know. If you are trying to solve the riddle of life, think of each person as a puzzle-holder, someone who holds puzzle pieces that fit in the gestalt called life—the input of each person is needed to comprehend the wider cognitive universe.

There is a paradox and an irony that we encounter as human beings; we have minds that are mutually exclusive (my hypothesis). At every turn, with every decision, we face this built-in irony and paradox; we must honor each individual Soul as we, also, equally honor the Ego that uses generalizations and statistics to allot individuals into judgmental categories. The Ego and the Soul are equal siblings in my worldview. Paradoxically, our two minds are like the Greek statue of Janus, fused viewpoints staring in diametrically opposite directions (see Chapter Four for an explanation).

With all these complex caveats fresh in mind, let us turn to Helen Keller and explore her life from infancy to old age using developmental scales as a guide. As you read, think of your own life, the evolution of your own mind. Helen Keller's cognitive evolution helps us put our own cognitive evolution into focus.

Helen Keller's Infant Mind

Helen Keller was born with normal eyesight and normal hearing; she was on track to developmentally unfold like any other child. She had a healthy brain and potentially above average intelligence. Then, in 1882, came a fever at nineteen months that destroyed her vision and hearing, and from that day onward, everything changed for Helen. Overnight, her mind lost two of the primary ways human beings learn about the world—through seeing and hearing. Her brain had to suddenly, and very rapidly, begin the process of rewiring itself.

A key question to ask at the beginning of this exploration of Helen's mental development is this: How evolved is a normal human brain at nineteen months—what can such a young mind do? What has a nineteen-month-old mind learned through experience and through normal maturation? The answer is revealing.

By nineteen months, the human brain has laid down the foundation for language, socialization, and for navigation through an environment. At birth, a brain is *potentially* ready to speak Mandarin, Urdu, Hebrew, Arabic, English, any language, depending on what the parents and community use to communicate. The infant brain is also *potentially* ready to move about any kind of domain, through a yurt located on the tundra, or through an apartment high rise in an urban setting. In other words, *the basics are in place by nineteen months* to master the language of the culture, to learn the rules and emotional signaling of the culture, and to navigate through the environment where the culture operates.

What is clear from the developmental evidence, is that a nineteen-month-old child has already built the neuronal networks that comprehend how space is laid out. At nineteen months, Helen unconsciously knew about floors, walls, ceilings, doorways, inside, outside, things above and things below, things in front and things behind. Helen's mind could use landmarks and pathways to navigate—the neurology was in place to enable rapid and efficient movement through space at nineteen months. To accomplish smooth navigation, the brain primarily uses vision and hearing. When vision and hearing suddenly disappear, the brain must use the other senses to enable navigation; however, by nineteen months, *the foundation is in place* for comprehending and moving through space *using whatever senses are available.*

Developmental specialists know that a nineteen-month-old child can walk, run, climb, push, pull, and bend over to pick up a toy from a standing position. A nineteen-month-old child can also bite, poke, scratch and hit others. Hand-and-eye coordination is quickly developing by the nineteenth month, and the sense of balance is becoming highly refined.

The child of nineteen months can say at least 10 to 20 words, as the dawn of language is blossoming; one of Helen's early words was "wah wah," for water. A growing proto-ego is emerging at this age and tantrums are not uncommon when that ego cannot get its own way. The child has a familiar home environment that has a sensory signature, familiar sights, sounds, and smells. There are familiar routines, eating, bathing, going to the bathroom, a bedtime ritual, a waking up ritual, familiar individuals (and pets) present in the environment. In a healthy household, there is a comforting sameness and security to life at nineteen months.

Caregivers reward some behaviors and discourage other behaviors—the child, at nineteen months, is learning what is considered appropriate and what is not. Sharing and cooperating with others in a social setting is just beginning to develop. The child is constantly watching and listening; she is learning to mirror the behaviors observed in those around her. The child can use imaginative play to mimic what is seen and heard. The child of nineteen months is also rapidly learning about actions and the consequences of actions.

One of the primary questions I asked myself as I started this book was about Helen's ability to navigate through space without hearing and seeing the environment. How can a person navigate without vision? Add hearing loss and the task becomes seemingly insurmountable. However, being normal for nineteen months affords a child a long head start. By nineteen months, Helen had learned what space is and how to navigate smoothly through it. Her domain was her house and the immediate area around the house. That knowledge—the subconscious memory of how the domain was laid out—was not lost when vision and hearing disappeared. Compared to Helen Keller, and her nineteen-month head start, a congenitally deaf-blind individual would have a far more difficult time understanding and negotiating space.

Each stage of a child's development is marked by how much of a domain that child has mastered. For example, an infant is carried everywhere and has no mastery of independent movement. A toddler begins to move around in a single room but soon can negotiate several indoor spaces. The toddler is still carried around a lot and often visits other domains as the parents go about their day. Through this means, the child becomes aware of the barn, the yard, the garden, the church, the grandparent's house, and so on, depending on the environment and family circumstances.

Without this head start, Helen Keller could never have become the wunderkind that she became. She had the basics in place, the foundation that Anne Sullivan would use to mold her mind.

Helen Keller's Archaic Mind

There is a fundamental first understanding underpinning developmental scales: the development of the mind of a child replays the development of the human mind throughout history. In other words, early in species development, going back tens of thousands of years, humanity had a collective mind that was not much more sophisticated than that of a modern nineteen-month-old child. Evidently, our very ancient ancestors had only rudimentary language, crude social skills, limited intellectual capacity for problem-solving, and undeveloped cultural emotions. Lifespans were brutally short in the caveman days—twenty to thirty years is a rough average—there was little time to develop wisdom, to learn from experience.[36]

Philosopher Jean Gebser identified an early phase of development— thousands of years ago—that he called the Archaic period. Presumably (theoretically), the people of the Archaic age had an instinctual, impulsive, reactive, *sensorimotor cognition*; we can surmise that there was a lot of sniffing and elbowing going on and no technological prowess beyond chipping flint to make primitive hand tools.

Another fundamental understanding about developmental scales is that human beings born today can exist an entire lifetime at one of these early developmental levels. For example, there are people with brain damage so severe that they are stuck at a cognitively infant stage of development where everything must be done for them. There are also individuals alive today who are stuck at the Archaic level. They also have severe brain anomalies that prevent them from developing beyond the Archaic stage of cognition. In other words, there are Archaic humans alive today who are sniffing, elbowing, and acting out of reactive instincts. Most of these individuals are in custodial care.

However, *compared to minds that came previously*, the healthy Archaic brain was relatively sophisticated. Archaic people inherited all the genetically evolved behaviors of their ancestors. Archaic Minds were also the foundation for more sophisticated minds that came later in evolution. Our modern minds hold the rudiments of our Archaic ancestors.

A sense of magic was (presumably) prevalent in Archaic people; they could perceive the world around them, they could move accurately through that world, but they could not explain the world. These people were understandably superstitious; they believed in unseen forces beyond and behind all that happened in everyday life. They were affected by events in the world, but they had little control over what happened to them. They had a home range where they could hunt and forage, but they could not conceive of worlds beyond their immediate sensations. To be superstitious is to have a primitive worldview; this worldview was a foundation upon which more sophisticated worldviews could eventually be created as minds evolved.

Modern adults stuck at this stage of mental development struggle just to fulfil basic survival needs. If these needs are not met, the Archaic person will rebel or withdraw into themselves. In the Archaic mind, other human beings are just objects for gratifying needs, not people with their own needs. Archaic minds feel that good people give to them what they want, while mean people do not give them what they think they must have. Cognition is simple and language is severely limited in Archaic people. At this stage, the individual has an inadequate understanding of the complexities of life, and they are easily confused and overwhelmed. The Archaic mind is a Narcissistic mind.

The Archaic mind is also an instinctual mind. Life just happens to this mind; there is no contemplation, little (or no) reflection on the past, and little (if any) future projection; everything is now. This primitive Narcissistic mind wants its own way and throws a fit if things do not go well.

Now, think of the young Helen Keller eating off everyone's plate, grabbing whatever she pleases, crashing to the floor her dolls when she is frustrated, kicking, biting, screaming, and pinching anyone who gets in the way of her immediate desires. She is literally living hand to mouth. Her communication is severely limited and emotionally demanding. She could have sat passively and disappeared into her void, but instead she displayed a ferocious willpower. That willpower, that thirst to know and communicate was the force that propelled her into more sophisticated levels of consciousness as she matured.

Helen's early life was limited by her immediate surroundings; her domain was small—there was no sense of living and dying, no sense that other minds also have instincts and thoughts, no awareness of the vast web of lifeforms beyond the walls of her house or the confines of her yard. Before Anne Sullivan arrived, Helen Keller had an Archaic mind, a mind that was blind to the pain of others.

Within this Archaic level of consciousness, (the Narcissistic mind), there is no empathy and no sense of responsibility to others. The Archaic mind is a basic animal consciousness, with no self-awareness and no self-observation. When Helen got older and reflected on her Archaic stage, she described her early self as a Phantom. In her 1955 book *Teacher*, Helen speaks of herself in the third person:

Phantom did not seek a solution for her chaos because she knew not what it was. Nor did she seek death because she had no conception of it. All she touched was a blur without wonder or anticipation, curiosity, or conscience. If she stood in a crowd, she got no idea of collective humanity. Nothing was part of anything, and there blazed up in her frequent, fierce anger which I remember not by the emotion but by a tactual memory of the kick or blow she dealt to the object of that anger . . . She did not know "shadow" because she had no idea of "substance." For her there was no beauty, no symmetry, no proportion. It was all want, undirected want—the seed of all wants of mankind. [37]

The difficulty of civilizing the Phantom was portrayed in the play and movie *The Miracle Worker*. The famous scene at the breakfast table stunned audiences. In *Teacher*, Helen tells the story from the Phantom's perspective:

Phantom was in the habit of picking food out of her plate and the plates of others with her fingers. Annie Sullivan would not put up with such behavior, and a fight followed during which the family left the room. Phantom acted like a demon, kicking, screaming, pinching her would-be deliverer, and almost throwing her out of her chair, but Annie succeeded in compelling her to eat with a spoon and keep her hands out of the plate. Then Phantom threw her napkin on the floor, and after an hour's battle Annie made her pick it up and fold it.

One morning Phantom would not sit down to learn words which meant nothing to her and kicked over the table. When Annie put the table back in its place and insisted on continuing the lesson, Phantom's fist flew like lightning and knocked out two of Annie's teeth.

Now that is a story you do not often hear: two of Sullivan's teeth were knocked out! That must have affected Sullivan's entire life; every time she ate, she must have been reminded of Helen's flying fists. Here is another rendition of what Sullivan faced:

The child she had come to educate threw cutlery, pinched, grabbed food off dinner plates, sent chairs tumbling, shrieked, struggled. She was strong, beautiful but for one protruding eye, unsmiling, painfully untamed: virtually her first act on meeting the new teacher was to knock out one of her front teeth. [38]

I guess we will not know for sure which teeth got knocked out or how many, but we get the point; this was no cake walk for Anne Sullivan. She was confronting an unevolved Archaic mind that had no interest in the concept of education.

Here is Helen's remembrance of the dawn of language (at the water fountain) and the emergence of a fully formed Egoic mind:

> I understood that what my teacher was doing with her fingers meant that the cold something that was rushing over my hand was water, and that it was possible for me to communicate with other people by these hand signs . . . The world to which I awoke was still mysterious; but there was hope and love and God in it, and nothing else mattered. Is it not possible that our entrance into heaven may be like this experience of mine? [39]

I love that final line: "Is it not possible that our entrance into heaven may be like this experience of mine?" At the point of death, will there be a flash of insight, a sudden *Aha Moment* that will reveal a hidden language, an unknown universe? Indeed, there is so much we do not know about our existence. Helen Keller is a mirror, a message, which enables us to reflect on the mystery and the hope that is our own unique life.

Despite this dismal description of the Archaic level of consciousness, there is a spark within this mind, a tiny light waiting patiently to be released. There are things hidden from view as we attempt to analyze this mind. There is Soul-potential and Ego-potential waiting to arise. This mind will blossom but only if the right kinds of experiences are offered to this hungry deaf-blind mind. Anne Sullivan would slowly and with great perseverance bring the experiences needed to cause a transformation in Helen's cognitive evolution.

Helen Keller's Tribal Mind

Something happens to Archaic Minds, maybe natural maturation brings about cognitive evolution, maybe a rite-of-passage occurs through deliberate rituals, or maybe a mythological bolt of lightning happens that widens the worldview of the Archaic mentality. Whatever the reason, an experience or internal revelation occurs that causes a transmutation from a lower to a higher level of consciousness. We know very well what happened to Helen Keller's Archaic mind, it was transcended at the famous water fountain and a new mind emerged, a Tribal mind.

Readers of the Helen Keller story know about the breakthrough, the miracle at the water fountain, when a spiritual force seemed to suddenly explode out of Helen's imprisoned deaf-blind body. Consider Anne Mansfield Sullivan and Helen Adams Keller at the dramatic water pump, when the blessing that was to become Helen Keller woke up and discovered a world beyond—your heart stops as you run this image over and over again in your mind, the water from the pump flowing over Helen's hand as Sullivan spelled "water," "water," "w-a-t-e-r," again and again, until Helen suddenly froze, in shock, as the miracle of language unveiled itself to her starving-to-death mind. She dropped to her knees, slapped her hand against the earth, her other hand outstretched, pleading for Sullivan to tell her the name for the ground she walked upon. Helen Keller's name for Annie Sullivan, what she wrote in a hand, fingerspelling each letter, was t-e-a-c-h-e-r.

Anne Sullivan said of the transmutation, of this miraculous moment: "It was a tremendous experience. Religions have been founded on less." [40]

This was a profound rite-of-passage, a movement from an exceptionally low level of consciousness to something vastly more complex and wonderful. However, there was more to this moment; not only did Helen leap from an Archaic consciousness to a Tribal consciousness, she also intuitively realized (sensed for the first time) that she had two minds; this was the moment when she *knew*, intuitively, that she had an Ego as well as a Self. (Dual consciousness is the subject of Chapter Four).

As a wild animal, an Archaic phantom, a creature driven by self-serving instincts, Helen lived in her whole body, in a totally Allocentric mind. She lived in the background without an awareness of individuality (except for instinctual needs). Until that moment at the water fountain, she did not know there was a universe of *seer and seen*, Ego and the Ego-of-others. Helen found her Egocentric mind that day at the water fountain; she suddenly felt like she was the center of the universe—

everything revolved around her. And all that revolved around her could be named and discussed. Helen suddenly had a way to communicate, a way to learn, and, eventually, a way to serve; she had found her place to stand in the universe.

Once she grasped "seer and seen," (Ego and Other), Helen understood that an avenue had opened, a reason appeared for her to communicate. So, in my opinion, it was not *just* language that threw opened a cognitive door when the miracle occurred, and it was not just a leap from Archaic consciousness to Tribal consciousness, it was also the intuitive discovery of a whole different mind—that is why we sense that Helen's cognitive leap was miraculous.

The Egocentric mind operates when the body is relatively still (see Chapter Four). Opposite to this, the Allocentric mind (The Self) operates when the body is navigating (in motion). Helen's "sudden freezing" is the important clue that the Egoic mind had suddenly emerged. Paying attention requires stillness. The more profound the attention, the more profound the stillness. Before the epiphany at the water fountain, communication was only about *signaling* needs, but suddenly, at that magic moment, *meaning appeared*—words were *symbols* and could be used to dialogue with others.

This transmutation from an Archaic mind to a Tribal mind was probably the most stark and stunning transformation that Helen Keller would experience in her lifetime. The Archaic mind did not disappear, of course, it was now simply the foundation upon which a Tribal mind could begin its evolution. The Archaic mind communicates through signaling, but the Tribal mind made the great (although rudimentary) breakthrough into symbol-based communication. From here, a slow evolution began as symbol-based communication became ever more sophisticated with each transformation of consciousness.

Helen went from kicking, biting, and screaming, to a lovable little girl who hugged and kissed others. This transformation was so remarkable because it occurred in a flash of insight, instantly. There was an ancestral memory inside Helen (as there is within all of us) wherein past (ancestral) cognitive breakthroughs are preserved. These earlier minds apparently lie within us as potential transmutations, awaiting experiences that cause profound changes in awareness.

The Tribal mind is related to the next possible transmutation called the Warrior mind, except the Tribal mind is gentler and like a hive brain (The Warrior mind is discussed below). In a hive brain, there is a buzz of activity that surrounds the individual; things get done by others as everyone fulfills their assigned roles. A social structure is perceived that dictates how everyday reality is supposed to work. Helen stayed in this level of consciousness for several years as her language and thinking skills slowly became more sophisticated. But Helen also moved through stages of consciousness faster than others (my speculation). Her vision and hearing did not constantly throw up distractions, as is the case with "normal" children who are bombarded constantly by interesting sights and sounds. Without distractions, Helen was able to concentrate with a profound focal power.

Think of our Neolithic ancestors (who had Tribal minds). For these people to survive, they had to cooperate. They had a sense that they were part of a (primitive) community with a shared social structure and a common (rudimentary) language. They had to trust each other, to accept a hive-like division of labor between the sexes and the generations, and they had to evolve an understanding that if you share, then others will share with you. Whereas the Archaic mind *perceived a world in which events simply happened*, the Tribal mind has a more evolved Ego; there is a strengthening understanding of an Ego that is separate from other Egos and separate from the things found in the environment—The Tribal mind *perceived a world in which events happened to an Ego.*

Tribal humans expanded their mastery of spaces and they journeyed beyond the range of the Archaic individual. There is also an increasing awareness of the activity of others as the Ego evolves. For the infant, the mother constitutes the world. The Archaic individual moves beyond the mother and becomes aware of a family unit. The Tribal individual increases the number of people that are perceived and monitored, an extended family; there is now an awareness of a small active community called a tribe.

In the Tribal stage, rudimentary independence emergences; dependence on the care of others is diminished. At this prerational stage of cognition, children learn to talk with more than one-word sentences and they begin to use symbols, however, they do not yet understand cause and effect. Modern adults stuck at this stage of development tend to use magical thinking to make sense of the world and their place in it. In the modern world, most people at this Tribal stage are disadvantaged and considered "uncivilized," from an academic perspective.

As I explained earlier, each level of consciousness has a coherent worldview supported by others who hold the same values. A given level of consciousness can look back and see the levels of consciousness below (Tribal man can perceive Archaic man), from which it evolved, but the notion that there exist more sophisticated minds is rejected or never conceived. Primitive minds cannot perceive more complex minds. In modern jargon, everything more sophisticated than a Tribal level of consciousness is "fake news;" every mind that is more complex than the Tribal mind cannot be seen, or heard, or believed.

Once Helen's Ego emerged, the violent, frustrated, biting, and kicking child faded. After the miracle at the water fountain, Helen is perceived as loving (she hugs and kisses everyone), gentle (she holds babies with great tenderness), and delightful (he explores with unselfconscious glee).

The concept of "us" also arises in Tribal consciousness; a collective of Proto-Egos share a common worldview. Religious ritual is a bonding force for the Tribal mind, religion gains ever more importance as evolution marches on. Human beings have an inherent need to gather in small groups and to identify with the worldview of these groups.

Language in the Archaic mind is sparse, literal, and primitive. In the newly emerging Tribal mind, language moves beyond the concrete and now entertains simple abstractions. Helen's early language was very literal. She got all her information about the world through fingerspelling and (increasingly) through books, as she learned to read braille. However, because vision and hearing did not distract her attention from her newly found ability to communicate, she rapidly went from literal words to abstract concepts. Helen had become aware of a vast reality beyond her Archaic mind; there was an entire universe to be explored beyond her body. She went after knowledge with a burning focus and kept her teacher constantly busy and constantly challenged.

Helen was still very literal, especially at the beginning of her voyage of discovery. Her questions were innocent, practical, and somewhat unsettling in there direct and honest asking. As she learned more and more about how the world worked, she became increasingly eager to know where everything came from. Why were things a certain way, she wondered. How did the world work? This led to esoteric questions (asking about what was hidden) and vague answers. For example, when she started to hear that the source of all things was a god, her questions were touching and literal. She asked questions like these (from *The Story of my life*, 1903):

- Who made God?
- Where did God get the soil to build the earth?
- Where is God? Did you ever see God? Show him to me.
- Does God have feet? Can he walk?
- Where is Heaven?
- How did God tell people that his home was in Heaven?
- When she was told that dead people go to Heaven, Helen asked, "How do you know where dead people go, if you have never been dead?"
- Where did Jesus go to school? Who were his teachers?
- Why must everything die?
- What is a Soul?
- Who made all things and Boston?

This obsession with God and Christianity would quickly consume Helen's interests and she began to search for answers that made sense to her literal mind. Once Helen realized the power of language, her mind became supremely focused, and her memory became extraordinary. The buzzing world around her went on without drawing her away from her cognitive obsessions. The leap from concrete to abstract was accelerated for Helen because of her deaf-blindness.

From a biological perspective, something profound happens in the prefrontal cortex of the human brain in late adolescence. The prefrontal lobe is critical for the evolution of personality, creativity, humor, problem-solving, impulse control, scenario building (planning for the future), and managing complex behaviors and abstract thinking. These higher-order executive functions are built on earlier stages of biological growth, however, only after the prefrontal transformation has occurred in the young adult do the new skills and nuances of personality become refined and sophisticated. After the pre-frontal lobe changes, it seems as if an adult mind has suddenly emerged after years of childhood. It is this prefrontal transformation that gives us the (incorrect) impression that cognitive development is complete in our twenties, and that the teenager has entered a finished stage called "adulthood."

Prefrontal changes are the trigger that transmutes a Tribal mind into a Warrior mind. Helen seems to have leaped into the Warrior stage in the preteen years, as if her prefrontal cortex had matured earlier than normal. Evidently, the evolution of the Warrior mind was accelerated in Helen's mind and, by the time she was in her teen years, the attributes of the Warrior mind were fully engaged.

Helen Keller's Warrior Mind

> She wanted no quarter, asked no one's pity. She had weapons "as strong as anyone else's." She had drawn strength at the beginning of 1916 by identification with Joan of Arc. Now she invoked the name of Jesus. ~ *Helen and Teacher*, 1980.

Helen Keller was 26 when she mounted her high-horse, picked up her "Joan of Arc sword," and headed into battle. She said, "I shall fight with the strength won from ceaseless battling with silence and darkness, with my faith, with my love, with the love of thousands that love me."

Helen Keller's Warrior mind was fully formed and on fire with virtue, conviction, and courage when she was just a teenager—now, in her twenties, her strength was at a peak and she was ready to face the Devil and his minions.

The Warrior stage of consciousness is a more aggressive development of the Tribal mind. In other words, the Warrior mind is also a Tribal mind, but it is slightly more evolved and more socially active. The Warrior mind is represented by a clan-brain rather than a hive-brain.

The hive mind was probably run by a queen bee. This mind was content to be part of the whole community, with no need to stand out, either as an autocratic leader or through rebellion. The Warrior mind, however, has evolved a personal/autocratic voice, and knows the power of social action. The Warrior mind is the idealistic rebellious mind of our youth, aware of a larger social sphere than Tribal minds feel. The Warrior mind can see a bigger picture—a collective of tribes.

I need to do a quick aside before I go forward with this perspective, especially as I use the term "patriarchy" in the discussion ahead. I imply in the coming pages that recent history has been controlled by males, by masculine energy. From a historical perspective, evidence shows that males have done the fighting, planned and built the technologies that kill, and then they have written the history of what happened after conflicts. Atrocities of every kind have been the work of the male of the species, not females. This is an easy generalization to make, but it masks something that needs to be clear. Love permeates all levels of consciousness and many of our most fervent advocates of love and kindness have been males living in patriarchal societies. Even in the heat of Warrior-mind fervor, the male poets, artists, statesmen, holy men, and sensitive souls wherever they are found, have stood for compassion and restorative justice alongside the females.

And, of course, being a female does not mean that you are not going through these levels of consciousness as your mind matures. For example, a woman can be just as Narcissistic, Ethnocentric or Traditional, as any male. I need to emphasize, however, that there have been female philosophers who have objected to Ego-development scales, saying they are male-driven—the same patriarchy at work in academia. In other words, feminine criticism has maintained that levels like the Warrior mind are much more indicative of masculine cognitive unfolding and much less so for the evolution of female consciousness. There is also a modern movement toward androgyny and transgendered-humanity that further casts doubt on the ability to use developmental scales broadly and without significant caveats. It is also true that Ego-development scales were first created by female researchers like Jane Loevinger and Susanne-Cook Greuter.

I am a male with two sons, a grandson, a granddaughter, and a daughter. The Warrior period for me and, hopefully, for my children and grandchildren, (as they develop their own worldviews) has been about standing for justice, equality, loving-kindness, and intelligent empathy. Using abstractions and generalizations (like "the patriarchy") to explain masculine actions/emotions detracts from the everyday, normal humanity of males. On the other hand, we have too often taken the young boys out of their path and turned them into soldiers who have killed others and been killed themselves. Males have been the primary victims of this era of "justified" violence. When you see words like *patriarchy* below (and you will) make sure you see it as complex and controversial. Here is Helen's comment about patriotism:

> I look upon the world as my fatherland, and every war has for me the horror of a family feud. I hold true patriotism to be the brotherhood and mutual service of all men. The preparedness I believe in is right thinking, efficiency, knowledge, and courage to follow the highest ideals. When true history replaces the lies and false teachings of the schools, the true call of patriotism will be a call to brotherhood and not to arms. [41]

Love is constantly, patiently, incessantly opposing hatred, violence, and greed. War is a failure of the human mind to evolve. Helen Keller was a pure force for good, as the quote above shows; she spent her life in the service of Love. By the way, I capitalize *Love* and *Faith* in this book when the words represent the *philosophy* of Helen Keller . . . plus, I want to add emphasis to certain abstract terms.

With each new transmutation to a higher level of consciousness, the size of the perceived social group expands; the number of people you will tolerate and include in your group expands as consciousness expands. From infancy through the Archaic period only the family unit was perceived as essential. In the Tribal mind, more people enter the sphere of awareness; an extended family (a tribe) emerges as an entity. For Helen, this extended family revolved around the homestead where she was born, and it included everyone who interacted there. The Warrior mind further enlarges awareness so that a wider community is perceived than the Tribal; for example, other tribes are recognized and (more or less) tolerated by the Warrior mind. There is also a geographical area, a range, that the individual feels comfortable navigating within and through. Think of a teenager who is bored with the neighborhood and so ventures out into the wider community. With each new level of consciousness, geographical awareness expands further.

As I said earlier, even though we evolve to higher levels of consciousness, all the earlier stages are still inside of us. The Warrior stage of the teenage mind is full of high ideals and great intentions. These ideals do not necessarily fade as people age—however, we can "get stuck" at this level as easily as we can stagnate on any part of the spiral journey upward toward more sophisticated cognition.

The Warrior mind is powerful and there is often a youthful internal fire, a determination to share insights and to champion worthy causes (or personal/Egoic causes). For Helen Keller, her Warrior mind began to develop (as a teenager) after her friend John Hicks introduced her to the Christian mystic and Renaissance Man Emanuel Swedenborg. Once Helen identified with Swedenborg's theology, she went on a spiritual quest to become of service to others. Swedenborg taught Helen that Love was the core of life and that a true Justice Warrior was a soldier in the service of compassion.

Helen's humanitarianism and her religious convictions started with her Warrior mind. She held close to this stage of cognitive evolution for several decades, all through her college years and well into midlife. Helen was attacked in the media for her rebellious views and her friends were baffled by her choice of religion. Because this time in her life was so fascinating and because it has such a cultural impact, even to this day, I will spend a while below exploring Helen's young adult history and her controversial Warrior mind.

John Hitz

How is it that a deaf-blind girl from Alabama could even know about the existence of someone so unusual as the Swedish Christian mystic Emanuel Swedenborg? To understand how that happened, we need to look at the relationship between the teenage Helen Keller and her elderly (and quite remarkable) hearing-impaired friend John Hitz.

John Hitz Jr. was the superintendent of Alexander Graham Bell's Volta Bureau. The Volta Bureau was Bell's research and development center which focused on technologies for the deaf. The bureau was founded in 1880 and still exists today in Georgetown, Washington D.C. Not only was John Hitz superintendent of the Volta Bureau, but he was also Bell's personal secretary and close friend. Helen and Annie met John Hitz through their mutual friendship with Dr. Bell.

John Hitz spent summers with Helen and Annie, six weeks at a time for several years. Hitz would routinely take Helen on nature walks and instilled in her a love for the natural world and wonderment for its existence; he also spoke often to her of God and spirituality. In Nella Braddy's book *Anne Sullivan Macy, The Story Behind Helen Keller* (1933), is this description of John Hitz:

> Closely associated with Dr. [Alexander Graham] Bell in his work for the deaf was his secretary, an old gentleman in the grand manner, Mr. John Hitz, who wore a long white beard and a flowing cape like an actor's. Mr. Anagnos [Director of the Perkin's School for the Blind] always referred to him as "the picturesque secretary." Mr. Hitz was born in Davos Switzerland . . .
>
> Mr. Hitz assumed a sort of spiritual guardianship over Annie and her pupil, calling Helen his *Tochter*. Helen called him her *Pflegevater*, and Annie called him *Mom Pere*. It was Mr. Hitz who took Annie incognita to Feeding Hills [Massachusetts, where she was born] to learn about her family, and it was Mr. Hitz who led Helen down a path along which her teacher was

never able to follow, for it was Mr. Hitz who introduced her to the religion of Swedenborg. [42]

John Hitz contributed to history in ways that few realize. He gave Helen Keller braille editions, many thick books, of the writings of Emanuel Swedenborg. What had yet to be translated into braille, he transcribed himself and spelled into her hand each word. Helen read everything she could find by Swedenborg, and consequently she became a very unusual kind of Christian, she became a devout Swedenborgian.

The first book that John Hitz read to Helen was Swedenborg's difficult and lengthy tome called *Heaven and Hell*. Remarkably, in the preface of Swedenborg's work is the story of a blind girl who is deeply affected by Swedenborg's philosophy. It is almost as if Helen Keller has invaded history and now appears in a book published in 1758. Here is Helen's telling of her first impression upon reading the preface to *Heaven and Hell*:

> When I began *Heaven and Hell*, I was little aware of the new joy coming into my life as I had been years before when I stood on the piazza steps awaiting my teacher. Impelled only by the curiosity of a young girl who loves to read, I opened that big book, and lo, my fingers lighted upon a paragraph in the preface about a blind woman whose darkness was illuminated with beautiful truths from Swedenborg's writings. She believed that they imparted a light to her mind that more than compensated for her loss of earthly light. She never doubted that there was a spiritual body within the material one with perfect senses and that after a few dark years, the eyes within her eyes would open to a world infinitely more wonderful, complete, and satisfying than this one. [43]

We do not know the blind girl who is mentioned in *Heaven and Hell*, but we do know that her experience affected another young blind girl a century later, a girl who also found an internal spiritual body residing within her physical body. It is no accident that Helen compares her experience at the water fountain with the discovery of Swedenborgianism. It was at the water fountain that her Archaic mind was transformed into a Tribal mind. In the pages of Swedenborg's book, and because of John Hitz, Helen's level of consciousness was guided from the Tribal mind to the Warrior mind, a profound transmutation.

John Hitz helped Helen find a purpose in life, a mission that her Warrior mind was hungry to champion. All Helen's subsequent humanitarian actions are in keeping with her religious convictions. She drew from her study of Swedenborg her determination to devote her life to the suffering of others:

> In giving me the golden key to the hidden treasures of the Bible, Swedenborg's books have lifted my wistful longing for a fuller sense-life into a vivid consciousness of the complete being within me. Each day comes to me with both hands full of possibilities, and in its brief course I discern the verities and realities of my existence, the bliss of growth, the glory of action, the spirit of beauty.[44]

Helen speaks of "the hidden treasures of the Bible." She is saying that we make a mistake if we take the writings in the Bible literally. There is a more serious set of insights hidden beneath the literal. We miss the core of Christianity (to love, to serve, to evolve human consciousness) when we fail to detect and explore the esoteric mysteries hidden within the Bible.

Emanuel Swedenborg

Below, Anne Sullivan's biographer Nella Braddy Henney writes about Helen Keller's struggle to explain her religion:

> Writing about her religion was a personal and isolating task. None of Helen's friends could comprehend her fascination with Swedenborg; it was tolerated rather than openly supported. Helen yielded to the temptation however, and at the request of the Rev. Paul Sperry, pastor of the Swedenborgian Church of the Holy City in Washington D.C., agreed to write the story of her love for the teachings of Emanuel Swedenborg. In writing *My Religion* Helen was singularly alone. To her teacher, Swedenborg's gifted madness remained madness, not religion, though it seemed to Helen that anyone who studied that wonderful life "must become as humble as a little child." Helen was overwhelmed by the magnitude of her subject, but

she felt that any effort which might bring to someone else the peace that she had found in Swedenborg was worth making. [45]

Swedenborgian churches are called *New Churches* because Swedenborg brought a new kind if Christianity to humanity and a new interpretation of the Bible. Below is a quote from the Swedenborgian website in an article entitled "New Church History Fun Facts: Helen Keller's Letter about Swedenborg (Oct. 10, 1926):"

[Rev. Paul Andrew Sperry] had first heard of Helen Keller through his Sunday school teacher, John Hitz, a friend of Keller and the man who introduced her to the works of Emanuel Swedenborg. In August of 1926, Sperry had written to Keller to ask if she would consider writing a book about Swedenborg. He had to wait until October for her reply, not because she was in any way ignoring him, but because she wanted to carefully consider whether she could meet such a challenge . . . Her letter made it clear that, although she had organizational and practical difficulties to work out concerning the proposed book, she strongly believed in the project. [46]

To find the powerful John Hicks in the role of Sunday School teacher is delightful. In an important way, besides all the other wonderful contributions of John Hicks, he was behind the effort to get Helen Keller to write about her religious convictions.

To care about others and to promote love, that is Heaven's mandate according to Swedenborg. Our purpose on earth is to serve others—to make the world a better place. Human life is not an exercise in self-advancement. Our goal is to locate the passion within us, to summon our willpower and intent for the betterment of other people. That is the message that drove Helen Keller her entire life. She was determined not to be pitied or fussed over; she was put on the earth to serve, to love, and to care about the welfare of others; she was too busy and too focused to dwell on her own physical limitations. In an essay called *How I Would Help the World* (1935), Helen wrote:

By "church," he [Swedenborg] did not mean an ecclesiastical organization, but a spiritual fellowship of thoughtful men and women who spent their lives for a service to mankind. He called it a civilization that was to be born of a healthy, universal religion—goodwill, mutual understanding, service from each to all, regardless of dogma or ritual.[47]

The philosopher Immanuel Kant, a contemporary of Swedenborg, wrote of an "invisible religion" that resided in the hearts of men and women, and which was not touched by the dogmatic traditions that had smothered the esoteric core of Christianity. Perhaps Swedenborg's "spiritual fellowship of thoughtful men and women" is the same as Kant's "invisible religion."

Emanuel Swedenborg became important to me long before I realized that Helen Keller followed his compassionate mission. In the early 2000s, I was working on my family history and had traced my Scottish ancestors to a small chapel near Almont, Michigan. This lovely white chapel sits in the woods near a dirt road in a rural area of Lapeer County. I assumed the chapel was Presbyterian, the Church of Scotland, but I was wrong— it was a Swedenborgian chapel. One of my friends surprised me when he told me that he used to attend this church as a boy, and did I know that Helen Keller was a Swedenborgian. Discovering that Helen Keller also knew the story of Emanuel Swedenborg made me realize that she had a depth of spiritual understanding beyond what is commonly known. *My Religion* (1927) and *Light in my Darkness* (1994) are about Emanuel Swedenborg and what he has to say about the good life:

> What others did in science and politics, Swedenborg did in religion. With massive arguments and thundering anathemas, he sent a continent's literature of pessimism, condemnation, and insincerity crashing down into the abyss. [48]

Like Swedenborg, Helen's own style is sprinkled with thundering prose; we marvel at the power of her language. Reading the above paragraph, we get a sense of the passion that burned within Swedenborg and then ignited the soul of a teenage deaf-blind girl. We also feel Helen's conviction that she has found her mission and is ready to wield her own stinging blade in the battle for kindness and service against those who champion hatefulness and excessive self-interest.

Emanuel Swedenborg influenced generations of artists and intellectuals from the late 1700s until the present day. Besides Helen Keller, the list of those who found him fascinating and worth study includes Carl Jung, Walt Whitman, Ralph Waldo Emerson, William Blake, Johann von Goethe, Immanuel Kant, Fyodor Dostoevsky, Thomas Carlyle, Elizabeth and Robert Browning, Samuel Coleridge, Henri Bergson, W.B. Yeats, and Jorge Luis Borges. This is a remarkable (and incomplete) list of artists and intellectuals who found a common bond with Swedenborg.

Honore de Balzac called Swedenborg "The Buddha of the North." Buddhist scholar D.T. Suzuki, who is credited with introducing Zen to the Western World, used Balzac's phrase and wrote a book for the Japanese public called *Swedenborg: The Buddha of the North*. Henry Ward Beecher wrote "No man can know the theology of the nineteenth century who has not read Swedenborg." Henry James, the father of psychologist William James and novelist Henry James was perhaps the strongest proponent of Swedenborg in the 1800s in America. In 1863, Henry James published *Substance and Shadow, the Secret Life of Swedenborg*. It is obvious, from this quick historical glance, that the teachings of Emanuel Swedenborg deeply influenced Western philosophy and Western literature.

When many of the greatest minds of a civilization stand up to speak with eloquence about a fellow human being, it catches our attention in a powerful manner. It is true that Swedenborg was fashionable among intellectuals and artists in the late 1800s and early 1900s especially, but the fascination came for a reason—which still resonates. What is it that Emanuel Swedenborg taught that caused such an upheaval within the creative community of Western civilization?

Essentially, Emanuel Swedenborg advocated five perspectives:

1. Swedenborg said the purpose of religion, of life itself, was to further the evolution of Love. We were to love each other, love ourselves, love the earth, love other creatures on earth, love life itself, and love the Source. When we truly flowed with Love, we would know that the highest order of things was to serve what we loved.

2. Swedenborg said the Bible was not meant to be taken literally. The Bible was allegorical, mythological, and it pointed the way to expanding Love. From this perspective, the Bible served more sophisticated, more evolved minds. Unlike Swedenborg and Helen Keller, human beings with low levels of cognition needed to be told what to do—they needed a literal Bible. But at the higher realms

of cognition, more sophisticated minds used abstract, allegorical, metaphorical language to guide their actions. Swedenborg was speaking to an emerging (more sophisticated) cultural mind.

3. There is an implied evolution to human consciousness in these proclamations. If we are to be in the service of Love, we are going to have to evolve the mind; most human beings do not know how to cognitively evolve their minds—they do not know the pathways which lead to greater spiritual unfolding. Swedenborg suggested a way forward.

4. A new kind of "church" was called for to serve these more evolved minds. This was an "internal church," where love was not mandated but rather flowed naturally from compassion. The Kingdom of God was within; there was no need to create sects, denominations, or any other kind of material church. This is the esoteric principle of concordance: all religions serve the same Source.

5. Swedenborg introduced his followers to what I call the *Twilight Portal*. He knew how to go out-of-body, and he knew how to retrieve information from beyond sensory appearances. This intrigued his followers, especially the creative artists, who felt that their artistic abilities also flowed from somewhere beyond the surface, beneath appearances.

Swedenborg lived at a time when the high end of cognitive culture was moving from less evolved minds (Tribal, Warrior, Traditional) to a Modern mind. Swedenborg had a scientific, Modern mind, he knew a cognitive revolution was underway. On the other hand, he was aware of the shortcomings and dangers emerging as the Ego expanded. Therefore, Swedenborg supported the Romantics who were fighting against the excesses of the Enlightenment. Swedenborg was keeping the esoteric mysteries alive, keeping the ultimate unknowns in the equations, keeping loving-kindness before his readers, even as he endorsed the scientific revolution.

The Twilight Portal

Looking for answers about the evolution of consciousness—as it related to philosophers like Swedenborg—eventually led me to the Monroe Institute in the Blue Ridge Mountains of Virginia. The Monroe Institute is a center for the study of consciousness, psychic ability, and most significantly at the time the institute was founded, the exploration of out-of-body experiences. Robert Monroe, the founder of the Monroe Institute, wrote about his curious and at times frightening journeys that happened when he was in a zone between sleep and wakefulness, called the *hypnagogic state* when it occurs in the evening, and the *hypnopompic state* when it occurs in the morning. At the Monroe Institute, I became fascinated with this state of twilight awareness and went on to explore the phenomenon in more detail when I returned home (after taking the Institute's Gateway Course). It seemed obvious to me, after studying Swedenborg, that he knew, from a remarkably young age, how to enter this altered state of consciousness and that his spiritual power came from his ability to go through the *twilight portal.*

Saints and seers throughout recorded history have used the twilight portal to experience visions; Swedenborg is neither the first nor the only person to discover this unusual state of consciousness. Pre-cognition, religious conversions, all manner of psychic capability seem to manifest in this level of semi-wakefulness. When psychics are observed going into a trance, for example, they seem to fall partly, but not completely asleep. Indeed, they slow their brain rhythms down from a restful state called *alpha*, to a slower brain wave frequency called *theta*. If they slip to a deeper state of wakefulness called *delta*, they fall asleep and dream. Therefore, between alpha and delta frequencies, in the state of slow brain wave activity called theta, consciousness seems to open a portal to extrasensory experiences.

I cannot prove that the theta state generates anything outside mental hallucinations. The personal experience I have with it, however, is enough for me to know that theta-perceptions are clear and feel more powerful—*more real* actually—than waking consciousness. There is no doubt that powerful insights, often accompanied by voices and images seem "vividly real" in this trance state of awareness. Swedenborg was a rational, scientifically-minded man. I think he would have appreciated the discussion below.

Before I dive (briefly) into the science behind out-of-body spiritual adventures, let me suggest that Helen Keller might have lived in an alpha-theta state of consciousness most of the time. Light waves and sound waves are two of the most powerful external influences on the human body. In different ways these powerful wave-like inputs drive the higher wakeful states of consciousness—like the *beta-wave* state of everyday awareness and the highly focused *gamma-wave* level of consciousness. Beta and gamma waves inhibit alpha, theta, and delta waves. Without this beta/gamma-inhibition, the slower, calmer, and more spiritually attuned wavelengths can more easily manifest. We have in the brain of Helen Keller a steady state alpha rhythm that perhaps accounts for her mild manner, her relaxed body, and her poised posture. It would have been easy for her to slip into the theta state—just below alpha—and into a more spiritual realm. It is entirely possible that out-of-body journeys came easily to Helen, although she might not have been able to articulate the experience as a phenomenon outside daydreaming or active imagination.

Permit me now to enter a brief sojourn into the science behind spiritual states of consciousness—this is an important discussion because it helps us better understand the reality that Helen Keller might have experienced daily.

Like psychics and mystics before and after him, Swedenborg went on *out-of-body journeys*, including numerous visits to Heaven and Hell (I suspect he was in the fog between Heaven and Hell) where he took notes and came back with a new understanding of Christianity: The Bible, according to Swedenborg, was allegorical and metaphorical; the Bible was not meant to be taken literally—that is what Swedenborg was told in Heaven.

To put it mildly, literal journeys to Heaven and Hell are hard for a scientific mindset to entertain (less so if we are talking metaphorically). But Helen Keller suspended her judging mind long enough (and often enough) to explore and consider esoteric (hidden, controversial) ideas—she did not shut down when confronted with mystery or with the implausible. I suspect that she went on many out-of-body experiences herself—using her imagination to open portals.

I remember as a boy of eight visiting the eye doctor for the first time, finding out that I was a high myope, and then realizing, after I got my glasses, that the blurry world that was my "normal vision" was not at all what other people were seeing. My new glasses felt like a miracle—colors were bright, I could see details on the leaves of trees, and there was a vivid clarity to the world that I had no way of knowing about before getting my thick lenses.

It could be that Helen had a vivid perceptual ability—coming from her proximity to the twilight portal—that enabled her to sense theta consciousness. The ability to use the twilight portal to gather information must have seemed normal for Helen; she probably assumed that what she was sensing was common to all humanity. But without the right "thick lenses," without the right prescription, most of humanity is perceiving only a blurry image of a greater theta-reality. Compared to theta consciousness, "normal" for most of us *Normals* might be a relative deaf-blindness. Helen could sense that her perceptions were different and unusual, but she had no way to explain her esotericism without a modern scientific background.

The Spirit Molecule

Theta consciousness feels like a portal opening into a spiritual realm. Psychics, saints, empaths, mystics, and scientists have experienced what I will call *theta-wave spirituality*. Scientists have for years explored possible physiological explanations for *theta-wave spirituality*, and they have found a possible connection in a remarkable chemical (DMT) that became popularly known as the *Spirit Molecule*.

The same set of experiences as are reported in *theta-wave spirituality* are also described by subjects taking N,N-Dimethyltryptamine (DMT); these experiences include out-of-body sensations, near-death experiences, contact with other sentient (alien) creatures, feelings of being one with a greater essence, profound peace, and ecstasy. But why, scientists wondered, would a brain rhythm that is halfway between wakefulness and sleep release DMT, a molecule originally understood to be related to great stress? The key understanding is that DMT is remarkably close in chemical composition to melatonin, which is released during sleep.

Melatonin is gradually released into the blood stream as a person drifts from wakefulness into an ever-drowsier state. Perhaps, scientists speculated, there was an intermediary transitional moment every evening and every morning when DMT spilled over into the blood stream, causing the opportunity for "spiritual experiences," especially for people who knew how to stay awake enough to witness theta-perceptions.

When the body is about to fall asleep, muscles are temporally paralyzed—this is a normal condition called *sleep paralysis*. Sleep paralysis occurs just before falling asleep, and just before waking. Being paralyzed, unable to move, is a severe shock to the mind. It may be that

DMT (a stress-related hormone) is naturally released because of this twice daily paralytic "trauma."

For a detailed review of DMT, see Rick Strassman's book *DMT: The Spirit Molecule: A Doctor's Revolutionary Research into the Biology of Near-Death and Mystical Experiences* (2000). The plant ayahuasca has become a favorite of researchers studying psychic phenomenon. The powerful effects of ayahuasca are derived primarily from DMT. Research continues to this day on *The Spirit Molecule*; see, for example, the work of the U.K.-based Berkeley Foundation. To review the history of psychedelic use, see Michael Pollan's book *How to Change Your Mind: What the new science of psychedelics teaches us about Consciousness, dying, addiction, depression, and transcendence* (2018).

Experiments with weak magnetic fields placed over the temporal lobes have also induced spiritual experiences. This scientific apparatus has been called *The God Helmet* because of the responses that subjects report, including: a sensed presence, altered states of awareness, and mystical experiences. The results of magnetic stimulation applied to the temporal lobes remain inconclusive and controversial. Trying to find a neural correlate to esoteric experiences is an ongoing effort.

I suspect that Helen Keller would find these scientific speculations interesting but would not accept that her Faith and sense of connection with her God could ever be completely explained through reductionist science.

The Light in my Darkness, the Voice in my Silence

Emanuel Swedenborg apparently knew how to tap into the twilight portal at will. He must have gotten exceptionally good at entering this worldly realm between wakefulness and deep sleep where theta-generated images can be witnessed and remembered. As a deeply religious man, coming from a family, a culture, and a time in history when Christianity was fundamental, Swedenborg's journeys out-of-body manifested as Christian. According to his now famous account, Swedenborg went to Heaven and he visited Hell. When he got back from these remarkable journeys, he wrote down his experiences, what he had seen and what he had heard. The experiences told him that Christianity had to evolve; that a *New Church* (a new kind of mind) was to be created based upon a higher evolution of human consciousness.

What Swedenborg found during his discussions in Heaven, what appealed to Helen Keller and to the greatest thinkers and artists of the era, was (as I have stated several times now) that the Bible was mythological, allegorical, and mostly about the internal transformation of the human soul, about moving through stages of cognitive and spiritual development—the Bible, seen as a whole, was about the evolution of human spirituality. The *New Church* that Swedenborg advocated was not a new religion; he was opposed to creating a new religious sect, even though many of his followers ignored his wishes. Swedenborg's *New Church* was a new perspective; he argued that a new kind of Christian was to evolve, one who understood the true nature of the spiritual teachings of Christ. Here is how Helen put it:

> The new thoughts about the unity of God that Swedenborg offered as a replacement for the old concepts are precious because they give one insight to distinguish between the real Deity and the repelling appearance that results from a wrong reading of the Word. The following extract from *True Christian Religion* shows how Swedenborg strove to supplant those unchristian concepts with a nobler faith:
>   "It may be evident how delirious they are who think, still more they who believe, and yet more they who teach, that God can condemn anyone, curse anyone, cast anyone into hell, predestine anyone to eternal death, avenge injuries, be angry, or punish. On the contrary, he is not able to turn away from anyone, or look at anyone with a stern countenance." [49]

From Helen Keller's perspective, Swedenborg brought back the message from Heaven that human beings, using the example of a loving God, were to be compassionate. Each human being should, Swedenborg argued, be working to elevate their own spiritually during their lifetime. Swedenborg's logic was that since God is compassionate, therefore, so should his creations be compassionate. A God of compassion would not condone torture or vengefulness. The journey through life, according to Swedenborg's logic, is about the evolution of individual compassion and wakefulness; there is a spiritual pathway that Christians should be following.

Swedenborg felt that we are on this planet to evolve our consciousness, to become ever more capable of serving others so that the human species can endure and evolve peacefully. *At the higher levels of consciousness, artists (creative people) come into being*—that is why so many of the most evolved minds on the planet were (and still are) drawn to Swedenborg. In perhaps his most famous book, *Arcana Coelestia* (Heavenly Mysteries), Swedenborg says:

> It may therefore be stated in advance that of the Lord's Divine mercy it has been granted me now for some years to be constantly and uninterruptedly in company with spirits and angels, hearing them speak and in turn speaking with them. In this way it has been given me to hear and see wonderful things in the other life which have never before come to the knowledge of any man, nor into his idea. I have been instructed in regard to the different kinds of spirits; the state of souls after death; hell, or the lamentable state of the unfaithful; heaven, or the blessed state of the faithful; and especially in regard to the doctrine of faith which is acknowledged in the universal heaven. [50]

Something was plainly different in Swedenborg's mind compared to a "normal" mind. From a scientific perspective, an unusual bio-quantum internal state must have been generating loving images and profound insights, even angelic voices spoke to him; and the insights he was given were well ahead of his time. I must leave it to others to speculate if Swedenborg had temporal lobe seizures or some other brain-based "anomaly." Something benevolent and helpful was coming from the soul-depths of Swedenborg's mind, so we—converts or skeptics— carefully and respectfully listen to his insights.

From a cosmic perspective, something in Swedenborg's mind opened and allowed communication between our earthly domain and more sophisticated realms; whether you buy that or not, it is how Helen Keller explained Swedenborg.

Swedenborg was not the first personage to experience messages coming from the twilight portal. We have no way to know how many important messages were "channeled" to human beings throughout evolution using this method of twilight-perceiving. Before Swedenborg, in the 1600's, for example, Rene Descartes was being "instructed" to change the face of religion and philosophy:

> . . . following a period of intense solitary meditations, Descartes
> [experienced] a vision and a three-part dream that revealed to
> him his vocation and the foundations of the science he was to
> create. He held fervently that this single episode was the most
> important occurrence in his entire life. [51]

The power of hypnagogic imagery, like that which visited Descartes and
Swedenborg, seems to move civilization forward, to challenge the status
quo, to provide insights into new possibilities for the evolution of human
society and for the evolution of consciousness. This resonates with Carl
Jung's archetypes, with William Blake's paintings and poetry, with the
entire creative world of the artist. Hypnagogic imagery is a language of
the intuitive mind, where fountains of wisdom and compassion bubble
upward into beta-consciousness. It is no wonder that poets, writers,
painters, and great thinkers of an age could sense and appreciate the
powerful messages that Swedenborg brought back from his out-of-body
experiences.

Besides the powerful impact that Swedenborg had on intellectuals
and artists, there was one theme he hammered home repeatedly
throughout his writings. Heaven had a message for all of mankind:

> Out of the wealth of influences . . . there was one theme of
> Swedenborg's works that had an impact on virtually all . . .
> individuals and movements: his often-stated insistence that
> what makes people most human is their willingness to turn
> away from the limitations of self—to love one another, and to
> show that love by serving society. [52]

This was also the well from which Helen Keller drew her spiritual energy.
Obviously, the ability to "go out-of-body," to leave behind a body that
was weak of sensory input, to sail wherever imagination could consider,
held great hope for Helen. And to know that Heaven was real because
a trusted saint had hung out there and took notes, was exceptionally
comforting to someone so sensorially isolated. One wonders what
Helen Keller was doing in the twilight hours:

> I was delighted to have my faith confirmed that I could go
> beyond the broken arc of my senses and behold the invisible in
> the fullness of the light and hear divine symphonies in silence.

> I had a joyous certainty that deafness and blindness were not an essential part of my existence since they were not in any way a part of my immortal mind. [53]

I wonder if Helen actively tried to "go beyond the broken arc" of her senses. Besides daydreaming, did she deliberately, systematically try to go out-of-body? There is no record of this in her books and articles. She certainly prayed, perhaps using contemplative mediation to expand her awareness.

Having studied hearing and vision my entire career, I am aware that these two senses can act as powerful filters. They could very well inhibit or mask other sensory abilities. I will discuss the role of proprioception in detail in different ways throughout this book series, but for now I will just note that out-of-body experiences would be much easier to experience without vision and hearing interfering with proprioceptive input. I would not be a bit surprised to learn that Helen Keller could easily travel out-of-body. She certainly was powerful and articulate; she seemed to have insights and a mission far beyond her culture. She seemed also to have evolved a direct channel to something beyond the visual-hearing veil.

Helen called Swedenborg "The light in my darkness, the voice in my silence." She says that Swedenborg best suited her needs, restored her to equality with those who had all their faculties:

> I cannot help laughing sometimes at the arrogance of those who think they alone possess the earth because they have eyes and ears. In reality, they see only shadows and know only in part. They little dream that the soul is the only reality, the life, the power which makes harmony out of discord, completeness out of incompleteness. [54]

Helen Keller considered herself an equal to the rest of humanity. The sighted and hearing population might harbor pity and a sense of superiority to "the disabled," but Helen Keller was not buying that arrogance. Her religion told her a greater truth. Instead of becoming a sad ward of sighted overlords, Helen became a spokesperson for God. She became the eyes and ears of an esoteric realm, a kingdom that the sighted and hearing could not perceive. *She was called to serve humankind* and she was, therefore, called to battle against that which was unkind in the world. Service to others is a central core of Christianity, so, of course, it was key to Helen Keller's personality.

Many people know that Helen Keller was a fierce fighter for social justice. She had a radical confrontational side combined with a remarkable way with words that got her views across vividly. This fiery energy came from her religious faith. Emanuel Swedenborg is not a lightweight in the esoteric world; his impact has been profound—indeed, he continues to influence evolving minds to this day. In her circle of friends and relatives, Helen stood alone as she defended Swedenborg, but her usual courage and stubbornness to speak her mind won out:

> The teachings of Emanuel Swedenborg have been my light and a staff in my hand, and by his vision splendid I am attended on my way. [55]

A Justice Warrior Goes to War

Helen Keller's religion became the foundation for her actions; in her articles and books, she went to war against ignorance and cruelty. Although she never framed her actions in this way, Helen Keller ventured out to fight against low levels of cultural cognition. She was, using modern terminology, opposed to the behaviors of Infantile (Narcissistic) minds, Archaic minds, and Tribal minds. Most importantly, she went to war against Warrior minds that held clannish aspirations to make war, to conquer, and to lay waste to the planet. Helen went after primitive worldviews, challenging low levels of consciousness. Essentially, Helen was opposed to the worldviews of an entrenched patriarchy—she was opposed to a class structure that kept so many people in poverty while a few held most of the wealth and power.

Helen Keller's thought processes, her depth of emotion, her spiritual convictions, and her consistent actions come from a remarkably high level of cognitive sophistication. To minds less evolved, Helen Keller's motivation and passion were mysterious and questionable. Her mental development and the product of her cognition—her convictions and actions—were hidden from minds with lower levels of cognitive unfolding. Helen was challenging such minds to evolve, much to their irritation.

Every level of consciousness—each of which generates a worldview— feels it is the pinnacle of cognitive evolution. The narcissist, for example, is sure that their mind is the best mind ever created, the most worthy and marvelous mind—a gift of a narcissistic god. For a narcissist, all other minds are stupid and unworthy compared to their own mind. At the narcissistic level of cognition, all information coming from higher levels of consciousness is "fake news." The narcissistic level of cognition is a baseline, (the lowest of the low) upon which all further mental development is built. Narcissistic minds living in her era did not like Helen Keller; to them she was an upstart, a troublemaker, a wrong-headed, weak-minded, crippled (imperfect) female, unworthy of a voice in the affairs of men.

The Ethnocentric mind, a step beyond the Narcissistic level, belongs to elite groups—collections of Narcissistic Egos. Ethnocentric (tribal) minds also feel their group to be the pinnacle of evolution. No mind is more special than the group-mind that Ethnocentric minds embrace. Ethnocentric gods look down with pride at their supreme creations, at their elite groups. The Ethnocentric mind is sure that the Narcissistic mind is more primitive than their own, but they are deaf and blind to all the "fake news" coming from the overhead spiritual clouds. Helen Keller was an annoyance to the Ethnocentric mindset; she was not part of their cognitive community. She did not share their unassailable worldviews; consequently, her views were rejected as religious and political blasphemy.

Here is the problem: Narcissistic and Ethnocentric minds sometimes become violent when confronted by more sophisticated worldviews. They feel threatened, afraid, and all their supporting memes seem under attack. The history books are filled with the atrocities perpetuated by these two primitive minds, the Narcissistic and the Tribal Ethnocentric—especially the Warrior Clan mind. Because these primitive people have historically been so dangerous, wisdom and knowledge, beyond what they can comprehend had to be hidden from them (so it was believed). However, Helen Keller ignored the danger. She was speaking hidden truths and those truths made Narcissistic and Ethnocentric populations furious. All the awe and goodness these same people had expressed for Helen when they thought she was a vulnerable cripple, was quickly over-shadowed by their hatefulness and defensiveness when she began to speak a more sophisticated language.

Narcissistic and Ethnocentric minds have been behaving barbarically for centuries, drowning witches, chopping heads off with guillotines, burning people at the stake, breaking people on racks, putting the "unworthy" into concentration camps and starving them to death, machine-gunning dissidents, on and on throughout recorded history. The actions of these primitive minds—almost all of which were males— were (and still are) horrific; I struggle to find the most god-awful terms in the English language to describe the things done in the name of religion and nationalism. You must hide certain kinds of knowledge from this cognitively unevolved crowd because they do not take criticism well (or at all). Cognitively unevolved masses are not ready to dialogue; indeed, they do not comprehend the concept of *dialogue*.

Esoteric knowledge is also rejected knowledge. You cannot reason with primitive minds because these minds have not evolved the capacity to reason. They are operating on memes and hateful emotions. You also cannot appeal to their empathy, compassion, and wisdom because they have not evolved empathy, compassion, and wisdom. Narcissistic and Ethnocentric minds cannot yet comprehend higher forms of spiritually, where all-encompassing love has supreme value. Finally, you cannot appeal to wisdom or experience because Narcissistic and Ethnocentric minds lack an understanding that wisdom comes from diverse experiences; these minds have little to no experience with groups (and ideas) unlike their own. Narcissistic and Ethnocentric minds know only themselves and only the in-crowd.

Scientists have also been notoriously rejecting of ideas that are outside accepted practices. This is largely good—to be skeptical of claims that are unsubstantiated, not tested by the scientific method or peer reviewed—but rejection of new hypotheses as superstition or New Age nonsense has at times hampered progress. Science also has a set of memes that disguise themselves as fact. Scientific memes serve as fences that inadvertently keep new ideas out. I discussed "scientific memes" in my earlier books and will not elaborate further. My point is simply that every level of consciousness has a set of memes that support their worldview.

I suggest that only a low percentage of the global population had reached sophisticated levels of consciousness when Helen Keller was alive. No wonder her humanitarianism and compassionate statements about love and tolerance were scorned. Very few people were kind enough, loving enough, wise enough, and spiritually sophisticated enough to have a clue what Helen Keller was expressing. Unfortunately, many Modern minds still seem to lack the capacity to understand Helen Keller's level of consciousness.

~

I always have the same angst every time I write about levels of consciousness (as I have done above and in my previous books), so I need to make two caveats. First, no one is at a stable level of consciousness; we all have a center of cognitive gravity. Since all the previous levels of consciousness (which we have transcended) still reside within us, it is possible for any of us—regardless how elevated our spirituality—to slip all the way down to an Egocentric (Narcissistic) mindset on a bad day. On a clear-headed day, we might reach integrated and compassionate levels. The point is that our moods and circumstances affect how our personalities and essential cognitive-core manifest. Everyone is on this spiritual journey—no one is excluded—and we each have a center of cognitive gravity. We need to be patient with each other (and with our own evolution) as we help each other to evolve.

The second caveat is that it is extremely dangerous to turn Ego personality scales into value hierarchies—that is not a good idea (and not what developmental psychologists support). Assigning value judgements is what the Ego does best, but caution is always necessary. The lower down on the scale of consciousness, the more likely we are to find people who severely (quickly) judge others. The higher up the scale, the more people we find who are cautious, patient, forgiving, and tolerant.

Of course, it is not okay to allow cruelty and indifference to rule our lives. I believe Helen Keller would insist that we should not use the excuse that we are too busy to do what is right, or that we have too many obligations to pay attention to injustice, or that we do not have enough information to act in the face of evil, or that we did not realize the seriousness of what was going on and, therefore, did not summon the courage to stand up for loving-kindness, wisdom, and intelligence. The good Christians of Germany and Italy (and the good Zen Buddhists in Japan) during the Second World War were just "doing their jobs," playing their cultural roles, doing as they were told, going with the cultural flow, and not drawing attention to themselves (for very understandable reasons). The result of indifference, cowardliness, and unevolved cognition was two world wars and suffering on a totally horrendous scale.

Helen Keller modeled a quite different worldview for humanity. The banality of evil, business as usual, was not acceptable to her. She was constantly in the face of evil. That is one reason why we admire her, and why we are in awe of such courage. As early as the 1930s, she could see that the German culture was heading for a bad future. Here is her journal entry for January 15, 1937:

> It is a matter of daily wonder to me how the German nation can live so despicably, submitting like fishes to every inhumanity which statesmanship and civilization have combated since the first recorded cry of oppression—large numbers beheaded for political offences to which no other modern country would attach the death penalty; forty-nine thousand people sent to concentration camps; criticism of art, drama, films; and books prohibited unless they be according to the Nazi point of view . . . then there are vast war preparations being pushed at an insane rate while the people are rationed on foods that do not build up resistance to disease or exposure. [56]

I was alarmed when I read that, as early as 1937, the Nazis already had concentration camps, and their war machine obsessions were well understood by the everyday person, even outside Germany. A shadow had spread over the landscape of Europe and the trajectory of the German Narcissistic and Ethnocentric worldviews were driving humanity toward catastrophe.

The populations that sanctioned and supported war were at an extremely low level of cognitive development. They did not understand people like Helen Keller—their only strategy for dealing with sophisticated minds, like that of Helen Keller, was hatefulness and vindictiveness. Nation states like Japan, Germany, and Italy (during the Second World War) routinely murdered people who had more evolved minds. Many of those put to death were poets, artists, academic scholars, and fervently spiritual individuals.

Historically, the liberals, the so-called radicals, the intelligentsia, have been murdered by authoritarian regimes—thinking and questioning (problem solving and reasoning) have not been universally accepted as religiously or politically good. Cognitive sophistication is perceived as dangerous to autocratic minds. Helen Keller's life would certainly have been in peril had she been a citizen of the Third Reich. She would have ended up in a concentration camp or been murdered for her worldviews.

The Nazis not only killed off the academics, artists, and intellectuals, but they also killed people who were blind and deaf because these "flawed beings" were perceived as "not pure." Not only were Helen Keller's Democratic and Socialist views intolerable to dictatorial minds, but she was handicapped, and, therefore, in the eyes of the Nazi regime (any autocratic government), her life was not worth preserving. The Nazi mindset wiped out generations of poets, saints, prodigies, and scientists; Helen Keller would have been one of the victims had she been living in Germany during World War Two.

This is from the U.S Holocaust Museum website:

> On July 14, 1933, the Nazi government instituted the "Law for the Prevention of Progeny with Hereditary Diseases." This law, one of the first steps taken by the Nazis toward their goal of creating an Aryan "master race," called for the sterilization of all persons who suffered from diseases considered hereditary, such as mental illness, learning disabilities, physical deformity, epilepsy, blindness, deafness, and severe alcoholism. With the law's passage the Third Reich also stepped up its propaganda against people with disabilities, regularly labeling them "life unworthy of life" or "useless eaters" and highlighting their burden upon society. [57]

Useless eaters: what a vicious phrase, the work of minds filled with hate. Unfortunately, that same hateful and intolerant cruelty still lives in our modern world. If the craziness is not stopped, the results may well cause history to repeat. Technological changes on the horizon are coming at an exponential rate and the changes are globally disruptive; *only cognitively evolved, tolerant, spiritually sophisticated, and intelligent minds should lead humanity at this perilous time.*

At the very least, we need a global debate that openly dialogues about "the nature of cognitive evolution"—what should future minds look like? How ought we to evolve? The time to dialogue about this challenge is right now; we are running out of time.

Helen Keller could perceive racism, bullying, and mean-spiritedness without having functional eyes and ears. She could perceive what was hidden, more so than many people with healthy eyes and ears. Helen Keller had a very sophisticated and highly evolved ability to read people; she also intuitively read worldviews; she could—so it seems in retrospect—surmise who was awake and kind, and who was (cognitively, relatively) asleep and hateful.

Helen's subtle abilities and eloquent opinions might have gone unnoticed, stayed under the cultural radar, but the media was alternately enthralled and abhorred by her statements and her activities—they kept her views in the public eye. In a letter published in the socialist publication *New York Call* on November 8, 1912, Helen attempted to explain her worldview. The letter begins with this sentiment:

> For several months, my name and Socialism have appeared often together in the newspapers. A friend tells me that I have shared the front pages with baseball, Mr. Roosevelt, and the New York police scandal. The association does not make me altogether happy . . .
>
> [After a scathing rebuttal, the article ends with this sentence]: If I ever contribute to the Socialist movement the book that I sometimes dream of, I know what I shall name it: "Industrial Blindness and Social Deafness." [58]

Helen could perceive that her culture was relatively blind and deaf. She lived in the waning years of the Industrial Revolution, so she called what she was seeing *Industrial Blindness and Social Deafness.* Helen's observation in the quote above is not just about individuals having vacant, soulless eyes; she is accusing entire governments, entire nations, of having a general level of consciousness that was unsophisticated and harmful—she was talking about collective groups with shared and, in her opinion, shallow worldviews.

The following comes from my first publication *Bugs, Blindness, and the Pursuit of Happiness* (2016):

> When a deaf-blind human being can unmask the political and economic hypocrisy of her time, it is unnerving to the power brokers. Helen Keller's writings and speeches were labeled Un-American by the right-wing element. It is no wonder they kept her under surveillance. However, the communist hunters in North America were not the only power brokers to fear Helen Keller. In 1933, the Nazi regime burned her books. They implied that she had an Un-German spirit. Here is her (now famous) response:

To the Student Body of Germany, May 9, 1933:

History has taught you nothing if you think you can kill ideas. Tyrants have tried to do that often before, and the ideas have risen up in their might and destroyed them.

You can burn my books and the books of the best minds in Europe, but the ideas in them have seeped through a million channels and will continue to quicken other minds. I gave all the royalties of my books to the soldiers blinded in the World War [WW 1] with no thought in my heart but love and compassion for the Germany people.

I acknowledge the grievous complications that have led to your intolerance; all the more do I deplore the injustice and unwisdom of passing on to unborn generations the stigma of your deeds.

Do not imagine your barbarities to the Jews are unknown here. God sleepeth not, and He will visit his Judgment upon you. Better were it for you to have a millstone hung round your neck and sink into the sea than to be hated and *despised of all men.* [59]

In *Helen and Teacher* (1980), biographer Joseph Lash suggests that Helen's book *Out of the Dark* was, perhaps, the only book burned by the Nazis. Of course, we will never be sure what works of literature were tossed in the flames:

> She had her own personal quarrel with the Nazis. At least one of her books had been thrown into the infamous bonfire in Berlin, the "burning of the books" that had attended Hitler's coming to power. Her German publisher denied that any of her books had been burned. In 1936, Otto Schramm, her German publisher, advised her that German Laws prohibited the printing of passages that expressed a friendly feeling toward the Russian experiment [with socialism] and that he "must cut out of the German edition of *Midstream* the part about Lenin."

Helen was indignant when she was told to edit out her pro-socialist worldview. She told Schramm to stop the publication of all her books in Germany. She would not be censured by any regime.

The population of Germany and the leaders of that nation held that a race of human beings, blond-haired, blued-eyed Aryans, were superior to all other of God's creations—that was the general (average) worldview of an entire nation state. That single insane idea led to the death of 70 to 85 million people during World War Two. This is from a Wikipedia page:

> An estimated total of 70–85 million people perished [in the Second World War], which was about 3% of the 1940 world population (est. 2.3 billion) . . . Deaths directly caused by the war (including military and civilians killed) are estimated at 50–56 million people, while there were an additional estimated 19 to 28 million deaths from war-related disease and famine. [60]

Unevolved, susceptible minds—the perceptually deaf-blind masses with the soulless eyes—have risen up throughout history, marched through the streets, sang patriotic songs, and then gone off to war, unaware what atrocities lay immediately ahead. As technology races forward in our era and our weapons become ever more horrible, it becomes an emergency to keep such minds from taking the reins of power again. Unfortunately, the technology of war has outstripped the pace of cognitive evolution; the dangers are more acute now than they were in Helen Keller's era.

I am recalling a song that was written by contemporary singer-songwriter Susan Werner called *Why is Your Heaven so Small?* That song holds a sentiment that Helen Keller would have embraced. Here is the chorus from Susan Werner's song:

> Well, I know you'd damn me if you could,
> but my friend, that's simply not your call.
> If God is great and God is good,
> why is your Heaven so small? [61]

The higher up the spiritual hierarchy, the more embracing, tolerant, and loving are the values, the ethics, and the intentions. The conception of a loving Heaven expands and expands as we ascend. As we look down from a sophisticated and loving height, standing beside Helen Keller, we see people with shallower worldviews below who envision small Heavens with few occupants. The ability to feel love and to be tolerant, progressively shrinks as worldviews become Narcissistic or Ethnocentric.

The masculine insanity that killed 70 to 85 million people during the Second World War, had no spiritual core; the hearts of the males who ran this horror show were as soulless and vacant as their eyes. Helen Keller's God was *not* small, and Heaven was not a club for old white males, for Warrior-Minded males who had the power to define God and Heaven in their own image. Helen got in the face of injustice and stupidity, she confronted the low level of consciousness of her time—for this she was attacked and trivialized. But she never backed off; she stood her ground for a lifetime. The image I see is that of a deaf-blind schoolgirl, a Joan of Arc heroine, facing down the heartless, soulless Nazi war machine.

Helen Keller also did not back down as she squared off against *all* the unevolved patriarchal societies of the world, including her own country. She was a militant suffragette; she had a lot on her mind, and she let the world know what she felt and thought. Women did not have the vote when Helen was speaking out as a young woman; she felt passionately that this male-dominated worldview was unjust and intolerable:

> We must know why a woman who owns property has no voice in selecting the men who make laws that affect their property. We must know why a woman who earns wages has nothing to say about the choice of the men who make laws that govern wages . . . We must know why our fathers, brothers, and husbands are killed in mines and railroads. We women, who are natural conservationists, must find out why the sons we bring forth are drawn up in line and shot. We must organize with our more enlightened brothers and declare a general strike against war. My father was a Confederate soldier, and I respect soldiers. But I grow more and more suspicious of the political powers that take men away from their work and set them shooting one another. Not all the military poems that I have read have roused in me a heroic desire to welcome my brother home with a bullet in his heart. We women have the privilege of going hungry while our men are in battle, and it is our right to be widowed and orphaned by political stupidity and economic chaos. [62]

In modern times, Helen's bold, heartfelt, and in-your-face articulateness would be met with threatening Twitter feeds, ugly Facebook posts, and harassment by thugs with automatic weapons. There is an open public channel in our modern social-media where political stupidity can shriek with hatefulness and pretend to be sane. Helen Keller would be deaf-blind to the madness; she would carry on with her mission; she would stand on the high ground and speak from her Soul.

Helen Keller also got in the face of the women who did not take a stand, women who accepted the status quo, women who did not examine their lives, their essence, women who, through their silent collaboration contributed to and supported the system that denigrated and enslaved them:

> I am not disposed to praise the educated woman, as we commonly use the term. I find her narrow and lacking in vision. Few women whom I meet take a deep interest in the important questions of the day. They are bored by any problem not immediately related to their desires and ambitions. Their conversation is trivial and erratic. They do not consider a subject long enough to find out that they know nothing about it. How seldom does the college girl who has tasted philosophy and studied history relate philosophy and the chronicles of the past to the terrifying processes of life which are making history every day! Her reputed practical judgment and swift sympathy seem to become inoperative in the presence of any question that reaches a wide horizon. Her mind works quickly so long as it follows a traditional groove. Lift her out of it, and she becomes inert and without resource. She is wanting in reflection, originality, independence. In the face of opposition to a private interest or a primitive instinct she can be courageous and vividly intellect. But she retreats from general ideas as if they did not concern her, when in point of fact civilized life is comprehended in general ideas.
>
> Such a woman comes to the gravest responsibilities like the foolish virgins who hastened to the marriage with no oil in their lamps. She is not prepared for the battle of life. Before she knows it, she may be in the midst of the fight, undisciplined and disorganized, struggling for all that is precious to her against an enemy whose position she has not reconnoitered. She sends her sons and daughters into the streets of life without the knowledge that protects. Ignorance gives her confidence, and she is fearless from want of understanding.
>
> . . . some of those who have suffered most cling to the ideal and pass it on to their daughters, as slaves teach their children to kiss their chains. [63]

Many women stood by their men during the wars and the injustices, but Helen Keller was having none of it. Her statement that mothers pass their ignorance and social blindness on to their daughters, *as slaves teach their children to kiss their chains*, is chilling. No wonder people got angry with her in-your-face rhetoric; she did not leave them any wiggle room to justify their weakmindedness.

It was lonely being a suffragette when Helen Keller was alive. The authorizes were still beating up women like Lucy Burns, Dora Lewis, and Alice Paul in their jail cells. The patriarchy was backed into a corner, like an animal with rabies; patriarchal males threw all their hatred at the likes of Helen Keller and her sister suffragettes.

In the era in which she lived, women could not get into positions of power, they were not in the government, nor were they in the publishing business—there are few books by women as we go back into history. Like slaves, women were property—clods of earth have no voice. Even in religion, the voice of the church, of theology, was masculine. Women were to stay silently in their place. However, deaf-blind Helen Keller refused to be silent. Hers was an early feminine voice in the fight for equality on all fronts. In 1911, she wrote:

> It makes no difference whether the Tories or the Liberals in Great Britain, the Democrats or the Republicans in the United States, or any party of the old model in any other country, get the upper hand. To ask any such party for women's rights is like asking the czar for democracy. [64]

Helen's distain for patriarchal low levels of consciousness was directed at all good-old-boy networks. It did not matter who was in power; if women were considered second class vassals, then that ridiculous worldview had to be confronted. Helen Keller's humanitarian, radical-for-the-times views made her a vocal and energetic champion of social change.

Throughout much of the early 1900s, Helen Keller's political opinions, according to her critics, were radical, utopian, dangerous, and not patriotic. Her saintly image was shredded every time she spoke out against social inequalities. Her deaf-blindness, her sweet disposition, and her soft femininity were inadvertently marketed in her youthful and innocent days. As a young girl, she was often portrayed in the media as a saint, a role model, or she was perceived as helpless and in need of champions. But when she became a young adult, her political and religious convictions clashed with this public image—much to the distaste of the same media. Her socialist views were in line with her religious convictions as was her opposition to the capitalism of her era. In an article for *American Magazine* in 1912 she wrote:

> I am the determined foe of the capitalistic system, which denies workers the rights of human beings. I consider it fundamentally wrong, radically unjust, and cruel. [65]

Global capitalism in our modern world has become so complex it is impossible to perceive the whole mechanism. We live in a much more challenging (and confusing) time than when Helen Keller stood against injustice and cruelty. Capitalism was a much harsher system in the industrial age. Consciousness has evolved since Helen's lifetime, and there are now many more people with Helen-Keller-Souls. There is still hope that Helen's vision of a more tolerant, loving humanity can win out over hate and self-serving greed.

Like many liberals of her time, Helen Keller was a self-proclaimed socialist, a supporter of the revolution in Soviet Russia, a member of the socialist labor movement, a pacifist (who did not entirely rule out force in defense of Democracy), a champion of causes for the disabled, and a fervent suffragette. She was later disgusted with Stalin and horrified by the Fascists in Germany, Italy, and Spain—she spoke out eloquently and courageously against these immoral beasts. Soviet and Nazi brands of socialism were not, in any way, the "Democratic Socialism" that Helen stood for. The Second World War threw her into a moral dilemma:

> At the time we entered World War I, my conscience was clear, and I succeeded in retaining my pacifism, but when the second conflict broke out, the issue seemed clear-cut to me—liberty or Hitler—and I did all in my power to help America and the Allies to overthrow a horrible tyranny. Yet I felt as if I had deserted the celestial standard of Peace and I am still troubled by it. ~ *Teacher*, by Helen Keller, 1955.

Despite her pacifist sentiments, Helen supported the soldiers who fought in World War Two and consoled the wounded on regular visits to hospitals after both world wars. History now suggests, in retrospect, that

Helen's youthful views toward communism, although well intended, were off the mark. Communism and Socialism, as these concepts were understood in Helen Keller's lifetime, did not bear compassionate and wise fruit as hoped in the Soviet Union. Neither Communism nor Socialism could drop the yoke of patriarchal worldviews—these social movements were still *old-boys-clubs* with differing uniforms. To be fair, Helen Keller was searching for a political movement that opposed poverty and war, and which was in line with her religious principles that service to others and love ought to be the focus of governments. Helen would be quite pleased, I think, to see what the Scandinavian countries have done under the banner of Democratic Socialism.

For Helen Keller, poverty, ignorance, and low social class were the primary causes of disability. The evidence of wealth inequality as a major cause of global suffering is solidly within Keller's purview. For example, the leading cause of blindness in the world today is from cataracts—this ocular impairment is a completely preventable, unnecessary situation. An ophthalmologist can replace a cataract with a lens implant in less than 15 minutes, restoring sight. As it stands now, more cataracts cause blindness every year than eye doctors can treat; consequently, the problem, on a global scale, is still getting worse instead of better. I am talking about right now, in our lifetime, not just when Helen Keller lived.

Why is this? Why are the injustices that Helen Keller fought against still with us? I suggest that Helen Keller would say that our social problems remain unresolved because poverty, ignorance, and class structure conspire against the best intentions of humanitarians. The affluent and well-educated do not go blind from cataracts, only the poor, the ignorant, and the powerless become unnecessarily blind, especially in Third World nations.

In the *New York Call*, in 1911, Keller wrote an article called "Social Causes of Blindness." In that short piece she wrote:

> Our worst foes are ignorance, poverty, and the unconscious cruelty of our commercial society. These are the causes of much blindness; these are the enemies which destroy the sight of little children and workmen and undermine the health of mankind. So long as these enemies remain unvanquished, so long will there be blindness and crippled men and women.
>
> To study the diseases and accidents by which sight is lost, and to learn how the surgeon can prevent or alleviate them, is not

enough. We must strive to put an end to the conditions which cause the disease and accidents.[66]

Helen was not arguing against medical intervention and rehabilitation, she was simply saying that the root cause of impairments and disease is to be found in class inequality. This inequality was quite blatant during the early years of the industrial revolution; Helen was a witness to the damage that was occurring to laborers and their families during her youth.

Anne Sullivan was Helen's spiritual ally in the fight against social inequity. Sullivan was a behind-the-scenes advocate for the same causes, but she was not a radical. Helen Keller was a Joan-of-Arc character, always on her high-horse and heading into battle. Sullivan was more subdued and cautious. Here are Sullivan's own words about disability:

> . . . you [Helen] are as sensitive as I am to the horrors of primary poverty and the sickness, debility, and want of decency it creates. I too have endured distress seeing poverty crushing people down and down in the social morass, but I have never believed that anyone intended to hurt others. And I am sure that no one foresaw how horrible, appalling, and enslaving industrial life would become—employers, landlords, and financiers as well as laborers caught in the toils of an economic and mechanical system that grew faster than human thought could have predicted. [67]

I do not think Helen Keller would have totally disagreed with her articulate friend and teacher. Helen was opposed to war, she was a pacifist, but she had great compassion for the soldiers caught up in the madness. She also realized that the populations of militant nations were swept up by the madness and had no voice to combat the evil. There was a global mental illness going on in the first half of the twentieth century; it was a disease of consciousness, a disorder which manifests evil repeatedly, decade after decade. I am struck by Sullivan's observation that the damaging side effects of the industrial revolution grew faster than human thought could predict. That is the same problem we face today; the slow evolution of human cognition cannot keep up with the consequences of exponentially arising destructive technologies.

Spiritual unfolding is happening at a snail's pace, falling far behind the advance of disruptive and (in a military sense) destructive technologies. Helen Keller knew that a spiritual unfolding, a blossoming of loving energy, could alter the minds of men and women and make the world more loving and accepting, but that evolution was painfully slow in coming. The battle we face, that Helen Keller so eloquently explained, was not over land claims or the right to rule—it was not even about power. *The battle was over the right to define consciousness,* the right to declare what a human mind ought to think and feel. That battle continues; the insane patriarchy that ruled recent history, waits in the wings, and the question remains: how should the cognition of humanity evolve?

Why did Helen Keller Become a Liberal?

True education combines intellect, beauty, goodness, and the greatest of these is goodness. [68]

For Helen Keller, loving-kindness and service to others were paramount ideals. They were ideals that came before intelligence. To be a liberal, in Helen Keller's passionate mind, was simply to understand the primary importance of love, tolerance, and forgiveness, and to act in accordance with those ideals. If the word *liberal* is offensive to you because it implies certain economic theories or Post-Modern judgements that feel unacceptable, then use the word *humanitarian*—for me, the two terms are essentially the same.

When we look at the charts and diagrams of the developmental psychologists, which show stages of cognitive evolution, we see that each level of mental development has a unique worldview, a unique way to perceive reality, a unique way to make meaning, unique memes that support generalizations, and a unique set of culturally entrained emotions. Each level of consciousness also has specific definitions for the same abstract concepts. For example, each level of consciousness, each reality, defines "God" differently—there could be, if developmental psychologists are correct, *at least* seven definitions of God. At the Narcissistic end of the spectrum, God would look pretty much the same as the Ego doing the defining; God would be an anthropomorphic mirror image of the Narcissistic Ego. In the Ethnocentric community, God would be an agreed upon anthropomorphic entity with love and tolerance only as large as the Ethnocentric (tribal) group would allow.

As we move up the scale, each level would have a more mysterious God, a less concrete God, a more complicated, loving, tolerant, and inclusive God. Judging from her character and actions, Helen Keller's God lived at the highest levels where Love was all-encompassing.

If we look at words like "liberal" or "conservative," the same thinking would apply: if there are seven definitions of God, then there are seven definitions for other abstract ideas, like liberalism, love, justice, etc. For example, a Narcissistic view of liberalism would be hostile and defensive because liberalism implies sharing and equality. The Narcissist is not capable of loving anyone else; there is no need for sharing with people who are not equally worthy. Ethnocentric groups are collections of Egos, not a harmoniously spiritual group (like we find at higher levels of cognitive evolution). These Ethnocentric tribes have shared memes and meaning-making habits that fit within a narrow worldview. Ethnocentric groups have historically, in knee-jerk fashion, rejected liberalism for the same "reasons" that Narcissists reject liberalism: because Narcissist groups are not capable of loving anyone outside their group; there is no need for sharing with people outside the chosen group who are not equally worthy. There is no need to love those unworthy of love.

At the elevated levels of cognitive evolution, the word *liberal* simply means *kind*. Ideally, liberals are generous, sharing, and they have broad and deep feelings for the suffering of others; liberals (humanitarians) feel a call to relieve pain and injustice. Helen Keller tried her whole life to be kind, to serve others, to feed the poor, heal the sick, prevent needless physical impairments, bring equality to women and to minorities, and reduce income disparities. Progress on all fronts has been made since Helen Keller lived, but these problems have not been solved; new generations face the same challenges, the same unfinished business that Helen confronted.

Because of her deaf-blindness, Helen was forced to use her whole body to access information about the world. She may also have been in contact with subtle vibrations that the sighted and hearing populations do not normally perceive (for example, through the twilight portal). I suggest that Helen could feel things, like subtle emotions, that others do not physiologically notice. *To feel* the emotions of others is what we mean by the term *empathy*. Sympathy is an Egocentric cognitive *recognition* of the emotions of others, but empathy is an actual non-cognitive (Allocentric) *feeling*. An empath senses and mirrors the emotions of others.

I am not sure that we can equate levels of consciousness to empathy; it is more the case that some people have an innate ability to notice and mirror emotions—regardless of their level of consciousness. One path to becoming a humanitarian (or political liberal) would be the ability to sense the pain and frustration of others and work to resolve the cause of their issues.

Empathy is on a bell curve, each of us is somewhere on the scale; some individuals have deep empathy, others seem to have almost no empathy. People with little to no empathy might gravitate together into religious and political groups. The same would be true with artistic Souls with powerful empathetic mirroring skills—they would join with others like them for political and religious reasons. Helen joined forces with those who could feel the pain of others and her religion and politics reflected this central core of her personality.

In his book *The Pattern Seekers* (2020), Cambridge University Professor Simon Baron-Cohen provides evidence that empathy is genetically inversely correlated with systemic thinking—(hypothetically) the more an individual is capable of empathy, the less they are skilled at systemic thinking. Contrary to this, the more a person is skilled at systemic thinking, the less they are capable of empathy—the two cognitive systems appear to be somewhat oppositional and oscillatory. In my Navigational Consciousness hypothesis (discussed in the next chapter), empathy is the product of Allocentric processing, while systemic thinking is the product of Egocentric processing. As such, we would *expect* to see the mutual exclusivity and the oscillatory nature of these two brain mechanisms.

Most people fall on a bell curve where the ability to be empathetic and the skill at systemic thinking are balanced, however there are extremes on either end of the bell curve. It is more the case that as we engage our systemic circuit, we inhibit or empathic circuit, and vice versa—they oscillate, taking turns manifesting.

Helen Keller's Traditional Mind

The reality that Helen was born into, a farming culture in the south, is called *Traditional* on developmental scales. The Traditional mind emerges from lower levels of consciousness; it is a transmutation beyond the Tribal mind and beyond the Warrior Clan-mind.

The Traditional mind is a great leap forward; it is a cognitive precursor to the scientific method and to the Modern mind. Reasoning skills become refined and valued in the Traditional mind, language becomes more abstract and sophisticated, literature evolves, the wisdom of the culture begins to be carefully stored and shared as education becomes more valued. Jean Gebser locates the root of this cognitive transformation between 300 to 500 BCE, a time when the Greek culture of Socrates, Plato, and Aristotle held court. There is an initial awareness, among these early thinkers, that human minds are dual, having both an Ego and a Self (my terminology). Traditional minds evolved out of agricultural communities where cooperation and communication were essential. Susanne Cook-Greuter says (in 2020) that about 75 percent of all humanity *still resides* at this Traditional level of consciousness.

The reality that Helen Keller was born into provides us with a good review of what a Traditional culture looks like. In Alabama, in the late 1800s, most people believed in an anthropomorphic god and they went to a church (a location for worship) on predetermined days. A family man (a patriarch) controlled the finances of the household, while his wife, a subordinate, managed the household. Women had few rights in early versions of the Traditional mindset because they were not considered by the culture to be strong enough or intelligent enough to deserve greater equality or responsibility. In the earliest days of the Traditional mindset, it was okay to have slaves (euphemistically called "domestic servants" after the Civil War) because a large plantation could not operate profitably without slave labor ("farm" labor). Slaves had less rights than women—they were barely considered human (or were often *not* considered human). In a Traditional culture, there are well-defined class and gender roles with attendant expectations and rules of conduct—evidently, a plantation (agricultural communities) required this regimentation.

Conflict is inevitable between Ethnocentric tribes; conflicts include divisions between black and white, male and female, old and young, my church and your church, my politics versus your politics, my ethnicity versus your ethnicity, and my country versus your country. Traditional level conflicts are not much different from Tribal conflicts, although the Traditional level of consciousness is much less violent than the continual Warrior-Clan conflicts that defined the Middle Ages.

Like every level of consciousness, Traditional minds have a set of beliefs that define reality and define behavior. Deviation from these beliefs is not acceptable within the group. Complex abstractions (like Faith and Democracy) are not fully developed in the Traditional mind. However, this mind is much more awake than the previous levels of consciousness; sympathy is slowly giving rise to empathy in more sophisticated Traditional minds. As amazing as this new mind is, it still cannot hold against the emotions that allow the Warrior mind or Tribal mind to reassert control over their worldviews. Traditional minds did not (and still do not) oppose war or retribution (an eye for an eye).

Helen Keller, whose mind evolved beyond the Traditional—beyond the reality she was born into—would still be fighting the same battles today as she fought in her day. The Traditional mind is still dominant in the United States (as I write this) and the belief structures that keep it alive are strong. However, this Traditional mind can be transcended, and *it has been* transcended by millions of people on the planet. It has transmuted into the Modern mind. But how did this happen? What caused the transmutation in Helen's mind from Traditional to Modern?

The human brain builds a model of the world that matches the external environment—physical, social, and emotional. This model *becomes hardwired* (but remains malleable) for the culture it finds itself in. The levels of consciousness that we are discussing here are anatomical and physiological brain states. That is why it is so hard to "change a mind." You must "convince" a mind at a low level of consciousness to (essentially) anatomically rewire itself—good luck with that. The concept of *reason*, the use of evidence to solve problems, and the appeal to a higher spiritual philosophy to guide decisions are not effective strategies against mindsets—like the Narcissistic, Tribal, and Traditional minds—that do not use sophisticated reasoning, evidence, or sophisticated spirituality to make decisions.

The anatomy and physiology of the brain is determined (in part) by the environment, by relatives and friends, and by the culture. However, and this is the key to transmutation away from the Traditional mindset, if you pluck a member of a community out of their familiar environment and place them in a foreign world, culture shock will occur. The brain/ body will go into an emergency mode (shock) and will begin to rapidly rewire itself to survive in the new circumstances. What might happen to a Traditional mind that would cause such a transmutation? How might a Traditional mind be plucked out of an environment?

The answer is (I suggest) that relocation and/or university-based (higher) education can cause the transmutation from a Traditional mind to a Modern mind, simply through moving away from accepted routines and beliefs. Helen Keller moved away from the Traditional culture in Tuscumbia, Alabama, away from an agrarian community, and relocated to Boston, to an urban environment. She was exposed to new teachers at the Perkins School for the Blind who understood things that Anne Sullivan did not. Helen Keller fell into a social community composed of highly evolved minds, people like Alexander Graham Bell, Michael Anagnos, Mark Twain, William James, and Oliver Wendell Holmes. Most importantly of all, Helen's youthful mind was exposed to a university setting (Radcliffe) where brilliant minds directed her to read the best literature, as well as the most astute works of history (as then understood). Consequently, Helen's rigidly-modeled Traditional mind was slowly rewired, and she went from being a woman with a Traditional mind to a woman with a Modern mind. [69]

But why did Helen Keller have such a remarkable mind compared even to the women who attended university alongside her? I believe this came about for biological reasons, which I will discuss in Chapter Four. However, there is another insight that explains not only her eloquence but also her rapid movement through levels of consciousness. Because she was deaf and blind, she had no visual images to identify, categorize, compare, and mentally manipulate; this freed up a lot of brain-processing space. She also did not have auditory patterns to identify, categorize, compare, and mentally manipulate. This freed up even more brain-processing space. So, what did Helen's mind do with all this excess processing power?

The brain comes equipped to construct meaningful patterns based on the environment it finds itself in. That ability to construct meaningful patterns was constantly starving for input inside Helen's deaf-blind brain. However, she did eventually find a "substance" that her mind could use to identify, categorize, compare, and mentally manipulate; that substance was *tactually transmitted language.*

When Helen Keller discovered language, particularly the language of her culture (Western civilization), she had something to construct meaning from—consequently, she incorporated the language, emotions, and concepts of the best thinkers in Western history as she read their works at a university level. Helen did not just learn *about* what great minds had said and what they accomplished in the past, Helen's hungry mind *devoured*, word for word, the great works that had defined history—she read the original documents (not summaries). The eloquent ideas of some of the Western world's greatest minds were the patterns Helen's brain used to craft her own remarkable mind.

If Helen's mind was crafted using the eloquence of poets and dramatists like Shakespeare, the concepts of the greatest Western philosophers like Kant and Hegel, the science of minds like William James, the religious convictions of Jesus and Swedenborg, and the cutting satire of friends like Mark Twain, it is no wonder she spoke so eloquently of the unseen world around her. It is also no surprise that her ideals, her spirituality, her emotions, and her biting eloquence, came together inside her mind and forged something cognitively unique. Helen's mind had nothing to do except absorb, play with, and remember the literature of her times. Her mind was composed using all that was assumed to be good in Western culture (through an early 1900's perspective): optimism, democratic ideals, freedom of expression, and belief in education.

In other words, Helen's mind based its reality on the realities she found in books. Literature, the captured voices of others, contained visual and auditory images that Helen used to craft her own worldview, her own reality, her own sense of right and wrong. Helen Keller's mind was created using the best of the best in Western tradition (from Radcliffe's perspective). She absorbed (inhaled) the world's knowledge; she became an amalgamation of historical insight. It was through reading great literature, and through discussions with sophisticated friends and associates that Helen's consciousness leaped forward. She shows us the power of relocation and the power of the written word to move minds from low cognition to higher cognition—Helen is proof that words experienced in novel settings can cause transmutations of consciousness. The Traditional mind evolved enough reliance on reasoning to open itself to further cognitive and spiritual evolution. *Words that transform* can be effective tools for transmutation within Traditional minds, while remaining ineffective for Tribal and Narcissistic minds.

There is another remarkable characteristic of the Traditional mind that enabled consciousness to develop further, leading slowly to the Modern level of cognition. Helen Keller had sufficient food, good housing, and a solid (functional) family that provided love, attention, education, and safety—she was born into comfort, into Love. Without enough food, love, safety, and shelter, a mind cannot evolve. There is no time or opportunity to spend "working on the self, crafting a better mind" if basic needs are not met. Traditional communities were far more sophisticated than anything that had come before. A stability was arising, a foundation, a way of life that would be a solid ground for further cognitive and spiritual evolution.

Paying attention to one's inner mentality *is a luxury* at the lowest levels of consciousness. Economic stability, spiritual guidance, and ever-advancing technologies enabled the move from Traditional mind to Modern mind. Helen Keller knew this; she spoke eloquently about the evils of poverty, neglect, ignorance, and hatred. She knew that human beings were victims of unevolved economic systems. It was not just that minds had failed to evolve, it was also that cultures, societies, and governing bodies were inadequate to the task of providing for suffering individuals.

Helen Keller's Modern Mind

The one thing that best defines the Modern mind is an awareness of the scientific method and the expert use of *reasoning*. The essence of the scientific method—the thing that makes science revolutionary—is the suspension of absolute belief, the very thing that earlier levels of consciousness relied on to justify their cognition. The Modern mind is open to dialogue, to alternate viewpoints. This openness, by itself, is a threat to all forms of consciousness that came before the Modern mind. Narcissistic minds, Tribal/Warrior minds, and Traditional minds are founded on belief structures that members of these cultures are expected to hold as unquestionable. The neural structure of the brain that had evolved in our ancestors—that had created their reality and meaning—was suddenly (during the Enlightenment period) challenged. Narcissistic, Tribal, Warrior, and Traditional minds that are based on a set of beliefs, intrinsically rebelled against the Modern mind (and still do)—even to the point of violence and murder.

Earlier I made a distinction between *belief* and *faith*. Faith is a very high-level *awareness*. It begins to arise within the Modern mind, even though this mind still confuses the two concepts and often rejects *Faith* as another term for belief. Lower levels of mind have tried to turn science into a justification for more primitive worldviews. This is called Scientism, an Egoic attempt to bring autocratic beliefs into science. Scientism misunderstands and misuses the scientific method (which requires a continual suspending of belief).

Like all the other worldviews, Modern scientific minds often feel that they have reached the top of the cognitive mountain. All other worldviews, from a scientific perspective, are the work of superstition and fake news. The Modern mind rejects the worldviews of Narcissists, Ethnocentrics, and Traditionalists, but fails to look upward at those with greater spiritual sophistication. As I write this from my own worldview (which is deeply committed to reason and science), I am speaking as if I am atop a mighty mountain, but I know from my study of levels of consciousness (and witnessing people more spiritual than I am) that I am ignorant of where the spiritual path leads from here. We are all on this road together; all of us are "stuck" at some level of cognition and emotion.

Unfortunately, Modern minds also do not fully comprehend duality; Modern man does not know that he has two minds, a Self, and an Ego. The Modern monological mind certainly knows about the Ego; indeed, the Modern mind is almost entirely Egoic. That is why there is so much angst, so much depression, so much despair, so much hopelessness, and so much barrenness in Western culture. Why? Because the Self (soul) is unevolved in the Modern mind. The Soul is the source of spirituality; Modern man has crafted a culture with little to no spirituality. I will tell you why I think this is so in Chapter Four.

Helen Keller blew right through the Modern level of consciousness. She found Faith early and she used it as a power source. Science was a tool, a curiosity for her, but it was not the answer to all things. The Modern mind was the last stand before (ironically) science itself revealed the sham of the monological perspective. The brain builds powerful models for how the world works, for what reality is, what meaning is, and how emotions should manifest—science brought us this wisdom, and science brought the developmental scale that I am ironically using to challenge the Modern mind as a half-thought-out methodology. Ironically, wonderfully, science is an evolution of esotericism—science is constantly searching for what is hidden, for the invisible, for the unknown and unexplained. Science is in the esoteric business.

Science discovered that the Modern mind, the mind that created science, was just another example of mind-building—a good one, but still fundamentally lacking. Helen Keller did not stay long within her Modern mind, she shot right up into the Post-Modern mind. Unfortunately, this put her exceedingly out-of-reach of most individuals in her culture. She was perceived as strange by her society, out-of-control, an uppity cripple, a mouthy woman who needed to be watched by the FBI and set straight by the patriarchal powers that ruled in her time.

If Helen Keller were alive today, she would not be out-of-place. There are many Post-Modern minds in the world today. These Minds are mediating, doing yoga and tai chi, exploring holistic and simple ways to live and communicate, developing loving-kindness as they pursue spiritual paths, and striving to live moment-to-moment. Post-Modern minds are reaching for compassion; they are a creative group, innovating (channeling) from the Soul, and they are standing silently, faithfully, as they stare compassionately down and offer a hand to less-developed minds. There are ever-increasing numbers of Helen-Keller-like Post-Modern people alive today. For many of them, Helen Keller is a spiritual role model.

Nicholas Humphrey, in his books about the evolution of human consciousness, concludes that human beings have evolved the relative ability to be *expert psychologists*, able to "examine and interpret" (to various degrees) the minds of others. This *inner-psychologist* slowly evolved through the eons, until it had become quite sophisticated in Modern minds. Some Modern humans have evolved the ability to intuitively "read" the minds of others. Some of the more talented *expert psychologists* can ascertain, through observation of body language, facial nuances, and the tone and cadence of voices, the intentions, motivations, and potential behaviors of those they are observing. *Expert psychologists* can read the mirror that is another's mind and can also become a mirror that others can interpret (not always accurately, of course). Humphrey says we have become expert psychologists through centuries of necessary practice.[70]

I suggest that this ability to relatively read other minds is present to different degrees depending on the level of consciousness a person has reached. The Narcissistic mind and the Tribal mind seem almost completely to lack this ability to *read* others. There appears to be a blindness to the sending and receiving of signals between individual human beings at the lowest rungs of cognition. I suggest that the inner psychologist begins to blossom in Traditional minds but is still primitive. It is only at the Modern level and above that the inner psychologist has the potential to become an expert at "mind reading."

I was puzzled why so many Americans could not perceive the Narcissism of our 45th president. No matter what he said or did, there was a sizable number of Americans who were impervious to his attitudes and actions. For a Modern mind, this mind-blindness (of those with lower levels of consciousness) is amazing to witness. In the year 2020, about one-third of all voting Americans seemed incapable of using an inner psychologist to read the reality around them. It was only after I encountered Nicholas Humphrey's insights that I considered the hypothesis that one-third of the American public might simply not have evolved the ability to use an inner psychologist. Another way to say this is that at least one-third of the American public had not reached the Modern level of cognition.

Humphrey's *Inner Psychologist* is related to Cambridge University Professor Simon Baron-Cohen's description of an *Empathy Circuit*. The empathy circuit is a uniquely human neuro-system that enables us to observe the emotions of others in real time, as well as monitor our own emotional flow from moment-to-moment. The empathy circuit allows us to imagine what others are thinking, intending, and wanting so that we can appropriately and emotionally react. Interestingly (but not surprising) Baron-Cohen says there are two empathy networks, *cognitive empathy* which considers and judges the emotions of others, and an *affective empathy* that allows for an appropriate emotional response—these two divisions appear in my schema to be examples of Egocentric (cognitive) and Allocentric (affective) processing.

Helen's astute ability to detect and interpret the inner psychologists of others is remarkable. She could also detect the inner psychologist of entire cultures, especially her own. That ability to extrapolate from the individual to the collective is evidence that she had evolved a Post-Modern mind. Baron-Cohen's empathy circuit is on a developmental bell curve; at low levels of consciousness there is little activity in the empathy circuit. A Narcissistic level of consciousness, for example, has essentially *no* empathy. From that zero point, each level above on the spiritual spiral attains a greater ability to use the empathy circuit. At a Post-Modern level, the empathy circuit is highly refined and sophisticated. Helen Keller had empathy for *all* mankind—that is a remarkable level of empathetic development.

As I write this, shortly after the 2020 elections in the United States, we find a drastic polarization in the population. Frustration is the rule, emotional exhaustion is widespread. I made my case (above) for one side of this debate and I hold that the reason for the divide is differing levels of cognitive evolution, differing levels of empathy and inner psychology.

However, I would like to also suggest another interpretation that is more global.

In Chapter Four, I will present the case (a hypothesis) that human beings contain two paradoxical minds. Essentially, we are a confused species because we have two contrary minds inside the same brain. We have (anatomically and physiologically) an Egoic mind and a Soul mind; these two are mutually exclusive and they are deaf-blind to each other.

The universal "forces" (circumstances) that brought about our dual cognition operate at different scales (as above so below). For example, the cognitive duality that defines our individual mental state, also operates at higher levels of organization causing bicameral divisions at different levels of social interaction. Therefore, we would expect to find (or could predict) a roughly 50/50 split in the American electorate, as well as a planet divided into a Western world "versus" an Eastern world, a split (battle) between individualism and collectivism, between conservative and liberal, and between Republican and Democrat—all these mirror image social structures are *to be expected* given our dual cognitive neurology. The biological duality found in our genetic makeup scales up, again and again (as over here, so over there), to playout at ever more global scales.

Below is a quote I like from the book *Jung and Steiner: The Birth of a New Psychology* (2002). This statement suggests that the split we saw in the electorate in the 2020 presidential election is not a new phenomenon:

> A proponent of individual psychology, E. Wexberg, had to confess in 1928: "The opposing forces of growing individualism and the personality cult on the one hand, and the necessity of developing a feeling of communality on the other hand, are causing insurmountable problems that so tragically show themselves again and again in the life of individuals as well as the life of nations."

This remarkable quote from a hundred years ago shows that the same duality we encounter today was recognized at the turn of the 20th century. This is no surprise if we understand cognitive duality and combine this understanding with the esoteric meme *as above so below.* Those who uphold individual rights above communal rights repeatedly go head-to-head against those who uphold communal rights above individual rights. On a body-centric level, this is the internal battle between our two minds. The Egocentric mind is individual, the Allocentric mind is communal. I also like the suggestion in the above quote that a personality cult can evolve from excessive individualism—this certainly seems to be what happened in the four years that the 45th president reigned in the United States.

It is as if the Egoic mind—which is dedicated to individualism—is at constant war with the Soul-mind, which is dedicated to collective cooperation. Egoic conservatism is constantly at war with Soulful liberalism. The amazing irony is that both these minds reside inside every human head, and manifest (are projected) inside the body politic. The question facing humanity is this: How shall the human mind evolve? How do we balance our internal conflicts? How do we not enter a final civil war between two minds deaf-blind to each other?

One more observation is exceedingly important in this discussion. As I will make clear in Chapter Four, the Egocentric mind requires a seer and a seen (an observer and an object/form to be perceived). The Ego is constantly searching for "objects" to attach to, both cognitively and emotionally. The Allocentric (Soul) mind does not attach. When an individual is overwhelmed by Egoic processing to the detriment of Soul-processing—when one mind, the Egoic, dominates (suffocates) the other mind—excessive attachments can occur. If a culture is composed of individuals who have yet to "find" their Soul minds, then cult worship can develop. The worshipping of monarchs, religious figureheads, and political dictators as cult figures results when human cognition is unbalanced. This has been and continues to be an extremely dangerous situation, especially as destructive technologies continue to appear at an exponential rate—the problems coming at us faster and faster require the skills of (at least) sophisticated Modern minds.

Helen Keller's Post-Modern Mind

Postmodernism is largely a reaction to the Modern mind's assumption that the scientific, objective worldview is the peak of cognitive evolution. It is a reaction against the Modern mind's tendency toward excessive materialism, which tends to be devoid of poetry and seems unable to give spirituality room for expression.

The Post-Modern mind is aware that worldviews and realities are crafted by individual minds. Therefore, Postmodernism is cautious and skeptical of generalizations which claim to be valid for all individuals and all cultures. Postmodernism relies more on experience (qualia) and rather less on abstract thinking and quantitative analysis. Whereas the Modern mind embraced the Ego and dismissed the Soul as superstition and ignorance, the Post-Modern mind returns Allocentric "Soul-thinking" to its rightful place as one-half of humanity's paradoxical duality.

Before I go further with this discussion, let me acknowledge the fierce infighting that is taking place around these worldviews. I especially see Post-Modernism attacked and denigrated alongside the opposing laudatory statements alleging the advances Post-modernism champions. This necessary and important debate is raging as I write these words. I will make two observations and then get back to my focus. First, as I said previously, we must focus on one individual at a time. We are each a miracle, and we need to treat each other with due respect—that comes before we start slicing and dicing each other's worldviews. Second, we are speaking here of generalizations and abstractions. We are engaged in an Egoic debate, which is fine if we have an overhead view of the debate and if we listen respectfully to those who seek to clarify or counter our words—we might even learn something new if we allow our worldviews to be malleable. . . . Back to business.

The Post-Modern mind does not need a supreme deity to dictate what humanity ought to be doing. It is okay *for humanity* to decide that *Love and Service to Others* is the highest calling for the species. The Source for "valuing life" can come from within the human mind (the Kingdom within); it does not have to have cosmic origins. There is no need to debate where the ultimate Source came from, or how anthropomorphic the Source ought to be, or what the rules are that some cosmic force laid down in the early days of eternity. Believe what you want (you be you), but—putting the origin debate aside—the Post-Modern mind accepts the challenge and begins the task *of applying* kindness, intelligence, and wisdom in the service of Love and Others. The Post-Modern mind knows that there is much work to be done; these advanced minds say, "Let us get on with the work and never mind about religious sects and political parties."

Helen Keller moved beyond her more primitive levels of consciousness when her life was given a purpose, a life-mission. When she was just in her teen years—after discovering Swedenborg's teachings—she decided to dedicate her life to the service of others. However, as a young adult, she had no expertise, no way to help. Her university education eventually changed that and so did fate.

Helen was eventually asked by the newly created American Foundation for the Blind (AFB) to work for the betterment of blind human beings, as their spokesperson. Helen accepted this offer; she needed an income and a place to put her aspirations. This association with the American Foundation for the Blind began as a national effort but soon became a global crusade to change minds, behaviors, and laws everywhere on the planet. Helen now had financial support for her life-mission, a way to use her Warrior soul, her Traditional values, her clear-headed Modern reasoning skills, and her Post-Modern Faith to make life easier for others who were less fortunate.

The Post-Modern mind has a mission and a practice. This practice is essential and is a primary feature of Post-Modern consciousness. For Helen Keller, (as far as we know) it was her constant reading of the Bible and her study of Swedenborg that was her daily practice, her foundation for Christian contemplation (meditation). Post-Modern minds know that there exists a "spiritual journey." Post-Modern consciousness has stepped onto the pathway and has begun a journey toward awakening. Helen was on this pathway; she was trying to become a more spiritual person; she was disciplined, focused, and she was actively trying to make a difference when and where she could. The spiritual journey is exhausting at times because the goal is constantly to subsume old models of reality and layer them with a more loving, tolerant, expansive, and productive model of reality.

Post-Modern minds also know what it means to "have a witness." Biologically, this witness is a proprioceptive system in the brain that *can watch itself* as the body and emotions go about their routine activities. The Post-Modern mind can create a witnessing Ego, which "floats above" and monitors the Ego-at-work; in other words, an Inner Psychologist develops. The Post-Modern mind knows about levels of consciousness and works toward further transmutations. This mind does not know what comes next along the spiritual path, but the Post-Modern mind does know that *something comes next*—and so a Post-Modern mind is always searching.

The Post-Modern mind is remarkably close to sensing the duality of mind. Post-Modern minds can dwell in the Self (Soul, Allocentric mind), suspending the stressful life of the Ego. When the human mind dwells for long periods within the Soul, stress drops away, and a sense of living in a stage play appears (signaling the advent of the Integral mind). Serendipity and synchronicity become "real" at this stage of "brain modeling." A new level of reality appears—and it feels incredibly good to live in what feels like virtual reality, an ethereal stage play where we are actors in a cosmic drama.

Having a Post-Modern mind, however, can also feel quite lonely. There are not many people at this level of cognition; it is, therefore, hard to find a community of such sophisticated minds. Helen Keller was lucky because *she did* find such a community (of the most evolved minds in her time) and she found this supporting community at a remarkably young age. In our time, there are relatively more Post-Modern minds than when Helen lived, and many Modern minds are poised to move upwards on the spiritual path—it is not as lonely as it once was for Post-Modern minds.

Cultures are a blend of levels of consciousness and these various levels are understandably in conflict. As I said earlier, cultures have an average level of consciousness. If 75 percent of the American culture resides at the Traditional level of consciousness, then a mere 25 percent make up the rest. Roughly, ten percent are still in Narcissistic and Tribal stages, ten percent are Post-Modern, and just 5 percent have Integral minds. This is a statistical dynamic rendering, so it is not a good idea to hold fast to these speculations; I am offering a very generalized overview.

Epigenetics, the latest revolution in genetic science, is said to cause the human DNA structure to *rewire on the fly* (just like neurons in the brain rewire as we learn); in consequence, the experiences of a previous generation are passed to emerging generations. Because of epigenetics, we can hope that higher levels of consciousness will become more often represented in evolving cultures, while lower Narcissistic and Ethnocentric minds will fade from history. Already, we can see that Traditional and Modern minds are "under review" and are slowly losing numbers to higher levels of cognition. Traditional and Tribal Minds are complaining of "cancel culture" as their memes, inadequate reasoning, and weak empathy fail to counter Post-Modern challenges.

If epigenetic speculations are correct, previous experiences are causing an actual hardwiring change in newly born minds. We have cracked the genetic code but not the epigenetic code, so we do not yet know how experiences are passed from generation to generation. However, there is a sense (an intuition) that suggests lower levels of cognition are being overrun by more sophisticated epigenetic changes.

It is the Post-Modern mind that finds esotericism fascinating. When this mind discovers serendipity and synchronicity—that all the world is a stage and that it is possible to live within this magic framework—then the Post-Modern mind begins to advocate for the return of the fairies to hedge and workshop. At this level of consciousness, we want to bring back the fairies (the magic) because we want the Post-Modern mind to evolve further, to express itself, to create, and to help other minds transcend.

The awareness that "all the world is a stage, and all the men and women are actors," is a deep insight that is more fully grasped within the Post-Modern mind. There seems to be, to the Post-Modern mind, an ethereal (perhaps metaphorical) membrane surrounding the body that oscillates; this membrane sometimes acts as a mirror and sometimes acts as a screen—cognition projects and absorbs, sends and receives. This membrane encases our field of consciousness. When we become aware of sending and receiving at the surface of the membrane, the sensation we feel is like an actor starring in a life-play, saying our lines on cue—we become a witness to our life unfolding.

At the Post-Modern level of cognition, we become aware of the membrane around our consciousness (which we can shrink or expand to fill a classroom—or a universe); we become aware of the cloud of sensations that define our moment-by-moment consciousness, and we become aware of the dual processes of Egoic-attending and Soul-awareness. I suspect that Helen Keller was in direct contact with the cloud of sensations that constitute dual-consciousness.

To develop a mind, to further the sophistication of consciousness, requires time, an awareness of the need to evolve, and an emotional and financially stable foundation (a healthy and fortunate lifestyle). People in poverty, struggling to get enough to eat, who have unresolved and unattended physical and mental health challenges, and who have little hope of a better future, are not going to attend yoga classes. Moving through culturally higher levels of consciousness will not be possible if we fail to help the least fortunate of our fellow humans.

Here is where we must leave Helen Keller; her mind sailed into the upper 10% of her culture, but she did not go beyond Post-Modern (as far as I can surmise). Hers was a mind heading for the Integral level of consciousness; however, she would also, I suggest, have had much to say about the Post-Integral (Post-Human) era that is now knocking at our door—I will discuss (muse about) Helen's speculative take on the Post-Integral mind below. First, however, we must understand the sophisticated Integral mind that comes before the Post-Human mind.

Integral Minds

Maybe Helen developed an Integral mind. I do not know, and I am not the one to judge since my own mind often dwells happily within the Modern and Post-Modern levels of consciousness. On good days, I am at the Post-Modern Level, but I cannot claim to have reached Integral or Post-Integral stages of cognition with any consistency.

To have an Integral mind means that you have an alchemical, or psychological, or experiential understanding that levels of consciousness exist. If you do not know there is an available spiritual path, and if you do not know what levels (landmarks, waystations) are available along the path, and if you do not know the methods available for transmutation, then there is no way for you to cognitively accept, study, or experience these levels. No doubt, Helen Keller knew there was a spiritual journey that could be followed but I do not know where her contemplative mind went during her explorations of spirituality. Certainly, she did not know the scientific theories I am using in this discussion—they were not formulated during her lifetime—and the Buddhist eightfold pathway was not commonly studied in the West. However, using her Christian perspective, Helen had Faith that Jesus was enlightened and had encouraged his followers to seek to know about the spiritual journey toward the heavenly state called *Christ Consciousness*.

Integral minds know the difference between the Ego and the Soul (the Self), and these sophisticated minds seek *To Be* as well as *To Become*. "To be" means to dwell within the Soul, within the Allocentric mind, to be aware, to flow, to enjoy being in the stage play of life, as opposed to the Egoic mind that is always busy planning to get somewhere, to accomplish, *to become* rather than to locate and reside in the present moment (the location of the Soul). There is a (hypothetical) physiological explanation for this cognitive duality, which I address in Chapter Four.

The Integral mind can perceive all the different levels of consciousness which are co-existing within themselves, within other humans, and within any given culture. The Integral mind is tolerant of all these levels of consciousness and uses loving-kindness, compassion, and education to help other minds become more self-aware and more accepting. The

Integral mind knows, for example, that a human being cannot just suddenly leap from being Narcissistic to being Post-Modern; there is a long road toward sophisticated spirituality, and it takes great discipline to keep trekking upward on the Path.

At the Integral level of consciousness, all of life is accepted—the crazy, the divine, the evil, the awful, the godly, the blessed, all the stages of cognitive growth are "appreciated and embraced." *Acceptance* is the rule—surrender to what is. The message is to, "stop mentally struggling." All the childish earlier minds reside inside us. We are composed of the minds that came before and now we are to become something else—new varieties of consciousness are becoming available. To reach these new levels of cognition, we must begin with a Faith-based acceptance of all that came before—after all, it is a done deal; everything had to be exactly as it was for this moment to manifest. This does not mean that we allow cruelty to go unchallenged or ignorance to go uneducated. It simply means that we stop wasting energy being angst-filled and constantly distraught at the state of things. No need to mourn the past, no need to obsess about potentially horrible futures. The task is right now.

Cognitive and spiritual growth is a slow process—meanwhile, we cannot keep up with our own technologies. The tortoise (human cognition) is racing the hare (technology). However, Love continues to expand with each step upward on the spiritual winding staircase— technology may continue to race forward but the pace of Love is constant, and it never rests. When the body dies, something still exists, something moves from a dead person into other living bodies—our ancestors live within us still, and not just epigenetically, metaphorically, or historically. Something "lost forever" never left. . . . I was somewhat amazed as that last sentence flowed onto the page, as if a mind more sophisticated than my own had taken control of the computer keyboard (smile). So, I leave the sentence there and wonder.

This enduring force that "never leaves," this energetic-structure, which we call *Love*, will not be denied; it cannot cease to be. Love will continue to guide humanity out of the cognitive dark ages. Helen Keller lives within us still; her Soul merged with the collective Soul. Helen taught us to ignore the darkness and the silence that defines our ignorance; she whispers to us, "Just keep moving, just keep seeking, just keep sharing, just keep loving—get up every day and try again."

The Integral mind stands on a mountain top and looks down at the entire history of conscious evolution. There is no use pitying or denigrating the Souls who struggle up the mountain, just as you struggled upward. What you see below is the movement of an entire species evolving—*it is what it is; it is going where it is going.* Rejoice in the awareness of consciousness and then journey onward; there is much work to be done, many global challenges ahead.

There is another viewpoint about the Integral mind which needs to be mentioned. In esoteric thought, our two minds—even though they are paradoxically deaf-blind to each other and mutually exclusive—have found a way to oscillate (cooperate). Look in the mirror at your anatomical mirror image halves—you are composed of a left side and a right side; that is a metaphor for your cognition. Your two anatomical halves found a way to cooperate so that you could move with a purpose: to use tools, to communicate, and to navigate straight-ahead. Your bilaterally includes two minds that can overcome their stark divisions to (optimally) function. In esoteric thought (exemplified in Carl Jung and Rudolf Steiner) an Integral mind is one in which our two minds have found a well-tuned resonance. Something of a higher cognitive order manifests when the oscillation between our two minds reaches an optimal frequency.

The Integral mind embraces the whole of humanity. We have a human heritage, an obligation to our species—we are on this Earthship together, on the third planet from the sun, isolated within a lonely solar system, lightyears from our nearest neighbors. We are an unfathomable mystery, a stunning conundrum, a motley assortment of Souls, a collective miracle. Working together, we have an obligation to preserve our fragile blue planet, to preserve our history, to honor and preserve all other species, and we have an obligation to enable a healthier, happier, safer world for those who inherit our work. The Integral mind knows that we are on this journey together; it knows it has an obligation to carry on the migration of the species; it knows that it is paradoxically both a drop in an eternal ocean (the Egocentric mind) as well as the ocean itself (the Soul mind).

The Perils of Unnatural Selection

If Helen Keller had her way, human minds would evolve to be ever more loving and ever more focused on being helpful. But Helen is gone from this reality; only her words remain to inspire and challenge us.

Helen is not alive today in this age of artificial intelligence, gene editing, psychotropic drugs, and neural implants. I fear that Helen's appeal to Love and Service is only heard by a select few Integral minds.

Most scientists do not know about levels of consciousness, they have Modern minds. These intellectually brilliant scientists are racing to develop robotic creatures that fit their Modern worldview, which too often lacks empathy and a focus on service. In a Capitalistic economic system, kindness and service are not profitable—the creation of smart weapons and intellectually savvy sex dolls may very well trump more honorable work.

American biologist Edward O. Wilson says (as have others) that we have entered the Age of Unnatural Selection. Biological evolution (natural selection) moves too slowly, so humanity has taken the reins— we have accelerated the rate at which we can alter our minds and bodies. We now have the power to alter the speed and direction of cognitive evolution. We will soon be able to tailor-make consciousness. What kind of unnatural creatures should we create? What kinds of minds will they possess? What worldviews will these unnatural creatures manifest?

This is no small question for the human species. Manmade cognitive evolution is as important a challenge as facing climate change, or battling pandemics, or avoiding nuclear war. Our ability to alter brain anatomy and physiology used to be a slow process. But those happy days of ignorant bliss are gone. The speed of brain/mind manipulation is accelerating, spinning out of control as science races forward like a run-away cement truck with no driver.

Of course, humanity has been messing with the mind for centuries, using caffeine, nicotine, alcohol, prescription drugs, and hallucinogens. But like everything else in our modern world, the speed of change is accelerating faster than lawyers and politicians can study and direct social adaptation.

How should the human species cognitively evolve? Looking back through history at all the wars and all the atrocities, it might *not* be a good idea to keep creating the same minds as came before. What happens to the spiritual pathway when we mess with natural selection? What happens to levels of consciousness? What happens to the interaction between Soul and Ego? Who gets to make the decisions about the evolution of cognition? How evolved are the decision makers?

One thing is noticeably clear to me; most of the people building advanced technologies have mathematical/logical brilliance. They are creating technologies, especially artificial intelligence, *in their own image, using their own Worldviews as a model.* However, these clever minds do not necessarily have spiritual brilliance. Empathy, compassion, and Soul-development are not often on their radar; Soul-Development is not their strong suit. Most AI researchers, I contend, have Modern minds, and they are unaware of more spiritual levels above their own development. Mathematical/logical prodigies are crafting the technological future, but I am not convinced that they should be given free reign.

Unfortunately, we have extraordinarily little control over the future that is raining down on us. It is too late to apply brakes to our technologies. It is too late to stop the flow of unnatural selection. Futurist Ray Kurzweil, who has made predictions that have come true over 80% of the time, predicted a singularity in the year 2029. Here is how polymath John Von Neumann defines the inevitable singularity:

> The ever-accelerating progress of technology and changes in the mode of human life give the appearance of approaching some essential singularity in the history of the race *beyond which human affairs, as we know them, could not continue.* (my italics)

In 2029, if Kurzweil is correct again, information processing ability will create unnaturally-selected entities capable of intellectual, emotional, and spiritual feats exceeding human ability. How will these creatures assess levels of consciousness? How will they define and judge *your* worldview? How will they decide if your worldview—or an entire culture's worldview—needs adjustment? Who will carry out the adjustment? How will these new computer wonder-minds alter the moment so that human affairs—business as usual—can no longer continue. All of which brings us to a discussion of the Post-Human mind.

The Post-Integral (Post-Human) Mind

Let us pause to reflect and suppose that Helen Keller was still alive today. What might Helen say about the artificially intelligent future raining down on natural humanity? What impact might the exponential march of technology have on her life and worldview?

One thing is sure, if Helen Keller were alive today, she would not be silent during the debate about humanity's future. She would find it irresponsible of citizens not to engage in dialogue about important events. At the very beginning of the debate, Helen would ask: Where is the furious effort taking place to engineer *artificial compassion* into the new robots? Why has loving-kindness been subsumed many layers deep under the definition of intelligence? Why is kindness not exponentially evolving alongside our technologies? Why is "fast and smart" (and profitable) perceived to be so much better than "thoughtful, helpful, empathetic, and free?"

Helen Keller was feisty, outspoken, and she fought for what she believed in: she believed in Love and she believed in using the power of Love to make the world a kinder place for every single person on the planet. If we are hell bent on creating robotic creatures that are highly intelligent, then Helen would insist that Kindness, Love, Empathy, Service, Trust, and Tolerance not be left out of our new creations.

This need to create artificial (robotic) compassion is, of course, not lost on scientists. There are researchers all over the world working on incorporating human attributes—kindness, curiosity, trust—into their robotic creations. There is an entire industry called "Machine Ethics" dedicated to the augmentation of heart and soul, concentrating on building machines that help humans make sound moral decisions, machines that understand the emotional and ethical consequences of human behaviors. Particularly in Japan, scientists are developing helper robots for the elderly, for disabled people, for people who are depressed or grieving, for children needing play therapy, and for people who just need a friend they can count on (or a sexual partner). In other words, *there are* sophisticated, compassionate scientists working in the best interests of kindness on a global scale—just as Helen Keller would wish.

However, the problem we face globally is that these well-meaning scientists are not in charge of governments or armies and there are few of them compared to the army of AI researchers focused on the creation of mathematical/logical creatures. Military and intelligence agencies have the money and infrastructure to craft combative, soulless, heartless, exceedingly efficient Robo-warriors. Humanitarians do not have an endless source of funds to further the advancement of loving-kindness and caregiving.

It is clear to me that Helen Keller would insist, from a very global overhead perspective, that we face an incredibly old problem: the *epigenetic mandate of the Y-chromosome*. Historically, scientists and futurists working on emerging technologies, military leaders, and politicians crafting laws that regulate the development of disruptive technologies, have been predominantly males at Modern levels of consciousness (or below). This is changing rapidly, especially in the developed world, but Modern males still dominate in many professions and in most of the world. Therefore, masculinity (I am channeling Helen), at Modern or lower levels of cognitive sophistication, have gone off on another obsession, a hyper-fascination with "intelligent" machines. Helen Keller would be constantly asking the world's cultures why loving-kindness is not *at the forefront* of our efforts to enhance human capabilities. And why are we not working on strategies for evolving (improving) outdated and dangerous worldviews like Narcissism and Ethnocentricity?

Helen Keller would also say, I think, that it does not matter how concerned and well-intended the scientists are when decision-making is in the hands of patriarchal politicians with low levels of consciousness. Helen Keller would be concerned that the patriarchy is still holding court, building a world in their own aggressive, self-serving, testosterone-driven tribal image. She would warn that peril awaits those who ignore empathy, relationship, imagination, spirituality, and the nurturing of the Soul. She would see (as have others) that Democracy is threatened by narrowly defined Artificial Intelligence (AI): Machines on algorithmic autopilot are ideal allies for autocrats who need surveillance technologies to control controversy and dampen dissident activities.

In September 2020, Netflix released a documentary called *The Social Dilemma*. I had been "preaching" about the dangers of AI for many years (mostly grumbling to myself), that a future was fast approaching where artificial intelligence would outpace the evolution of human consciousness. What this Netflix documentary showed was that "the feared future" had arrived several years ago, and the list of dangers that many had warned about had already been uncaged. It was almost too late to save Democracies, too late even to continue the evolution of human cognition (natural selection).

Social-media algorithms, running on A.I. autopilot and driven by profit motives, operate on Facebook, Google, YouTube, and other social platforms. These algorithms are controlled by the machines, there is limited human oversight (once the algorithms are unleashed), and there are limited laws to protect consumers. Social media companies like Google, Apple, and Facebook are the richest corporations to ever exist on the planet. How did they get to be so profitable, where is the money coming from that fuels their empires?

Essentially, algorithms continually feed users what they have indicated their interests to be. For example, if you believe that Covid-19 is a hoax, Facebook and YouTube, will give you a constant dose of confirmational newsfeeds that support your view—few contrary news items will appear in your web-feed. The result is that the machines themselves (your phone and computers) create bubbles around social groups, reinforcing specific levels of consciousness. The result is an artificially-induced Tribal mentality that pits one tribe against another. This is a perfect algorithmic recipe for destroying Democracies by reinforcing Narcissistic and Ethnocentric minds.

What I realized, after seeing this documentary and after reviewing Professor Shoshana Zuboff's book *The Age of Surveillance Capitalism*, was that AI algorithms are essentially freezing human minds at low levels of consciousness through constant reinforcement. If a mind is Tribal it gets only tribal confirmation on social media. There is never any challenge to tribalism, no move to the Modern mind, no acceptance or understanding of the scientific mind. In the same way, the Modern mind cannot evolve to a Post-Modern level because it never gets a chance to even glimpse higher minds at work. AI has glued every mind to a wall and fed that mind exactly what it already knows.

Unnatural selection, driven by AI algorithms, is preventing the usual route to cognitive evolution. We are being programmed, every one of us, all day, every day, as we use our social media. Cultures are being ripped apart as I write this. The social media companies are "mining attention," using "AI manipulation engines" and a business plan called the "attention attraction model." The tech giants have found a way to use the weakest links in human mental processing to turn humanity into attention-products, into automatons, into walking, organic, rabidly-consuming flesh-based robots. That would be you and me.

The horror of this—as if we needed more horror—is the effect on young minds holding social media in their hands. All those young people with their noses toward their phones are addicted. It is an *AI-planned* addiction, a deliberate method to sell things and make a profit. A young preteen mind is extremely vulnerable to this manipulation. Depression and suicides of teens and preteens have been trending upward since the advent of these AI algorithms. The human brain, under normal conditions, rapidly evolves until the twenties when anatomical and physiological changes slow down. We have no idea how these algorithms are altering the minds of an entire generation of super-vulnerable kids. This is a mental health emergency, but little is being done. The situation may be worse in countries outside the United States where military governments and autocratic systems know how to use these algorithms to develop obedient and fervently supportive populations. We have built a gigantic, ungoverned, unregulated, out-of-control propaganda machine running on autopilot.

On February 3, 1937, Helen wrote in her Journal:

> It seems to me more urgent than ever to foster in the present young generation a spiritual philosophy and imagination that shall keep the morning dew in their souls when an age arrives that knows not the muses or the Graces. [71]

"An age that knows not the muses or the Graces"—are we already there? Are we ignoring compassion and tolerance now? If we build our future in the imagine of the Y-chromosome, will we end up with a poetry-barren surveillance culture? Will the future be dangerous, soulless, lacking imagination and devoid of good humor? Esotericism, the home of the Muses and the Graces, is a counterforce to Y-chromosome expression/aggression—Helen seemed to know this intuitively.

If Helen Keller were alive today, I suggest that she would hold history up for sight-dominated minds to review. First, she would show us World War One—over a hundred years ago. There were poets and diplomats, empaths, scientists, doctors and nurses, educators, religious leaders, and spiritual justice warriors in the world when The Great War to End All Wars started. These good (Modern and Post-Modern) souls lost out to the Narcissistic madmen who wanted to fight each other, to conquer, to slaughter, to rule, to glory in victory. The insane patriarchy that caused World War One invented innovative weapons of war: tanks, barbed wire, machine guns, air combat, and nerve gas. The war machine also created propaganda, pitted boy soldier against boy soldier, and caused the death of innocent civilians. But the Great War to End All Wars did not end all wars—it was just another epic slaughter in the history of mass murder. The Y-Chromosome was still driven to soldier on. Just one generation later, the same epigenetics that murdered eleven million soldiers between 1814 and 1818, started another world war.

Helen Keller would now hold up the images from World War Two (September 1, 1939 to September 2, 1945). "This is you," she would say to the Narcissistic and Ethnocentric males on the planet. "This is your doing. Although, this time you created more effective weapons and more advanced mind-control."

The big (dumb) boys wanted to fight again in the 1930s and 1940s, to conquer, to slaughter, to rule, to glory in victory. It was the same madness as last time around. There were poets and diplomats, empaths, scientists, doctors and nurses, educators, religious leaders, and spiritual justice warriors in the world when the Second World War started. But these good souls *lost out again* as the madmen began the slaughter. An estimated 100 million people died because of that second global war, because of the Y-Chromosome, because of an epigenetic sequence that (evidently) cannot learn or evolve (a pandemic mind-virus). That "World-War-Two Patriarchy" is still with us as I write these words, still just as shallow, still cognitively unevolved, staring out from vacant eyes, still spiritually clueless.

Now Helen would show more wars in Korea, in Vietnam, all through the Middle East. Genocide in Africa. Tribal warfare is still raging throughout the world, male against male, shallow mind against shallow mind, Y-Chromosome against Y-Chromosome. Always there are exponentially more sophisticated weapons, amazingly effective propaganda, more effective mass killing strategies as the weeks unfold. Always the landscape gets more barren and there are fewer and fewer poets.

Now, Helen would show us the present. She would show us a picture of the United States Congress. On the Republican side we see the same tired epigenetically crippled patriarchy, still in power (I write this in December 2020). Republicans dress alike in the uniform of the patriarchy, suits and ties (I call them *Penguins*). Historically, these Penguins have all been males, these Republicans, with an occasional token female or minority male thrown in to feign Democracy (thankfully, this is changing). On the Democratic side of the isle, we see America: male and female, ethnic diversity, sexual diversity, racial and religious diversity—the whole melting pot stands in opposition to something ancient and un-evolving. [72]

There used to be some honor in the term "Republican;" the word used to stand for individual rights, cautious reason over unquestioning emotion, family (Christian) values, and fiscal responsibility. Now (as I write this), the Republican Party has shrunk to become a Narcissistic, Ethnocentric, Traditional throwback to a Middle Ages mindset—I write this with the Trump presidency thankfully about to step away from power. There is (obviously, my own politics have exploded onto the page) a lunatic fringe in America that is being fed through social media; there are politicians who are using these brainwashed millions to further their need for attention, for Egocentric power, and for profit.

Patriarchal worldviews are still the norm in many countries. The National People's Congress in China, for example, is chillingly like old versions of the American Republican side of Congress, except there is no second body in China that matches the Democratic side of Congress in the United States, where variety, plurality, and femininity can be seen. The huge Hall of Governance in China is filled with males wearing suits and ties (Chinese Penguins) or males dressed in military uniforms. The Devine Female is rarely in sight, rarely in positions of power in Asia or in the Middle East. The dictatorship of China is racing ahead with genetic manipulation, surveillance mastery, and empire building. China is on a collision course with the United States and the loser will be the planet. The same kind of male mind dominates the Middle Eastern and African nations, except now the patriarchy has a different uniform and the males are often autocratic religious figures.

Helen Keller would now ask whether the Y-Chromosome, this epigenetic-monster, will be allowed to craft the Age of Artificial Intelligence. Will AI be used to make better weapons, better propaganda, more effective mass killing machines?

The answer is *yes*. AI will be used by patriarchal males to build weapons. It is happening now on a massive scale. Poets and well-meaning scientists are cautiously (naïvely?) optimistic, despite the history of the Y-Chromosome. Meanwhile, Slaughter Bots are rolling off the assembly line. The Y-Chromosome-driven epigenetic madmen are poised for their next murderous insanity.

Meanwhile, the AI gurus are talking about how wonderful our world is about to become because of exponentially advancing science. I do not (entirely) buy it and I doubt Helen Keller would have bought that deaf-blindness either, without serious reservations. Somehow, we must modify the epigenetics of masculinity, and soon. We must figure out a way to accelerate loving-kindness and spirituality.

Given this bad news, there is, fortunately, some hope on the horizon that the bad guys will not annihilate the planet again. In the Western world, we are witnessing a counterforce to the unchecked flow of the patriarchy; we see a renaissance of the feminine perspective. Women are rapidly gaining power and taking leadership positions.[73] There is great hope in the West that democracy, spirituality, and loving-kindness will grow and thrive. However, in other locations on the globe, males with low levels of consciousness still dominate, and they rule as if we still lived in the Middle Ages. There are still countries that are staunch dictatorial patriarchies, and their perspectives are often militant. My point is that even though concerned, sophisticated scientists in the Democracies will strive to keep technology and science in check, male-dominated countries (East and West) will turn technologies into weapons; ethics will not stand in their way—Love is not the primary agenda in the war rooms.[74]

In 1917, Helen wrote:

> War is negation of life, blasphemy. So long as men are murdered, and go forth to murder, and *employ their peaceful years in preparing tools of murder*, the Gospels and The Prophets and the Law are an insult and a mockery.[75]

I italicized the words above because they are true and need to be remembered. There is an incessant arms race to create ever more powerful weapons because we do not trust each other (for good reason). This might be the case until there is a global government, which I feel we must inevitably develop. For now, it seems, no one can stop this techno-arms race. If Helen Keller were alive today, she would be holding up the mirror of history, saying: "Look! Look at yourself in the mirror, gentlemen. Is this barren madness your gift to the next generation?"

Helen Keller knew, of course, that an ocean of emotionally sophisticated men were humanitarian allies in the struggle to keep peace and love at the forefront, but she also knew that there was something genetic, something aggressive, potentially and irrationally violent inside masculinity that had clearly been outed by history. I suspect that Helen would caution us to be very suspicious as we race into the blades of a future controlled by masculine forces existing at low levels of consciousness.

Helen's contemporaries (men and women)—in her view—were stuck within rigid worldviews, at low to moderately-evolved levels of consciousness, unaware of cognitive developmental levels and oblivious to the need for spiritual evolution (my terminology). Helen would remind us that many contemporary policy makers and scientists still have limited levels of consciousness, guided by a monological gaze that is blind to dual-process and blind to the need for spiritual growth. In other words, many scientists still do not see clearly enough that they are building their own cognitive worldviews (limitations) into their creations.

There is also the problem of trust. Helen used to say that she loved her dogs because "you could trust them to be loyal." I believe, then, that Helen would say that AI does not yet understand *trust*—not as a human being might. There has been no urgent drive to build sophisticated morality and spiritual depth into AI—because the designers of intelligent systems have not adequately defined or understood morality, emotional intelligence, trust and spirituality; even systematic intelligence itself is left inadequately defined. Helen Keller would have challenged scientists to build their creations to be emotionally and morally trustworthy.

I am sure Helen Keller would have used sharp-tongued and compassionate language to get her views and her sense of alarm across in her writing and speeches. I have done my best to channel her anger and her in-your-face rhetoric. However, there is another side to Helen Keller that we must honor as this debate about the future rages. Helen Keller's faith was not a religious belief, not dogma, not frozen tradition. Faith was her essence, her knowing. She had faith that an outside, all-encompassing loving force exists, a compassionate power that is outside the current comprehension of the smart boys and smart girls. Faith, Helen's heart would insist, will win in the end.[76]

Unfortunately, the Y-Chromosome sneers at Faith, hissing at the meme that declares Love to be supreme—the Y-argument is that Faith and Love are pollyannaish, naïvely dangerous forms of ignorance. The idea that Faith and Love will eventually win against dark forces is rejected by the patriarchal mind as esoteric nonsense. This is the backlash Helen faced her whole life as the patriarchy fought back against her courageous, emotionally powerful words.

Another of Helen Keller's admirable traits was her conviction that courage ought to be at the forefront of our approach to life. Below is a famous quote of hers about courage. I referred to the quote earlier, but here are the full paragraphs from her book *Let Us Have Faith* (1940). Keep in mind that she wrote these words just as World War Two was beginning:

Security is mostly a superstition. It does not exist in nature, nor do the children of men as a whole experience it. God himself is not secure, having given man dominion over His works! Avoiding danger is no safer in the long run than outright exposure. The fearful are caught as often as the bold. Faith alone defends. Life is either a daring adventure or nothing. To keep our faces toward change and behave like free spirits in the presence of fate is strength undefeatable.

Serious harm, I am afraid, has been wrought to our generation by fostering the idea that they would be secure in a permanent order of things. It has tended to weaken imagination and self-equipment and unfit them for independent steering of their destinies. Now they are staggered by apocalyptic events and wrecked illusions. They have expected stability and find none within themselves or in their universe. Before it is too late, they must learn and teach others that only by brave acceptance of change and all-time crisis ethics can they rise to the height of superlative responsibility. [77]

I believe Helen would say that being fearful and retreating from challenges is in no way helpful. Bring the courage necessary to face the challenges as they arise. Confront the dangers, act with compassion, do what must be done to establish order and kindness. Helen is also reiterating the message that change is part of the fabric of nature, integrally woven into the structure of humanity. Stability, guaranteed safety, and absolute belief are not real—we are in a river, flowing, there is no enduring picture of reality.

Helen Keller was also an incurable optimist. If she were alive today, she would realize and acknowledge that computers are already a wonderful contribution to the evolution of our species. She would see that our world is already digitally interdependent; technologies are globally linking the whole of humanity. No one is giving up on cell phones (digital communications), medical technologies, and social media despite serious and disruptive problems. The culture may dangerously evolve, but goodness will prevail in Democracies: the police will do their job with honor; the military will protect us honorably; our teachers will educate us with dedication; well-intended politicians will continue to debate and modify laws as needed. We will not give up on each other; compassion, courage, and optimism will prevail—that is the voice of Helen Keller flowing through my mind into yours.

In her Journal written in Europe in 1936 and 1937, while German and Italian soldiers marched in the streets, Helen wrote these words:

> Often, I am asked if I do not think the machine is destroying the best attributes of man. I reply: No, each machine is an extension of man's mind over matter. [78]

In other words, even faced with a potentially horrific future, Helen Keller's faith, courage, and optimism would prevail.

I am sitting at my desk, hammering out these controversial words, hoping that Helen Keller would approve of my emotionally heavy interpretations. Obviously, I have used Helen as much as she has used me. But our goal is the same: a world where loving kindness, tolerance, and spiritual sophistication prevail. Helen Keller was a humanitarian and a peacekeeper. I am quite sure that she is smiling down over my right shoulder as I put controversial words into her mouth. I have alluded to dual-process theory and levels of consciousness, and Helen Keller knew nothing of these concepts. However, I do feel that I got her sentiment right.

I will let Helen have a final word before we leave the complex challenges of politics, technology, and the future:

> The test of a Democracy is not the magnificence of buildings or the speed of automobiles or the efficiency of air transportation, but rather *the care given to the welfare of all the people.* [my italics] [79]

CHAPTER FOUR: OUR STRANGE DUET

Sing once again with me
Our strange duet.
My power over you grows stronger yet.
And though you turn from me to glance behind,
The Phantom of the Opera is there
Inside your mind.[80]

12 Steps that Lead to the Hypothesis of Navigational Consciousness

I realized during my career that thinking about the evolution of thinking was what I had been doing for decades. All my musing about the brain and mind eventually coalesced after my retirement from teaching and I ended up with my own version of dual-process theory, which then evolved into a hypothesis about dual-consciousness.

When I laid out my map, my hypothesis, and viewed it from above, I found myself staring at a strange paradox, a mirror-image. Metaphorically, I was staring at the Phantom of the Opera playing inside the human mind. I was mesmerized by the image of the Phantom's mask that covered one side of his face, making his countenance a Yin-Yang symbol. I also remembered the Greek statues of the God Janus—two joined heads looking in opposite directions, two mutually exclusive worldviews forever linked but never agreeing about reality—never knowing the oppositional reality of a mutually exclusive twin.

I could see from my map, from my hypothesis, that a powerful duality sings within the human mind; we sense this to be true because we each have such a paradoxical mind. After years of study and musing, I found myself staring at a hypothesis which seemed to explain *how* our paradoxical, yet glorious "strange duet" evolved. I also realized that human consciousness could only be understood from an evolutionary perspective; we had to find the simple correlates, millions of years ago, that started the "consciousness process." We had to answer the question, "How did life go from a *glimmer of awareness* to the human mind?"

I now look back at my books with amusement and bewilderment, wondering what caused me to follow such a strange path at my advanced age. I eventually realized that a self-proclaimed cognitive philosopher did not have to be totally correct to hold forth with hypotheses; I did not need ten post-graduate degrees to think about thinking. In other words, it was okay to be an Optometrically-educated Orientation and Mobility philosopher. The profession of Orientation and Mobility has only a few philosophers, so I am confident that my ideas will eventually be heard and considered. For reasons that will become clear as you read, I decided to call my version of dual-process theory *Navigational Consciousness*.

Just a quick aside: I will keep reminding you that this logic-flow is "my hypothesis." I am doing this *not* for Egoic reasons or to sell copies of my textbooks. I am simply taking responsibility for this logic-flow; I am acknowledging the many complex theories of consciousness coming out of neuroscience, philosophy, and psychology that do not totally share my conclusions. I am aware that many others have theories and intuitions different from my own. I do not want to imply, in any way, that my philosophy is totally sanctioned by neuroscience, philosophy, or psychology. My perspective concerning Navigational Consciousness is unknown to other disciplines (as far as I know). My hypothesis evolved because of an unusual blending of two professions, Optometry (visual science), and Orientation and Mobility (the art and science of blind navigation).

Whenever I try to explain Navigational Consciousness, I find myself going through a sequence, trying to slowly, step-by-step, show the logic that gave rise to a new way to understand the emergence and evolution of human cognition. Navigational Consciousness is so foreign a concept that it takes a while to fully grasp the essence and the implications of the idea. However, I will do my best to put this important concept in simple terms using Helen Keller as a focus.

If you do not have a background in science, this discussion will probably be somewhat "painful," especially as the discussion progresses. I initially went down this path to assist my profession, Orientation and Mobility,[81] so the ideas were not initially meant for public consumption. On the other hand, as I reflected on the hypothesis of Navigational Consciousness, I saw that it was important that these insights be shared with a broader public. It is worth the effort, I think, for anyone sophisticated enough to care about Helen Keller's complex mind, to grapple with these difficult concepts.

The question I am asking (for the purposes of this book) is this: *How was Helen Keller able to navigate through her environment without vision and hearing?* Throughout history, blind and deaf-blind people were left immobile most of the time, only allowed to move if a sighted person could be a guide. To this day, many blind people are still relegated to accepting sighted guides or put into wheelchairs in airports and other settings and pushed about while their affairs are managed for them. Unfortunately, this is still the worldview commonly adhered to in many regions of the developed and undeveloped world. In other words, very few people outside the profession of Orientation and Mobility would even entertain the idea that a deaf and blind person could get around independently. But Helen Keller *could* negotiate familiar spaces on her own. How did she do that?

There is a film clip of Helen Keller coming into a room with a tray of food—giving Polly Thomson breakfast in bed. How did Helen know where the bed was and how did she go directly from the door to the bed? How was she able to walk up the steps to the second-floor bedroom, find the doorway to the bedroom, pass through the threshold without tipping the tray, and all the while keeping track of her location? In other words, how is it possible to navigate accurately and efficiently without using vision and hearing? Helen Keller could do it, so obviously it is possible. I will address that question, using dual-process theory as a foundation, in the pages ahead.

The outcome, the conclusion, of the difficult thought-process that leads to Navigational Consciousness, is that human beings have *a very strange kind of dual-cognition, which came about (my hypothesis) because of the evolution of navigation.* This dual consciousness has a neurological and anatomical foundation that makes perfect sense when it is understood. As I mentioned earlier, I wrote two textbooks explaining this theory/hypothesis as precisely as I could. I was working out the logic as I wrote *Consciousness: A New Slant on an Old Conundrum* (2017). The second textbook explored the responsibilities that come with dual cognition and it contained a fresh summary of dual-process theory; that second book is called *The Confusion Caused by Being Your Own Twin* (2018). I also wrote a science fiction novel called *A Martyr for Mandelbrot* (2019) so that I could introduce these difficult concepts in layman's terms.

I began my study of dual-process theory with the books and insights of Dr. Jonathan Evans and Dr. Keith Frankish (see the bibliography). These two professors have an online paper (quite dated now, but still relevant) that contains a history of the study of dual-cognition in human beings. Each of these professors also wrote a book (and numerous articles) about dual process theory.

The foundations of dual-process theory in America probably originated with Harvard Professor William James. James held that there are two kinds of thinking: associative thinking and analytical reasoning. James claimed that associative knowledge came from past experiences; he described associative knowledge as "only reproductive." James believed that true reasoning could handle "unprecedented situations.

In 2013, Nobel Prize winner, Daniel Kahneman, wrote a best-selling book called *Thinking Fast and Slow*. Kahneman's book was the chief avenue for getting dual-process theory into the public domain. In a way, Kahneman explained a process that we can sense; we intuit that we have dual minds—we know that Kahneman was on the right track. However, we still struggle to explain *how* our mental duality might anatomically and physiologically work. And *why would evolution craft two kinds of cognition?* Earlier textbooks about left-and-right brain and fast-and-slow brain did not answer this fundamental question.

For a while, left-brain versus right-brain (or female brain and male brain) was the popular science-related avenue (meme) for exploring/ explaining dual-cognition. Fast and slow thinking is a newer perspective, but neither approach identifies the neurological evolution that would lead to dual-cognition. What I have done in my own work is offer a biological and evolution-based perspective that purports to explain *why* we evolved two brain hemispheres and two processing speeds.

On a lighter note, many of us were introduced to dual-process theory by Dr. Seuss in his book *Cat in the Hat* (1957). Dr. Seuss intuitively created two mischievous thinkers who were hell-bend on getting innocent children into trouble. He called his free-spirit creations *Thing One* and *Thing Two*—this remains my favorite image for our two mutually exclusive minds. Delightfully, our dual consciousness has a paradoxical sense of humor.

A key beginning point is this: Helen Keller had a normal (whole-body) anatomy and a normal physiology despite her sensory depravations. The loss of vision and the loss of hearing (the main external sensory systems) did, indeed, affect her cognitive evolution, but the effect was not enough to prevent her from becoming the extraordinary phenomenon that she eventually became. The human mind (and human consciousness) can work perfectly fine without vision and hearing; Helen Keller is the evidence.

Below is the step-by-step logic that underpins the hypothesis of Navigational Consciousness and explains how Helen Keller could navigate on her own. It is a long journey, which gets more complex and hypothetical as it unfolds. However, the beginning of the journey is easy to grasp.

Of course, Helen Keller's navigational abilities were sometimes halting and often inaccurate, but she *could* move independently, and she *could* accurately get to intended locations, primarily in familiar settings. There is a video clip available on YouTube that shows an older Helen moving independently in her house (using the walls as a guide). For those interested in video evidence, there is an entire YouTube channel devoted to Helen Keller. Importantly, Anne Sullivan's earliest letters about Helen depict a continually active little girl, getting into everything, racing up and down stairways, going in and out of the house. Therefore, not only was Helen Keller aware of her surroundings and able to navigate familiar spaces, but she was also quick to do so; her movements were fast and fluid, especially when she was a young girl moving about her familiar home.

A note of caution before we begin this exploration—I am not talking here about Cartesian Dualism, the theory that Rene Descartes elaborated centuries ago. Descartes pitted the ethereal substance of mind against physical substance—he said the two were made of different elements, as if the mind was made of spiritual juices and the universe of atomic juices. However, I do wonder if the translations of Descartes' work were misunderstood. I am inclined to think that Descartes grasped what I am exploring here (dual-processing) and like other philosophers struggled to define what he was introspecting. There is a long-standing practice of beating up on Cartesian Dualism, but I wonder if Descartes' worldview has been misinterpreted. My intuition tells me that Descartes was grappling with dual processing.

I am also not talking about the popular notion of left-brain and right-brain or fast-brain and slow-brain—*these are observations* of dual-processing at work. Furthermore, I am not discussing female verses male brains in this section, although I often use the terms *divine feminine* and *divine masculine* to refer to Allocentric and Egocentric differentiations (discussed below). This "divine" (esoteric) terminology refers to processes—masculine and feminine forces—that are present in both males and females. What I am doing in this chapter is providing a biological explanation for *why* we have two cognitive processing systems.

Step One: Purposeful Movement

Human beings have brains attached to nervous systems so they can move in a purposeful and adaptive way.

Neuroscientists say that the reason we have a brain attached to a nervous system is so that we can *move in a purposeful and adaptive way.* This makes sense and the evidence is clear: all creatures that *move around a domain*—bugs, fish, birds, reptiles, amphibians, mammals, human beings—have brains attached to nervous systems. Contrary to this, all plants—living things that do not move through a domain—*do not* have brains attached to nervous systems. Plants also do not have muscles attached to nerves, nor do they have an embodied sensory system that operates in synchrony with a neuro-motor system. *A biological brain is essentially useless unless it has a body to purposefully move (control).* Brains evolved during evolution to control movement. Therefore, every sensory system and every neuromotor system serves the goal of *movement with a purpose.*

Scientists also say that the brain and nervous system evolved *to manage bodies.* Everything that a body does is enabled, controlled, and monitored by the brain and the nerves attached to the brain. In other words, *the brain must have a body to manage.* Building a disembodied brain—like a computer brain that sits on a desk—makes no sense if the goal is to mimic (replicate) the human mind. Historically, AI researchers have built knowledge-acquisition systems but have failed to build experience-acquisition systems; this oversight has come about because early AI scientists missed the fundamental understanding that brains and bodies are inseparable. To be fair to the brilliant minds that are embedding processing systems into objects and into sentient beings, the goal of AI is not to necessarily replicate human cognition—the goal is *to build tools* that support human cognition, tools that assist, augment, and amplify human intelligence.

It does make sense to give a robot a brain because there would be a body for the mechanical brain to control. It also can be argued that a virtual brain (inside a computer) might control a virtual body. Indeed, our brains already create virtual minds as well as imaginary domains for virtual minds to explore ("we hallucinate our world," according to Professor Anil Seth[82]). Robots and virtual minds aside, in the everyday biological world that human beings inhabit, brains and nervous systems evolved to enable living organisms to purposely move about a domain.

Step Two: Straight-ahead Navigation

Human beings have brains attached to nervous systems so they can navigate straight-ahead.

The neuroscience perspective—that brains plus nervous systems evolved to control movement and manage bodies—can be refined further. Purposeful movement is a broad way to consider evolution's intentions, but the initial reason nature developed brains attached to nervous systems (my hypothesis) was to enable straight-ahead navigation. Our whole anatomy and physiology attests to this observation. Our feet point straight-ahead. Our eyes point straight-ahead. Our face points straight-ahead. Our muscles are designed to move the whole body forward. Every creature we observe moving through a domain is traversing the environment straight-ahead.

The purpose of a brain and all the systems that feed information to the brain through peripheral nerves serve this primitive forward-striding navigational network. Even though input from some sensory portals (eyes and ears, for example) can become non-functional, the overall total-body purpose is not changed. The whole body is designed to navigate straight-ahead; all systems, sensory and motor, serve this navigational purpose. The muscles (and remaining sensory systems) designed to move Helen Keller's body forward through space were normal.

Scientists have also speculated that brains evolved to make predictions about the future. Certainly, brains did evolve to examine alternate futures, however, I believe this is a function of our navigational brain, which had to master perception of space in front of the body. We are forward-facing creatures. While traveling at a certain speed straight-ahead, we must decide the path we will follow, what obstacles to avoid, and where our final destination will be located. We have choices and we select from the offerings. We predict the fastest and safest routes—or the most scenic, or the route that takes us by a friend's house, etc.

Navigation has been evolving for a half billion years. It is not surprising that we internalized futurism. We are masters of navigation; we love navigating and discovering. It is no wonder that the study of the future became an esteemed profession and that scientists would suggest that the brain evolved to muse about and plan for plausible futures, i.e., that the brain was designed to make predictions. However, from my perspective, navigation straight-ahead came before other human behaviors, including making predictions about the future.

Step Three: Bilateral Creatures

Evolution designed bilateral creatures to enable straight-ahead navigation.

From the understanding that brains and nervous systems enable straight-ahead navigation, we can now ask the next logical question: What did nature design—what was the engineering plan—that enabled straight-ahead navigation? The answer is that evolution designed bilateral creatures. Every creature that navigates uses a bilateral alternating gait to move straight-ahead. Bugs, birds, fish, mammals, and human beings are all bilateral creatures that use an alternating "gait" for forward movement. A half billion years ago there was an explosion of new creatures on the planet—all these new creatures employed bilateral movement to travel straight-ahead.

Helen Keller's bilateral anatomy was in no way altered by the loss of vision and hearing. She could move about (move forward) because her brain was still getting signals from every muscle in her body that said in unison: "Move forward using alternating strides."

Step Four: Excitation and Inhibition

Evolution designed a muscular system (controlled by nerves) that enabled bilateral creatures to navigate straight-ahead. Signals to sets of muscles alternate (oscillate) so that excitation and inhibition switch off and on.

A creature designed with mirror-image halves (a bilateral creature) can only move if a neuromuscular control system is in place that enables and modulates movement. This control system is in the brain, although there is a distributed network of nerve centers (clusters) throughout the body that inextricably operate synchronously with the brain. The job of this whole-body neuromuscular-control system is to provide the energy necessary to get the body in motion, to keep the forward momentum going, and to precisely stop the forward momentum as needed. This neuromotor system is also responsible for sending messages to the two sides of the body, telling one side to move forward and the other side to stabilize. Also, very significantly, the brain—in conjunction with this distributed nerve network—must "stitch" the two mirror-sides of the body together in a continuous and seamless harmony.

Therefore, there is a muscular system (an engineering design) in bilateral creatures that enables straight-ahead movement. Let me emphasize that this design system uses inhibition and excitation to stabilize some muscles while activating other muscles.

It is important to understand a fundamental, foundational principle of nature (maybe all physics, as well): *everything oscillates (at many scales)*. We find this oscillation (excitation alternating with inhibition) everywhere we look. For example, there are positive and negative poles in molecules and atoms, left and right chemical structures, breathing in and breathing out, systole and diastole in the heart, alternating gait controlled by oscillating neurons, and excitation and inhibition of muscle systems used to carry out tasks. In other words, movement alternates with no movement, action with inaction, instability with stability, feedforward with feedback, and chaos oscillates with order. Oscillation is a law of nature.

Between oscillation cycles there are gaps. These gaps are fundamental to any oscillation system because the gaps are the turn-around-space where the pendulum pauses before heading in the opposite direction. For example, we could not hear without the gaps between utterances— language would not be possible without gaps (silent spaces). We also could not read without the gaps between letters, words, braille dots, and paragraphs. It is no surprise to discover that a human being moves around using an oscillating mechanism—rather, it is to be expected. Also, I suggest, the mind itself must oscillate and must have gaps to function. The mind and consciousness are scaled-up versions of atomic and molecular oscillatory behavior (as above so below).

Creatures that fly use a different kind of oscillation to enable straight-ahead navigation, but the foundational algorithm—inhibition alternating with excitation—matches that of creatures that walk using alternating strides. Flying creatures flap their wings (excitation) and then glide (rest in an inhibition phase). When sets of muscles are activated other sets of muscles are stabilized in both creatures that fly and creatures that walk.

The neuromuscular system in the brain and body that fires alternately and synchronously was normal in Helen Keller. Her gait was alternating like anyone else's stride. She was not ataxic; she did not have cerebral palsy.[83] Helen's brain delivered smooth and accurate signals to the muscles which then gave accurate feedback to her brain.

Step Five: Figure and Ground

Evolution designed a sensory system (working in exact harmony with muscles) that enabled bilateral creatures to navigate straight-ahead. This sensory system must also alternate between excitation and inhibition to be in harmony with muscular activity.

To walk, to fly, to do any kind of movement, some muscles must move while other muscles must provide stability. Nature designed a system that was mutually exclusive: when one set of muscles is activated, a corresponding set of muscles are inhibited. It logically follows that the development of the senses would be in harmony with this primary movement physiology. Indeed, that is the case, the senses operate in a mutually exclusive fashion and in exact harmony with the muscles.

When muscles are activated, a corresponding set of sensory systems are simultaneously activated. When muscles are inhibited, a corresponding set of senses are simultaneously inhibited. Just like the muscles, the senses operate in a mutually exclusive fashion—the senses also oscillate.

The primary and evolutionary purpose of the senses, in my hypothesis, is to enable straight-ahead navigation. Every *sensory* system is simultaneously gathering information about the background (scene, gestalt) as well as the foreground (form, pattern, figures). For the purpose of accurate navigation, *the senses must solve the puzzle of figure/ground*: What is the figure and what is the background in which the figure is embedded? Navigation is made possible because we can find and follow pathways around the solid objects in our domain. The senses are solving the figure/ground dilemma in exact harmony with the activity of the muscles.

It is also true (my hypothesis) that the navigational brain oscillates between perception of forms (shapes/figures) and perception of the ground—the combining of figure with ground happens at a fast and unconscious rate. The more we attend to a figure, the less information we can gather from the ground. The more we defocus on figures, the more we can process information from the gestalt (the total scene).

Helen Keller's navigational system could resolve the figure/ground problem without using vision or hearing. Her mind understood concepts like pathway, background, foreground, object versus no-object, animated versus non-animated. Helen's internal maps for managing space were structurally normal. Like all human beings, she came "factory-equipped" (right out of the womb) to eventually navigate straight-ahead through a land-based domain.

Step Six: Dual Minds

A dual sensorimotor system is required to enable straight-ahead navigation. From this anatomy and physiology—after eons of evolution—came two separate kinds of mind, one mind specializing in stabilization, the second mind specializing in movement.

Bilateral movement emerged about 600 million years ago in the Cambrian Age. Over the past 600 million years, evolution kept experimenting and modifying bilateral movement, building evermore complex and capable creatures. The result of over half a billion years of evolution is that the two sensorimotor control systems—a system which activates muscles and senses balanced against a system which inhibits muscles and senses—eventually became quite sophisticated. In other words, the oscillating neuro-control system of bilateral creatures became so sophisticated that eventually dual-minds emerged—one mind specializing in activation of movement and the other mind specializing in stabilization (inhibition) of movement. These two minds evolved to be mutually exclusive and (essentially) simultaneous. This is the essence of my Navigational Consciousness hypothesis. The rest of the logic detailed below rests on this simple proposition.

This hypothesis of the navigational brain replaces the notion that we have a right brain and a left brain. Anatomically, bilateral brain hemispheres are to be expected in a bilateral creature. The activities of the two brain hemispheres inform us about the operation of the overall navigational system, which is a whole-body phenomenon. In other words, there is an incompletely thought-out truth to left/brain and right/brain (and, also, fast-brain, slow-brain).

I came to the proposition that the evolution of bilateral movement led to dual minds through two rivers of thought. Besides following the logic outlined here, I also examined current and historical knowledge. I found that wherever we look, in philosophy, in psychology, in education, in religion, in esotericism, and in science generally, we see the same duality. In other words, scratch the surface of any professional discipline and you will find a history of thought in which a mutually-exclusive duality eventually emerges as a (bewildering) focus. Indeed, the evidence for an innate oscillatory duality is everywhere in our literature.

The hypothesis that there is a left-brain reasoning system separate from a right-brain creative system was enthusiastically embraced when it first appeared (even though it was later found wanting) but why was the left/brain right/brain hypothesis so popular? The reason, I believe, is that *we instinctively know* that dual-consciousness is true—we sense our duality, even though we struggle to define this strange cognitive manifestation. I examined duality in various professional fields of study in my book *The Confusion Caused by Being Your Own Twin* (2018), and I will pick up this thread below.

Helen Keller's dual minds were normal. She had the same potential as any other person to contemplate, emote, create, imagine, and react to environmental variables. The whole-body oscillation necessary for navigation still worked in Helen Keller despite her having no vision and no hearing. Like everyone else, Helen Keller had two highly evolved (and completely normal) minds.

Nobel Laureate Gerald Edelman showed us that neurons are engaged in Darwinian natural selection. Neuronal patterns inside each brain are in a survival-of-the-fittest environment—the mental patterns that are used most (our mental habits) win out over less used patterns of neuronal action. Darwinian natural selection in neuronal networks supports the Navigational Consciousness hypothesis. The repeating oscillation—excitation (movement) versus inhibition (stabilization)—necessary to walk straight-ahead or to use familiar tools has operated for more than 500,000 years. That is a long time to fire the same sets of neurons. The body (nervous system) fine-tuned these neuronal patterns until we ended up with dual minds, the *Ego* and the *Self.*

Helen Keller was forced to refine her mind, to enhance her *internal* sensory acuity, and she inhaled knowledge as fast as she could—because it made her feel alive and connected. Darwinian neural selection crafted Helen's remarkable mind and made it more robust and more acute than many of her contemporaries.

Step Seven: Dual-Process Theory

There is an established scientific discipline that studies human cognitive duality. The history of language also establishes that two minds are at work as human beings record and create.

When I was writing my two textbooks on the evolution of consciousness, I used an established theory (using the logic I outlined above) to make the case that all creatures that move straight-ahead had to have evolved two minds. This established scientific discipline is called Dual-Process Theory and it has a long and respected history in specific scientific communities. All I did was take an established discipline and ponder ways that it might be altered or expanded to fit my own field (human navigation, Orientation and Mobility).

Dual-process researchers explore the anatomical and physiological details that suggest a fundamental duality-principle in nature and in the design of the human body. There were initially some simple applications of the theory in the social sciences and economics. However, I extended the theory to the hard sciences and especially to my own profession. I made the connection that the evolution of navigation required dual sensorimotor systems, and I coined the term navigational disability to describe what happens when dual-processing is damaged or thrown out of balance. I also used the terms Allocentric and Egocentric (as used in my discipline) to describe how our dual cognition operates. I will explore the concepts Egocentric and Allocentric later in this discussion.

If the initial reason we are engineered bilaterally is to navigate straight-ahead, and if navigation requires dual processing, then we would expect to find duality whenever we attempt to explain the mind or explain consciousness. It is not surprising, therefore, that from the two mutually exclusive sensorimotor control systems evolved two ways to gather information about the environment: either through Egocentric attention or through Allocentric awareness. In other words, attention and awareness are not the same thing; indeed, they are mutually exclusive ways to gather information about the world.

This observation—that there are two ways to attend—is the beginning of our understanding the origin of binary language; we find mutually exclusive terminology in all the realms of cognitive exploration. Here are some examples:

1. In psychology, we find these dualities: conscious and unconscious, subjective and objective, anima and animus, Ego and Self. [84]
2. In philosophy, we find these dualities: empiricism and rationalism, noumena and phenomena, mind and body, intellect and reason, deduction and induction.
3. In religion, we find these dualities: faith and belief, duality and non-duality, right-doing and wrong-doing, spirit and soul, the divine feminine and the divine masculine.
4. In science, we find these dualities: feedback and feed-forward, background-processing and foreground-processing, serial-processing and parallel-processing, short-term memory and long-term memory.
5. In education, we find these dualities: knowledge and experience, creativity and reasoning, art and science.
6. In literature, we find these dualities: intelligence and wisdom, facts and metaphor, verbal and non-verbal, Dr. Jekyll and Mr. Hyde.

If we study the dual words found in various professions, we find that the words reference either Egocentric processing (the *Egoic perspective*) or Allocentric processing (the perspective of the *Self*). To give some examples: Egocentric deals with duality, Allocentric deals with wholeness (non-duality); Egocentric processing uses neurofeedback systems, Allocentric processing uses neural feed-forward mechanisms. Egocentric processing is serial (temporal) while Allocentric processing is parallel (spatial). I have also speculated that *Spirit* is an Egocentric concept and *Soul* is an Allocentric concept. I give more examples in my textbooks, but hopefully you agree that our literature holds evidence of dual cognition.

The duality we find in all disciplines of study also shows that concepts exist on a bell curve. We observe, for example, that there is a duality between conscious (awake) and unconscious (asleep)—exact opposites. However, on careful observation, we discover a gradient between the extremes. We discover that there are degrees of wakefulness that exist between totally awake and totally asleep. To give another example, we can observe two kinds of thinking, deductive and inductive. However, when philosophers closely observe this phenomenon, they find or postulate gradients/degrees that exist on a bell curve between the opposite concepts.

Looking at Helen Keller, we see that her attention system (her Egocentric processing) was negatively impacted (damaged) by her inability to visually fixate and track. She could not use the Egoic visual system to separate figure from ground. Hearing has a parallel attention versus awareness mechanism; Helen could also not fixate or track using hearing. In other words, Helen Keller's Egocentric processing system was severely impacted by the loss of vision and hearing.

Therefore, Helen's Allocentric *awareness* system had to become more acute to compensate for the loss of Egoic *attention*. She had to learn to non-verbally sense the environment using her whole body. Helen Keller's subconscious (Allocentric) *awareness* system, her intuitive skills, her esoteric depths became hyper-alert to compensate for her inability to consciously (focally) *attend* using vision and hearing.

Step Eight: The Paradox

Our dual cognition is paradoxically deaf and blind: The Ego can never know the Self and the Self can never know the Ego (like the Janus head). Movement can never know no-movement. The Ego pays attention. The Self is aware. Awareness and attention are mutually exclusive.

I called the mind that works when the body is relatively still (stable), the Egocentric (attending) mind. I called the mind that works when the body is in motion (navigating, flowing), the Allocentric (aware) mind. When we concentrate, attend, we are using the Egocentric mind. When we do not concentrate, when we relax the Egoic mind, when we move purposefully through space, when we experience flow, we use our Allocentric mind. These two minds separately evolved over eons of evolution, each becoming more sophisticated as time passed. Eventually, the Egocentric processing system evolved what we call the Ego (the stable entity). The Allocentric processing system evolved what we now call the Self (the flowing entity, the Soul).

As I said above, knowing about the duality of the sensorimotor system enables us to speculate that there would be two ways to gather information. That is, indeed, what we find: we can pay attention to something, or we can be aware of ourselves and the environment as we navigate around objects and follow clear pathways. Just like the alternating neuromuscular system, attention and awareness are mutually exclusive yet simultaneous activities, when one system is excited, the other system is inhibited. For example, we cannot attend to an object-of-regard the very same time as we take in (are aware of) the background scene. Therefore (as I said above), there is an attention system (Egocentric processing) that operates in harmony with the mind that sends the don't-move (stabilize) system, and there is an awareness system (Allocentric processing) that operates in harmony with the mind that sends the move signal. Attention operates when the body is not purposefully moving through a domain. Awareness operates when the body is moving through space.

Egocentric processing, which operates in stabilization mode, requires a seer-seen process. The Egocentric mode occurs when we (as an entity, an *Ego*) lock-on (pay attention) to objects in a domain. To locate an object in the environment requires a sense of *Ego* as separate from an object. The process of locating an object and holding it in the mind long enough to approach, consider, or avoid the object, necessitates this seer-seen dichotomy, an "Ego and Other-than-Ego" perspective. Contrary to the Egoic mode, The Self does not require a seer-seen dichotomy. The Self is non-verbal, and it does not categorize or judge.

I know this is complex; it took me two textbooks to explain my hypothesis. However, our anatomy and physiology dictate this duality and these two global kinds of information-gathering systems. Awareness is a whole-body phenomenon, while attention (a head-space phenomenon) is a focused activity that is relatively inhibited when there is whole-body sensory awareness.

After she became deaf and blind, Helen Keller was primarily forced into a whole-body sensing mode. The eyes and ears are in the head and, therefore, give us a sensation that our minds reside in the head. However, without eyes and ears, this head-based bias fails to solidly materialize. Helen Keller was not lost in a head space like so many of her seeing and hearing fellow humans. Helen Keller absorbed the world *all at once* through a very sophisticated, highly evolved Allocentric processing system—her *awareness* skills were stellar. Egocentric attention (for Helen) was accomplished through touch—especially through her very perceptive hands and feet—as well as through a highly evolved sense of smell. The acquisition of language gave her an internal "tactual voice." After Helen got her "internal voice," her Egoic, head-bound, mind (her Ego) rapidly developed and eventually became extraordinary.

Helen Keller, like all humanity, had two kinds of consciousness (two ways to get information about the world), through the Egocentric mind and through the Allocentric mind. Both processing systems became highly evolved and balanced in Helen Keller's amazing deaf-blind mind. She intuitively knew this. That is why she could argue (like Kierkegaard did, see below) that Faith and Intellect were mutually exclusive and yet equally important.

The Egoic mind eventually evolved into a sophisticated system that names, categorizes, analyzes, and remembers that which is perceived (attended to) by the external senses. The Egoic mind (the Ego) operates only regarding manifest entities, "attaching to" (fixating or tracking) these entities. The Egoic mind also creates emotional labels that become associated with objects-of-regard: we avoid that which is distasteful or harmful and approach that which is beneficial or pleasing. The Ego can also use language and can attend to an inner voice. Contrary to the Ego's complex set of skills, the (Allocentric) Self has no access to verbal language, although there is a rich Allocentric system for interpreting body language, musical expression, and facial expression, which are non-verbal automatic (dynamic) communication systems.

Helen Keller miraculously developed a highly refined Ego. Her language ability quickly became astounding as she worked with Anne Sullivan. I would suggest that Helen's mind had evolved beyond its (historic) time frame, several rungs up the spiritual ladder from most of her contemporaries. Helen Keller is proof that the Ego is not entirely linked to vision and hearing. A complete, complex, emotionally stable, and highly evolved Ego can exist independently of the two primary external senses, vision and hearing.

The Self/Soul (the Allocentric mind) eventually evolved into a sophisticated system that *projects, mirrors, and remembers* animated navigation (flow) maps. The brain stores animated maps of territories and routes (pathways) through various domains. The Self does not attach or have emotions regarding entities in a domain—the Self flows dispassionately past landmarks and follows along pathways. The Ego and the Self are mutually exclusive, but they operate simultaneously (figure and ground appear together). In other words, we operate using two minds that are simultaneous, but which have mutually exclusive (contrary) activation (information-gathering) systems, Egoic attention, and Allocentric awareness.

In the introduction, I said that I would offer a (speculative) scientific explanation for *You are That* and for Jung's concept of the unconscious. Here is my speculation: The Ego, especially when meditating, can, at rare moments, sense a presence. This presence is the Ego's twin, the Self, which can only fully manifest when the Ego disappears. The Ego cannot perceive its twin mind because as soon as it turns to look, the second mind is not there (think of the Janus head turning to look for its twin)—the Ego cannot locate and observe the Self. The Egoic mind, which requires stability to perceive, cannot perceive the mind that is in constant motion. The static mind cannot perceive the dynamic mind. What we call the unconscious is the Allocentric mind, the mind that only functions during movement.

Meditators call the *felt presence* (awareness of a Self) "the real you, your essence." They say, "Never mind the Ego because *You Are That*— you are that sensed, unnamable something. Another name (arguably) for the Self (the Ego's twin) is the *unconscious*, which is what Jung labeled that chilling thing he felt below Egoic consciousness.

Below is a summary review of our two minds, a comparison between the Ego and the Self. I cover this discussion in greater detail in my two earlier textbooks, so this is an incomplete summary. Also, this exploration is an on-going cognitive philosophy; with each new book, I seem to see the overhead view with greater clarity—I have slowly gained confidence in my navigational hypothesis as I reviewed the evidence for each new publication.

The Egocentric Mind (the Ego) and The Allocentric Mind (the Self)

The Egoic mind gives rise to the Ego, which perceives as if it is the center of the universe. Eyes and ears, as the main external senses, give the human being the impression (the evidence) that they are the center around which everything and everyone else revolves. Therefore, the Ego perceives that it is in the head, protected by the skull, and is the center of everyone's attention.

I love this observation by comedian John Mulaney: "I don't know what my body is for except to take my head from room to room." That observation makes me smile. It seems we are talking heads that need a bodily transport system to take the eyeballs and ears from domain to domain.

An interesting paradox is the sensation that we have no head—think about that for a moment as you look around the room, where is your head? Our head, our face, our eyes and ears are hidden from everyday awareness and *yet we think we are located within this head space.*

The Self *is aware* that it is not the center of the universe and not in the head. The Self is an integral, inseparable, networked whole-body *process*; the Self cannot be dissected out from the universe.

In the language of network theory, the Ego is a node, and the Self contains flowing links that connect nodes to other nodes. Networks require nodes (no-movement), which are connected by movement through bridges and pathways.

∿

The Egoic mind (the Ego) is verbal; it is built around language, around internal dialogue as well as spoken dialogue. The voice in the head is further evidence (for the Ego) that the head is the center around which the universe revolves.

The Allocentric mind (the Self) is non-verbal. There is no internal or external spoken dialogue associated with the Self; The Self *does have* non-verbal language, including facial expressions, body language, and musical expression—the Self analyzes *flow.*

∿

The Egoic mind defines concepts, creates categories, and judges value.

The Self does not concern itself with concepts, categories, judgements, or with anything we associate with conceptual thinking.

～

The Egoic mind exists only when there is a seer observing (perceiving) something. In other words, the Egocentric mind must have a seer-and-a-seen to function.

The Self does not need a "seer and a seen" to function.

～

When we consider figure and ground (foreground and background), the *figures arise from the Egoic mind.* The Egoic mind disassembles pictures (scenes, gestalts) into tinnier and tinnier pieces—it is a reductionist mind.

When we consider figure and ground (foreground and background), the *background arises from the Allocentric mind.* The Self creates scenes (the canvas, the page). The Self expands rather than reduces. The Self is a wholistic mind.

～

Egoic processing functions best when the body is relatively still. The Ego becomes deaf and blind when the body moves.

The Self functions during movement; it is driven (created) by flow. The Self is never still; it is always in relative motion. The Self becomes relatively deaf and blind when the body is still.

Allocentric processing is a response system (related to movement), while Egocentric processing is a gathering, organizing, recognizing, anticipating, and predicting system (related to *getting ready* to move with a purpose).

Breathing in and breathing out (flow) is Allocentric. The gap (no flow) between breaths is Egocentric. You cannot think during the act of breathing in or out. That is why the breath is used in meditation to cool down overactive Egocentric processing.

The Ego receives, the Self gives.

~

The Egoic mind is the fountainhead for Belief and for the emotions bundled with beliefs.

The Self is the fountainhead for Faith; no emotions are bundled with faith—it just is. (*I am That*)

~

The Ego feels like it is in the head because the mouth, eyes, nose, ears, and brain are in the head.

The Self is not located in the head. The self is a whole-body sensory system.

~

The Ego gives rise to the attention system.

The Self gives rise to the awareness system.

Attention and Awareness oscillate (at an imperceptible velocity).

~

To navigate through a domain, the Egoic mind uses landmarks.

To navigate through a domain, the Self flows along pathways relative to more stationary objects. The Self is a GPS-based, birds-eye-view system rather than an earth-bound landmark-based system.

~

The Ego is the source of duality. The Ego is convinced that we live in a binary universe.

The Self is non-binary. The Self is convinced (simply knows) that we live in a non-dual universe.

~

For the Ego, "all men are islands" isolated by space and time from all other beings.

The Self knows that everything is connected, part of dynamic networks; therefore, "no man is an island."

⌇

The Ego is awake (beta, gamma, and lambda brain waves appear during the conscious state). The Ego believes that *it alone* defines consciousness—it denies any other definitions.

The Self operates below Egoic (head-level, verbal) consciousness. The Self is associated with alpha, theta, delta, and epsilon brain waves.

⌇

The Ego evolved through the acquisition of knowledge. Intelligence is related to knowledge acquisition, so intelligence is an Egoic function.

The Self evolves through the acquisition of experiences. Wisdom is related to experience. Wisdom is the result of Allocentric processing.

Knowledge and wisdom are derived from different minds and are, therefore, oppositional and oscillatory.

⌇

The Egocentric mind (especially in males) is a predatory mind, connected to a nervous system designed to find prey, hunt them down, and kill them.

The Allocentric mind is a defensive mind, connected to a nervous system designed to protect the organism from predators, to hide, to flee, and to protect.

⌇

The Allocentric mind, in every way, is the opposite of the Egoic mind; the two minds are mutually exclusive; when one is on, the other is off. The two human minds oscillate, are deaf-blind to each other, and are held in bondage: a positive pole and a negative pole revolve around a force (occupying a gap) that keeps them together. The image of Janus heads fused back-to-back is a brilliant depiction of our cognitive dilemma.

From a physiological perspective, one mind is not better than the other; our two minds co-evolve and are co-dependent. However, the Ego and the Self *seem to independently* evolve, one mind can (it seems) become more complex than the other. For example, when we observe human behavior, it appears that human beings can have highly evolved Egos and shallowly evolved Selves—or the opposite can be true.

There is a problem with this line of thinking that bothered me for some time. To navigate or, indeed, to perceive reality, the two minds must be equal in power and in value. We could not survive without cognitive oscillation (at various spatial scales). However, if the two minds are so tightly linked and co-dependent, how is it that one mind can be so much more sophisticated than the other mind? The answer, I suggest, lies in the way we attend to the world.

Two attention systems can be independently employed. For some reason, human beings can get locked into *attention*—the Egoic system for attending to a domain—and be unaware of and underuse *awareness*, the Allocentric attending system. It seems to be the norm (in Western cultures especially) that the Ego attends too much, and the Self is aware too infrequently. One side-effect of this disparity is that we tend to think of Egoic attention as the only existing system for surveying the surround. We often fail to understand that we have a twin Allocentric mind. For example (this seems to be the norm in Western cultures), Egoic attention can be highly evolved and sophisticated, but awareness might be little evolved and unsophisticated.

Another way to say this is to observe that at a sensory and perceptual level of processing (early gathering of data), we have two minds in balance. However, at higher conceptual and behavioral levels of processing, the two minds can diverge, one or the other can become more sophisticated.

Like any human being, Helen Keller had two minds; she had an Ego, and she had a Self. Both of her minds were highly sophisticated and highly evolved.

⁓

We must now make an adjustment to the original proposition that the reason we have a brain attached to a nervous system is so that we can move in a purposeful and adaptive way. After the invention of bilaterality and after two minds emerged and became sophisticated enough to evolve dual cognition, *purposefulness itself took on two meanings*.

For the Egocentric mind, purposefulness implies intention, concentration, conceptualization, planning, and a thirst for exploration. In the Egoic sense, "purpose" equals wakefulness and thinking/

attending. The Ego's role is *to seek* moments of stability. *The Ego is about Striving-to-Become.*

For the Allocentric mind, "purpose" refers to flow, to navigation, moving somewhere efficiently and safely. We cannot say that the Self perceives and acts purposefully (consciously)—no *wakeful thinking* occurs in the Allocentric mind. The Soul's role is *to go with the flow . . . to just Be. The self is about Being (experiencing in the moment).*

Step Nine: The Mind is the Sixth Sense

The mind can be thought of as a sixth sense. This means that subjective consciousness (as an extension of the mind) is also a sense. The mind is a super-sense because it combines patterns from all smaller portals (eyes, ears, nose, skin) and seamlessly combines these inputs into a coherent whole.

> She fought the debunkers who, for the sake of a spurious honesty, would denude her of landscape and return her to the marble cell. She fought the literalists who took imagination for mendacity, who meant to disinherit her, and everyone, of poetry. Her legacy, after all, is an epistemological marker of sorts: proof of the real existence of the mind's eye. [85]

The quote above from Cynthia Ozick's article in the *New Yorker Magazine* is brilliant and of the high caliber typical of *New Yorker* articles. Cynthia Ozick says that Helen Keller is proof of the existence of internal vision; proof of a "mind's eye." My gut and heart tell me that Ozick's observations are correct. However, as a researcher, I need further evidence. Is there a mind's eye? Where is it? Poets intuitively say "yes, of course, there is a mind's eye," and skeptics say "no, the mind's eye is imaginary, there is no anatomical evidence for an actual "eye in the mind." In other words, as we would expect using dual-process theory, the Flowing-Self (the Poetic Soul) says *yes*, and the (literal, skeptical) Ego says *no*. We need to take a closer look at "the mind."

One of the key insights I got as I was puzzling out my hypothesis of Navigational Consciousness was that the Greek philosopher Aristotle had thrown us off the scent about 2500 years ago. Aristotle told us that we had five senses. From then on, throughout modern history, we have been repeating that questionable meme. How many senses we list depends on how we approach the question. I will not go into the intricacies of the arguments, but I will suggest that it is helpful to think that *we have six senses*, not just the favorite five. There are, indeed, five complex external sensory systems—which are really *sets of systems*—that gather information from the outside world, but there is also an *internal* set of senses that monitor the body and the brain. If we do not understand the internal sensory systems, we cannot begin to comprehend the mind and subjective consciousness.

The internal senses that were left out of the discussion (for 2500 years) make all the difference when we are thinking about cognitive evolution (and Helen Keller). This internal sensory complex was overlooked because it operates *within* the body. The five familiar senses *are portals* through which *external* vibrations *enter* the body. However, the *internal senses* monitor what is happening *to* the body and *within* the brain. There is an internal portal called proprioception through which information flows to the brain from muscles and tissues beneath the skin. Proprioception is the orchestrator of the internal senses. I discuss proprioception in the next section.

Eastern religious philosophy regards the *mind itself* as the sixth sense. This is a difficult idea to grasp at first, especially from a Western perspective. To qualify as a sense, there must exist a portal through which patterns impinge on a body. For example, the two eyes are portals that let in quantum energy. This quantum energy hits the retinal surface where initial visual processing takes place. The two ears let in compressed air waves (frequencies) that hit the hairs of the cochlea where initial auditory processing takes place. If portals are necessary to enable the collecting and interpreting of sensory information (coded as wave patterns), what kind of portal is the mind using?

The answer, I suggest, is that the mind is sensing the sum of all sensory input from every portal (external *and* internal). Importantly, the mind is aligning the input from every smaller portal to make one gestalt (one big virtual portal). For example, the mind is combining visual wave-based input with auditory wave-based input to sense a combined simultaneous multisensory input. Likewise, all tactual and olfactory input is matched with visual and auditory wave patterns. The mind is "Making Sense" of all input to create a coherent and coordinated big picture of reality.

The mind is sensing the body (including brain activity) as well as sensing the external world. What the body is doing moment-to-moment must correspond with the information attained about physical reality. Internal processing must exactly match external processing. The mind is sensing three variables: the internal state of the body; the activity of the brain; and the state of the physical world (in the moment) and combining two sets of input (external and internal) into a single gestalt—this is obviously an extraordinarily complex process.

∾

There is a powerful anatomical argument supporting the mind as a sensory organ. Everywhere we look within the neocortex of the brain, we see a similar neural architecture. The neuronal arrangement in the visual cortex, for example, is strikingly like the architecture in the auditory cortex. Likewise, the design of the neocortex in the somatosensory area and in the frontal processing fields of the neocortex are similar in design. What this implies is that the mind is gathering wave-based patterns (from all portals), combining the cumulative data, and then processing the information *in the same manner*, using the same wave-based pattern-analysis—the same bio-algorithms are used repeatedly.

If we look back a half billion years (the Cambrian Age) at the dawn of bilateral movement, at the beginning moments when the bicameral mind began to function, we can speculate that the brains of all creatures—bugs, birds, fish, rabbits, frogs, etc.—had to evolve similar functional systems. That is, indeed, what we find. When we look at the brain of an ant, or a bird, or a human we see vastly different anatomical arrangements (organ shapes). However, when we examine the *function* of specific areas of brains, we see that all bilaterally-derived brains evolved similar functions. To move straight-ahead, for example, requires a brain that can solve the figure/ground dilemma, while making future-oriented judgments.

Two Israeli scientists, Simona Ginsberg and Eva Jablonka, theorized that the dawn of subjective consciousness occurred during the Cambrian Age. Their theory, which looks at the necessary functions that had to be in place to enable consciousness, is carefully explained in their book *The Evolution of the Sensitive Soul* (2019). Their findings, which highlight the evolution of consciousness from the Cambrian Age, match my observation that bilaterality also emerged at this time and gave rise to dual-processing.

~

Given all that has been said above, we must answer the question, "Why didn't other primates develop minds as sophisticated as humans?" If bilaterality required the engineering of two minds, then all creatures that move straight-ahead have dual minds—this is a commonality, not an anomaly. However, something accelerated the human mind; something caused human cognition to evolve alongside the evolution of bilaterality and navigational competence. What was it that made the difference in the human mind? Can looking at Helen Keller's mind help us answer this question? I think the answer is yes.

Deaf-blindness caused the isolation of Helen's mind, drove her inward and forced her mind to adapt to the loss of vision and hearing by concentrating on the remaining senses, even the "hidden" internal senses had to be amplified. Helen's mind carried out this adaptation by refining the acuity of her inner sensory system—just as smell and touch had to step up, so did Helen's mind have to step up; her processing of internal signals had to become more conscious (and less on autopilot).

For Helen, no thoughts were arising in her mind before language— she says she was just a Phantom before language, sensing and reacting instinctively. But after the epiphany at the water fountain, Helen's mind discovered that *Naming* led to communication, and communication led to the internalization of language. Once an internal voice developed, then self-reflection, review of the past, and speculation about the future was enabled. With language, Helen's mind had something to do; it had an avenue to receive symbolic patterns that her mind could then remember, refashion, and express.

In addition, we need to understand that, as a human being, Helen *was born with* the ability to understand causality. About 100,000 years ago (some say less), human beings developed a brain that could innovate and invent. Humans began to speculate about the future, make predictions, and innovate. No other animal could think causally, and no other creature uses language. Human duality became exceedingly more complex and sophisticated compared to our closest genetic cousins, the primates.

Therefore, I suggest (as have many others) that it was language, and the ability to understand causality, that drove the human mind to become obsessed with its dual self. Language drove humanity to daydream, to build mental artifices, to plan for the future, to react in the moment, to share ideas, and to review history. Knowing "as above" enabled humanity to predict "so below." I am writing these words because the human mind is (especially in our era) trying to understand itself—it knows that it is the result of causes that preceded the present moment, and it knows that it can evolve further. Collectively, we are driven to evolve cognition through self-examination.

Bilateral creatures, which did not develop language, and did not develop sophisticated if/and/then cognition, could not evolve minds with an internal self-reflective voice. Only the human mind was set on a journey of self-reflection and self-obsession. Therefore, we must add language-plus-causality to the equation to make the understanding of dual-processing complete. Language combined with the ability to think systemically is why we developed an understanding of the Self and the Ego.

The human mind monitors knowledge and experience and then makes intentions to further enhance knowledge and attain further experiences. Our minds learned to self-evolve. Helen's mind had little else to do except "self-evolve." She went after knowledge and experiences constantly—her world travels gave her wisdom-experiences, and her thirst for knowledge drove her to obsessively read the literature of her age.

The human Ego eventually discovered its isolation. However, wisdom came from moving from domain to domain, from greater and greater exposure to foreign environments and foreign minds—thus, the *Self* discovered *the network* it was intricately enmeshed within. Together, the Ego and Self point to a species migration—we are heading somewhere that feels almost predetermined by our unstoppable thirst to know and to invent.

Step Ten: Proprioception is the Internal Portal

Proprioception is the portal through which the mind senses all (internal) muscular and sensory activity. The body's ability to animate, to "behave," is controlled by proprioception. When human beings claim to be conscious, they are, in part, acknowledging this awareness system.

The mind is constantly receiving and combining patterned information from several internal sensory portals. The vestibular system, for example, gives the mind information about gravity, from which the mind can determine (maintain) balance, momentum, and posture. In my earlier textbooks, I used the term proprioception to mean the sum of all internal portals. Proprioception, in this wholistic sense, is key to understanding the mind and consciousness.

Proprioception monitors what the body is doing at every moment, using a neuronal network that links all our muscles and subdermal systems together synchronously. Every muscle in the body—using a massively distributed and intricately networked set of nerves—is constantly sending the brain information. The muscles are reporting whether they are in excitation mode or inhibition mode. Therefore, the mind knows where all our limbs (body parts) are at any moment (right hand on the computer mouse, for example) and what the body parts are doing. Here is the most important take-away from this observation: The body's ability to animate is controlled by proprioception.

The word behavior refers to exact movement sequences. Proprioception remembers all movement (animation) sequences. In other words, proprioception remembers purposeful (behavioral) movements. All our postures, facial expressions, and action-habits are governed and monitored by proprioception. Our ability to walk, to talk, to gesture, and to use tools (all purposeful movements) result from proprioception. Without the proprioceptive neural network, human beings could not walk, talk, reach, gesture, grasp, or "behave" in any way.

Most importantly, *animation* gives human beings their (Allocentric) sense of Self. We *sense* that we are animated creatures; we sense our wholeness, we sense our movements, and we sense ourselves as separate from the world around. When we say that we are *aware* of being conscious, we mean that *we can sense* our animation (our proprioception). This is one of the realizations that Buddhist meditators discovered as they watched their own bodies (their own minds) operating.

Proprioception is a whole-body phenomenon that operates below conscious thought and (mostly) without conscious control. Proprioception is automatic; we do not need to think about walking or talking or posture or facial expressions—these activities just flow. Egoic Consciousness *can* intercede and override some of the automatic functions of proprioception, but most often the proprioceptive system operates on autopilot.

Purposeful Movement and Meditation

In my book *Consciousness: A New Slant on an Old Conundrum* (2017), I have a chapter called "Blending Eastern and Western Thought." In that chapter is a subsection called "Why did the Buddha sit under a tree?" Buddha was meditating and his act of sitting was entirely purposeful. This is from *Consciousness: A New Slant on an Old Conundrum*:

> After centuries of exploring the powers of meditation, Buddhist monks and Hindu gurus arrived at a common beginning [for meditating]: first, you sit down and plant yourself on the earth; second, you close your eyes; third, you pay attention to breathing. If you do these three things for a few minutes every day, you will discover that you are happier, more at peace, and you have become a kinder person. How could this possibly be?

Put another way, when we meditate, we do three things that make us calmer, happier, and ultimately kinder:

1. We stop all gross movement of the muscles. This calms the proprioceptive system. Indeed, meditation inhibits the whole body from sending animation signals to the brain. This is like inhibiting the eyes by closing the eyelids or shutting down hearing using ear plugs. *Rule one is to consciously inhibit the sense of proprioception.*
2. We induce artificial blindness by closing the eyes while meditation is occurring. *Rule two is to consciously inhibit the sense of vision.*
3. We become aware of breathing in and breathing out. Rule three is to consciously activate the Allocentric mind by "going with flow." A correlate to *Rule Three is to consciously inhibit the Egocentric mind (which cannot operate during flow).*

The job of the mind is to control the body, to allow for purposeful movement. Meditation goes against the main reason the mind exists. Meditation negates purposeful activity. The mind suddenly has nothing to do (freeing up a ton of energy). Under these conditions, during meditation, the mind must learn to *Be* rather than to *Do*. The mind must *wake up to experiencing* rather than striving/longing to accomplish goals. Meditation is a method for discovering the existence of the Ego's twin, the Soul.

~

People were unnerved when they witnessed Helen Keller's stillness. She could be tree-like, motionless like a statue. When she did decide to move, she did so with unexpected vigor, with sudden animation. People were startled by this unusual behavior.

Vision and hearing did not interfere with Helen's perception as she became totally open to proprioceptive input. During her moments of stillness, she was picking up vibrations from the environment that arrived at the surface of the skin. Helen had a profound ability to consciously inhibit proprioception. She could still her animation—the motor (output) component of proprioception. This left the sensory component of proprioception wide open and ready to gather and process subtle input.

So, the first rule of meditation was easy and well-refined for Helen; she could hold her body exceedingly motionless. Her vision and hearing were totally gone so the second rule of mediation was also easily satisfied. We find nothing in the literature about Helen's daytime breathing. But when we are very still, we become hyper-aware of breathing. Breathing is automatic, it cannot be stilled, it flows and flows.

We cannot generate thoughts or problem solve when we are *actively* breathing in or breathing out. Only at the turn-around point, the gap between breaths, can thoughts intrude.

It seems that Helen Keller may have been in a meditative state routinely, as part of her everyday existence. Her calm demeaner, her gentle aura, her ability to sustain concentration may have reflected her meditative state. She was "toying" with enlightenment, even though she might not have been able to articulate the process.

Meditation reduces stress which cleans out the debris from cells and organs which then extends life (Helen lived almost 88 years). Optimism is a form of resting-detox, a de-stressed mind state. Helen's optimistic personality blended with her meditative state. Or, maybe, because she was routinely in a meditative state, her optimism—her faith-based worldview—naturally developed.

Insights seems to arise from the meditative state, as if a channel is opened that allows our guardian angels to provide us with eloquence, energy, and creative direction. Help arrives when we still the overheated Ego. Helen's eloquence is undeniable as is her spiritual goodness and stubborn determination. I sense that a meditative state enabled her spiritual aura to blossom and allowed insights to eloquently arise.

Step Eleven: The Ego Arises from Proprioception

Proprioception is the source of inner dialogue and as such it gave rise to the Ego. Allocentric awareness is a total-body sense of animation and as such it gave rise to the Self. Egocentric attention is a head-based sense of identity. Taken together, our attention (Ego) and our awareness (Self) give us our feeling of being dually conscious creatures.

The human brain, like all organic creations, was constructed using the principles inherent in the physical world. According to quantum scientists, everything is made of energy fields. Energy is a duality, partly wave (flow), partly particle (no flow). If the body and brain are products of a dual universe, then the mind had to be created as a dual structure. I content that this is exactly what we find. Duality is built into our bilateral bodies, built into our dual-brain hemispheres, and built into our dual-processing systems (Egocentric and Allocentric) because the physical universe is based on duality—a wave-particle paradox.

Because there exists in human beings two mutually exclusive cognitive systems, we expect to find (and we do find) two kinds of vision, two kinds of hearing, two kinds of touch, and two kinds of proprioception: Allocentric and Egocentric. Allocentric processing operates during movement; Egocentric processing operates during no-movement (stabilization). As we animate a set of muscles (Allocentric action/flow), there is always another set of muscles that stabilizes the body (Egocentric stability). If all the small sensory portals (eyes, ears) provide dual-processing, it follows that the mind itself uses dual-processing. Consciousness is a more sophisticated sensory system than the mind, but it is also dual.

Proprioception is key to comprehending consciousness. Like vision and hearing (and every sense) proprioception has both an Allocentric and an Egocentric component. We located the Allocentric half of proprioception: it is the system that allows for awareness, for a sense of Self that can *animate* and can *flow* through environments. What, then, is the Egocentric component of proprioception; what gives us our sense of having an Ego?

To a large extent, our Ego arises because we can talk to ourselves. Our inner voice is often who we think we are—we equate internal verbalization with being an Ego separate from everyone else and from an environment. Inner dialogue leads to an inner sense of identity—we *feel* that *we are* this internal voice. According to psychologist Zoltan Torey, *the inner voice is proprioceptive memory of actual speech.* Therefore, proprioception is causally linked to our sense of Egoic consciousness.

This is not a small revelation. It is quite shocking when you first comprehend what is happening. The voice in the head is a recording based on muscle memory. When we use our internal voice, our mouths subtly move, our jaws and facial muscles move, and vocal-cords quietly vibrate in an exact duplication of actual speech. If we make the same set of movements repeatedly, we get the same behavioral result. We can say the same things repeatedly because our brains know the sequence of muscles to activate to generate speech. Later, in evolution, Zoltan Torey suggests, muscle memory could be activated internally (silently) by duplicating (but not activating) actual speech, and then a voice in the head was heard. When this first happened in evolution, the inner voice scared the bejesus out of our ancestors—the Gods were speaking directly to them!

Helen Keller could not routinely produce speech accurately (even though she gallantly tried). Therefore, she had no, or few (verbal) muscle-memory habits—she had no (or extraordinarily little) internal voice. In a sense, she was meditating in silence continuously, which is perhaps why she presented as so serene. However, she did fingerspell while sleeping; her hand movements played-back during sleep when she was unconsciously "talking to herself." Her hands and fingers also moved as she daydreamed, according to observations by her friends. In other words, Helen Keller's "images" and her proprioceptive speech maps (stored in the brain) were generated primarily by muscles in the hands and fingers, not by jaw or lip muscles, or vocal cords. Of course, it is not that easily explained because Helen did feel lips and vocal cords and she did learn to speak. The truth is always embodied and more complex than our hypotheses.

Helen Keller's inner voice was tactual and animated, a strange correlate to the voices in the head of those who can "hear" internal speech. This unusual kind of inner voice was her Egoic world, the thing that gave her a sense of being the center of the universe. This centered feeling could not have the same impact (I surmise) when compared to powerful visual images and matching (simultaneous) auditory images that clearly depict our body at the center of all activity. Sound is a 360-degree phenomenon with Egoic attention as the center. Helen's Egoic sense was weakened by her sensory losses and yet her behaviors show the world a fierce sense of inner strength—Helen's Ego somehow emerged strong and determined using vibratory messages (energy patterns) that were neither visual nor auditory.

Helen's *Self* (her Allocentric consciousness) was also seriously impacted by the loss of her major external senses, hearing and vision. She could not see the gestalt (the visual scene), nor could she see her relative place in the gestalt as she moved about. She could not perceive the sound clues all around her, (especially spoken language) that would have given her a sense of community. Yet, she clearly had a sense of relationship and community. Somehow, her *Self* emerged as strong and as powerful as her *Ego.*

For me, Helen Keller shows that the evolutionary march of *the Ego* and its twin *the Self* can manifest without vision and hearing. Somehow, the proprioceptive sense, that inner world of animation that gives rise to dual human consciousness, can shape both the Ego and the Self without any input from visual or auditory images.

Helen Keller was animated, energetic, and full of life. Her proprioceptive system, her sense of being alive, her dual consciousness (Ego/Self), evolved to be (through extensive adaptation) completely normal. Because of the loss of vision and hearing, we can also suggest that *Helen Keller's proprioceptive portal was enhanced to compensate for the loss of external input,* just as smell and touch were enhanced to compensate for the loss of vision and hearing. Consequently, Helen Keller's mind (consciousness) became extraordinarily complex and, as I will discuss in Chapter Six, enabled her to become both a language prodigy and a spiritual prodigy.

Helen Keller may have lost the ability to see and hear, but *her mind was extraordinary,* and her mind was dual. Consider what it would be like to have no eyes or ears. What would your mind be doing most of the time? I suggest that a deaf-blind mind—that is otherwise normal—would develop the sixth sense (the mind) to a remarkable degree, *compensating for the loss of vision and hearing.* Helen is evidence for this hypothesis—she developed a sophisticated, highly active sixth sense, a marvelous mind. Helen says she looked out at the world using "the eyes of my soul," as if the non-seeing, non-hearing mind could still acutely perceive and could still make sense of the physical world.

Helen Keller had a normal-to-extraordinary proprioceptive system—that is the key to understanding her navigational abilities; she could walk, communicate, reason, use tools, and explore without input from vision or hearing.

Step Twelve: The Mind as a Movie Projector

The human mind not only senses a world around, but it also "projects" a 3-D map that enables straight-ahead navigation. This is a brain-based, apparent-projection, not an actual projection.

The visual scene in front of us is happening inside the brain; what we "see" is just a best-guess (usable) rendering of physical reality (which we cannot directly perceive). We can hypothesize—and I suggest it is true—that the visual scene in front of us is an animated 3-D map initially designed to enable straight-ahead navigation.

We can further surmise, because of embodiment, that all the sensorimotor systems must coordinate synchronously with vision to create the 3-D animated map that is projected (rendered) all around us. Therefore, all the senses contribute to the body's "movie projector." The ability to project the world is a behavior we are born with. Projection can operate without hearing or vision because proprioception, touch, thought-generation (the mind), and olfaction are also part of the whole-body human projection mechanism. Helen Keller naturally projected a world outside/beyond her body using her remaining (embodied) sensorimotor systems. Like any other human being, Helen Keller had a built-in ability to project a spatial world.

In the field of Orientation and Mobility, we postulate the existence of zones of space that human beings use to navigate; below is a general list of the spatial zones our minds can innately project:

- Body-space: a skin surface separates us from the domain we are in. Body-space (encased within our skin membrane) gives us our sense of being an animated organism distinct from the surroundings.

- Personal (emotional) space: Personal-space is the protective region around our body within which we do not like others to enter (without prior agreement).
- Peripersonal-space: when we use tools (instruments, implements), the mind incorporates the tools as if they were part of the body. Tools blend with body-space as if they were part of the skin boundary. The combination of body-space with tools gives us peripersonal-space.
- Communication-space is the zone of space wherein we feel comfortable communicating, not too close and not too far away.
- Landmark-space is the area round a body that is filled with information which can be used by our navigation system for orientation.
- Beacon-space: Beacon-space is a distant region that contains clues to navigational position, such as the location and height of the sun or the sound of a distant train.

Philosophically, we can suggest that these spatial zones are like auras, layers of space that can be explored and interpreted. There is meaningful information embedded in each spatial zone. When we move our Egoic attention into a zone—where we can perceive information and make predictions—all other zones are naturally inhibited. However, our Allocentric system is still operating unconsciously and on auto-pilot below Egoic attention.

Another important hypothesis is that zones of space are energy fields. We are familiar with the visual field and with our ability to direct the eyes to various depths of space. Fields have a size and a volume and can be explored by Egoic attention or Allocentric awareness. Our eyes can examine any location within their field horizontally, vertically, and in depth. Hearing also has a 360-degree field that can be explored for meaning. The field of hearing must overlap and energetically coordinate with the visual field. The human 3-D projection system uses the total amount of information combined from all the senses. When we probe our spatial zones, we are looking for specific kinds of meaning related to navigation (to figure/ground analysis).

In the introduction, I talked about imagination as a key principle in esoteric cosmology. Imagination is part of the human projection mechanism. We can project our imagination into spatial zones, into the future, into the past, and into the moment (and to various spatial depths).

Likewise, *we can project our emotions* into the surrounding spaces; emotions, too, are embodied, projected energy fields. The projection of imagination and emotion are huge fields of study; I mention them here to emphasize that the human 3-D projection system is extraordinarily complex and networked.

Our projected 3-D map has two components, figure and ground. To navigate we must see objects (forms) and we must see pathways around the objects. Evolution has created scenes filled with objects and pathways. Everything is always moving in our physical universe. Therefore, our 3-D map must flow; it cannot freeze-up—it must be animated. We also need two processing systems to simultaneously gather meaning from spatial zones; the Egoic processing system generates and interprets objects (figures/forms/patterns), while the Allocentric processing system creates gestalts and flow-pathways through scenes.

During meditation it is possible to see that reality, as we project it, is paradoxically also a mirror—we send, and we receive. The world our mind creates is constantly adjusting as the environment moves (vibrates, animates). There is a mutually-exclusive oscillation at work as we switch from Egocentric projection-mode to Allocentric receiving-mode (mirroring). One moment we project a 3-D map to navigate through and the next moment we are noticing (receiving from the mirror) landmarks and salient objects. Allocentric and Egocentric processes oscillate at the plane of perception.

Helen Keller shows us that the human 3-D projection system does not disappear when vision and hearing are lost. She could project a world just as others could, but she did her projecting using her remaining senses. Helen had access to the spatial zones mentioned above because her mind, as a cumulative super-sensory system, came "factory-equipped" to make guesses and predictions using the information to be had within the various spatial fields. Her imagination and emotions could, as well, probe these fields in the absence of vision and hearing.

Let me end this complex reflection by once again emphasizing the hypothetical nature of my speculations. I have suggested an overview (a scientific worldview) for the evolutionary purpose of the human brain and nervous system. From that beginning, I built a case for dual-processing, which led to dual-physiology and eventually to dual-cognition and then dual-consciousness. This scientific worldview is one of many possible explanations for how the human mind works. I called my first book *A New Slant* on an old conundrum (consciousness). I was careful not to infer that I had solved the dilemma of consciousness. I know that I am limited by my own knowledge base and experiences. I also know that I can only add, in some small way, to the greater dialogue about the evolution of consciousness.

A Complex Journey

This has been a complex journey. I debated whether such a diversion into brain science and cognitive philosophy had a place in a book about Helen Keller. However, my intention from the beginning has been to show how the phenomenon called Helen Keller could have evolved in the absence of vision and hearing. How could Helen, such a powerful force of nature, have arisen in our midst?

Helen Keller's sixth sense, her mind, was not normal, it was extraordinary. Her sixth sense compensated for the loss of hearing and vision by becoming more alert, more attuned, and more unusual compared to "normal" minds.

Navigation through life is a tricky business, it is easy to lose our way. We need guides that we can trust. Helen Keller is such a guide.

Here is a summary of the steps leading to the hypothesis of Navigational Consciousness:

1. Human beings have brains and nervous systems so they can *move in a purposeful and adaptive way.*
2. Human beings have brains attached to nervous systems so they can *navigate straight-ahead.* Because of this ability, human beings became masters of prediction (what lies ahead; what does the future hold for us individually and as a species).
3. *Evolution designed bilateral creatures* to enable straight-ahead navigation.
4. *Evolution designed a muscular system* that enabled bilateral creatures to navigate straight-ahead. Sets of muscles are either in stabilization mode or movement mode.
5. Evolution *designed a sensory system* (working in exact harmony with muscles) that enabled bilateral creatures to navigate straight-ahead. This sensory system *also alternates between excitation (movement) and inhibition (stabilization).* The result of this design is that the dilemma of "figure and ground" is biologically resolved.

6. Therefore, a dual sensorimotor system is required to enable straight-ahead navigation. From this anatomy and physiology—after eons of evolution—*came two separate kinds of mind,* one mind specializing in stabilization (inhibition), the second mind specializing in movement (excitation). This is the core idea within the hypothesis of Navigational Consciousness.

7. There is an established scientific discipline that studies human cognitive duality, dual-process theory. *The history of language also establishes that two minds are at work* as human beings record and create.

8. *Our dual cognition is paradoxically deaf and blind:* The Ego can never know the Self and the Self can never know the Ego. Put another way, *movement* can never comprehend *no-movement* and *no-movement* cannot understand *movement.* . . . The Ego pays attention. The Self is aware. *Awareness and attention are mutually exclusive.* You cannot simultaneously be aware of the whole gestalt (scene, big picture) *and,* at the same moment, examine (pay attention to) details embedded in the gestalt. Oscillation gives the illusion of oneness—figure and ground seem to appear together.

9. *The mind can be thought of as a sixth sense.* This means that consciousness is also a sense—an elaboration, an extension of the mind. The mind is a super-sense because it combines patterns from all smaller portals (eyes, ears, nose, skin) and seamlessly combines these inputs into a coherent whole.

10. *Sensory systems presuppose portals. Proprioception (with nerve end-organs located in the skin and muscles) is the portal through which the mind senses all muscular activity.* The body's ability to animate, to "behave," is controlled by proprioception. When human beings claim to be conscious, they are, in part, acknowledging this awareness system.

11. *Proprioception is also the source of inner dialogue and as such it gave rise to the Ego.* Allocentric awareness is a total-body sense of animation. Egocentric attention is a head-based sense of identity. Taken together, our attention (Ego) and our awareness (Self) give us our feeling of being dually conscious self-aware creatures.

12. *The human mind* not only senses a world around, but it also *"projects" a 3-D map that enables straight-ahead navigation.* The reality we perceive is *totally* constructed inside our skulls—we

literally make our shared (and yet, very individual) reality inside our brains.

So, how was Helen Keller able to navigate through the world despite being deaf and blind? She could navigate because she had a normal brain (an extraordinary mind), a normal Ego, a normal Self, a proprioception system that was normal (maybe extraordinary), and she was provided diverse opportunities to explore the world around her, including availability to some of the Western world's best writers and historians. The loss of vision and hearing did not prevent her navigation skills from developing using her remaining senses; of course, her navigation was not completely "normal," and it was not always efficient and accurate, but Helen *could* determine her position in space, and she *could* get from one location to another in familiar settings.

Chapter Five: Why Navigational Consciousness Matters: Supporting Worldviews

I have lost only two of God's gifts. I still have many powers, and the greatest gift of all is mind—mind that can be cultivated, and through which I can enjoy most of God's blessings. ~ *Helen and Teacher*, by Joseph Lash, 1980.

Helen Keller and Søren Kierkegaard

Nietzsche called attention to the fact that within every human being another is hidden. This is taken to be a poetic way of speaking, but it is no such thing. In every human being another *is* hidden! This human being is often much more intelligent than the one that is visible. ~ *Becoming the Archangel Michael's Companions*, by Rudolf Steiner, 2007.

Both Nietzsche and Steiner understood levels of consciousness; they could see that all earlier evolutionary developments of consciousness still reside within our mind. In the quote above, Steiner is pointing out another complex idea that he understood (a hundred years before science explored levels of consciousness). Steiner is saying that the Ego has a twin mind, a Soul mind that is often wiser than the intellectually endowed Egoic mind. As I looked at the history of philosophy, I saw repeatedly that the world's greatest thinkers had discovered humanity's fundamental cognitive duality long before science sanctioned the study of consciousness.

Since we are discussing dual-process theory, let me turn your attention to a remarkable thinker who discussed cognitive duality long ago, Danish philosopher Søren Kierkegaard.[86] I could have chosen any number of famous philosophers to reinforce my contention that cognitive duality was a common theme throughout history, but there is a parallel with this book and Helen Keller that allows Kierkegaard to stand out.

I was amazed when I read Kierkegaard's discussion about *Knights of Faith*—his contrast between faith and intellect was so in-tune with Helen Keller's *Knights for the Blind* volume that I felt the need to link the two worldviews. I do not know if Helen Keller encountered Kierkegaard's philosophy when she was at Radcliffe—she probably did—but the emotional correspondence between her mind and Kierkegaard's is remarkable. Both Immanuel Kant and then Friedrich Hegel used similar terms and logic as Kierkegaard, so Helen may have also come by the faith-versus-intellect debates through the German Idealists—which she surely studied at a university level.

Søren Kierkegaard is the first of the existential philosophers. He lived a short, intense, and sometimes painful existence, from 1813 to 1855. Besides being a philosopher, he was also a Christian theologian, a poet, and a social critic. Kierkegaard thought and wrote with a ferocious intensity and he published a wealth of philosophical insights in just a few decades. He died at age 42, so it is fortunate that he was driven to share his inner musings as a young man.

Much of Kierkegaard's writing deals with the Christian concept of love. This is the first correspondence (associative link) between Keller and Kierkegaard: both influential souls considered love to be at the core of human activity: we are on earth to care about others and to actively embrace and expand love. Both Keller and Kierkegaard were critical of Christianity as it was understood and practiced by the organized leaders of the church; for Keller and Kierkegaard, the church had lost its mystical heartbeat. Both thinkers also felt that the common man failed to grasp (or act upon) the essential message at the heart of Christianity, which is love.

The second correspondence that links Keller and Kierkegaard is their insistence that human beings have the power to choose. You can become a powerfully loving Knight filled with faith and determination, or you can turn your back and live a deaf-blind life. You can choose to live an unexamined and uncourageous life, or you can get on your horse and ride off to confront injustice and cruelty. The life you choose is the life you get. Keller and Kierkegaard did not mince words—their convictions challenged us: *decide* what kind of a human being you are to become, and then make it happen. In her book *Let Us Have Faith* (1940), Helen wrote:

> Faith is not a cushion for me to fall back upon; it is my working energy.

Faith is an energy source that wells up from the Soul. You *do not analyze* faith; *you use faith* to change the world for the better. Faith, in this context, does not mean deep belief, because faith is the opposite of belief. People who believe are capable of murder and extreme cruelty, as history plainly shows. Faith is non-verbal energy, an Allocentric flow of loving energy into and out of the body. Indeed, it is true that there *does* exist a connotation for faith in the common vernacular which implies unquestioning belief—however, that is *not* what Helen Keller meant by the word, nor Kierkegaard. Faith is Allocentric; belief is Egocentric— these two minds are deaf-blind to each other.

To Kierkegaard we owe our understanding of *objectivity* and *subjectivity*—he is purported to have coined those terms. He also told the world that science was about objectivity. Contrary to objectivity, Christianity, according to Kierkegaard, was about subjectivity, or should be. Scientists, he said, can learn about the world by observation, but observation *cannot* reveal the inner workings of individual minds. Kierkegaard, from my perspective, was telling the world that we have two kinds of consciousness, which he called subjective consciousness and objective consciousness.

When I was writing my textbooks about consciousness, I repeatedly encountered a similar revelation by Western philosophers; they all seemed to understand that a polarity existed in the human mind. All the major philosophers that I encountered seemed to grasp duality, but, unfortunately, they each gave the duality different names— like subjective and objective, phenomena and noumena, anima and animus, the *being* mind and the *becoming* mind, or the fast mind and the slow mind, (there are as many names for the polarities as there are philosophers). As a result of this failure to recognize that everyone was talking about the same polarity, we ended up with a linguistic nightmare. We now have a blizzard of dual terms that all point to the same simple polarity. The early philosophers also had no scientific data to suggest where human duality might be coming from, so they all speculated on the source.

Both Keller and Kierkegaard saw that Intellect, the work of the Egoic mind, had nothing at all to do with Faith, which seemed to be arising from an entirely different kind of mind—this is a third correspondence between the two thinkers: they could both sense dual-process. They both realized that Intellect had to be dropped if Faith were to manifest. Kierkegaard called this a *leap of faith*: a person had to abandon logic long enough to jump over a dangerous chasm. On the other side of the chasm was not knowledge, but the *process* of knowing. The goal was not to prove anything, *the goal was to experience* the joy of being alive. Here is Helen Keller writing about this conundrum:

> Reason hardly warranted Anne Sullivan's attempt to transform a little half-human, half-animal deaf-blind child into a complete being. Neither science nor philosophy had set such a goal, but faith, the eye of love, did. I did not know I had a soul. Then God in a wise heart drew me out of nothingness with cords of human love and the life belt of language, and lo! I found myself. [87]

That is an amazing paragraph from a remarkably sophisticated mind. Helen Keller knew that it was love and trust that enabled her to discover the world. Intellect, talking, logic, none of that wonderful Egoic processing would have saved her from silent oblivion—she would have ended up locked away in some awful asylum had she not had the parents she did, and without Anne Sullivan. The doctors suggested as much— that she be locked away. My mind shivers at that bleak scenario. I wonder how many times in history we have wasted the life of a remarkable human being—locking genius away to rot in obscurity.

Like so many of the existential and phenomenological philosophers, Kierkegaard and Keller could articulate a duality that differentiated an Egoic mind from a Faith-based (Allocentric) mind. Both Helen Keller and Søren Kierkegaard knew the same truth about Faith. However, neither had the scientific background to argue for a quantum/biological derivation of the Soul (the Self, the Allocentric Mind), from wherein Faith arises.

Kierkegaard also coined the term *angst*, which I relate to the Buddhist concept of *Dukkha*, the suffering that comes simply from being a sentient creature. We know the life cycle: human beings are born, grow old, and then die—there is no way out; there are no exceptions. No human being escapes angst, the daily anxiety that is a sidekick to wakefulness. No matter what we feel or think, there is always doubt, worry, even dread. Surety is not a given in our universe. Along the life-journey, we encounter perils and grief, depression and dread, shame and guilt mixed with joy and a sense of responsibility-heavy freedom. We are never on totally solid ground within this fluid Earth-reality.

However, for Kierkegaard and Keller, there is a choice. We can embrace doubt, accept uncertainty, and we can confront suffering—we can stare down the bad news and live a full life, despite inevitable bouts of angst and sadness. We were put on Earth to relieve suffering, our own suffering, and the suffering of others; let us get on with this task. Helen Keller was an optimist, she used angst, dread, grief, and suffering to make herself strong:

> I can say with conviction that the struggle which evil necessitates is one of the greatest blessings. It makes us strong, patient, helpful men and women. It lets us into the soul of things and teaches us that *although the world is full of suffering, it is also full of overcoming it.* [88]

I italicized that famous sentence because it needs to be remembered. We live in a sea of suffering, but we do not have to drown in it. With Faith, we can learn to walk on these deep waters.

As I was writing about Helen Keller and her relationship to philosophers, it occurred to me that she had every right to take her place among the great minds of Western civilization. We are used to our philosophers being old white guys with enough time on their hands to write about ideas. History has been cautious (or hostile) to the notion that a great thinker might be a woman with disabilities.

Helen Keller still impacts generations; she still inspires, and she still causes us to stop and consider her words and convictions. I think she is one of America's greatest Philosophers of Faith. I will let the philosopher Helen Keller have the final word. This is from her journal, December 9, 1936 [italics are mine]:

The order of nature will always necessitate pain, failure, separation, death; and these will probably become more menacing as the complexities and dangerous experiments of a vast world civilization increase. The delicate task will remain ours to ensure God's gift, joy, to His children. Many persons have a wrong idea of what constitutes true happiness. It is not attained through self-gratification but through *fidelity to a worthy purpose.* Happiness should be a Means of accomplishment, like health, not an End in itself. Every human being has undeniable rights which, respected, render happiness possible—the right to live his own life as far as may be, to choose one's own creed, to develop his capabilities; *but no one has a right to consume happiness without producing it,* or to lay his burden upon shoulders merely to fulfil a personal desire. [89]

Helen Keller and Rudolf Steiner

In the section above, I used the philosopher Søren Kierkegaard to represent all Western philosophers. My point was that Western philosophers, one and all, grappled with duality. They each used their Egocentric mind to locate this duality, to label it—each in their own way—and they puzzled over the conundrum. There were also many others, not philosophers (by profession), who used their explorations to discover the same duality. It is this second non-philosopher group to which I now turn.

I could have called this section "Helen Keller and Carl Jung," or Helen Keller and William James." Or I could have substituted Johann Wolfgang von Goethe or Albert Einstein, or Samuel Taylor Coleridge for Rudolf Steiner. These are all names of individuals who understood that there were wonderful mysteries hidden beneath human understanding (beneath everyday appearances); these Allocentric thinkers dared to dance on the fringes of acceptable behavior—they challenged our understanding of knowledge and reality.

Let me stick with Rudolf Steiner (as an example) because he was a prolific and determined individual and he left us a wealth of books, lectures, and technical papers to support his ideas. Steiner was a Goethe scholar, so he can speak for Goethe as well as for the other esoteric thinkers listed above. In his youth, Steiner was essentially trained as a scientist, even though his clairvoyant nature was inherently dominant.

Steiner is quite hard to understand without considerable background knowledge. He wrote in German about esoteric science and abstract concepts—his translators probably did not fully understand what he was talking about. He also used alchemical (ancient) languages and he used the symbolism employed by different esoteric disciplines. This approach is bewildering to Modern minds.

I am also sure that Steiner cannot be understood without an understanding of humanity's dual cognition, he speaks of spirit and soul as if it were a forgone conclusion that cognition was dual. Nevertheless, we can profitably use Steiner's ideas if we understand that he was talking about the evolution of energy states in the human body—he was giving us a history of the evolution of consciousness, just as Jean Gebser did (and Susanne-Cook Greuter and Ken Wilber).

Steiner asserted that we could learn to self-adjust our energy fields; essentially, he was saying what Socrates had said, "know thyself and you will be able to change thyself." We can alter our level of consciousness if we know how to work with bio/quantum energy. During meditation, we alter our energy states, and then slowly we move our consciousness to more sophisticated levels.

Partly because of his education, Steiner was committed to science. He insisted that whatever esoteric alchemy was being brewed it had to stand up to vigorous scientific scrutiny. If there were fairies and magic wands hidden behind appearances, Steiner demanded proof of their existence. Going forward with stubborn scientific determination, which was mixed with Allocentric and esoteric perspectives, Steiner soon found himself an ironic leader and spokesperson for the Occult Era in European history. Steiner was comfortable with this unorthodox role because he had a foot in both everyday reality and esoteric reality—which he (and Goethe) considered to be revealed by two different kinds of science (Allocentric and Egocentric, using my terminology). Steiner studied not only hardcore materialist scientists, but he also hobnobbed with advocates of the Occult, people like theosophists Madam Blavatsky, Anne Bessant, and Indian philosopher Jiddu Krishnamurti. The philosophy and practice of Theosophy was embraced by Steiner as he forged his reputation as a spokesperson for esoteric thinking.

Steiner, like Goethe before him, understood that duality was inherent in nature. These individuals, these early cognitive explorers, did not have dual-process theory in the 1800s to support their thinking, but they did realize that human beings were a confused species because every human was born with two minds in conflict. Goethe's famous play Faust is a classic study of the human cognitive conundrum.

It took Goethe sixty years, off and on as time permitted, to complete *Faust*. Some say that his own cognitive development and his life experiences can be seen reflected in the play. The story of Faust (the man) has a long history predating Goethe. In the earlier history of Faust (as a work of symbolic art), we find the classic standoff between the Ego and the Soul. It is within this broader context that I make my claim that *Faust* is a classic rendition of humanity's cognitive dilemma. From a dual-process perspective, Faust, the main character in Goethe's play *Faust*, makes a deal with the Devil (Mephistopheles); essentially, Faust sells his soul (the Self) to enrich his Ego.

I suggest that *Faust* is a study of the evolution of human consciousness, a study of duality from an artistic perspective. The play was a way for Goethe to lay his own dual mental life, as a Soul-Poet and Egoic-Philosopher before our eyes. In the stage play of *Faust*, the Ego is shown his Twin sister, the Soul. The Ego slowly discovers that the world is a barren wasteland without his poetic sister.

Steiner speaks of a fundamental duality inherent in the biological make-up of human beings; it is almost assumed by Steiner, as he writes, that we all agree there is *spirit* and there is *soul*. He also speaks of paradox and polarity, and he asserts that *the spirit arises from the soul*. Essentially, Steiner saw the conundrum of duality that was inherent in humanity long before biological evidence began to accumulate. He did not say where this duality might have come from, but he seems to have understood the essential challenge of having two minds in balance. Steiner understood the figure-ground oscillation behind mental processing; he called the soul "the ground" and the figures that emerged from soul "the spirit." He does not use the terms Egocentric and Allocentric, but he would, I suggest, have had no trouble comprehending my Navigational Consciousness hypothesis.

Rudolf Steiner (and Immanuel Kant before him) assigned the term "Intellect" to Egoic (reductionist) processing and "Reason" to Allocentric (wholeness) processing. Both Intellect and Reason are needed for balanced cognition, but Reason is too often ignored or undeveloped in the unevolved human mind. That *Reason* is used as another name for *Soul* is bewildering (I want to bang my head against Goethe's coffin). The point is that Kant, Goethe, Steiner (and so on and on) discovered and discussed human cognitive duality. Helen Keller intuitively understood that Reason was Soul-based, different from Egoic Intellect. In the quote below, she indicates that her powers of reason separate her from others of her time:

> I have the advantage of a mind trained to think [to reason], and that is the difference between myself and most people, not my blindness and their sight. ~ Helen and Teacher, by Joseph Lash, 1980.

As I said above, Steiner insisted that there had to be a science behind esotericism (whatever term we wish to use for the Allocentric mind—Soul, Self, Reason, etc.); there had to be a scientific explanation for why the brain housed the duality that Steiner called Intellect (Ego) and Reason (Soul). Steiner called his perspective "Spiritual (or Esoteric) Science," to contrast his worldview from Materialistic Science. This dual insight was well ahead of its time and few people understood what he was getting at (indeed, few understand his views even today . . . and I do not wish to imply that I fully grasp the extent of Steiner's vast knowledge).

Essentially, what Steiner learned from Goethe was that scientific materialism was an Egocentric reductionist activity—the scientific mind dissected everything into ever smaller parts. Egoic Science required an observer (seer) and objects of study (the seen). Steiner, following Goethe, argued that we should (*in addition* to reductionist science) also study process, flow, connectedness, the operation of the whole organism. In other words, we should not just dissect existence, we should also merge our minds with the networked processes of nature. In figure/ground terms, Steiner and Goethe insisted that we should study the *ground* as well as study the figures embedded in the ground. The blank canvas or blank page are just as important as the drawings or words painted/printed on the background. From the background, figures flow into existence. Steiner and Goethe said we needed to study this flowing-in and flowing-out of existence.

Steiner eventually distanced himself from Theosophy, forming his own field of study called Anthroposophy. Theosophy was based on Eastern religious perspectives. Steiner was a Christian, so Anthroposophy was more in harmony with Western religious perspectives. Both Theosophy and Anthroposophy took duality for granted—as if we all agreed from day one that human beings were dual creatures. Steiner held that between the two minds (Ego and Self) was a gap, a flow that contained oscillating energy. It was in the flow where we would find thoughts suddenly appearing as if out of nowhere and out of nothing. It is not enough to postulate a Spirit polarized from a Soul; we must also ask about the mysterious gap between the two minds out of which "thoughts, images, and insights" arise. Steiner held that through mental exercises (meditation), a person could become a witness to the emergence of insights. Several of his books and many of his articles contained meditation exercises. Steiner's science of esotericism (the occult, any mystery) was best served by:

1. Being Allocentrically *aware* (of the background).
2. Being Egocentrically *attentive* (to objects arising from and returning to the ground).
3. Being a *witness to the gaps* between the two minds from which insights appear. (This is what poet Leonard Cohen meant when he said, in his song *Anthem*, "There is a crack in everything— that's how the light (insights) get in".

Ego, Self, and the gap between the two are needed for a full understanding of cognitive reality. Science, in Steiner's era, was ignoring—or not aware of—the Ego's twin, the Allocentric Soul-mind and so missed half the world's available knowledge. There was also no attention paid to the oscillatory nature of existence, to the energy gap, the polarity that held the two minds frozen (dancing) together.

Steiner lectured that in the modern era, the Ego had lost connection with compassion. Evolution seemed to be pushing the Ego to become ever more autistic. The Ego seems to be trying to separate itself more and more from its twin sister, the Soul. I believe that Helen Keller could sense this evolutionary trend—*thinking* devoid of empathy—and she was abhorred by this unfolding, as was Steiner.

In Steiner's first book *Goethe's Theory of Knowledge* (1886), he says, "one who has a rich mental life sees a thousand things that may remain unseen by one who is mentally impoverished." The reason Helen was so remarkable was because she evolved a rich mental life that enabled her to perceive what others could not. Here is a quote from *Helen Keller, The Open Door* (1957) that states Helen's view on spirituality:

> I know there are people who are bored with spiritual ideas. They are bored because they do not know their own capacities and consequently miss the multitude of bright, illuminating interest that would come if they learned to think inwardly.

Steiner could not have said this any clearer, and he would have agreed with Helen—the human mind contains potentials that lay hidden from (and yet are within) most people. Steiner was all about the hidden capacities of the human mind. He wrote several books explaining the sequences to be followed *to create sophisticated minds.*

Significantly, Steiner had clairvoyant abilities from a young age; he knew something about his own mind, that it was wired in such a way that he could see beyond the physical everyday world (so it seemed to him). His Esoteric Science was a philosophy, a method, and a knowing that explained how it was possible to look through physical space— past sensory impressions, past appearances—to something that was normally hidden, but which could be perceived by the mind if that mind was professionally trained. I suggest to the skeptical reader that they temporarily suspend their scientific, rational mind (the Modern Level of consciousness) and probe what Steiner tried to tell humanity a hundred years ago. Steiner is hard to comprehend for various reasons, but it is worth the effort to study his philosophy.

If Steiner is right that there are additional perceptions (or perceptual methods) beyond what eyes and ears observe, then Helen Keller may have experienced a world different from what we customarily assume to be normal. Helen said that her view of the spiritual world was as clear to her as the physical world was to beings with vision and hearing. Had she known about Steiner, Helen might have been a supporter and advocate for his viewpoint—just as she supported Swedenborg (and for similar reasons).

Over the past few decades, neuroscientists have probed and embraced Buddhist mindfulness (meditation techniques). Neuroscientists learned, for example, about the Buddhist eightfold path toward enlightenment. It became clear to researchers that it was not enough to just understand the philosophy of Buddhism, it was also necessary to "do the work" that could change cognition, as monks had shown to be possible. Buddhist monks can change their energy states through intention and methodology. Neuroscientists—hooking monks to MRI machines—are discovering the brain pathways that are affected (changed by meditation) as the monks self-alter their brain biology.

Steiner was influenced by Buddhist teaching. He knew that there were methods and there was a pathway to follow in Buddhist practice. Steiner says the same thing about his Esoteric (Spiritual) Science, that there are methods and there is a pathway that leads the mind to perceive the world beyond the physical. Steiner's methods and Buddhist methods overlap and intertwine—problems arise because of terminology and translations. Steiner's energy bodies (ether, astral, etc.) were partly based on Buddhist thought. Importantly, however, Steiner was not a Buddhist, he was a Christian. He felt that Christianity, the Bible, and the teachings of Jesus, also offered a pathway to be followed that enabled the human mind to evolve. The Christian pathway, in Steiner's view, was analogous to other spiritual systems, including Buddhist insights.

Steiner also discussed the idea of hiddenness. There is a hierarchy of hiddenness. For example, much is hidden from the mineral world—a rock does not know much. Less is hidden from the world of plants, which can sense and respond to environmental changes. Even less is hidden from animals that can navigate, search, and relate. Human beings have much less hiddenness than plants and less spiritually evolved animals. There is a pattern revealed in this observation: there is an evolution toward revelation, away from hiddenness. Is it not logical (would it not follow) that *more remains hidden*, waiting to be revealed if only a more sophisticated mind was created, or a correct pathway followed? Steiner says yes, more is hidden, but with experience and practice our minds can learn to perceive in additional ways, moving beyond the appearances of everyday reality.

Steiner and Goethe both held that Spiritual Science was not magic or based on superstition and ignorance. In my terminology, they were simply saying that the Allocentric mind can be trained, fine-tuned, and used to perceive in ways that are different from what the Egocentric mind can perceive using the external senses. Steiner argued that using the internal senses, including the mind's skill at imagination, intention, and flow-perception, human beings can grasp spiritual realms. These so-called *spiritual realms* are not based on magic or superstition, they are simply energy systems (levels) that can be felt, understood through experience, and then used by the mind to bring about conscious change to the Self and to the world around.

In a fascinating way, Steiner was simply showing humanity that the brain had evolved this thing called "the mind." He was implying that prior to recent evolutionary advances in cognition, humanity could not

Reason. The ability to reason is what Steiner means by "the Supersensible Mind." If Steiner saw the world that exists today, he would observe that there are still many human beings who have not evolved supersensible minds. If we assume that others have mental capacities like our own, we might very well be wrong. It could be that Narcissistic, Ethnocentric (Tribal), and Traditional minds have yet to refine the capacity for Reason—they lack supersensible minds.

The internal senses (including the mind) give rise to Allocentric processing (awareness). The reason awareness is constantly being interrupted is because the external senses—which give rise to Egocentric processing—inhibit internal processing. For Helen Keller, this Egocentric inhibition was drastically reduced, so her ability to process Allocentrically became greatly enhanced. Therefore, I suggest that she was able to sense the hidden spiritual energy fields that Steiner discussed.

I must leave this line of thought now because Steiner's world holds the whole of esoteric history and this is a book about Helen Keller. Many volumes have already been written about Steiner's work and his methodologies. My goal has been to show you that a discussion of "fairies and magic wands," the scientific study of the Soul, of the Allocentric mind, is not New Age nonsense or unscientific prattle. There is something here that is fundamental and extremely important to understand. Helen Keller's humanitarianism, her fierce determination to be a champion for Love, Faith, and Service, comes flowing out of her Soul onto the pages of her books and speeches because she could sense the messages (patterns of energy) flowing from her Allocentric mind into the world.

Quantum Navigation

In my second book *Consciousness: A New Slant on an Old Conundrum* (2017), I speculated that the retina was a quantum computer. Experts in multiple fields are busy debating this speculation and experiments are on-going to prove or disprove the quantum nature of retinal processing. However, my statement that the retina was a quantum processor is a hypothesis; I used logic and analogy to suggest that the retina *already* exhibits inherent and fundamental quantum behaviors.

Because of embodiment, I further suggested that our whole human make-up *had to be* quantum—if vision has quantum properties (which direct the development of human anatomy and physiology), so too must hearing, touch, smell, proprioception (each sensory system), and the mind itself (the combination of all sensory systems) contain quantum-like behaviors. In esoteric terms, I used *as above so below* to compare scales of reality—in this case, comparing effects in the quantum world with the much larger world of molecules and cells in the retina.

The breakthrough for me came when I asked myself why it was that the retina had two processing systems, a system driven by rod cells in the peripheral retina and a second system driven by cone cells in the foveal (central) retina. These two vision systems track through the brain along separate processing streams; they are biological evidence for dual-processing on a vast whole-brain scale. When we explore what these two vision systems primarily do, we discover that the rod cells in the peripheral retina can be understood to measure momentum and the cone cells can be surmised to measure location. That observation hit me like a bolt of lightning when I realized that this design mirrored a fundamental property in the quantum world.

Werner Heisenberg's famous *Uncertainty Principle* in quantum physics says that—in the electromagnetic world—it is impossible to measure momentum the very same time we measure for location. In the quantum realm, we can measure either momentum or location but not both simultaneously. The eyes use electromagnetic energy (light-waves) to create vision. Therefore, it makes sense that the retina would incorporate the mathematics of quantum mechanics to create our visual world.

The eye, because it is dealing with quantum energy, evolved to measure momentum (movement) as well as location (no-movement) in two separate processing systems. The only way the retina could use quantum properties was to evolve two systems of measurement and then to "combine" them though superfast oscillatory processing (or perhaps through additional mechanisms). The insight that hit me was that the retina was using ultra-tiny quantum effects and reproducing the *Uncertainty Principle* at a macro-level. At an exceedingly high scale of processing, the result was dual-cognition. But that revelation was just the beginning of my journey as I compared micro and macro correspondences. Let me set up this discussion with a story.

One evening in December 2020, I watched a Ken Burn's documentary on the birth and evolution of Country Music. I watched as Burn's told the story of how Country Music legend Hank Williams came to write "I

Saw the Light," using an old gospel tune as the foundation for the song. That night, with the song fresh in my mind, I had a dream about "seeing the light."

In the dream, I found myself at the bottom of a deep and quite narrow vertical shalt, underground; I was looking up—I had been pushed into the narrow shaft and had fallen deep within the earth. Whoever pushed me was not letting me return. As time went on, the shaft grew smaller and more distant, as if I were steadily sinking ever deeper down, away from the surface.

I soon realized there was no way back to Earth-Reality. A terror, like drowning, fell over me—a feeling of suffocation. I eventually saw a tiny light in the distance (as I turned to look behind me) and—having no other option—began to move in the direction of the light. In the dimness of the light, which had gotten slightly brighter as I approached, I came to a wall. The light seemed to be on the other side of the wall.

It was then that I realized I had no body; walls were no longer barriers. Without a body, I had no need to breathe or to be afraid; I had no need for oxygen or bodily sensations. I moved through the wall. On the other side of the wall, I could still perceive the light. My only option, the only journey available to me was to continue toward the light. I was no longer terrified of being trapped underground surrounded by darkness and without oxygen. Now the sensation was one of being lost and needing help.

As soon as I felt the need for help, a personage appeared, a felt presence that could communicate with me. "What help do you seek?" it asked. The first thought I had, the first need that arose, was for companions in this new dark world. As this thought came, so also did a multitude of other personages arrive—these were my ancestors. I was comforted and reassured, although no one spoke.

Then I was shown a book—it floated in front of my consciousness. I could sense that the book was meant to help me, that it was a benevolent book. It was not the Bible or Koran or any earthy document. The book was a universal vessel for storing knowledge (it was actually a portal, as subsequent dreams revealed).

Sleep was fading and I was slowly waking, but I needed to look in the book—I did not want to wake up! In the twilight, in the Theta-wave state, I suddenly got a message from the book. It was as if the multitude was helping me with my earthly challenges. Here is the complex message from the book: *Infinity and eternity are the two basic tools of the human mind*. I felt that I understood this strange message because it supported what I had already written about in my previous books—the message was an affirmation of dual-process theory and my desire to apply the theory to the evolution of human consciousness.

The human mind, so I was instructed in the dream, constructs reality within itself using two tools, infinity and eternity. Evidently, minds can construct endless time (eternity) because every mind has a bio/quantum fractal system for constructing time, moment-to-moment, using the *particle nature* of electromagnetic waves. The (second) mind can also simultaneously construct endless space (infinity) because it has a bio/quantum fractal system for making space using the *wave nature* of electromagnetic waves. Using my Navigational Consciousness hypothesis, I could see that Eternity is the work of the Egocentric (temporal) processing system, while Infinity is the work of the Allocentric (spatial) processing system.

At my desk in morning, as I reconstructed the dream and the message (which I have gotten before in other dreams and wrote about in my other publications), I pondered hiddenness and Helen Keller.

My first thought was that Helen Keller's mind—just like any other mind—could construct space and time, infinity and eternity, without using light waves or sound waves. This proves embodiment; the whole body is a quantum system, a combination of synchronous wave forms that the neocortex decodes. We can remove some of these wave forms (as with blindness or deafness, for example), *but the embodied bio/quantum processing system remains.*

Second, if the whole body is quantum and uses dual processing—Egocentric and Allocentric—then all the spooky stuff of quantum mathematics must also be present within us. The magic of the quantum world may be hidden from our surface mind, but it still functions whether we are aware of the process or not. Helen Keller's fairies and magic wands might have a quantum basis.

Third, using quantum spookiness, we can speculate about human behaviors and potential. For example, if the particle nature of physical reality comes in discrete packets (photons have a particle-like structure), then so would manifestations of energy at the macro level appear in discrete packets. If we look at the atom, for example, we find that electrons occupy *distinct* orbital regions around the nucleus. This requirement that energy must be bundled in energy packets would explain things (I am making a huge leap to the macro world) like the personality types of the Enneagram and the Myers-Briggs personally styles. Human beings may be individually unique, but we also arrive at birth with discrete *energetic structures* (personalities and potentials) that unfold as we mature.

Psychologist Howard Gardner defined distinct human types of intelligence (broadly conceived), which are *energetic structures* that enable specific kinds of innate abilities. If human beings are quantum creatures, constructed by bio/quantum fractal (building blocks), we *would expect to find* what we, indeed, do find: human beings are born with discrete personality types, categorical ability-types (musicians, mathematicians, athletes, writers), and an Egocentric mind that manifests figures from an Allocentrically-generated ground.

Before we go any further with this complex set of analogies, let me point out what appears obvious: The human mind (and body) was constructed using the building blocks of an electromagnetic particle-wave based physicality. Because of this architecture, the mind can construct a real-time representation of reality. We can use this internal construction to create endless time and endless space. However, this just sets the parameters of our abilities—all else is hidden. In other words, there may actually be *no* infinity, *no* eternity, *no* reality that matches what our minds construct. There may very well be illusory barriers that we can walk through, and places where we can go that do not require breathing or sensing—spooky places, hidden places, esoteric places.

Additionally, if the human mind and body are quantum, then the quantum phenomenon called *entanglement* must, by analogy, also be contained within us. Helen Keller felt that Swedenborg's ability to go out-of-body was a valid way to attain wisdom. From a standard scientific perspective (from a non-quantum perspective), going-out-of-body is nonsense—from a Modern level of consciousness, this kind of "thinking" is superstitious, wishful, and ignorant. The only way a Modern mind would entertain out-of-body experiences would be through verifiable experimentation. There is no such solid evidence today, primarily because scientists are exclusively using Egocentric processing to do their searching. The appeal to quantum logic is perhaps an opportunity for the Modern (scientific) mind to pause and allow a hypothesis.

Carl Jung's concepts, especially serendipity and synchronicity, feel like quantum entanglement at work in a world that was created by quantum effects. We are embedded in this quantum soup and, indeed, we are made of the same soup—we affect the environment as the environment affects us. Quantum Magic at the subatomic level appears to also play out at the macro level.

We probably have the ability (potential) to navigate at a quantum level. However, our primary senses, vision, hearing, and proprioception, mask this navigational ability. It seems that only in our dreams and in our imagination can we move through the quantum soup. Or perhaps, the subtleness required for quantum navigation is closer to the dream I had, where a bodiless "entity" can move fearlessly through walls to encounter energy beings. The whole focus of this book has been on Helen Keller's esoteric abilities. Vision and hearing did not block or interfere with her connection to subtle energies. If navigation at a quantum level is a reality, then Helen Keller might have been closer to subtle experiences than any other human being has ever been.

All the while I was engaged in fleshing out the Navigational Consciousness hypothesis, I was bothered by a large question: How do the two minds work together if they are mutually exclusive, deaf-blind to each other? That does not feel intuitive. We feel ourselves to be a unified creature, we do not feel dual as a matter of everyday experience. If we are quantum-derived creatures, however, there is a possible answer. Think of the power of quantum computers. They are dual machines using bits of ones (something) and zeros (nothing), on-and-off gates (excitation and inhibition). Regular computers also use ones and zeros for processing. However, in quantum computers, there is a third state that allows for unity, a both/and gate. If we are quantum, we might also have minds that can process with both/and gates.

I am quite sure (I say this with a guilty grin) that I have long ago sailed past the focus of the everyday admirer of the Keller/Sullivan mythology (and most neurologists and philosophers)! However, my goal from the beginning has been esoteric hidden worlds—this avenue has allowed me to speculate, muse, and dance on the edges of things.

If human beings are quantum creatures, then, so also was Helen Keller a quantum being, but her connection to the spookiness inherent in Quantumland was not masked by vision and hearing. We must listen carefully to what she told us in her books and articles and in her speeches, because she knew some things—many things (probably unconsciously)—that we do not yet comprehend.

～

When I discussed the Law of Correspondence in Chapter Two, I noted that the human neocortex evolved the ability to work with patterns—this is well accepted in cognitive psychology and neuroscience. Our ability to think, to have thoughts, to postulate, to systematize, to assimilate, to scale up and down as we examine the world, evolved for a reason—*there is a cause* that resulted in our problem-solving minds. What is this cause?

The answer, I suggest, is that the navigational mind had no choice except to create such a problem-solving mind. It is quite simple, really: in order to navigate straight-ahead, we must perceive an animated map of what is in front of the body. That "projected" map is what we use as we move about; the map must contain pathways around objects. Evolution, using the Egocentric (quantum-particle) mind, developed a way to perceive forms (figures)—these forms are just patterns (grid lines on reference frames).

The neocortex evolved to recognize and remember repeating patterns. The neocortex also evolved to manipulate patterns, to work with partial patterns, to categorize patterns, and to dissect or combine the patterns we call objects (forms, figures)—this is Egocentric (quantum-particle) processing. Evolution, using the Allocentric (quantum-wave) mind, developed a way to perceive flow—the perception of space (the ground), which holds forms. Notice that the "if" side of the if/and/then equation refers to the ground (background state)—for example, if the background is in a specific energetic state—the result will be a "then," a figure manifesting from the background. This ability to use an if/and/then algorithm for navigation eventually generalized to what we call systemic thinking.

This dual neocortical processing system had to use if/and/then logic to enable navigation through a domain. *If* there is an object in the path, and you need to continue on the path, *then* go around the object. *If* the way ahead is clear, and you wish to take this path, *then* you may travel faster. *If* you travel from landmark to landmark, and you continue to employ landmarks, *then* you will arrive at a destination. Using the animated map projected in front of us, we can predict how navigation will unfold before we even move. *If* a scene looks like this, and we perceive pathways, *then* flow (movement) through the scene and along a path will look like that. The navigational mind learned to project (predict) in real time using a repeating if/and/then algorithm.

After the Navigational brain evolved if/and/then logic capability, the acquisition of language enabled humanity to communicate experiences. Cognitive sophistication evolved in parallel with navigational sophistication. Vision and hearing contribute to the quantum navigational mind, but their loss does not shut down the operation of our miraculous minds. Helen Keller's quantum navigational mind was not only normal, but it was also extraordinary.

Simon Baron-Cohen, Jeff Hawkins, Ray Kurzweil

I am going to briefly examine three books about the human mind, which were influential in the development of my own cognitive philosophy. The authors of these three books are brilliant thinkers who have vast knowledge and decades of experience in their respective professions. I have read more than one book by these three and I find myself in harmony with the general direction of their conclusions.

I am well aware that this deep dive into science momentarily takes our focus off Helen Keller's life. However, what these authors show (for our purpose) is that Helen's mind was normal (or extraordinary) even at the level of brain neurons.

My Navigational Consciousness hypothesis suggests that the human brain is entirely designed to enable navigation straight-ahead. The brain developed to comprehend and survive within space. Therefore, the brain measures and makes predictions based on spatial coordinates overlaid on the physical world. Temporal calculations come into play as the body moves through space.

We would expect to find that the brain has systems for parsing and quantizing space. This perspective *expects* that grid cells, place cells, straight-ahead cells, border cells—any specialized neuron built for navigation—would be found in the brain. We would also *expect* to find that some cells measure flow (excitation), and other cells measure stability, the absence of movement (inhibition). We would also *expect* to find a pattern-seeking and pattern-solving fractal in the brain tied intimately to navigation. We would *expect* to find duality and oscillation built into the brain at all scales. To navigate requires a dynamic neural system that can solve the figure-ground challenge; we would *expect* to find such a mind, and we do.

The Pattern Seekers: How Autism Drives Human Invention (2020) by Simon Baron-Cohen

Dr. Simon Baron-Cohen has written several important books of which *The Pattern Seekers* is the most recent (see the bibliography). A basic tenet of his new book is that the human mind has two fundamental neural processing systems, an empathy circuit and a systematizing circuit. The empathy circuit is concerned with interconnectivity, relationships, sharing, and emotional bonding; it is a loving-kindness system, which presupposes that other humans also have minds and emotions. The systematizing circuit is concerned with pattern analysis, problem solving, and invention, which presupposes that other humans also have minds that can reason and innovate.

For me, this designation of two neural circuits is another example of dual-process theory. Baron-Cohen's research and his observations of human behavior have led him to conclude that not only do human beings solve problems, but they also care about and sense the emotions of others. These two circuits evidently evolved separately (in parallel), so that one or the other can be dominant. In an autistic mind, especially, the systematizing circuit is powerfully developed, often at the expense of the empathy circuit. The two circuits are somehow linked and to an extend can be understood as mutually exclusive (when one goes up, the other goes down).

I am reminded of the first book I read by Dr. Baron-Cohen called *The Essential Difference: Male and Female Brains and The Truth About Autism* (2009). I was startled (and delighted—because it fit my own worldview) by his observation that autism and the generic male brain share basic processing behaviors. In other words, there is something within males, in testosterone-driven masculinity generally, that is like autism. Males tend to have stronger systematizing circuits at the expense of their empathy circuits, which is the beginning of the argument that males cause wars and all manner of hostilities because they (relatively) lack empathy—many males have a weakly developed empathy circuit. Commonsense and the history of aggression support Dr. Baron-Cohen's research; certain kinds of males, with weak empathy circuits, are the cause of much of the planet's chaos.

The Pattern Seekers is an exploration of the systematizing circuit and the link to autism and to the male mind. Baron-Cohen states that about 70,000 years ago, a remarkable transformation occurred in the brains of Homo Sapiens—the systematizing circuit evolved to enable highly sophisticated innovation. From that point in time, human beings started to invent at an unstoppable rate; creativity exploded and eventually gave birth to the privileged lives some of us are now experiencing.

Systematizing uses if/and/then neural circuitry. Baron-Cohen argues that when this if/and/then circuity became sophisticated about 70,000 years ago, it was the catalyst that differentiated Homo Sapiens from Homo Erectus. Baron-Cohen also acknowledges that language emerged at about the same time. However, he argues that it was not language that primarily changed Homo Sapiens, but rather the systematizing circuit.

From a Navigational Consciousness perspective, I would add that the systematizing circuit and the empathizing circuit must both have an evolutionary history—there must have been circuits in the hominid brain that were the foundation for the new, more evolved circuits. For example, if/and/then circuitry was present in primitive cells 3 billion years ago. Bacterial colonies align toward a light source to enhance collective survival. *If* light is present *and* energy from light is needed for survival, *then* align to the light. The first true eyes evolved rapidly 500,000 years ago during the Cambrian explosion. The eye is a supreme if/and/then processor. Baron-Cohen's hypothesis is that this primitive brain circuit slowly evolved until some new biological addition expanded and accelerated the capability to use if/and/then processing; this change enabled the human species to innovate and invent.

Baron-Cohen is aware of the early examples of primitive if/and/then processing, but he is arguing for the capacity to invent, which is a highly advanced evolutionary form of the systematizing circuit. From a dual-processing perspective, the advent of invention is a further development in the Egocentric processing system and is a further advancement in the ability to navigate. Navigation went from a purely mechanical system for moving through the physical world, to a sophisticated mechanism for navigating within the brain using mind-navigation, which included the ability to navigate into imagined futures, and to navigate through history to remember prior successful strategies for survival.

To navigate along open pathways (gaps) and to identify, approach, or retreat from objects, the brain had to solve the background-foreground (figure/ground) puzzle. If/and/then processing had to develop because of navigation. *If* there is a pathway around objects ahead, *and* you need to go that way to get to a location, *then* follow the pathway. If there is food ahead, and you are hungry, then focus on the food and move toward it. Rapidly evolving *If and then* processing dates back *at least* a half billion years.

Besides adding to an understanding of Navigational Consciousness, Baron-Cohen's perspectives address two other themes in this book. Helen Keller raged against a masculine mind that was aggressive and unkind, leading to wars, murder, neglect, and indifference to suffering. Baron-Cohen shows us why unkind aggressiveness might be present more in testosterone-driven creatures compared to estrogen-guided creatures. Males cause wars because overly aggressive males lack fully evolved empathy circuits. If most politicians are male, and if most military leaders are male, and if most of the scientists building AI systems are male, then we should expect a lack of empathy to govern behaviors and decisions. This is becoming an increasingly dangerous situation as we race into the blades of an AI dominated future.

There are autistic females, of course, many of whom are engineers, mathematicians, brilliant people with highly systematic minds. Presumably, these females may have less activated empathy circuits. As such, these females are part of the problem if they build creations that disregard empathy.

The second theme that relates to Helen Keller is that her if/and/then neuro-circuitry and her empathetic system were normal and well balanced. Indeed, Helen had a highly refined ability to use her systematizing circuits to compose eloquent and elaborate prose to express her worldviews. She was a clear-headed and brilliant thinker. Her empathy circuit was hyper-evolved, enabling her whole essence to become dedicated to Love and Service. Helen's loss of vision and hearing did not disable her systematizing and empathizing circuits; if anything, these systems were enhanced by deaf-blindness.

On the basis of his research, Baron-Cohen found five personality clusters:

- *Empathizers* (Type E): These are people with empathy skills that are more evolved than their synthesizing skills. About one-third of the population is type E. This type is twice as prevalent in women as in men.
- *Balanced Empathizers and Synthesizers* (Type B): These people have a steady, balanced ability to switch back and forth from empathy to synthesis. About one-third of the population is Type B; men and women are equally likely to have this skill.

- *Synthesizers* (Type S): These are people with synthesizing skills that are more evolved than their empathy skills. About one-third of the population is Type S. This type is twice as prevalent in men as in women.
- *Extreme Empathizers* (Extreme Type E): These people are rare in the population. Extreme Type E is more common in women than in men.
- *Extreme Synthesizers* (Extreme Type S): These people are rare in the population. Extreme Type S is more common in men than in women.

From a Navigational Consciousness perspective, it is clear that the extreme types of Empathizers and Synthesizers are primarily deaf-blind to each other. There is also a clear differentiation between males and females; females on average are more empathetic, while men on average are more systematic. It appears that there is a *relative* deaf-blindness to the skills and personalities of others, especially between the genders. From an evolutionary perspective, women give life to babies and nurture them. The men went out on adventurous hunts to kill animals so that the tribe could survive. Different hormone systems evolved over millions of years, which may partially explain how we got to this conundrum.

We are under a false assumption that the minds of others are the exact same as our own minds. The more we learn about the brain (and the mind it channels), the more we realize just how different each of us perceives and conceptualizes.

Helen Keller was Type B. She was capable of compassionate, powerful empathy, but she was also a brilliant synthesizer. Her cognition was well-balanced.

A Thousand Brains (2021) by Jeff Hawkins

As I was finishing this book, I received Jeff Hawkins' new text *A Thousand Brains* (2021), which I had pre-ordered. Jeff's company *Numenta* is using the human neocortex as a template for machine intelligence. *Numenta* is essentially a theoretical company, working on what I call cognitive neuro-philosophy, except their practical goal is to model systems that will eventually operate on neural-computers.

I began following Jeff Hawkins' insights after I read his earlier work *On Intelligence*, which was written in 2004 in collaboration with Sandra Blakeslee, a science correspondent for *The New York Times*. I was anxiously anticipating *A Thousand Brains* because I could sense that Jeff's discoveries and perspectives—his *Thousand Brain Theory*— would inform my Navigational Consciousness hypothesis. As I read *A Thousand Brains*, I looked for how Jeff's thinking supported or challenged my own cognitive philosophy.

I had no idea when I started writing that I would embed an entire cognitive philosophy in the middle of a book about Helen Keller's mind. However, this discussion of *Numenta's* work provides biological support for the philosophical, psychological, and physiological perspectives discussed above.

Most significantly, the *Numenta* team found evidence at the microscopic (cellular) scale that points to the brain being an organ built for navigation. The brain is constructed not just for external navigation through diverse environments, but also for internal (mental) navigation. The *Numenta* team did not conclude, as I do, that the brain was built with navigation as the driving force, but they are, step by step, providing evidence that supports my Navigational Consciousness hypothesis.

From within the framework of Navigational Consciousness, I postulated that a universal algorithm—a wave/particle duality—was crafting physical and biological creations. Research at *Numenta* appears to support this proposition; they are finding that the neocortex is built to operate a universal algorithm.

According to Hawkins, the neocortex is composed of repeating copies of a basic circuit. We are smarter than other creatures because we have more copies of this circuit. The basic circuit (algorithm) is slightly different in different regions depending on what it is connected to. If connected to the eyes, for example, the basic circuit enables vision. If connected to the ears, the basic circuit enables hearing. Presumably, the basic circuit also enables the synthesizing and empathizing neuro-networks that Simon Baron-Cohen found in his research.

The *Numenta* team reasoned that if we figure out how the basic circuit is engineered, we can better understand how the external senses, like vision and hearing, are derived. Understanding the basic circuit would also improve our understanding of behaviors like empathy and systematic thinking. Everything a human being does, senses, and thinks, is tied to this basic universal circuit.

When explaining the universal circuit, Hawkins draws a parallel between the concepts of Charles Darwin (1809–1882) and the ideas of neurophysiologist Vernon Mountcastle (1918–2015). Darwin identified a basic circuit (algorithm) that theoretically explained the diversity of life through natural selection. Mountcastle identified the basic circuit (algorithm) in the neocortex of the brain that theoretically explained the diversity of human abilities. In my cognitive philosophy, I suggest a universal algorithm that purports to explain the diversity of the biochemical universe. The esoteric concept of correspondence (As above so below) suggests that a universal circuit is constructing (modeling) systems at various temporal and spatial scales.

The basic circuit that Darwin and Mountcastle saw is the same foundational circuit that built the biochemical universe. That is why "As above, so below" is such a profound insight. At any scale, we can observe the universal basic circuit duplicating itself. From my philosophical perspective, the basic circuit is *movement balanced with no movement* (flow/excitation balanced with no-flow/inhibition). In the beginning, the unmoved-mover moved and began to create a universe in its own oscillating (pulsating) image. This basic fractal, after innumerable replications, also built the bicameral mind.

The neocortex uses a general-purpose method to learn, which is founded on the basic universal fractal. Hawkins says, "Being able to learn practically anything requires the brain to work on a universal principle."

In 2016, Jeff Hawkins made a conceptual breakthrough when he envisioned that the neocortex used reference frames to build models of the world at ubiquitous spatial scales. Reference frames are populated with links to other reference frames, they have internal integrity, and they are nested.

What I had been arguing with my navigational hypothesis was that the brain was initially designed as an organ for navigation. It made sense that map-like reference frames would play a central role in a navigational mind. Hawkins agrees, saying that reference frames evolved to enable navigation through the physical world (in the old brain), which were then internalized in the neocortex to allow us to mentally navigate objects—and then, later, internalized further to allow conceptual navigation.

The breakthrough that Jeff and his team made in 2016 was that neocortical columns attach reference frames to objects—all objective manifestations are assigned a reference frame, a grid overlay. The hands and fingers know where they are relative to the grid overlaid on any object. The fingers navigate over a 3-D surface just like the body navigates through a scene.

The *Numenta* team asked themselves, "What kind of function, or algorithm, can create all aspects of human intelligence?" Their answer is that *reference frames* are used to store any kind of knowledge. "Each column in the neocortex—whether it represents visual input, tactual input, auditory input, language, or high-level thought [empathy and systemic thinking]—must have neurons that represent reference frames and locations."

Therefore, all mental operations *require movement* through neural reference frames—from location to location in any given neural matrix. *Mental movement is internalized navigation* using the same spatial-temporal algorithms that enable movement through physical space. Thinking is a form of moving through reference frames, invoking location after location on a matrix.

All human activity is a form of navigation; this includes thought generated by spoken or written language, mathematical thought, and musical thought. Music and spoken language are forms of sound-navigation. Mathematics is visual-spatial navigation. Written language and musical scores are also forms of visual-spatial navigation. Memory happens as we move through stored (familiar) sequences on a neural reference frame (like moving through rooms in a house; each room filled with different objects that differentiate the room from any other).

Hawkins proposes two generic kinds of neurons, *type one* that fires when the brain is registering something, and *type two*, when the brain is predicting that it is about to register something. This is more evidence for dual-process theory: Egoic processing yields conscious manifestations, while Allocentric processing yields unmanifest and unconscious backgrounds (where predictions and objects originate).

Hawkins is in the materialistic camp regarding consciousness. He feels that science will explain the phenomenon, sooner rather than later, given the pace of brain research. I wrote about the debate between the "materialists" and "spiritualists" in *Consciousness: A New Slant on an Old Conundrum* (2017). From my perspective, this debate is between our Egocentric mind and our Allocentric mind, between those who *believe* that atoms and quarks crafted everything, and those who *know* that a universal consciousness (information) created matter. Alan

Wallace, who wrote the *Taboo of Subjectivity* (2000) says, "There is little to distinguish religious ignorance from scientific ignorance." In other words, when we search for origins, everyone—priest or mathematician, spiritual guru or material neuropsychologist—finds the same delightful unknowable mystery. The *Numenta* team is focused on practical applications, so Jeff feels he does not have to join the unsolvable origins debate.

Hawkins also believes that AI machines will someday be conscious. As I stated in earlier books, we are heading to a future in which machine intelligence and human intelligence *will merge* in various invasive ways—humanity *will become* the hyper-conscious "machines" of the future. My musings suggest that Robosapiens will arrive before stand-a-lone machines develop some hybrid form of consciousness. Given what we know about the importance of movement to perception and learning, the AI conscious machines of the future will need a body to control (robotic or virtual)—my guess is that human beings will offer their bodies as a substrate for AI innovations.

Prediction is a ubiquitous function of the neocortex. Neuroscientists say that the brain must predict what will be true from moment to moment—this was an opening assumption from which *Numenta* could explore engineering designs. The brain needs a model of reality that is stable, which can notice change; the ability to predict is essential to neural design.

Hawkins further states that predictions come in two forms: when the body in *not* moving, and when the body *is* moving. Again, this is dual-process theory. Egocentric processing occurs when there is stability, a lack of flow, while Allocentric processing occurs when there is movement.

I was troubled by one conflict that seemed at first to challenge my cognitive philosophy. I have postulated that the retina is a quantum processor that follows Heisenberg's Uncertainty Principle. Rod cells in the retina are an old system in evolution, which has low acuity (20/200), sees only in black and white, has supreme low-light sensitivity, and is highly motion sensitive. The cone cells—newer in evolution—process for color, perceive only in high intensity light (daylight), have 20/20 acuity, and process for objects that are "frozen in a location."

The neurons leaving the retina divide into two processing streams (the *rod-cell stream* and the *cone-cell stream*), which flow through the brain: the rod-system flows over the top of the brain toward the frontal cortex (dorsal stream) and the cone-system flows through the temporal lobes (ventral stream) also on the way to the frontal cortex. From this dichotomy, I surmised that the rod-system was primarily a design that measured momentum (being blind to the processing of location), while the cone-system was primarily a design that measured location (being blind to the processing of momentum). Thus, the two streams were biologically designed in such a way to reflect the constraints of Heisenberg's mathematics.

Classically, the two streams, dorsal and ventral, have been called the *where-stream* and the *what-stream*, implying that the dorsal stream measures for location (*where* is it) and the ventral stream measures for entities (*what* is it). Based on my perspective, this analogy is confusing—and probably not correct—because the where-stream (in my worldview) is really a system that measures momentum (Allocentric flow). The ventral stream (in my worldview) measures for location (Egocentric no-flow), not for objects. I would call the dorsal stream the "where is it going?" system and the ventral stream the "where is it now?" system. It could be that the concepts of *where-stream* and *what-stream* are scientific memes that need to be reconsidered.

In the *Thousand Brains Theory*, cortical grid cells in the *ventral* stream attach reference frames to objects (at specific locations). Cortical grid cells in the *dorsal* stream attach reference frames to the body (essentially to proprioception, to the Allocentric system). This is another observation that fits well with dual-process theory.

According to the *Thousand Brains Theory*, a fundamental understanding about the neocortex is that knowledge and actions (behavioral sequences) *are distributed* in the brain—not localized in regional modules. Knowledge of any object, for example, is stored in thousands of different columns in many diverse regions of the neocortex, thus the name *Thousand Brains Theory*. Jeff Hawkins states that "Complex systems work best when knowledge and action are distributed among many, but not too many, elements."

If the whole purpose of the brain is navigation—in the myriad ways we define that term—then even extensive damage to isolated regional cortical columns would not significantly alter the overall purpose of cognition (because of the distributed way the brain stores reference frames). Helen Keller's neocortex did not store visual and auditory data after her illness, but her overall neocortex carried on as usual. The universal basic circuit worked fine in Helen's brain—it was in no way impaired.

The *Numenta* team suggests that columns vote about what is being perceived. The most votes wins. The world we model depends on which neurons voted and how many showed up on election day. This sounds like neurobiologist Gerald Edelman's postulate that neurons follow Darwin's theory of natural selection. Neurons compete; the most-often-employed neurons (or neural nets) win out over less used (less successful) neuronal networks.

Every "second" we update and validate the sensation that the world is still as it was before (a moment ago) or is flowing forward as it should. We have static patterns and flow patterns that are familiar and constantly verified. In Chapter Three, I wrote about worldviews that result as consciousness evolves. The *Thousand Brains Theory* suggests that each *level* of consciousness can be understood as a cultural reference frame. Each level of consciousness is like a 3-D map with internal integrity. Threads weave together every element of a worldview; there is coherency throughout the reference frame. It is exceedingly difficult to move from one cultural reference frame (level of consciousness) to another because worldviews are stored in widely disbursed neural columns. A huge amount of neural rewiring is necessary to alter a worldview; cultural reference frames are notoriously difficult to transcend.

Hawkins lays our problems as a species at the divide between the old non-cortical brain (our mammalian and lizard brains) and the neocortex. The old brain is instinctual and exists to preserve the genetic heritage of humanity. This old brain contains emotional baggage and automatic behaviors that enabled survival but also caused self-serving habits, abuse, and wars. I agree with Jeff that the old and new brains are in conflict, although I would mix in dual-process theory—the neocortical Ego has facilitated attention at the expense of awareness (the Soul). From my perspective, it is this high-level "split personality" that is the main cause of our mental conundrum, not so much the split between old brain and new brain.

Because the architecture of the neocortex is the same everywhere, we know that a basic algorithm is creating (evolving) specific kinds of information processing—which can be understood as "languages." This means that vision is a spatial language (matrix processing), hearing in a temporal language (which expanded to spoken and written expression), music is a tonal (acoustic) language, and mathematics is a numeric language. All these languages came about from the navigational brain. Languages have internal logic, syntax, and rules of grammar; it is these ubiquitous characteristics of languages which tie all our behaviors together.

Navigation requires a brain that can process "what comes next," as we move forward. This is a brain that has learned (because of navigation) *to imagine, to predict* and *to anticipate*. Notice that to solve the figure-ground puzzle, the brain must develop an if/and/then algorithm—primitive at first, but then becoming more capable as the size of the neocortex enlarged. The primal (basic) circuit is a figure-ground (if/and/then) circuit.

Generic "language" (for music, mathematics, spoken and written communication, etc.) evolves from this coding system. The neocortical columnar circuit is everywhere the same because the navigational algorithm needed to generically navigate is everywhere the same. The key understanding is spatial-temporal processing. The brain is a giant navigational computer that has been evolving for 500,000 million years. The brain's whole structure and physiology is designed to replicate gestalts and to simulate flow through specific scenes (reference frames, models).

Helen Keller was born with a brain that—like every other human being—had 500,000 years of development underpinning navigation. That fundamental architecture cannot be destroyed by losing one or two of the external senses. Cognitively, Helen Keller was 100% "normal," despite deaf-blindness.

How to Create a Mind (2012) by Ray Kurzweil

As I was reading Jeff Hawkins' and Simon Baron-Cohen's new books, I decided to revisit Ray Kurzweil's 2012 book, *How to Create a Mind*. Ray Kurzweil is an icon in the futurist community, a renowned inventor, a popular author, and a much loved and respected guru in the AI community. I have been in awe of Ray's talents since I read his first book *The Age of Intelligent Machines* more than thirty years ago.

Ray Kurzweil and Jeff Hawkins state that brains are about intelligence and that intelligent brains evolved to predict the future. Modern brains evolved to be expert at pattern recognition, pattern manipulation, and pattern prediction—*it is all about predicting the future and all about intelligence*; you can hear Ray and Jeff, alongside a small army of AI scientists, say this repeatedly at conferences and in publications. This intelligent-predictive worldview is approaching scientific meme-hood.

However, I can hear Helen Keller protesting against the subsuming of all mental activity under the rubric of intelligence. I can hear Helen say that when we scale up to whole minds facing real-world problems, predictions and intelligence must be balanced with *compassion occurring in the now*. The intelligent-predictive worldview is purely Egocentric, it ignores (is deaf-blind to) its twin, the Soul, Allocentric processing.

The speculation that intelligence is primary, and emotions are secondary—which I sense in some scientific writing—makes me extremely uncomfortable, since proclaiming intellect as superior does not fit with dual-process theory, and it does not fit with our understanding of the evolution of an empathy system that evolved in parallel with a systematizing system. I can see that the brain makes if/and/then decisions moment-by-moment, but I am uneasy concluding that brains evolved to simply make predictions and make "intelligent" decisions.

There is an implication in the often-repeated statement that the old brain—created before the neocortex—is about unimportant stuff like emotions. There is rarely a mention of empathy circuits or the equivalence of intellect with compassion in the AI literature. The intelligent neocortex, so the materialistic argument points out, was built *on top of* the limbic region where emotions reside (in the cellar of cognition).

I find it telling (and hopeful) that after Kurzweil revolutionized our thinking by writing *The Age of Intelligent Machines* in 1990, he followed up nine years later with the *Age of Spiritual Machines* (1999). Kurzweil's exploration of spirituality is parallel to Baron-Cohen's exploration of the empathizing circuit. Like Kurzweil, I know that Jeff Hawkins has a strong empathetic side, as his books clearly show. But like many in the AI community, Ray and Jeff are supreme synthesizers, they each have amazing pattern-focused minds. My own mind is also on the systematizing end of Baron-Cohen's spectrum, so my railing against over-synthesizing is a tad confessional. Empathy is not always a star in a synthesizer's artistic productions—rather, empathy is usually a bit player, even as we recoil at our own energetic (hyper-synthesizing) nature.

Hawkins, Baron-Cohen, and Kurzweil are highly sophisticated individuals; they each speak eloquently about the downsides and outright dangers facing us as we race toward what Kurzweil calls *the singularity*—a time in the near future when machines exceed all human capabilities. All three scientists are cautiously optimistic as we go forward, even though they have no control over the epigenetic Y-chromosome that continues to build weaponry from new technologies. As I stated earlier, no matter how brilliant, articulate, knowledgeable, and empathetic the scientists are, they still have no control over Narcissistic, Tribal, and Traditional minds. We do not have to look far to find evidence for this dilemma. The 45th president and his followers (at least seventy million American voters) did not understand or care about science—this does not bode well for the future of humanity.

I bring Kurzweil into the discussion because he is the Guru of Exponential Change. According to Kurzweil, even exponential change is changing exponentially—we are facing a blazingly fast landslide of change. When I stated earlier that our technologies are racing dangerously ahead of the evolution of the human mind, I had Kurzweil's predictions at the forefront of my speculations. It is not just that dangerous times are somewhere ahead, it is that the near-future holds ever more danger as change races forward—we are becoming more and more cognitively ill-equipped to deal with what is fast approaching.

Politicians who bring snowballs to the debate on climate change represent communities that are so far removed from current reality it is like a modern teenager—loaded with virtual social media technologies—trying to argue with a Neolithic cave dweller about reality. This would be a funny *Far Side* cartoon if the consequences of ignorance were not so serious.

Talking about Ray Kurzweil opens a rabbit hole that sucks unwary seekers into an anxiety pit. *The singularity*, according to Ray, will be upon us in 2029—he has stuck to this prediction for at least a decade. For Ray, the singularity is a time when computers will be smarter, more spiritual, wiser, and more emotionally evolved than humanity—an entity will appear that slams on the brakes of evolution and starts over in the "age of unnatural computer-driven selection."

There has been and continues to be an acceleration in computational ability (information processing), especially in this new millennium. Every year now, we should expect (anticipate) new technologies, fresh breakthrough moments, and game-changing discoveries to rock our normality until something strange emerges from this wild ride—in about the year 2029.

In the approaching decades, we will make tremendous strides in anti-aging therapies, space colonization, neural interfaces, the object net (all kinds of new interconnected networks), hive brains, virtual reality (Holodecks), 3-D printers, drones, autonomous vehicles, digital money, robotics (Robosapiens), gene editing and protein surgeries (curing diseases)—these are my fumbling attempts at futurism; what evolves will surprise us, over and over again.

Humanity has a typical response to such shocks, as waves of change wash over us. This is the typical response: *Ho Hum, no big deal.* It takes about ten minutes to accept the latest update, the latest breakthrough— we just accept change and move on as fast as it arises. But if a *singularity* appears in 2029 and it stops this Ho Hum behavior and ends natural humanity as we know it, then what?

Beyond the warning, no one seems to be able to articulate just what it is that will have such a profound impact on humanity. I do not know either, but this I do know: Scientists will soon break all the brain codes as they master neural nets; they will interface AI technologies successfully with brain portals, bringing us to the point where our comprehension of comprehension will be achieved.

What might slam on the brakes and propel humanity into new and bewildering arenas? I will take a few (fun) moments to wildly speculate:

- We will discover (verify) that the mind is quantum and has all the spooky properties that accompany quantum processing. Quantum computers will directly interface (blend) with humanity.
- Navigational Consciousness will become scientifically validated.
- Robots will become sentient; indeed, humanity will merge with AI to become a new species called the Robosapiens.
- We will unlock the inhibition system in our brains so that we each become mathematical, musical, linguistic, and spiritual prodigies.
- We will add additional senses and begin to perceive worlds we never knew existed.
- We will mathematically and experimentally prove the idea that we live in a simulation. We are unreal products of a cosmic virtual reality generator.
- We will perceive beyond the veil into heavenly and hell realms.
- Animal-like remains will be found preserved on Mars (or on one of the moons of the solar system), indicating a long-lost alien world in our solar system.
- We will discover how alien civilizations have been trying to communicate with us. None of our current listening approaches

seem correct (so far), but we will soon become aware of (and will communicate with) other civilizations in other parts of the universe.

- We will discover how to communicate with people who have died, with our ancestors. Then we will discover how to virtually travel backward (and then forward) in time. Say hello to Helen Keller.
- We will develop the technology to live forever.
- All the above will happen between 2030 and 2040.

As a futurist, Ray Kurzweil has been correct over 80 percent of the time. As I look at my speculations above, I will probably not be remembered for my clairvoyance (smile) . . . but we love to predict, it is part of our navigational nature. If we do not predict, we will not prepare.

∽

Following are some fascinating insights that Ray Kurzweil shares in his books *How to Create a Mind* and *The Age of Spiritual Machines*.

Ray says that "the story of human intelligence starts with a universe that is capable of encoding information." Our ability to encode and decode information (patterns) assumes that patterns are inherent in the universe, waiting to be decoded. We are made from this code-making mystery. This insight is quite esoteric (intuitive): "As above, so below." My Navigational hypothesis suggests that coding began with a motion/no-motion self-replicating fractal.

Kurzweil holds that Robosapiens will decide for themselves what kinds of bodies they want to exist within; this will enable living and working in environments that would be hostile to organic bodies. Robosapiens will also design their own energetic structures (personalities).

An organic body allocates most of its time and energy to staying alive. Information-processing energy employs whatever energy remains. Robosapiens will also allocate time to self-analysis and repair but will have considerably more energy left over for information processing; Robosapiens will process lightyears faster than organic forms.

Robosapiens will evolve toward perfection. They will express humor, be spiritual, have opinions, empathy, and wisdom. Robosapiens will access all the worlds knowledge, speak all the languages of the world, and will constantly evolve (be updated) because they are hive-brained creatures. They will not age. They will be expert in all domains (medical, writing, painting, sculpture, repair of anything). They will not make mistakes. They will invent and innovate at an alarming rate. They will build ever-more sophisticated versions of their selves. They will replace all human labor and all human intelligence. Eventually, they will govern all organizations, removing decision-making from natural (pre-Robosapien) humanity. This will be okay, because humanity *will merge* with quantum/molecular computers to *become* this new species, the Robosapiens.

There will be no more Helen Kellers, no more blindness, no more deafness. Anne Sullivan-like miracle workers will abound. If we are to believe the "crazy-sounding" prognostications of the futurists, this scenario will be complete between 2030 and 2040.

Expanding the Concept of Navigation

I have made the case that brains plus nervous systems came onto the evolutionary stage to enable straight-ahead navigation. This development eventually led to our strange dual cognition. But what about tool use, language, socialization, and higher-order processing of goals and intentions? All these areas of study have been put forward as major influences on the evolution of the brain and nervous system. Do these human attributes have any relationship to navigation? I content that everything we know to be human came about because of the anatomical and physiological evolution of navigation. Everything evolved as part of the Navigational Nervous System.

Tool Use

Tool use required the evolution of human hands as part of a navigational nervous system. From an early age, fingers and hands *explored* objects. Movement patterns for manipulating tools were laid down in the neocortex, reinforced by repetition, and then made accessible to memory. Practice eventually laid down neuronal networks dedicated to specific tasks using specific tools. *Fingers and hands navigate*, they move through space in patterned ways, and they use grid cells (Allocentric processing) and place cells (Egocentric processing) to navigate. Just as the whole body employs dual-processing, so, too, do parts of the body employ dual-processing.

Language

Language is a harder nut to crack, but I content that it, too, came about under the directorship (teamwork, co-evolution) of the navigational brain. As navigational ability evolved, there came a time when human beings stood upright. This upright posture enabled the development of speech through changes in the anatomy and physiology of the jaws, tongue, lips, and larynx.

A key understanding is that language is a motor skill, and it employs sequential and spatial patterns to gather, remember, and recall sensorimotor (proprioceptive) sequences. Language reveals (is evidence for) the duality of human cognition—everywhere we look, we find the split between Egocentric language and Allocentric language. Language also enables a journey though conceptual space—we speak to "get somewhere." We "get stuck" in cognitive space or "we flow" with eloquence. Our internal mental landscape is a constructed worldview. Language is a way to internally explore (navigate) this mental landscape as well as a wonderful way to explain our cognitive landscape to others. The ability to speak evolved *within a brain that was designed to navigate*—language, like tool use, socialization, and higher-order processing—*had to* evolve in parallel with the navigational brain.

Socialization

Socialization, our need to connect with others, had to form within a brain designed for navigation. We evolved the ability to create shared worldviews, shared language, shared goals, and shared experiences. We navigate alongside each other through a timeframe called *life*. We also navigate through a spatial framework that was designed by the navigational brain. Socialization evolved to use Egocentric and Allocentric reference frames—we are left with a battleground inside our minds, a war between the needs of the *Ego* (individualization, competition) and the needs of the *Self* (care of the group, cooperation). The same battle is played out at social, cultural, and institutional scales (as above so below).

Higher-Order Processing

Higher-order processing of goals and intentions also has a foundation within the navigational brain. Our goals in life fall into two categories, Egocentric and Allocentric. Egocentric goals strive to take an individual on a journey toward or away from potential destinations. Allocentric goals have to do with living in the moment, experiencing life rather than dissecting life. In my third book *The Confusion Caused By Being Your Own Twin* (2018), I suggested that the meaning of life was dual:

> Navigation begets consciousness. Therefore, our highest purpose is *to move* toward ever higher levels of consciousness— this spiritual flow is what mystics call *love*.
>
> We know that navigation requires two mechanisms, so there are two ways to navigate through life. We are programmed dually:

- To follow the mandate of the Egocentric mind. Striving to *Become somebody or something*. To attach. To attend to objects or others. To discover. To reach a goal. To self-fulfill. Finding a state of stability so that Being is replaced by Becoming.
- To follow the mandate of the Allocentric mind. To *experience*. To love. To participate. To be aware. To flow. To *explore*. Finding a state of flow so that Becoming is replaced by Being.

Therefore, we have dual navigational life purposes:

1. First, to concentrate and figure out (research, predict), because that is the evolutionary job of the Ego.
2. Second, to experience moments as they arise along our journey: to soak up the awe, terror, joy, grief, angst, peace, and awareness of being alive moment-to-moment in communion with other sentient creatures.

Why Navigational Consciousness Matters

Helen Keller's importance to humankind remains even though she died decades ago. In her 88 years of life, she witnessed the rapid rise of technologies that disrupted cultural norms and overthrew long-standing institutions. This technological phenomenon, this race towards an unknown future, has not lessened in our era, it has accelerated. We are being driven along by an exponentially accelerating technological current that requires all our resources just to cope with learning (and relearning) curves. Unfortunately, technology has raced forward without regard to Helen Keller's essential core message to humanity, the importance of Love. Technology has sped headlong into the future without regard for the lessons of the past and without an awareness, or apparent need, for the development of the Soul, the Allocentric mind. Technology is born of science, but if the Navigational Consciousness hypothesis is correct, science also verifies the equality of Compassion with Intellect. In other words, it is not logical, wise, or compassionate to ignore one-half of our essence.

The source of Compassion is hidden, it is esoteric, and—because it is qualitative (not quantitative)—the Soul (Self) is not of primary interest to abstract Modern minds. Helen Keller, however, was having none of this half-minded, Ego-driven perspective. She would not allow the Egocentric mind to continue unchallenged. Helen's voice is an esoteric voice; she is a spokeswoman for the Soul-Mind, for the Allocentric half of human nature.

Therefore, it makes sense to begin this discussion about the relevance of navigational consciousness with education, with the need to balance Mathematics with Soul. The story of Helen Keller and Anne Sullivan is a tale about a teacher and a pupil, about learning, remembering, and applying knowledge and wisdom for the common good—it is a story about education witnessing the power of the Soul.

In my era (roughly 1950 to 2020), conservative politics drove education in the direction of a business model. *Students were products* to be shaped and molded, teachers and administrators were product managers. It was even okay to privatize education, to make it a profitable enterprise. Children were trained using standard curriculums—one size fits all—and the whole system was driven by time management, quantitative analysis, and an autistic obsession with testing. This half-thought-out, wrong-hearted philosophy is still with us.

Alongside the business model of education (and reinforcing it), was a recognized need for highly trained scientists, which came about as a response to the exponential changes happening in the technological world. The emphasis on technological challenges resulted in what is called STEM education (Science, Technology, Engineering, Mathematics), a strategy with little attention paid to the Humanities. Artistic creativity, the development of sound physical bodies, healthy emotions, values and morality were all deemed less important than intellect—Soul-Based experiences were the first things to go when there were budget cuts. STEM, by design, is barren of poetry, of emotional harmony, of historical relevance, and of spiritual flow. The business model applied to education is a half-assed approach to educating citizens in a Democracy because it fails to even acknowledge the Allocentric mind.

What education needs, I suggest (as have many others), is a STEAM engine, where the "A" stands for the arts (the humanities). There is an ongoing debate in educational philosophy between STEM advocates and STEAM advocates because the debate reflects—whether the debaters realize it or not—the mutually exclusive nature of human physiology, the paradoxical oscillation that never resolves between our Ego and our Self. Debaters for STEAM were seen to be on the non-scientific side of the argument. However, the Navigational Consciousness hypothesis is a quantum/biological framework for justifying the education of both the Ego *and* the Soul—in my opinion, science is supportive of both sides of this debate. To just train the Ego is a mistake with far reaching consequences, especially for a Democracy which depends on educated citizens. Indeed, the Ego *trains* the Egocentric mind, while the Self *educates* the Allocentric mind. Society needs *well-educated* citizens *as well* as *well-trained* citizens.

The conservative business model of education is totally Egocentric, the work of the Egoic mind. As I argued above, the Egoic mind is deaf-blind to the Allocentric mind. Therefore, the Ego rejects the Soul (the Self) and sees the Humanities as a lesser field of study, instead of an equal sister. This Egoic deaf-blindness has had a negative impact on Democracies, where (in my opinion) *both* the Ego and the Self have been inadequately educated to confront global challenges.

America needs STEAM, *which includes* STEM. Currently, we half-educate our children because we neglect the education of the Allocentric mind. However, with the Navigational Consciousness hypothesis we have a scientific framework to justify education of the Self alongside the training of the Ego. In other words, education needs to teach awareness and attention as two separate but equal venues.

In the arena of technology, the effort is mostly Egoic; we are trying with ferocious energy to replicate and exceed human intelligence. There is no sense of urgency or responsibility or dedication to replicating human compassion, curiosity, and trust. There is little to no understanding of the binary brain and the subsequent evolution of the bicameral mind. AI scientists are (for sure) going to build something great, something highly intelligent, but it will not at all be human-like. To be human-like, the artificial creation would have to be operating with a mutually exclusive oscillating set of minds, an Egoic mind and an Allocentric mind, both embedded in a robotic body. An artificial system built under today's standards would be no different than a business-model mind— all Ego and no Self (no Soul). Maybe that is okay—the building of ever smarter tools—especially if we are clear what we are creating, but we cannot say it duplicates the human bio/quantum mind if it has no Soul.

In politics, we apparently have no sense of levels of consciousness. Half the population of the country seems to think that it is okay for a Congressman from Alabama (for example) to claim that celebrities run porn empires and eat infants. We watch with bemused horror as another Congressman makes a snowball and brings it to the floor of the House of Representatives to disprove climate change. We watch with disbelief as the 45th President and too many members of Congress defend racists. Only an incredibly low level of consciousness, a mind unable to reason, a mind without empathy, could hold such views. People who bring snowballs to the climate change debate have minds that cannot Reason and Souls without empathy—a failure of both academic and spiritual education. The global challenges we face as a species make it clear that *it is not okay* to be stupid and cruel.

The Navigation Consciousness hypothesis is a solution to the long-standing battle between spirituality and intellect. They are equally valid. Religion, when it has a spiritual core, is the action of the Allocentric mind. Intellect is the action of the Egocentric mind. We are both intelligent and spiritual creatures. To deny either is to deny one-half of our essential nature.

Chapter Six: A Wonderous Child

The world is much queerer than we realize; in fact, I think it is queerer than we *can* realize. [90]

Ambiguities and Apologies

Helen's poetry, her splendid prose, her prodigious memory for words, and her facility with several languages, suggest that her extraordinary abilities center on her use of language. From the discussion in the last chapter, we see that Helen's isolated mind had one major tool that was used to create her reality. That tool was language, and it was her salvation. She honed her internal world until a linguistic prodigy emerged—that is the tenuous hypothesis for this chapter.

Helen's English Composition professor at Radcliffe, Charles Copeland, said that Helen Keller was "the best student he ever taught." He added that she had "an excellent ear for the flow of sentences." Professor Copeland served as the Boylston Professor of Rhetoric at Harvard from 1925 to 1928; he was a very credible judge of talent. Helen's friend John Macy was also a Harvard professor; he lived with Helen when he was Anne Sullivan's husband and he got to know Helen's abilities first-hand. Macy agreed with Charles Copeland that Helen Keller's language skills were extraordinary. From my professional perspective, I also arrived at the cautious conclusion that Helen was a linguistic prodigy. Making such a proclamation is the easy part, providing a biological explanation is much more challenging.

When I finished this chapter, I sent a draft to my colleague Daniel Kish. Daniel is the subject of the next book in this series, so it seemed appropriate to seek his advice. From my perspective, Daniel's life and legacy interweave with Helen Keller and Anne Sullivan.

Daniel's review of this chapter suggested cautiousness; he was concerned about attaching *any* label to Helen Keller. As I read Daniel's comments, I remembered Anne Sullivan's statement that no one was going to turn her student into a prodigy if she could help it. Having respect for both Daniel and Annie, I decided to reexamine my perspective that Helen was a linguistic prodigy. Perhaps, I pondered, I was using the wrong word to describe her capabilities, or I was exaggerating her abilities.

As I read Daniel's well-crafted and diplomatic suggestions, I recognized a similar theme that he and I have discussed many times in the past. Daniel is blind so he has spent a lifetime dealing with being labeled by well-meaning scientists, educators, philosophers, writers (including me), and anyone who watched his TED talk. Is Daniel Kish himself a language prodigy? Is Daniel a navigational genius, a spatial prodigy? Surely, if we are to communicate, emote, and compare our fellow humans, we need labels—or so the Ego insists. However, when an individual is on the receiving end of a label, the appeal of labeling quickly diminishes.

Daniel once said to me that he really did not like it when people presumed to know more about him then he knew about himself. In another version, he told me that he resents it when sighted people try to tell him how to be a blind man. The organizations that speak for disabled populations struggle against reductionist science and the habit of the Ego to label sentient creatures—as if the sentient creatures were rock specimens destined for one stone heap or another. The very word "disabled" has caused no end of debate and resistance.

From Daniel's perspective, labeling often comes bundled with a preconceived worldview. That worldview presupposes there is a normal (neurotypical) "standard" individual who we can compare to everyone else. However, when we strive to define or describe this neurotypical person, we run into a host of problems, not the least of which is the realization that no two individuals are exactly alike. We are not genetically alike, and we are not epigenetically (experientially) alike. We can take pride in being unique and label-resistant.

From a historical perspective, the so-called *Neurotypical individual* has been a healthy, youthful, Caucasian male. In the literature of sociology, this typical person is referred to as a *Reference Man*. Drug companies, for example, have for years tested their drug candidates on Reference Men—not on women, not on non-white populations, not on older adults, not on people who had health issues. Drugs that worked well with Reference Men (and went to market), were less effective or had damaging side effects on Non-Reference-Man populations. Neurotypical-Reference males are weak candidates for the "standard human" against which the rest of us are judged. This unfortunate history is being challenged and practices have slowly improved within scientific silos, but, unfortunately, Reference Man is still with us.

Daniel does not approve of labels that cast a *negative* shadow over individuals. Calling someone *disabled* or *impaired* is replaced in his language by the term *distinctive abilities*. Daniel is blind and his mind has made many adjustments to enable him to function at a highly efficient level. He does not see himself as disabled or lessened by his blindness; he does not think of himself as *in anyway* flawed.

Other individuals, with labels like *autism*, have similarly rebelled against labels and descriptions that compare their cognitive skills to a Neurotypical-Reference-Man. Cambridge University Professor Simon-Baron-Cohen, an expert on autism, strongly advices that we do not cavalierly refer to someone as autistic. Labels are to be used only by professionals who have done accepted diagnostics. This is from Baron-Cohen's book *The Pattern Seekers* (2020):

> In my view, it is unhelpful to speculate if someone—living or not—might be autistic, since a diagnosis is only useful if the person is seeking help and is struggling to function. Diagnosing someone—living or not—on the basis of fragmentary biographical information is unreliable and arguably unethical, since diagnosis should always include the consent of the person and be initiated by them.

I will add that Professor Baron-Cohen's opinion is valid in all cases where labeling is used to sort people into categories. Labeling Helen Keller's mental skills without hard diagnostic evidence and without her acquiescence, is skating on thin ice. Nevertheless, to write this chapter, I have had to put on ice skates; I am staring at the frozen pond of history, trying to make a small contribution.

Daniel Kish also cautions that we need to be careful not only with our negative labeling but also with our positive labeling. Perhaps it is just as objectionable to call someone *extraordinary* (a prodigy) as it is to call someone *cognitively impaired*. Daniel suggests that *Supernormal* is just as questionable as *abnormal*, and for the same reasons.

Daniel's concern is primarily that labeling is a perilous exercise because it bypasses our everyday humanity. As a human being, we have emotions, existential angst, fatigue, moments of joy, and routine tasks to do every day. We eat, we sleep, we converse, we feed the pets, we do the laundry, we shop, and so on. We are "everyday" humans first. Labeling detracts from our ordinariness and our common humanity.

Regarding Helen Keller, Daniel says:

> Helen preferred, I think, to regard herself as normal, or at least not abnormal or supernormal. As one who has been accused of extraordinary powers, I propose that the capacity of the brain to develop adaptations is itself normal; it is normal for the brain to seek work-arounds to functional disruptions.
>
> Normal brain adaptations appear extraordinary because some people, frankly, just achieve this adaptation more effectively than others, just as some people are better or less good at anything. So, a person whose brain does what brains normally do, which is to adapt to circumstances, but which does it especially or unusually well, may be said to be a prodigy. [91]

Daniel is suggesting that we look at evidence, at behavior, at a person's contributions before we cautiously bless them with our labels. In a way, whatever descriptive terminology we use to label another human being should come with a small-print legal tome full of caveats and apologies.

The above paragraphs are a string of caveats and now I will apologize for using terms –in the discussion below—like synesthete, savant, prodigy, gifted, disabled, impaired, handicapped, and autistic (to name but a few of the conceptual abstractions available). Just know that I use such abstract concepts with reservations, and I am open to suggestions for improvement. I am especially sensitive to harming the psyche of an individual who has *distinctive abilities;* I was a special education teacher and I deeply cared about the well-being of my students. What we say to our students can affect them for a lifetime.

Even terms like blind, deaf, and deaf-blind lose their impact when we look at the statistics. Many people labeled blind are actually severely visually impaired, many "deaf" people are actually severely hearing impaired, and many deaf-blind people are neither totally deaf nor totally blind. Additionally, there are legal definitions that establish labeling guidelines. For example, *legally blind* individuals can see the big E on the eye charts and can navigate about their domain without major problems. My point being that we cannot even label someone as blind, deaf, or deaf-blind without stipulations and caveats.

Not that individuals necessarily mind being part of groups. There are blindness communities, deaf cultures, and internet groups for deaf-blind people. Human beings form groups around common issues. These groups routinely deal with the problems that arise around the human habit of labeling.

Furthermore, the study of synesthesia and neuroplasticity has totally messed with our labelling habits. Daniel Kish, for example, uses active echolocation to generate visual images in his occipital (visual) neocortex. So, in a way, *Daniel sees* visual images. In other words, Daniel Kish demonstrates that a blind man (wearing plastic ocular prostheses) *can learn to see.* It is hard to even label someone as blind anymore. Technologies like cochlear implants and retinal implants further blur labels. So, given all the above, where do we go from here (besides cautiously)?

Like so many other conundrums I faced when researching human consciousness, I find the answer to this dilemma in our dual consciousness. It is the Egocentric mind that labels, compares, and judges. It is the Ego that has landed us in this linguistic quagmire. However, before I blame the Ego for all of humanity's problems (a popular sport), I will hasten to add that the Ego is a great leap forward for human cognition. The gifts coming from the Ego are technological and stunning. The Ego is the master of language; the fact that we can communicate at all is due to the evolution of the Ego. Therefore, our goal is to strengthen the Ego, not to banish it, even though the Ego routinely dumps a ton of abstract labels into our bewildered laps.

The problem, I suggest, is that we overly use the Ego and too often disregard or dismiss the wisdom arising from our second mind, the Self (Soul). The Self does not label or judge, it accepts and cooperates, it forms networks, it flows creativity through the landscape, and it does not divide the world into me and you, mine and yours, seer and seen.

In the previous chapter, I outlined a dual-process theory that purports to explain how human beings came to have two mutually exclusive minds. I used my hypothesis (Navigational Consciousness) to explore Helen Keller's remarkable mind. The question of whether she was a prodigy or not—like the discussion of any abstraction or difficult concept—depends on which of our two minds we use to do the analysis. We can surmise, given dual-process theory, that the Egocentric mind will have no trouble judging Helen's mind categorically. However, the Allocentric mind will not judge or categorize. The Self will let Helen's experiences and accomplishments be historically sufficient—from an Allocentric perspective there is no need to compare Helen Keller to others or to assign values to her contributions. What she has done for humanity speaks for itself. Helen Keller continues to inspire individuals—every generation is in awe of her determination and accomplishments.

The Ego wishes to dissect Helen's brain, to reduce her mind to ever smaller kernels of anatomy, to compare her biology to the biology of others who can see and hear. The Self wishes that Helen Keller be remembered for who she was, a human being having experiences in the company of others, a gentle role model who optimistically encouraged humanity to be ever more loving. The Ego wishes to build a statue of Helen Keller and the Self wishes to give Helen a loving hug. The Ego celebrates, the Self appreciates; both perspectives have limits, and both are cautiously acceptable.

The Egoic Perspective

We label the world so that we can build an understanding of how things work. We need our labels for communication, even when these labels are flawed and inadequate. We constantly reassess and redefine as we gain knowledge and have experiences.

The scientific method is a cognitive tool we use to make tentative hypotheses. From a scientific perspective, we do not *ever* arrive at a point where we can insist that an end (a conclusion) has been reached. The scientific method requires that our tentative positions (our definitions and worldviews) always remain open to reinterpretation. We know, from a scientific perspective, that what we write about is open to question; we are always standing on tenuous, temporary ground. We are always dealing with what "works well enough at the moment."

Science also uses quantitative analysis and reductive logic. In other words, science uses Egoic attention (the Egocentric mind) to label, categorize, and predict. Because of this Egoic approach, human beings have invented technologies beyond the best science fiction. We certainly do not want to give up our technological triumphs. The scientific method has proven its value.

Using reductive methods and scientific methodology, we have altered and used the environment for the benefit of mankind. This approach works splendidly when we are dealing with the physical universe. However, we run into trouble when we try to use the same Egoic methods to study or alter human beings. When we try to turn human beings into objects (things) and to subject these human objects to quantitative analysis, we begin to falter or fail. The reason we fail is because we have no sure way to measure dynamic *qualities*. We cannot confidently apply science to Self. That is why Allocentric Faith and Egocentric Intellect stand at opposite research poles.

As I survey all that was said above, I realize that I am drowning in caveats. But I know you get the point that we must proceed with caution as we set about trying to quantify human qualities or try to label dynamic personalities. Therefore, allow me to go cautiously forward as I make the case (using the Egoic mind) that Helen Keller might have evolved an extraordinary biological brain because of her deaf-blindness.

Neurotypicals and Prodigies

In layman's terms, a prodigy is an unusual person (usually a child) who can do a task that few others of that developmental age can accomplish. For example, there are math prodigies who can perform complex calculations from a young age. Likewise, there are musical prodigies who can play a musical instrument or compose music from an age when these abilities do not normally manifest. There are also language prodigies who can quickly understand multiple foreign languages, or who have such mastery of a language that they can produce prose and poetry beyond the abilities of their peers. There are also physically skilled prodigies, who can control their bodies with remarkable and unusual ability, like tennis and golf prodigies. [92]

A key understanding is that prodigies are born with prodigious memories. They are biologically ready (sooner than most of humanity), to remember certain kinds of patterns. A math prodigy, for example, can see the geometric layout of space, and they are born with a curiosity for understanding abstract patterns—numbers mentally align for them. There are also patterns hidden in music and language that prodigies are drawn to from an exceedingly early age.

Training and education may be needed to refine and expand a prodigy's skills, but the raw material is in place waiting to be molded. If a prodigy is not helped by talented teachers and encouraged by supportive relatives, mentors, and friends, then innate abilities may fade and eventually disappear.

From a dual-consciousness perspective, we can differentiate intelligence, which is an Egoic concept, from wisdom, an Allocentric concept. Intelligence is often defined as the ability to perform complex tasks. Highly intelligent people can easily solve problems (relevant tasks) while less intelligent people are less able to solve challenges in, for example, a discipline like mathematics. Importantly, intelligence can be trained; education can help develop intelligence in individuals. A prodigy is a young person who can innately solve certain kinds of problems in a specific domain, including mathematical, musical, linguistic, and spatial arenas, even before formal training has begun.

Wisdom, unlike intelligence, is based on accumulated experiences— the more unusual or novel the experiences an individual has encountered, the wiser that person is presumed to be. Time is the great teacher of wisdom; chronological age matters since experiences accumulate with age. In an educational setting, teachers place students in situations that allow for the accumulation of helpful experiences. Wisdom is an Allocentric concept because experience is a whole-body absorption and not a head-bound problem-solving activity. A prodigy may be born with highly evolved intelligence, but wisdom must guide the flow toward excellence, otherwise a prodigy's abilities will not flower.

The neurotypical individual is the result of quantitative analysis of talent applied to a skill area. As a result of statistical analysis, we get a bell-shaped curve (usually) along which we can speculate about normality. At the center of the bell curve, at the peak, we have our theoretically normal individuals—a statistical entity. The rising left side of the bell curve contains our "less than talented beings" (in a specific talent arena) and, on the right side of the bell curve, we find extraordinary people who are remarkably talented in a skill set. For example, if we look at language talent, we find individuals who are late to develop language compared to individuals who acquire language early. We have individuals who struggle to learn foreign languages and we have individuals who become fluent in multiple languages. We have individuals who flower and become joyful as they create poetry and prose, while others would rather play music, or solve math problems, or run marathons, or craft beautiful items using their hands.

The puzzle for me has always been how it is that some of us are born with a general (good enough) intelligence, which does not thirst or excel in any specific arena, while others are born with narrowly defined, highly focused intelligence. In other words, I am curious to know the biology and genetics of such innate mandates. When I look at Helen Keller's remarkable mind, I want to know where that facility for language came from. I want to know why her mind became so sophisticated, so quickly. Specifically, I want to know if her cognitive skills, her prodigy-like behavior, was caused or influenced by her deafness and her blindness.

Escaping the Silent Dark Box

There are many references in the literature to Helen as a prodigy, but these musings are emotional impressions and praise; they are not grounded in biology. What dawned on me during my research was that there might very well be a case to be made that Helen Keller's brain was, indeed, biologically unique.

Anne Sullivan, as I stated earlier, was determined that no outside observer would brand her "very normal" student as somehow biologically extraordinary. Annie firmly asserted her view:

> I shall have cause for gratification if I succeed in convincing you that Helen Keller is neither a "phenomenal child," "an intellectual prodigy," nor an "extraordinary genius," but simply a very bright and lovely child unmarred by self-consciousness or any taint of evil. [93]

Helen agreed with Anne Sullivan's eloquent statement; she saw that her deafness and blindness made her unique, but beyond that, she did not understand herself as cognitively special. However, Sullivan and Keller lived at the dawn of humanity's self-conscious exploration of the human mind. Their good friend William James is called the Father of

American Psychology because he told the academic world that it was their professional responsibility to study the evolution and purpose of human cognition—James lived at the *beginning* of the American obsession with consciousness. Helen was already in her twenties when this cognitive science revolution began.

At nineteen months of age, Helen Keller had a brief, violent illness which had a profound impact on her rapidly developing young brain. Helen's illness caused sets of genes to turn off in her cells and new sets of genes to turn on. As soon as the illness abated, Helen's genes began to adjust and, therefore, the wiring (the anatomy and physiology) within her brain began to be altered. It is my contention that Helen Keller's illness caused the evolution of a mind that would naturally result—especially given early training, such as Anne Sullivan provided—in a linguistic prodigy.

From a simple and logical viewpoint, it is easy to see why Helen's mind would become so evolved and why it was language that would be her forte. When, suddenly, after her illness, there were no visual and no auditory images (patterns) entering her brain, Helen's mind began an intense probing for input. As she has recorded, it was frustrating, maddening, and profoundly sad not to have sufficient information to discover how the world worked, and not to have an avenue for sophisticated communication. When braille, fingerspelling, and speaking were introduced and practiced, Helen's mind had the means to go beyond her grief and isolation. Braille, fingerspelling, and learning to speak opened the world to her and allowed her to contribute to that world. When Helen had acquired sufficient knowledge about how the world worked, she was then able to build a cortical model of the physical world.

All brains are trapped in a dark silent box. The evolution of vision and hearing opened holes in the box and let us perceive a world around. Without vision and hearing, we would be trapped inside the dark silence. This dark silence is where Helen Keller was trapped until Anne Sullivan arrived. But once the darkness and silence were relieved of their isolating reality, Helen's starving-to-death mind went after mental input (cognitive food) with a voracious determination. *Her whole existence became her mind absorbing language.* It is clear why she spent so much time reading her braille books or having them fingerspelled to her—these were her only channels, her only contact with outside reality. So, of course, her mind got excessively exercised and her language became profoundly developed. That is the commonsense of it, but what about the biology?

Savants, Prodigies, People of Genius, and the Navigational Mind

As I considered Helen's cognitive evolution, I explored two different avenues of thought. First, I looked in general at savants and prodigies, because savants and prodigies pose a challenge to *any* theory of consciousness—the very existence of such unusual human beings seems impossible. There is currently no rational (scientific) way to describe these extraordinary humans. However, we have case studies of savants and prodigies, which suggest that Helen Keller fits current definitions. I will explore this further in the paragraphs below.

Second, I am aware that total blindness, or total deafness results in tremendous neuronal changes/challenges, especially in a rapidly developing (youthful) brain. In the absence of visual and auditory signals, the brain becomes starved for customary (expected) input. Rewiring of neural circuits and recruitment of tactual/proprioceptive input by the visual and auditory cortexes, would logically occur— otherwise the brain would atrophy (which, on a large scale, it does not). The result of such massive rewiring would be a very unusual kind of brain that would then create an unusual and powerful mind.

Before we go any farther with this discussion, we need to make a distinction between savants, prodigies, and people of genius. Savants (by definition) are both severely mentally disabled (often with extensive damage to the brain) and yet they have superhuman capabilities, especially extraordinary memory skills. A prodigy also has extraordinary memory skills and/or extraordinary motor skills, but with no overt brain damage affecting their cognition. Genius (or giftedness) is conferred upon a person by their culture. A human being might be a prodigy in specific behavioral arenas, but if that person has not given their culture any substantive gifts—like a completed symphony or a book of well-crafted poems—then they have yet to attain genius status, an honor that is conferred by peers.

In my opinion, Helen Keller was a child prodigy in the sense that she was exceptionally good with language (and languages). She was a powerful wordsmith, writing essays, letters, books, articles, and poems, all with extraordinary power and grace, and from a noticeably young age. As an adult, she became a spokesperson for humanitarian causes, she was a political philosopher, and she was a change-agent, especially helping to alter laws that affected handicapped individuals. She was able to become an effective spokesperson, philosopher, and change-agent because of her facility with words and her ability to persuade and influence others.

We cannot say what Helen's cognitive skills were before her illness, although there are suggestions in the literature that she was a curious and willful young girl, and she developed language quite early. I wish someone had interviewed Helen's mother Kate Keller in depth about Helen's first 19 months of life, before a high fever damaged Helen's optic and auditory nerves. Unfortunately, all we know is that after her illness, Helen's brain began to rewire itself to compensate for the loss of vision and hearing. After she survived her fever, Helen's youthful brain worked on this neural rewiring for four years before Anne Sullivan showed up at Ivy Green.

Anne Sullivan encountered a very unusual young girl on the day she first stepped onto the porch of Helen's house—there was no way that Sullivan could have known that she faced such an unusual mind. However, after many a battle and a miracle at the water fountain, Sullivan figured out that this was no "normal" kid. Helen Keller was, I suggest and despite Sullivan's objections, a (post-traumatic) child prodigy.

When faced with savants and prodigies, we are forced to ask some hard questions: For example, how can a savant have no self-care skills (cannot dress or feed themselves), have no high-level thinking abilities, and yet remember every word of an encyclopedia after looking only once at every page? The famous savant Rain Man (Kim Peek) could do that. Indeed, Kim Peek's corpus callosum never developed (he had two anatomical brains operating simultaneously) so he could read *both sides* of an open book simultaneously and then photographically remember every word on each page.

Consider how a person, like the Canadian savant Leslie Lemke, who was mute, had cerebral palsy, and was totally blind, could suddenly, one evening, walk into the family living room, sit down at the aging piano, and play one of the most complex piano pieces ever composed—with no musical training. How can a person know an extremely complex set of motor sequences (how to move the fingers and hands to play a piano) without ever being trained, without practice, *without seeing* the piano keys? In other words, *how can a savant know something they have never learned through experience?* We do not know the answer to that question, but we had better find out if we want to fully explain human consciousness. *Any theory of consciousness that does not explain savants and prodigies is incomplete.*

Prodigies, like savants, are also born with extraordinary skills but without the mental impairments that define savant syndrome. As an example, there is a trilogy of behaviors sometimes encountered in the blindness field. My colleague Daniel Kish has worked with several students who (more or less) fit this profile. The children Daniel has worked with are totally blind (or severely visually impaired), "autistic" (to various degrees) and they are extraordinary piano players. As remarkable as this is on the face of it, there are several caveats that need to be made around this observation.

I know as a special education consultant that many parents recoil when professionals label their kids with trending jargon. Terms like *autism* are especially hot button topics. Children are individuals first; they are unique and should be categorized very cautiously. Autism is probably like synesthesia, a set of evolving cognitive styles that confer advantages and disadvantages under different circumstances. In other words, this trilogy—blindness plus autism plus piano prodigy— is speculative and needs more analysis before we can make solid hypotheses. All we can assert now is that a few mobility specialists have noted the peculiar triad of traits found in some students. Daniel has encountered more of these children than most specialists because of his unique international practice.

It is also true that kids born with this trilogy do not simply grow up to be virtuoso piano players or composers. They must practice for many years with topnotch teachers before their talent can blossom. Here are Daniel's comments about one of his remarkable students:

> While my student's gifts with the piano are hard to deny as "giftedness" (even prodigy), there is also no question that his current extraordinary level of performance on the piano is hugely supported by massive amounts of highly qualified instruction, not the least of which came from his mum in the early years painstakingly working on every element of basic form and technique which, it must be said, he utterly lacked. His gifts and talents, his prodigy we might say, most definitely

gave him a significant, perhaps even necessary boost, but it is unquestionably hard, hard work that has brought about his extraordinary performance capacity. [94]

Daniel also added that using the term "autistic" to define the children who fit this trilogy, is highly problematic. These children often have distinctive cognitive styles compared to neurotypical children; these mental skills should not be judged as better or worse—they are simply different. After reading Simon Baron-Cohen's book *The Pattern Seekers*, I am inclined to use the phrase *extraordinary systems thinkers*, rather than autism.

Daniel also asked that I make it clear that this so-called trilogy has not been scientifically explored or validated. From Daniel's perspective, whenever we indulge in analogy or draw conclusions from limited case studies, we need to confess that our suppositions are speculative. Unfortunately, savants and prodigies are rare, and we are always dealing with limited examples. In my own defense, what I am doing in this section is making the case that blindness results in neural rewiring, with often puzzling consequences. There is potential research here waiting to be embraced.

We "Normals" are amazed when we witness savants and prodigies because we know it is impossible (for us) to play a musical instrument without learning the motor sequences needed to play notes—let alone streams of coherent notes. We must spend hours a day, over many years, practicing motor skills before we can play the piano with proficiency. What this means is that—contrary to our own experience—it is possible to be born with the ability to play the piano, an instrument that was invented in about the year 1700. Given what we know about how our biology works, this is a mind-boggling conundrum. You can watch numerous blind piano "prodigies" on YouTube. Many in-depth documentaries have also been created about these blind kids; they were born with the ability to play the piano without ever seeing the keys— the proof has been documented. Daniel pointed out to me a strange conundrum. These same blind prodigies may wander aimlessly around a room hunting for the piano (they have poor orientation skills) and yet when they get to the keyboard, they seem to know the layout and the patterns needed to turn the 88 notes into music.

Billy Joel and Elton John are two professional artists who were also piano prodigies—each of these musical geniuses was born with a mysterious ability to understand musical structure. There seems also to be a synesthetic component to their mastery. Watching Elton John's movie *Rocketman*, I was amazed that he could stare at lyrics with no musical notation and turn the words—almost instantly—into stunning music that went right to the heart of the listener. Stadiums full of human beings are swept up in a hypnotic collective trance by a musical power that both Joel and John possessed. We can speculate that genetics is involved, but we have no idea how that genetics works.

Which begs the question: Why the piano? Are there saxophone prodigies? Hammer dulcimer prodigies? What other motor skill sets might we be born with? Why are there Chess prodigies but few Checker prodigies? Can we be born knowing how to speak French or Mandarin? Are great athletes born knowing skill sets like pole-vaulting or hurdle leaping? Are great singers born knowing how to sing opera or hip hop? Why does Enneagram research suggest that there are a limited number of personality styles? Why are there only a limited number of Jungian archetypes? Something is at work behind known (non-quantum) science; something esoteric is messing with us. As I discussed earlier, if we are quantum creatures, as I suggested, then all this savant/prodigy weirdness might make sense when associated with quantum spookiness.

At the moment, we do not know the logic, the scientific explanation, or the epigenetics that might even begin to provide answers. And speculating about quantum weirdness does not offer concrete evidence. We do know that a person, like Jason Paget, for example, can be beaten by thugs (to near-death) and then, after physically recovering, wake up as a mathematical prodigy. We also know that people waking up from a coma have been documented speaking a foreign language—a language they were never exposed to and never studied. Psychologists call the phenomena *bilingual aphasia*.

Musical savants can play anything they hear only once and then play back a musical composition note-for-note. A language savant can repeat, word-for-word, what they have read, although words are not required to be meaningful for the savant—and quite often *are not* meaningful. For a linguistic *prodigy*, however, where no brain damage has affected higher order thinking skills, the memory for words and word structures is extraordinary. The important point is that *memory is key to extraordinary behaviors in savants and prodigies*. Many of Helen Keller's biographers and friends commented on her extraordinary memory abilities. She got into trouble as a preteen over what came to be called "the Frost King plagiarism scandal" because of her near photographic memory for language. She reproduced a book that had been read to her as a young child, not realizing that the words were not original.

I made the case in Chapter Four that our brains were created to enable straight-ahead navigation. To extend our understanding further, we must consider memory skills. Many neuroscientists now believe that our brains are dynamic memory machines—every behavior is backed up by exact memory sequences. We could not navigate unless we had a massive capacity to remember landmarks (objects, forms, features), routes, and scenes (backgrounds, gestalts). Following dual-process theory, we can speculate that there are two generic kinds of memory, one for remembering backgrounds (gestalts, scenes, flow-patterns), and one for remembering the objects (features) that are embedded in the background. This is dynamic memory; the two memory systems are constantly adjusting as we move about relative to a dynamic environment—everything is in flux.

If we understand the brain as a dynamic memory machine, then savants and prodigies are examples of the memory machine being altered and making adaptations. In other words, after impact (injury) to the developing brain, we would expect that memory would be a featured adaptation—memory would be enhanced or reduced depending on the extent and locus of injury.

What the existence of savants and prodigies suggest is that memory skills are inherited—*whole behaviors* are remembered generation to generation. So, not only are physical attributes passed from generation to generation (blue eyes, red hair, Roman noses, etc.), so, too, are behaviors, like piano playing and mathematical prowess passed to offspring. Even personality types could be genetically transmitted. For example, Enneagram studies suggest that we are born with established personalities. Nine possibilities (nine kinds of basic personality) are suggested by the research. How could it be that we are born with built-in personalities? Why are there only a limited number of personality types?

Indeed, how can it be possible for a person to have multiple personalities? Multiple personality disorder (MPD) is characterized by two or more distinct and relatively enduring personalities—two or more minds (personalities, neuro-substrates) in the same brain. Let us consider for a moment, as an example and for simplicity, that a person has just two personalities (rather than multiple personalities).

Twin personalities can be diametrically different, one might be (cognitively) blind, for example, or have a lisp, while the other personality is fully sighted and articulate. We do not have the science to explain these strange, implausible phenomena. The quote below is from a *Scientific American Magazine* article called "Could Multiple Personality Disorder Explain Life, the Universe and Everything?"

> In 2015, doctors in Germany reported the extraordinary case of a woman who suffered from what has traditionally been called "multiple personality disorder" and today is known as "dissociative identity disorder" (DID). The woman exhibited a variety of dissociated personalities ("alters"), some of which claimed to be blind. Using EEGs, the doctors were able to ascertain that the brain activity normally associated with sight wasn't present while a blind alter was in control of the woman's body, even though her eyes were open. Remarkably, when a sighted alter assumed control, the usual brain activity returned.[95]

The authors of the above quote also acknowledged that something is going on beyond the reach of present scientific understanding:

> Although we may be at a loss to explain precisely how this creative process occurs (because it unfolds almost totally beyond the reach of self-reflective introspection) the clinical evidence nevertheless forces us to acknowledge something is happening that has important implications for our views about what is and is not possible in nature.

The reason that psychologists stopped using "multiple personality disorder" and adopted "dissociative identity disorder," is because they came to believe that their patients did not have *multiple* personalities. Instead, the patients had *fragmented* personalities—they were unable to form a single stable personality, a reliable identity; therefore, they were not able to consistently present to the world a stable persona. These patients could not pull together *one* personality.

I was unable to find a critique of the German study cited above, so I do not feel confident presenting this single case (of blind and not blind showing up in the same brain) as entirely substantiated. I am simply exploring the esoteric, pointing out mysteries yet to be scientifically clarified.

Related to personality disorders that manifest as blind and not-blind in the same individual, are near-death experiences in which blind people claim to be able to see again, or, in the case of congenitally blind people, to see for the first time. This is from the U.S. National Institutes of Health:

> Vision in near-death experiencers that are blind, including totally blind from birth, has been described in many case reports. This, along with the finding that vision in NDEs is usually different from normal everyday vision and often described as supernormal, further suggests that NDEs cannot be explained by our current understanding of brain function. [96]

An extensive and critical study of blindness and near-death experiences called "People Born Blind Can See During a Near-Death Experience" was published by Dr. Kenneth Ring, Professor Emeritus of Psychology at the University of Connecticut and Sharon Cooper, Research Assistant at the time of the study. The study was funded in part by the Institute of Noetic Sciences. Like multiple personality disorders, this arena of investigation is only supported by a few case studies. I am not comfortable presenting these viewpoints as conclusive. As I said above, I am simply exploring the esoteric edges of science.

In 2021, Netflix ran a four-part special called *Surviving Death*, in which paranormal topics were explored. Part one dealt with near-death experiences, part two with mediums, part three with ghosts, and part four with reincarnation. Because of my own background and experiences, I was especially interested in the depictions of near-death and reincarnation. The people interviewed for the series were entirely credible. They had obviously experienced something profound. Skeptics and careful researchers might be able to present important challenges to the explanations offered for the origin and biology of near-death experiences and reincarnation, but the humans who had the experiences seemed genuinely baffled by what had happened to them.

Longitudinal studies of reincarnation, at the University of Virginia, show hundreds of cases—everywhere in the world—in which children were born who remembered their most recent past life. When a five-year-old child can tell you details about a past life, including their previous names, where they lived, who their parents and siblings were, and how they died, we are left bewildered. When, in addition, a child's statements can be verified, when we find the records of the people who had reincarnated, we face a conundrum that challenges all our attempts to explain the evolution of consciousness. Something is going on that we do not yet understand. Great mysteries await great scientific/spiritual researchers who can piece together all the bewildering puzzle pieces. At the least, we seem to be living in a world that is far more mysterious and far more fascinating than we have so far considered.

I am inclined to think that quantum patterns play out at macro levels (as below so above). Once these quantum affects are applied to humanity, to genetics, we will then begin to understand all the mysteries, from reincarnation, to blind piano prodigies, to near-death experiences.

∼

The world of animal migration is also full of inexplicable conundrums. Monarch butterflies, for example, are known to fly from North America to Mexico and back. This is an incomprehensible feat. If you have ever watched a Monarch fly, you see that they flutter this way and that without any apparent direction or intention. What most people do not realize is that Monarchs die in-route. Their children take over and head off in the direction the parents were going before they died. Then the kids die in-route and the grandkids take over. Navigational routes and intentions are somehow built into the genetics of Monarch Butterflies (and many other creatures). *Migration is a species phenomenon,* especially in creatures like butterflies.

This insight made me wonder if navigational intentions (species migrations) are passed from generation to generation in other creatures (besides Monarch Butterflies). For example, what if each human being is born subconsciously knowing that they are to continue navigating in a set direction, on a prescribed course, toward a distant destination. This knowing would be Allocentric, an awareness-based system that was unknowable to Egoic consciousness. We navigate in an emotional, intuitive (instinctual) direction, evolving toward a preset goal.

What goal? How would navigational knowledge (species migration) be passed to the newly born? How do we transmit navigational coordinates to offspring? How do Monarchs (and people) know when they have *reached* a preordained goal (location)?

When Helen Keller says that Love is the spiritual heartbeat of Christianity, she is talking about our shared journey as a species. We are supposed to be traveling a spiritual path because at some unknown time in some unknown future, humanity will reach a Goal. Just like Monarch butterflies will die before the destination is reached, our children, our grandchildren, our great grandchildren will continue the species migration. We are born preordained to travel into the future with a mission. Some of us will flutter here and there, never moving closer to the goal, but others will find a mission, they will sense the species mandate, and they will move Love forward toward that unknown location. . . . and then what? Do we head back North?

All the above observations—from savants to butterflies—suggest that something is going on in nature, in our physical universe, that we do not yet understand. We are confronting hidden knowledge, esoteric knowledge. We might eventually find scientific evidence to explain what researchers observe (and I think we will), but, for now, these observations remain mysterious.

Esoteric (Hindu) lore suggests that there is an Akashic Record (a cosmic collective unconscious) where all knowledge is stored. Presumably, the human mind can potentially access the Akashic Record. For some reason, there is a mechanism within most minds that filters and blocks access to this universal library (if such a thing exists). However, when trauma occurs to the human brain, access to the Akashic Record arises automatically and unconsciously, resulting in savants and prodigies. Therefore, when I suggest that Helen Keller was in contact with something subtle that most of us are not aware of, it might very well be this cosmic collective unconsciousness that she is sensing.

If you do not like the idea of *esoteric lore*—if you want biological evidence—the place to look seems to be epigenetics. *Experience* dynamically rewrites genetic coding, turning genes on and off to enable or disable behaviors. The human genome is not static; it is constantly adjusting. Experience defines who we become. What science is missing is the epigenetic knowledge that demonstrates how whole behaviors are transmitted. For example, how are kids born with Mozart-like abilities—how did epigenetics learn to channel Mozart?

I do not have a clue what the answer is to all these conundrums (sorry), but there appears to be something in the human genetic (potential) repertoire which:

- Can create blind, cognitively distinct, piano prodigies.
- Can create people who can be blind one moment and not blind the next (as in dissociative identity disorder or dear-death experiences).
- Can create mathematical, musical, linguistic, and artistic prodigies at birth, or shortly after severe trauma.
- Can reincarnate, remote view, travel out-of-body, survive death, and can (when unfiltered) peer into the future.
- Can operate using/sharing a collective unconscious.

∼

Something is going on here, on the fringes of science (in the land of the esoteric fairies), outside acceptable theories of consciousness. And, somehow, blindness is part of the puzzle. So, perhaps, (I am musing) Helen Keller's deaf-blindness is part of the solution.

There is something that happens—especially around blindness—that rewires the brain and enables sensorimotor "anomalies" to manifest in miraculous ways. Visual and auditory processing constitutes much of the brain's real estate. When this real estate "goes up for sale," we wonder what neural processes take control of the abandoned audio-visual neuro-nets?

Why would blindness be central to the puzzle, the conundrum? The answer, I suggest, becomes clearer if we accept that the human being is a quantum creature. Light is what crafted the eye (as Goethe said), but then vision became the centerpiece for crafting the brain, the nervous system, the entire body. We are solar powered and solar-designed creatures, and the strangeness of the quantum world is somehow integral to our essence, to our behaviors. If we remove the visual stream, when we become blind to the patterns of light, we shut down a major power source and we cause the whole body to adjust, adapt, reconfigure. Helen Keller may be an example of such blindness-related rewiring.

∼

As I was crafting this chapter, I assumed that it was not possible for Helen (for a deaf-blind person) to be a piano player; she certainly could not be compared to the blind prodigies documented today—so I did not search the literature for any exceptions to my assumptions. Then, quite unexpectedly, I came across a remarkable newspaper article written by deaf-blindness expert Job Williams called "A Wonderful Child," published by the *Hartford Courant*, Friday, February 20, 1891.

I must confess that before I saw her for the first time a little over a year ago, I could not believe that the reports concerning her progress in language were not grossly exaggerated, but after seeing her and talking to her myself through the manual alphabet, I was prepared to believe anything regarding her progress in that direction. I never knew of a child deaf at so early an age as was Helen . . . who made such rapid progress in the knowledge of the English language.

But the greatest wonder was yet to come. Soon we heard that Helen was trying to learn to talk. That seemed the most absurd thing in the world. To think of teaching speech to a child totally deaf and blind was preposterous. Yet that seeming impossible thing has been done. The age of miracles is not yet past.

Last Monday morning I sat down beside her and carried on a running conversation concerning a great variety of subjects for nearly half an hour, and during all that time her part of the conversation, which was animated and sprightly and fun, was conducted entirely by speech and speech so distinct that I failed to understand very little of what she said. She seemed never at a loss for language to express an idea nor even to hesitate in giving it orally. It was an intelligible speech in a pleasant voice, and it was wonderful.

In the course of our conversation, Helen informed me that she could play the piano, and when I asked her to play for me, she sat down and played the air of a little song with her right hand and played the same part with her left hand an octave below. It would hardly pass for first-class music, the time not being very accurate, but it was music. Then, at my request, she sang for me a line of the song she had just played, and the singing was more accurate in time, though less so in tune than the playing.

Her memory is as remarkable as her grasp of language and her power of speech, and probably is the chief source of her success in both these. She grasps an idea almost before it is given to her, and once hers it seems to be ineradicably fixed in her memory. A few days ago, a book of poems printed in raised letters was presented to her. She opened it and read the first poem over twice, reading it aloud as she passed her finger over the lines. Then the book was laid away, and not referred to again until the next day, when it was found that she could repeat the whole poem of seven stanzas of four lines each, without missing a word.

Laura Bridgman was a brilliant example of what can be accomplished under great difficulties. Helen Keller is a prodigy. There is no one, nor ever was anyone to be compared with her. [97]

Job Williams was the principal of the American Asylum for the Education of the Deaf and Dumb in Hartford, Connecticut from 1878 to 1913. Prior to being named the school's principal, he taught deaf students for 13 years at the Asylum, the oldest permanent school for the deaf in the United States. In other words, Job Williams was a trustworthy observer; we cannot dismiss his observations as exaggerated. Furthermore, in the longstanding debate (in the deaf community) between those who favor sign language over those who favor oral communication, Job favored manual sign. He did not necessarily support the teaching of oral language to Helen Keller. Yet he was in awe of her oral skills.

Williams says that he witnessed Helen Keller playing the piano and singing. That is mindboggling. That she was not great at either skill is beside the point. How in the world did she play the piano without hearing the notes or the melody? How could her left hand be playing something different than her right hand? I suppose, of course, she was shown how to play the piano, but the fact that she learned to do so is remarkable.

There is controversy in the literature concerning whether Helen learned to use sign language. I am guessing that the teachers in the schools for the deaf at least tried to show her the basics of sign language, just as someone showed her the basics of piano playing. I suspect that she could learn and remember signs very quickly—she just did not need signs in her daily life.

Job Williams also emphasized Helen's extraordinary memory skills and he gives us an example. Williams also ends his observations by stating empathically that Helen Keller was—without doubt—a prodigy.

≈

After a brain is damaged, it slowly rewires itself over time, this is called *neuroplasticity*. Neuroplasticity is a recent scientific discovery; not many years ago scientists believed there were limited numbers of neurons in the brain connected to each other by rigid networks—scientists believed that if neurons were damaged, there was no hope of recovery. The new theory of neuroplasticity is that brains are dynamic, that neural tissue can heal, that new neurons can form, and that brains contain dynamic mechanisms for rerouting and rearranging neural networks.

Neuroplasticity means that the human brain can restructure itself through learning—indeed, the brain *must* be able to rewire dynamically, on-the-fly, otherwise there would be no such thing as *learning*:

> . . . the human cerebral cortex has revealed impressive capabilities to change its functionality and even its architecture during the process of education. [98]

We could not learn if the brain was not capable of changing its biology. Every moment of every day our brains are changing in response to experiences. When the brain is injured, it can detect the damage and then respond by rewiring itself. Therefore, a brain will adjust to blindness or deafness, or to any impairment. The extent of rewiring depends on many factors, including the extent and location of the injury, the age of the person, and environmental circumstances. Helen Keller had a deaf-blind brain that was crafted by neuroplasticity. It was, therefore, an exceedingly rare brain.

Rewiring sometimes connects regions of the brain that were never intended to be directly connected, as happens in synesthetes. Synesthesia is a neurological phenomenon in which stimulation of one sense leads to involuntary experiences in a second sense. The rewired brains of synesthetes result in people who, for example, can hear colors, or taste words, or see days of the month floating in space.

Science is discovering new kinds of synesthesia yearly. The number of known brain variations is currently (in 2021) debatably about 80. Synesthetes result when senses overlap or blend in ways that are "not normal," although the more we learn about the brain, the more the concept of "normal" comes into question. Most synesthetes regard their mental skills as a gift rather than an impairment. Synesthesia is increasingly seen as a normal set of variations that can evolve during normal brain development (or after injury to the brain).

The question for us is this: "How did Helen Keller's brain rewire itself when it no longer received visual and auditory information?" What areas of her brain were recruited to replace vision and hearing? What purpose was served by the rewiring? Helen's brain had to adjust in extraordinary ways after her sudden illness destroyed the nerves that connected the eyes and ears to her brain. It is worth the effort to speculate about neuroplasticity and the resulting rewiring that had to have occurred in her brain.

It is entirely probable that Helen Keller became an unusual kind of synesthete after her brain rewired itself. Helen was often accused in her lifetime of knowing things that she could not possibility have known—that is one definition of a savant or a prodigy, to know things you were never taught or had never perceived. Helen knew things, like visual images and auditory images, and yet she had no eyes to see or ears to hear.

Helen's friend, the great psychologist William James, used to tell his students that there is no sharp line between normal and abnormal, between mentally healthy and mentally unhealthy, between extraordinary and ordinary. There is always a fluctuating mixture of characteristics. Therefore, we can never quite find the borderline between extremes. Labeling each other is an imperfect practice—sometimes we seem spot-on with our suppositions and the next moment we look foolishly naïve. Let us go cautiously forward.

Helen Keller and Synesthesia

Helen Keller lived in a vibrational universe. The pure vibrational energy of the cosmos was there for her to experience, to explore, and to master. There is a quote by Jacques Lusseyran, another remarkable blind individual (the subject of volume three in this series), which shows he also discovered this vibrational universe; Lusseyran sensed the vibrations as pressure:

> I discovered that the universe consists of pressure, that every object and every living being reveals itself to us at first by a kind of quiet yet unmistakable pressure that indicates its intention and its form. I even experienced the following wonderful fact: A voice, the voice of a person, permits him to appear in a picture.

> When the voice of a man reaches me, I immediately perceive
> his figure, his rhythm, and most of his intentions. Even stones
> can weigh on us from a distance. So do the outlines of distant
> mountains, and the sudden depression of a lake at the bottom
> of a valley. [99]

Lusseyran was (I suggest) a synesthete; sounds evoked actual visual images for him because his senses overlapped. We now know that synesthesia can develop from sensory deprivation, so it is not outside the realm of possibility that Helen Keller also developed some variety of synesthesia. The question for me has always been *"What kind of synesthesia was Helen Keller gifted with?"* Or: "What varieties of synesthesia are possible without vision and hearing?"

I find it puzzling and fascinating that Lusseyran would say that he could read a person's intentions using a non-visual sense (and presumably without just judging voices). Helen seems to be saying the same thing, although she could do this reading without vision *or* sound. This means that the ability Lusseyran and Keller used to understand the world was outside our customary understanding of the known senses. I suspect that brains/minds are so different that the ability to register subtle vibrations, even unconsciously, falls on a bell curve; some people (empaths, for example) can experience what Helen Keller and Jacques Lusseyran could sense, but other people have no such ability. Most people fall somewhere in between these extremes. There is also the question of whether we can relearn or enhance the ability to sense subtle vibrations.

Some synesthetes register sounds and visual images during tactile exploration. In other words, during exploration of surfaces with the fingers, the auditory cortex and the visual cortex can also be simultaneously activated. Helen Keller's eyes and ears were disconnected from her brain by a high fever, but her auditory cortex and her visual cortex were not damaged (as far as we can conjecture). Helen would not know to call what she was experiencing internally either *sound* or *vision*, but it could very well be that her visual and auditory cortexes were active as she perceived the vibratory/tactile universe. In other words, beyond the poetic, the "Soul" might actually (biologically) be able to "see" and to "hear."

It could very well be that Helen Keller had some form of auditory-tactile synesthesia (hearing-touch synesthesia). This is a rare condition observed in normally sighted and hearing people, but perhaps it is not so rare in deaf-blind people. I am just speculating, of course, but science did not know about synesthesia in Helen Keller's time. When her biographies were being written, synesthesia was not a subject available for consideration. In other words, Helen Keller might have been stimulating her auditory cortex while exploring a surface, a face, or when communicating through fingertips and palms of the hand. If besides being an auditory-tactile synesthete Helen Keller was also a visual-tactile synesthete, then her occipital lobe (visual cortex) would also have been activated during tactile exploration. In other words, visual and auditory neural networks might have been active in Helen Keller's brain even though her eyes and ears were dysfunctional.

Some synesthetes experience more than one variety of synesthesia. For example, synesthetes may (at various moments) *see* sounds, *taste* words, or *feel* certain olfactory scents. It is likely, in my opinion, that Helen Keller had rare and extensive varieties of evolved-synesthesia. Smells, vibrations, and direct touch might all have been registering in her auditory and visual cortexes in some manner. This sensory overlap could hypothetically arise because of embodiment; our senses (under normal conditions) *never* act in an isolated manner.

A remarkable set of discoveries were made in the later decades of the twentieth century. Scientists doing fMRI scans saw that braille, when explored by the fingers, registered in the visual cortex. Later research showed that active echolocation, made popular by Daniel Kish, also registered in the visual cortex. As Daniel told me over dinner one day "The visual cortex is misnamed; it is really the *image-forming cortex*— any kind of sensory pattern is automatically registered *as a form* in the "visual" cortex." Other research suggests that the occipital cortex is a multisensory organ—it gets input from all the senses. What this suggests is that a blind brain would not necessarily have to "rewire," but, rather, that non-visual sensory input would gain neural territory as cortical visual cells diminished over time.

Therefore, we can speculate that Helen Keller was getting *image formation* in her occipital (visual) cortex as she scanned braille, stone walls, the face of friends, etc. Any time she used her fingers and hands, her brain registered patterns simultaneously in the visual and auditory cortexes. *Helen Keller might have been "seeing" and "hearing" using touch.* As crazy as this sounds to a lay person, it is entirely plausible to modern scientists. We have no way to comprehend how Helen perceived patterns arising in the visual and auditory cortexes. But we do have the evidence of her remarkable language, which was rich in visual and auditory references.

Research also suggests that the occipital cortex is active during language processing.[100] Visually processed words are exact forms (specific shapes); it makes sense that letters and word formations would be processed in an "image processing cortex." That Helen Keller became a language prodigy might be less of a surprise given this ability to perceive language forms within the "visual" cortex.

It took me years to realize that my colleague Daniel Kish was *seeing* images using projected sound clicks. Daniel is an amazing blind navigator because he can perceive forms and pathways without using visual input from a retinal system. I will briefly discuss Daniel's abilities in the next chapter. Essentially, what Daniel's abilities show is that sound images (phonetic forms, spatially derived images) are processed in the "visual" cortex just as braille and written language trigger neurons in the occipital (visual) lobe.

Given what research has found to date, I strongly suggest (cautiously conclude) that Helen Keller might have been seeing and hearing without functional eyes and ears. What I mean is that her healthy auditory and visual cortexes were still functioning in her brain—they were just using (embodied) tactile images, smell-patterns, and proprioceptive patterns to generate images and scenes. Here is an excerpt from a letter Helen wrote in 1930 that hints at synesthesia:

> I am conscious of an infinite variety of images, relations and degrees of brightness and darkness, void and fullness, space, height, depth and conceptual harmonies which I transmute into sound and color. [101]

Helen Keller was criticized in her writings for using auditory and visual descriptions. Embodiment, synesthesia, and occipital lobe imaging all point to actual cortical triggering of sound-like and sight-like perceptions in some blind individuals. In Helen's publishing years, during the early and middle twentieth century, there was almost no understanding of cortical processing; her critics were simply ignorant of the operation of the human nervous system. Of course, we are still ignorant about the operation of our cognition, although we are more knowledgeable compared to the decades when Helen Keller lived.

In *Helen and Teacher*, biographer Joseph Lash writes: "Helen sought bravely to demonstrate what a gifted blind writer, even a deaf-blind writer, can achieve through empathy, intuition, insight." If Lash had been born in our time, he might have added that Helen Keller's giftedness had a biological underpinning.

Helen's intuitive ability, her curiosity about how her mind worked, led her into the exploration of extrasensory perception (ESP). In her later years, she wrote a letter to Robert Duffus, after having had a discussion of Dr. Joseph Rhine's experiments in ESP at Duke University. Helen wrote:

> It has always been a strong belief with me that there are powers in many animals which can be developed beyond the physical senses, and it is a gratification to note that orthodox scientists are beginning to seek other causes than mechanical ones to explain telepathy and the incredible travels of migratory birds flying from the North to tropical countries and seeking out their old nests, eels finding their way swimming thousands of miles to the Sargasso Sea and back to the waters of Scandinavia. Surely, if creatures without the reasoning faculty can perform such wonders, Man endowed with spiritual and intellectual powers can achieve phenomena not to be explained by mechanical but by laws still waiting to be discovered. [102]

Helen is suggesting that science will eventually catch up with what psychics and empaths have been telling humanity for centuries: we have not uncovered all the laws of the cognitive universe. Helen lived in a vibratory world; she knew firsthand that our physical world held information that both vision and hearing could not directly perceive. Let me hasten to add that, from a scientific perspective, we have, indeed, answered many of the questions about animal navigation; there is no reason we will not also come to explain other mysteries such as "psychic ability." I predict that quantum biology will eventually explain unusual human abilities. There is evidence now that quantum effects in the retina allow birds to see the magnetic field lines of the earth, which they use to navigate long distances during yearly migrations.

It is not surprising that Helen Keller became interested in extra-sensory perception (ESP) as soon as she heard about it in the media. She was, herself, an example of extra-sensory perception; she knew that something was going on in her mind that was being described in the esoteric literature of her time (but not in the scientific literature).

According to Helen, Annie Sullivan visited her after Sullivan's death and assured her that she should continue the work they had started. That is a remarkable statement, and we should not dismiss it as "just imagination or wishful thinking." The implication is that something subtle exists even after death; some core of consciousness survives the death process.

As an interesting aside, I have communicated with others who are working on "Helen Keller projects," and we agree that we have a sense that Helen and Annie are channeling to us. The miracle is still performing miracles. I say this with a grin, and I do not care if it sounds like New Age daft, because it certainly feels like we are getting help from an esoteric spaceship. When I meditate, I say, "Thank you," and I request that the spaceship remain in orbit (smile).

A Spiritual Prodigy

> Helen herself said, "Blindness separates us from things, but deafness separates us from people." Helen was faced with significant challenges that imposed separation from both things *and* people, but she managed to develop strategies to connect with both things and people anyway. She did this, not to a minimal or marginal degree, but to a degree that exceeds the demonstrated capabilities of most human beings. In my humble estimation, this points to a prodigy level brain capacity. [103]

In the quote above, psychologist Daniel Kish makes a significant observation about human perception. Daniel is separating our perception into two avenues, one towards inanimate objects and the other to living creatures, especially human beings. Adaptations are necessary for blind and deaf individuals and skillful adaptations fall on a curve from inadequate to remarkable. Helen Keller and Daniel Kish are off-the-charts on the remarkable end of the adaptability scale.

In my own philosophy, I have called blindness a disability of the Allocentric processing system and deafness a disability of the Egocentric processing system. I created a conceptual duality, as did

Daniel in his above quote. Egocentric processing attaches to objects, keeping a separation between an Ego and Other-than-Ego; the Ego, in my philosophy, is devoid of Love and communion—the Ego works well with objects, with things, but not so well with people. However, the Soul (Self) flows like a circuit in a network—there is no separation of the Soul from the Source; Love and community are central to Allocentric processing. In Daniel's language, Helen overcame the limitations of blindness as well as the limitations of deafness to function essentially normally in the world—a remarkable feat that, by itself, qualifies her as a prodigy.

We relate to Helen's essence, to her Soul, and we marvel at her ability to function and contribute as a valuable member of society. I understood this as I read Daniel's note to me, but I felt there was more to consider; Daniel made me realize that I was missing something.

A rather significant insight appeared to me while I was pondering Daniel's quote. I had just revisited Harvard psychologist Howard Gardner's work on multiple intelligences and Daniel's ideas were blending with Dr. Gardner's worldviews as I was musing. The insight that came to me made me pause; I was dumbfounded by the oversight that had followed me around as I crafted this book.

I had spent more than two years putting this book together, reading everything I could get my hands on about Helen Keller and Anne Sullivan, making the point, almost on every page that Helen Keller insisted that mankind elevate Love and Service to the highest rungs of our collective value system. And here I was trying to show that Helen had, in Howard Gardner's language, a suburb Linguistic Intelligence. Which is true, Helen's Linguistic Intelligence was so remarkable we could call her a language prodigy, but my god, I had missed the obvious: Helen Keller had a prodigy-level *Spiritual Intelligence*. It is on every other page of this book (and throughout Helen's writing): Love, Love, Love.

Not every human being has such suburb empathy as Helen Keller. For example, the masterminds of artificial intelligence who are working to build machines that match their own highly evolved mathematical/logical abilities have an exceedingly valuable kind of human ability. But most of this cognitive brain power seems to come at the expense of Spiritual Intelligence. There are also people with musical prowess, people in Gardner's Musical Intelligence category, who can (remarkably) decode the tones of the universe. However, musical intelligence is a full-time passion—there is not a lot of processing power left over inside a musical mind to develop saint-like spirituality. The same is true of mathematical prodigies, or any kind of prodigy—there is not much processing room left over for working on Spirituality. We must choose our mission in life based on our innate gifts—we cannot be all things to all people. Here is the list of *categories of intelligence* that Professor Howard Gardner taught in his courses at Harvard:

1. *Verbal-linguistic intelligence*: these are people with highly developed verbal skills who have acute sensitivity to the meaning and rhythm of words. Examples include writers, poets, journalists, and orators—people like Helen Keller.
2. *Logical-mathematical intelligence*: these are people with the ability to think conceptually and abstractly, with the capacity to understand and create logical and numerical patterns. Examples include scientists, researchers, and mathematicians—people like Albert Einstein.
3. *Spatial-visual intelligence*: these are people with the ability to think using images, with the ability to visualize space abstractly. Examples include sculptors, painters, dancers, and blind navigators, like Daniel Kish.
4. *Bodily-kinesthetic intelligence*: these are people with the ability to precisely control their body movements, to control tools, and to use highly refined and accurate muscular sequences. Examples include athletes, dancers, pilots, and rock climbers—people like Babe Ruth.
5. *Musical intelligence*: these are people with the ability to create musical scores and to perform masterfully on musical instruments. These individuals can decode and recode the universal language of sound. Examples include musicians and composers—people like Mozart and Bach.
6. *Inter-personal intelligence*: these are people with the ability to use empathy to decode human emotions. They can respond appropriately to the emotional needs of others. Examples include teachers, nurses, doctors, care-givers, psychologists, social workers, and religious leaders—people like the Dalai Lama.
7. *Intra-personal intelligence*: these are people with the ability to know their own inner dynamic, those who are aware of their internal feelings. These individuals can understand intuitively

how their own values, beliefs, and thinking are processed. Examples include philosophers and leaders of all kinds (political, religious, educational)—people like William James or Rudolf Steiner.

8. *Naturalist intelligence*: these are people with the ability to sense embeddedness in the natural world, people who can sense inter-connectivity, who recognize (sense) the interrelationship of plants, animals, humanity, and inanimate objects in nature. Examples include naturalists, farmers, and environmentalists—people like John Muir.

9. *Existential intelligence*: these are people with the capacity to visualize and ponder big existential questions such as, "What is the meaning of life? How do we learn from the past? How might the future play out? How do minds work? What is consciousness? Examples include philosophers, futurists, and historians—people like the futurist, inventor, and much-loved guru of science Ray Kurzweil.

Howard Gardner said that if we lived forever, we would probably all develop each of these intelligences to high degrees. However, lifespans are limited, and genetics has predetermined many of our potential capabilities. Consequently, we either develop moderate abilities across the entire range of intelligences, or we develop one (rarely two or three) of these categories to an elevated degree. If you are driven to be a great golfer, for example, you must practice, practice, practice. However, that does not leave any time in a day to practice the piano, or write poetry, or tackle the big existential questions. In a way, the limitations of time force us to choose where we will put our efforts and, consequently, how our minds will inevitably evolve and how we might contribute to the evolution of our species.

Helen Keller's sensory limitations denied her certain avenues for intellectual development. It is no surprise that she evolved an exquisite linguistic intelligence, that she honed her abilities in the inter-personal and intra-personal skill sets, and that her naturalist and existential intelligences were highly evolved. I am inclined to combine these kinds of intelligence under one category, especially when the skills are as evolved as they were within Helen Keller's remarkable mind. When you have *extraordinary* talent (intelligence) in the set that coalesced in Helen's mind (linguistic, inter-personal, intra-personal, naturalist, and existential), the result is a *Spiritual Prodigy*, a person who would naturally tell you, repeatedly, that Love is the answer.

Practice lays down neural networks in the brain. Learning, overlearning, intention, devotion, discipline, all these result in a brain that is specifically wired to perform certain behaviors well and other behaviors less well. Where there is damage to the human brain/and nervous system, especially when it is severe as in Helen's case, neural rewiring is extensive.

~

What kind of unusual abilities were created in Helen Keller's brain by neuroplasticity, by cross-wiring, or by synesthesia? My first guess was that Helen's *language capacity*, her Linguistic Intelligence, was greatly enriched through neural cross-wiring, enabling her to be the prose-prodigy she became. Here is a letter to her Aunt Eveline written when Helen was just 8 years old while attending classes at The Perkins School for the Blind. Helen is already learning languages:

> To Miss Evelina H. Keller
> [So. Boston, Mass. October 29, 1888]
>
> My dearest Aunt,
>
> I am coming home very soon, and I think you and everyone will be very glad to see my teacher and me. I am very happy because I have learned much about many things. I am studying French and German and Latin and Greek. So agapo is Greek, and it means I love thee. J'ai une bonne petite soeur is French and it means I have a good little sister. Nous avons un bon pere et une bonne mere means we have a good father and a good mother. Puer is boy in Latin, and Mutter is mother in German. I will teach Mildred many languages when I come home.
>
> Helen A. Keller [104]

This is an eight-year-old girl who cannot see or hear, yet she is brailling (or typing) a very cogent letter. She is already interested in languages and she has already absorbed the rudiments of four languages (in about the 3rd grade). By the time she graduates from college just over a decade later she will have mastered these languages, even considering becoming a translator as a possible profession. I suggest that this is the activity of a girl who is a linguistic prodigy.

But being a prose master, having a thirst for expressive language, is not the whole story. Helen had a highly refined, exquisitely sensitive Allocentric mind. She processed subtle vibrations with her entire body; she was part of the nature she moved through. Therefore, her Naturalist Intelligence was profoundly developed—she was tuned to the energy of the natural world. This ability to sense with the whole body, to pick up subtle energy, also gave her extraordinary Inter-personal Intelligence. Her empathy swelled as her body matured; she emotionally reacted to the pain she perceived all around her, from the personal pain of wounded soldiers to the global pains of a war-torn planet.

Helen also had extraordinary Intra-personal Intelligence. She did not receive visual and auditory input, therefore, her isolation inside her own mind was profound. She had all day, every day, for a lifetime to experience "living inside her own head." She used her isolation to study her own cognitive processes—she understood quite well Socrates' dictum "know thyself." Not surprisingly, as Helen came to understand her own cognition, she could project her knowing onto others— she began to understand intuitively how minds work. She evolved a remarkable inner (expert) psychologist. This naturally led to her interest in the big existential questions. Now add Linguistic Intelligence to this powerhouse mind and you end up with a woman who had the tools and knowledge to speak with great eloquence about the challenges of her time.

∾

I will end this section with a couple observations that Anne Sullivan made soon after she began working with Helen. Many of Sullivan's letters and notes were lost to fire or water damage, but newspapers (across the United States) recorded and preserved important insights. This is from an article called "A Deaf-Mute Evolution: How a body may get on with only one sense," published by *The Sun*, New York, New York on July 11, 1887. It is a story primarily about deaf-blind Laura Bridgman but includes important comments about Helen Keller, age 7:

Quoting Anne Sullivan: "[Helen's] sense of touch is so acute that a slight contact enables her to recognize her associate. She can even distinguish readily puppies of the same litter and will spell the name of each as soon as she touches him. So nice is her sense of smell that she will recognize her own clothes from those which belong to others."

So quick is she to grasp the thoughts and ideas that it is desired to express to her that she seems to possess a power beyond ordinary comprehension; and as an illustration this instance is given: "She has never been told anything about death or the burial of a body, and yet on entering the cemetery for the first time in her life, with her mother and myself to look at some flowers, she laid her hands on our eyes and repeatedly spelled "cry, cry." Her eyes actually filled with tears."

"On one occasion while walking with me she sensed the presence of her brother, although we were distant from him. She spelled his name repeatedly and started in the direction by which he was coming. When walking or riding she often gives the names of the people we meet about as soon as we recognize their presence. Frequently, when desirous of making suggestions to her, outside of the routine of her studies or her daily life, she will anticipate me, by spelling out the very plan I had in mind." [105]

Something is going on here that is currently beyond our science. I believe science will eventually offer satisfying explanations, but for now a strange mystery remains.

Can we call a person with such an unusual brain *a prodigy* (linguistic and spiritual) if observed (extraordinary) behaviors suggest we should? I am inclined to answer in the affirmative. I think we can safely call Helen Keller a prodigy.

That observation aside, I will repeat what my colleague Daniel Kish emphasized earlier. It is Helen Keller's accomplishments, her gifts to society that draw our attention. She also deserves the title of *genius*, which peers (like you and I) confer on extraordinary members of a culture in recognition of outstanding contributions. Let us end this stream of musing and say *Thank You* to Helen Keller for her loving leadership, which still blesses us, and which will bless generations to come.

The Problem of Medical Records

As I read the letters that Anne Sullivan wrote during her initial months at the Keller homestead, I was struck by Sullivan's descriptions of Helen's movements. Helen raced from place to place in the house, up and down stairs, into the yard, through the garden, and visited the animals in the barns—that was the impression I got as I read the accounts. Helen and Annie also played hide and seek; Helen searched everywhere, under beds and desks, behind closed doors, on shelves, and under papers resting on a desk. There is also the famous story of Helen locking her mother in a pantry, tossing away the key, and then sitting on the porch giggling with glee.

These activities are quite amazing, implying a spatial understanding and spatial fluidity that is miraculous for a deaf-blind kid. Indeed, in my thirty-year career in special education, I have never seen such a grasp of spatial layout and such fearless movement in a deaf-blind child. Even in a child who is totally blind (with normal hearing), there is usually much more hesitation, more time spent lost and disoriented, much more deliberate, and cautious movement.

As a mobility specialist, I am troubled by our assumption that Helen Keller was totally deaf and totally blind after her illness. In most cases, (in modern times) when we examine a child with severe hearing loss and severe vision loss, we find islands of sensation. In other words, it is extremely hard for injuries or illnesses to totally wipe out our hardy senses, we almost always find residual vision and/or residual hearing during careful examination. Helen's actions as a child of seven are much too fluid, too sure, and too extensive for me to feel comfortable defining her sensory losses as total. I could be wrong, of course, but my experience as a teacher for thirty years, makes me wonder.[106]

We have two vision systems; one is called *central vision* and the other is called *peripheral vision*. These two systems play different roles in the visual process. Central (cone cell) vision is supported by delicate blood vessels and tiny nerves and it is a relatively recent development in evolution. Peripheral vision is an older system, going far back in evolution. Peripheral (rod cell) vision is tough, redundant, and extremely hard to totally knock out. If Helen had *any* kind of residual vision, it would no doubt have been peripheral vision. The chief function of peripheral vision is mobility—the ability to perceive movement and navigate around obstacles. Also, light perception and shadow detection are often retained in the peripheral retina, even after severe damage. A small amount of light perception can aid in navigation. If peripheral vision is totally knocked out—as it is in some hereditary disorders—smooth accurate movements become exceedingly difficult. Helen's movements, as described by Anne Sullivan, suggest that Helen had residual vision—at least for a while—when she was young. Keep in mind that I am musing as I reflect.

Peripheral perception is primarily unconsciousness—there would be no way for Helen to even surmise that her movements were being aided by automatic and unconscious perceptions. There would be no way for Helen to realize that she was using the peripheral vision system and no way for her to report the existence of retained islands of sight. Peripheral vision usually fluctuates with physiology and with environmental conditions. In one situation, Helen might have had usable residual vision and then, moments later, in another physical space she might lose that ability.[107]

We have no medical records, no ophthalmological reports, and no audiological records for Helen (or Anne Sullivan) besides the general comments of Anne Sullivan that doctors did not find evidence of vision or hearing during their examinations. No records survive (as far as I know) to establish what tests were administered and what specific results were documented. We are also talking about the late 1800s; therefore, even when tests existed, they were much less accurate and less revealing by today's standards. The bottom line is that we cannot say for sure that Helen's hearing loss and visual loss were both total in the weeks and months after her illness. What we do know is that those around Helen felt that her losses were total. In a report to the Perkin's Board of Directors in 1888, Anne Sullivan left this summary statement:

> During the past year Helen has enjoyed excellent health. Her eyes and ears have been examined by specialists, and it is their opinion that she cannot have the slightest perception of either light or sound.

Sullivan feels that it is Helen's extraordinary sense of smell that allows her fluid and accurate mobility. Helen identifies flowers, individual animals, rooms, and people using her highly refined olfactory abilities. Despite these observations, I remain skeptical. It could be that she had islands of vision and/or shades of hearing that contributed to her fluid and accurate movements as a child. With age, these residual abilities might have declined.

We do not know the facts, so we can carry on with the mythology. However, I also think it is okay to sow some doubts about the totality of her condition. There might have been a time, especially in her early years, when residual vision aided her navigation. That would explain the reports of her rapid, fluid mobility mentioned by Anne Sullivan.

Helen's eyes were enucleated in her twenties. After that operation, speculation ends; there could be no residual vision after her eyes were removed. I am not an expert on hearing, but Helen's inability to hear her own spoken voice indicates a very profound (probably total) hearing loss. Functionally, she did not seem to have any degree of hearing as an adult.

Also, the way Helen behaved in public settings reinforces that her loss was functionally total. She seemed sensorially oblivious to what was happening around her and she relied heavily (as Sullivan recorded) on olfaction. Below is a note Anne Sullivan made in a letter to Sophia Hopkins, April 16, 1888. Captain Keller had insisted that Helen go to church, but for Sullivan it was an ordeal. Helen would not stop sniffing, hugging, and kissing people around her:

> When the communion service began, she smelt the wine, and sniffed so loud that everyone in the church could hear. When the wine was passed to our neighbor, he was obliged to stand up to prevent her taking it away from him.[108]

This level of olfactory skill could only have evolved if vision and hearing were so impaired as to be severely (if not completely) dysfunctional. I will leave my musing there.

Chapter Seven: Passing the Torch to the Visionaries

I do not identify as a blind person. I am not blind. I see acoustic images. When I first realized I could see acoustic images, I thought "I am seeing!" If I closed my eyes, the after image, the memory of the image, was still there! I said, "I swear to you that I actually see! [109]

The Blind Teaching the Deaf-Blind

When I told my friend and colleague Daniel Kish that he was the feature of volume two in this Knights for the Blind series, right after Helen Keller, he had an emotional reaction, not unlike many others. Daniel did not enjoy being compared to Helen Keller *or* Anne Sullivan. Yes, he acknowledged their contributions, he saw them as allies in the battle to educate the sighted population, and he saw that Helen Keller was a Justice Warrior fighting against worn out paradigms and ignorance. But Daniel is his own self-made man, and his journey is his own. He lives in a different time, surrounded by technologies and juggling more knowledge than has ever been, so far, accumulated. Besides, who wants to be compared to a global mythology, to legendary icons, to a miracle and a miracle worker, to Helen Keller, a person who has been compared to Jesus Christ and Buddha? A hard act to follow, to say the least.

I understood Daniel's concern. However, I disagreed with my friend. I do think Daniel is the right person to follow Helen Keller in this series and I do think his contributions deserve to be highlighted and remembered in history. Daniel Kish is his own miracle.

After one of his visits to Michigan, Daniel was packing up to leave my house when I remarked that I had been writing about him—this was back in the early 2000s.

"Oh," Daniel said, "I have been thinking about writing a memoir. Show me what you wrote." So, I fired up my computer and I read these lines to Daniel:

> Daniel Kish travels the world with no guide dog and few technologies besides his I-phone and a long cane. Mostly, he travels alone. He flows through landscapes without awkwardness. When we are together at conferences, walking the streets of Toronto or Reykjavik, for example, I find myself intermittently jogging, trying to maintain his pace. He is careful, alert, but he is also fearless. He strides forward with great confidence.
>
> Using a self-developed cane skill, which he calls the *feather technique*, and his highly evolved echolocation skills, which he calls *Sonar-Vision*, Daniel *has walked alone* through the streets of Calcutta, India, at his fast pace along the teeming roads of Jakarta in Indonesia, through the streets of Moscow and Edinburgh, in Cape Town, South Africa, and in remote regions of Mexico—to list but a few of his adventures.
>
> I have stood with Daniel Kish on a mountain top and on a glacier in Iceland. He required no guiding on the mountain trails or on the slippery ice fields. The press calls him Bat Man and marvels because he can navigate any environment, any terrain, be it city streets, wilderness ways, or urban malls and transit stations, all without need of help. He can even ride a bicycle, not just on city streets, but along mountain pathways. For many years, he had a group of blind mountain-biking friends; they called themselves *Team-Bat*. Daniel's nickname, coined by his friends within this talented group, was *Sir Crash-a-lot*, which puts some humility to his superhuman reputation.
>
> Daniel lost both his eyes from cancer before he was two years old [Daniel: "I lost my first eye at 7 months and the second at 13 months. For simplicity's sake, I sometimes say I lost both eyes by the time I was about a year old. In truth, my vision

by all reports was pretty trashed long before then."]. Daniel's amazing navigational abilities have nothing whatsoever to do with residual eyesight—he wears two plastic ocular prosthetics. Whenever I watch Daniel move through space with such ease and confidence, my emotions are that of a teacher. I wonder how students the world over might also travel expertly if only they knew the secrets that Daniel discovered and then highly developed.

I also wonder how Daniel got to be such a normal navigator of physical space and of life without the use of his eyes. I am somewhat grief struck that—as a young teacher myself—I was not able to provide my students with the skill set that Daniel evolved on his own. I simply did not know about active echolocation when I was a young teacher. The tragedy here, in my opinion (and in Daniel's as well) is that teaching institutions across the globe *still* fail to provide blind students with the perceptual tools that would enable them to navigate like Daniel.

We must conclude that something is wrong with global philosophy and traditional practices in the fields of blind rehabilitation and special education. Fortunately, Daniel Kish decided to go on a mission, a hero's journey I call it, to save blind children on the planet from a life of culturally-induced slavery. Daniel Kish became a Knight for the Blind in the Battle against Darkness when he put his ideas into practice.

I later wrote these two paragraphs and read them to Daniel:

For some reason, a blessing for me, I got to know Daniel Kish well enough, as a friend and colleague, to realize what he was doing and why. It fell partially to me, therefore, to translate his ideas and teaching strategies in a way that my sighted colleagues and the public could comprehend—it took me years to figure this out, that I had a role to play, a responsibility to record this time in history.

The field of Orientation and Mobility is changing because of Daniel Kish and his blind colleagues at *World Access for the Blind*. Daniel's co-workers Brian Bushway and Juan Ruiz are remarkable individuals with skills as exact and graceful as Daniel's. Brian and Juan were among Daniel's first students;

they are proof that Daniel's skills can be replicated and even improved upon.[110]

Daniel Kish has two master's degrees, the first in developmental psychology, the second in special education (Orientation and Mobility). He is also the founder and CEO of *World Access for the Blind*, which his team is now calling *Visioneers*. The motto of Visioneers.org is: *We teach blind people to see with SonarVision*.

As the motto says, Daniel and his team teach totally blind people to see images and scenes using sound. *In other words, blind people can learn to see again*. It is a unique kind of seeing, of course, a kind of "low vision." *SonarVision* enables the seeing of objects, scenes, and pathways and, therefore, enables blind people a means to navigate in a way that looks and feels like sighted navigation. The world has never seen anything like this.

To witness Daniel navigating about the environment (using occasional tongue clicks to generate echoes) is amazing. I do not bother to help him anymore—not that I ever helped much. I see him as another "sighted" friend, because that is how he acts—like someone who can see (because *he can* see).

Like me, Daniel Kish is an Orientation and Mobility specialist. We are both fascinated with brain science and navigation and with the underlying philosophical core of our profession; we have spent hours discussing complex ideas during his visits to Michigan or when I have joined him on one of his teaching adventures. Because of these discussions, Daniel influenced the unfolding of my Navigational Consciousness hypothesis.

I have firsthand evidence of Daniel's genius. I have seen him navigate using *Sonar-Vision*—it is uncanny how fluidly he moves around, and, like Helen Keller, he may be an unusual kind of prodigy (another idea he is not comfortable with). I will leave that speculation for his own book. I have also seen Daniel work with students, a true rendition of the blind leading the blind. He is as competent as any sighted instructor— probably more so, given his empathy for blind kids and his personal experience as a blind man. How he manages to teach blind kids to navigate—the neurophysiology of the skill—I will discuss in his book.

One early morning over coffee, I began to daydream—a "what if" musing—that Helen Keller was alive in our time, a young deaf-blind girl in Tuscumbia, Alabama receiving instruction from a severely visually impaired teacher named Anne Sullivan. In my reverie, Anne Sullivan has been struggling to read with her bloodshot, exhausted, pain-stricken eyes; she is trying to figure out how to teach a deaf-blind kid.

Sullivan knew about fingerspelling because of Samuel Gridley Howe and Laura Bridgman, but she wondered if there was anything more important that she should be doing. That is when she came across a website called *Visioneers.org* and read the name *Daniel Kish*. It did not take long for Sullivan to convince the Keller family to hire Daniel to teach both Sullivan and Helen Keller about the field of Orientation and Mobility. Within a few weeks, Daniel Kish had moved in with the Keller family at Ivy Green, their homestead.

Moving in with a family is what Daniel Kish routinely does and it is one reason I felt comfortable comparing him with Anne Sullivan. Daniel lives with a blind student all day in the child's home. In this way, Daniel works with a child (and with parents and siblings) for hours during the child's normal routine. Daniel does this intensive training weeks at a time.

Daniel comes into a family with a philosophy, with discipline and focus, and he has a set of well-tested principles that he uses to impact a child's life. I will review a few of Daniel's teaching practices below under the title "Rules of Orientation and Mobility."

Imagine this scene on the porch at Helen's Ivy Green house: Daniel, who is totally blind, has just arrived to help a severely visually impaired teacher and her deaf-blind seven-year-old pupil. How will the trio communicate with each other? How does a blind mobility specialist work with blind children or with a deaf-blind child? I will paint myself into this picture as a narrator (external observer) because often, when I am with Daniel on a trip, I photograph him at his work and take notes for my book about him.

Daniel will use fingerspelling and braille to communicate with Helen and he can talk with Anne Sullivan, no problem there—it will all work out he tells Helen's mother Kate Keller, who is not so sure as she surveys the trio. Daniel explains that for a few days all he wants to do is follow Sullivan around as she works with Helen. We will assume that the breakthrough at the water fountain has already occurred and Helen has discovered a passionate desire to learn everything she can, as fast as she can.

It only takes a few hours of observation for Daniel to see that Anne Sullivan has an understanding that would have made her a good

Orientation and Mobility specialist. Sullivan understands the First Rule of Orientation and Mobility: *Blind children must move.* Many blind kids across the world are not allowed to move because sighted folks think that vision is required for navigation. These well-meaning caregivers are wrong; *immobilizing a blind child is devastating to the child's cognitive development—not allowing a blind child to move about is an ignorant strategy (unsupported by research), physically and emotionally debilitating, and irresponsibly cruel.* I have to be emphatic and in-your-face with this statement because the practice of immobilizing blind kids is happening right now all over the planet.

An individual's feeling of well-being is intimately linked to movement: the more we purposefully move (the more we interact within the world and with others) the more mentally healthy we become. Opposite this, the more we sit and do nothing, the more at risk we are for depression and physical deterioration. Anne Sullivan had Helen Keller moving from place to place all day long, everyday—the two were always active. This was brilliant on Sullivan's part, even though she was acting intuitively. Sullivan had no idea that these daily adventures were driving Helen's brain to rewire itself. Learning requires movement; Helen Keller evolved such a complex and eloquent mind because she explored her world.

It is not only well-being that is affected when we restrict a blind child's movements. The anatomy of the brain is also crafted (altered, trained) through movement. Neuroscientists have become intensely interested in a small brain region called the hippocampus. The cells in the hippocampus (for example, place cells, GPS-like grid cells, border-detecting cells, Vector Trace cells, and straight-ahead cells) await purposeful movement before they can grow and develop sophisticated connections. If purposeful movement does not occur, hippocampal cells atrophy, fail to grow connections, and, consequently, the ability to navigate decreases. In other words, the essential act of navigation, getting from location to location efficiently (purposeful movement), develops the biology and physiology of neurons. Reduce navigation and you inhibit the brain cells responsible for navigation. The brains of blind kids are being biologically harmed by the practice of restricting movement.

The Second Rule of Orientation and Mobility is this: *Blind children must learn to explore their surroundings on their own.* Self-discovery is the best kind of education. Experiences are needed in many kinds of environments, but a blind child's movements should not be constantly guided by others. Daniel says that the amount of time spent guiding a blind child should be drastically reduced and replaced by self-driven curiosity, passion, and self-discovery. This quote is from Daniel's pending book:

> When a blind child is guided through an environment, we are not allowing for the neurodevelopment of what is called in cognitive science *executive functioning*. The pre-frontal lobes of the brain, the seat of executive functioning, create personality, drive, and creativity. Therefore, hampering executive functioning has global and long-lasting effects on drive, creatively, and ultimately on personality. Our cognitive CEO makes choices, decides meaning, makes judgements, and organizes affairs; it is no surprise that many blind people struggle with all these skills, especially those blind individuals who have been guided everywhere. [111]

Sullivan got this rule right, as well. She encouraged Helen to unleash her curiosity, to get into things, to run her fingers over everything, to wade into the river, to climb trees, to search through drawers, to walk in the rain. Helen Keller was set free to explore and discover on her own. Sullivan was watching, of course, interceding as any teacher might, but she did not restrict Helen's curiosity.

There is a direct connection between movement in space and movement in thought: the greater the freedom allowed in the real world, the more powerful—more fluid, innovative, and expressive—the mind becomes. A fundamental reason Helen Keller developed such a free-spirited personality, and such powerful cognitive skills, was because she could explore the physical world on her own; she followed her curiosity. Mobility specialists know that it is okay to "crash a lot," to allow blind kids to bump their heads, scratch their arms, and to accrue some minor bumps as they learn how the world works.

Most modern-day Orientation and Mobility professionals agree that a child learns best when they are motivated to explore the environment on their own. A main job of the external senses is to alert attention to variables in the environment. If the environment is not "speaking to a child," then that child is not motivated to move. That is why many blind and deaf-blind kids are passive—nothing in the environment is beckoning them. The first task of the mobility specialist is to discover what might motivate a child to move. Curiosity needs to be encouraged and nurtured as the blind child sets out on their lifelong learning adventure.

Anne Sullivan was a masterful motivator; she exposed Helen Keller to every environment available. The two of them did few lessons at a desk. They got outside into the orchard, climbed trees, picked fruit, smelled the roses, and got pricked by thorns. They went down to the river and waded into the water. They went from experience to experience, *making friends with the environment* (as Daniel Kish puts it). Deliberate exploration of different kinds of domains—gardens, kitchens, orchards, carriages, bedrooms—in different kinds of weather, gave Helen a firsthand understanding of the physical universe she was born into. It was as if Anne Sullivan had studied with John Dewey, the great American philosopher of the pragmatic, the man who insisted that experience was the greatest teacher. John Dewey would have been proud of the conviction Anne Sullivan expressed in this letter to Sophia Hopkins:

> I am beginning to suspect all elaborate and special systems of education. They seem to me to be built up on the supposition that every child is a kind of idiot who must be taught to think. Whereas, if the child is left to himself, he will think more and better, if less showily. Let him go and come freely, let him touch real things and combine his impressions for himself, instead of sitting indoors at a little round table, while a sweet-voiced teacher suggests that he build a stone wall with his wooden blocks, or make a rainbow out of strips of colored paper, or paint straw trees in bead flower-pots. Such teaching fills the mind with artificial associations that must be got rid of before the child can develop independent ideas out of actual experiences.[112]

Sullivan takes Helen from one venue to another; every day they are off on another adventure of discovery. They even climb trees which especially pleases Daniel because tree climbing was freeing and exhilarating for him when he was a boy. Plus, Daniel's tree climbing obsession scared his mother, which is a plus for a young lad. Sullivan lets Helen touch the rose bushes and get jabbed by thorns. She lets Helen get dirty and wet, scratched, and bruised as Helen learns what is safe and what is not, what works and what does not. Experience is the best teacher and Sullivan gets high marks for her teaching strategy.

Daniel is quite pleased after watching Annie and Helen for a few days; he gives Sullivan exceedingly high marks for knowing intuitively the right thing to do. The Third Rule of Orientation and Mobility training, closely related to the first two rules, is this: *Do not over-protect blind children.* Daniel tells Sullivan that the rule in his profession is to "treat a blind child the same way you would treat a sighted child of the same age."

"Well," Sullivan asks Daniel, "is that it? I take her to different places and let her explore on her own, and I do not overprotect her? I let her bump her head and fall into ditches. I am already doing that. What else should I be doing?"

"There is a tool," Daniel tells Sullivan, "that we use in the field of Orientation and Mobility. It is called *the long cane.* Like all blind people, Helen needs a long cane, a cane tailored for her height and her walking speed. Modern canes for blind people are slender and quite long [i.e., not a support cane]. A long cane will allow Helen to move very quickly without fear of crashing into stuff or falling downstairs. Learning to use the long cane is quite easy. Once Helen understands how the cane works, she will take it with her everywhere, especially outside or in unfamiliar locations. The long cane will eventually feel like an extension of her arm. We will start the training in the morning. I have a cane for you, as well, Annie. People with severe visual impairments also use canes."

A curious child with a long cane can explore and quickly master a location, especially if the child is motivated. The child also needs to know that parents, teachers, and caregivers support the use of the cane. Parents, relatives, and friends need to allow (encourage) unaided, independent mobility. The problem is that sighted people do not often believe—deep in their heart—that a person with no vision is capable of independent travel. One of the primary reasons that blind and deaf-blind kids fail to become independent travelers is because of the ill-informed and quite harmful attitudes (assumptions) of the sighted population. Sighted individuals often do not see the value of a cane because of their initial belief that navigation requires vision.

The fourth rule of Orientation and Mobility is this: *use a full-length cane and the feather-touch technique when moving through space.* Daniel Kish redefined cane length in the profession of Orientation and

Mobility. Instead of using the term *long cane,* he uses the phrase *full-length cane.* Daniel determines cane length by measuring the distance between outstretched arms; this results in a cane much longer than is routinely prescribed by the profession. Daniel will have Helen stretch her arms out to the sides and he will measure the length from fingertip to fingertip—that will determine how long Helen's cane will be. New canes will be issued as Helen gets older and taller.

The *feather technique* was invented by Daniel and his staff to maximize perceptual input up the cane shaft. The cane glides very lightly over floor surfaces, barely touching them. In this manner, the cane user can pick up subtle differences in the terrain; the floor becomes an orientation map. Deaf-blind travelers especially need the subtle information coming from the ground. The *feather technique* gives them information needed to verify location and to navigate along pathways.

The fifth rule of Orientation and Mobility training is this: *Blind children need to systematically explore space.* Blind kids need to study space because space has a language with its own rules, syntax, and grammar. The language of space is complex, and it requires long years of study to master.

Blind kids need to study space as they become developmentally ready. Once they do this—year by year—they slowly discover that space is redundant and reliable, that the architecture of space can be used to navigate. A teacher is needed at this point, someone who understands human navigation and spatial concepts. It is at this juncture that Orientation and Mobility specialists introduce a developmentally appropriate teaching strategy, tailored to the child. Anne Sullivan had her hands full teaching Helen Keller about the entire world; we can forgive her for not teaching spatial concepts. However, it is at this point that history fails Helen; she could have become a highly accomplished role model for independent travel had she gotten a full-length cane and developmentally appropriate instruction.

Here is a quote from Daniel, in which he explains to a young mother how to work with her blind child:

> Continue to work on foundational building blocks. This comes in part from conceptualizing and using basic, reasonably predictable environmental elements. These include some conventions such as:

- Walls are generally straight and flat.
- Walls usually meet other walls at some point in things called corners.
- Walls generally hold something up called a ceiling.
- Walls are supported by floors.
- Walls often have doors and windows that can be opened and closed.
- People often put things against walls; you can trip over these objects.
- Walls often run parallel to other walls.
- Corridors (hallways) generally run straight and are defined by parallel walls and by floors and ceilings (also parallel).
- There are often intersections where hallways come together, usually at right angles.
- Walls often have doors which may stand open or closed. Watch out for half-opened doors.

Acoustic spaces are generally made up of three types of sound-image signatures:

- Open (no boundaries), like perceiving open fields or large parking lots.
- Closed (boundaries), like "looking" down a hallway.
- Present (objects are there but not boundaries), like a park filled with trees and benches.

Fences are an exception; they are open boundaries. ["What I said about acoustic spaces here may also pertain to vibro-tactual spaces for a deaf-blind person."]

The ground is either flat or not, and it may go up or down. It is generally more or less invariant, meaning that what was there before is likely to be there again. Deaf-blind people have been observed to use this (ground-based) information extremely well to learn and orient to new spaces very quickly.[113]

Sighted individuals take the world for granted as they navigate; no one needs to explain to a sighted kid about walls, doors, windows, floors, ceilings, and so on. However, we cannot assume that a blind child will know about the design structures of the built-environment.

Daniel speaks of *environmental literacy*; he is talking about how expertly a blind child has learned the language (the rules, syntax, and grammar) of space. Without systematic training, a blind child will be environmentally illiterate.

Sixth rule: if you must be assisted by a human guide do so in a manner that preserves as much personal independence as possible. In other words [speaking to a blind person], do not totally surrender your awareness of the environment and your independence to another person; their judgment and attention may not be stellar. Stay aware of your location, keep the cane in front of you, and use active echolocation to protect yourself and to maintain orientation.

Cultures differ in their interpretation of the needs of blind individuals. An almost universal belief is that blind people will get hurt if they are allowed to move about without a sighted guide. Blind individuals—especially sophisticated travelers like Daniel Kish—must cope with the insistence that they relinquish their independent movement to a third party. If this happens, Daniel suggests that the blind individual not stop monitoring the environment; that they maintain their sense of orientation. Here is Daniel speaking of his experiences in India in which he was not allowed to move about without a helping hand:

> What was fascinating to me is that, even though I was guided everywhere, more or less motored through virtually every activity in the interest of what I will call social flow, . . . the perception of my companions maintained that I was the most independent and capable person they'd ever met. When I queried one of my guides more deeply, he said he had never met a blind person, so he had no idea what to expect, but, as he put it, "You can do everything!", this after several days of having done nothing outside my hotel room without "hands together" to guide the process. Upon reflection, I believe this perception [that the blind need constant "hands-on help"] arises from the sense of casual and graceful social flow that can result from this well-coordinated transpersonal dyad. I have experienced the traditional model to be sluggish and cumbersome by comparison, marginally effective and relatively distasteful. If I dare speak for Helen, I think she might say something similar, although doubtless more eloquently.

Every culture has unique characteristics. Daniel speaks of the "traditional model," which is a sighted guide technique used in the United States (and elsewhere in the Western world). In India, there is a social element, a need to flow from social experience to social experience. A blind person from the U.S. might find that their guide in India wishes to hold their hand as they move about. Daniel is respectful of cultural practices even as he teaches alternative techniques and philosophies.

I recall a story Daniel told me about a day in Calcutta when he was exploring the street where his hotel was located. He came to a set of downward steps, which his cane picked up immediately. Before he could start down the steps, he heard a great commotion behind him, and two young men rushed up to "save him from sure calamity." They each took an arm and lifted Daniel into the air and carried him to "safety" at the bottom of the steps. Daniel was stunned, much annoyed, but managed to be polite and express gratitude for the (unwanted and unneeded) help. I believe this is what Daniel was expressing in the above quote; there is a kindness and helpfulness within the Indian culture, well-meaning and gently expressed. Daniel was contrasting this "social flow" with models of guidance he had experienced in less gentle cultures.

Daniel was in India because he had been invited there. He told me once that he only goes where "the wood is ready to burn." "There is no use," he told me, empathically, "to go uninvited where the wood is green and will not catch fire." The analogy refers to people who are ready to learn and ready to change, compared to places that will not budge from centuries of habit and ignorance.

Wherever he goes, Daniel experiences a sighted population that believes vision is required for navigation. This is an understandable cultural ignorance found throughout the world. Part of Daniel's mission is to confront this unfortunate practice. Wherever he journeys, he dialogues about the "best practices for allowing blind people to develop independent and happy lives." He also teaches the Principles of Orientation and Mobility reviewed above.

Redundancy

As Daniel explained to the young mother in the quote above, blind kids must learn about the various kinds of environments that exist in our physical universe. Each environment has *invariables*, dependable objects and dependable spatial relationships. In a garden, for example, you find plants, shrubs, and pathways laid out in a logical, deliberate fashion; plants are of various kinds that can be recognized, categorized, and used. A modern kitchen has a refrigerator, stove, pots and pans, a sink, and so on. A kitchen is often filled with a rich variety of pleasant smells, especially if meal preparation is happening. A bathroom has a different set of smells and dependable objects. Each specialized room has a general purpose, and each room presents an opportunity for exploration, self-discovery, and for guided learning. A student learns to "read" specific environments.

Blind children can learn environments because the physical world is dependable. The same set of principles are found everywhere we go in our land-based, gravity-dependent world. For example, if I ask you to draw a landscape, you will have a set of assumptions that you can use to build *any* landscape. Another human will have the same set of assumptions so they will be able to interpret what you have drawn. These environmental redundancies include this (incomplete) list:

- *Up and down* will be assumed. Everything has a ground (earth, floor, surface). There are things above the ground and things below, but always there is a framework with a ground and a horizon.
- Almost all movement of sentient creatures in a domain is straight-ahead, and there is assumed purpose to movement—movement is primarily directed toward a destination or a goal.
- The physical world has bilateral symmetry. We perceive mirror images all around us. All mobile sentient creatures have mirror-image right and left sides. We also perceive bilateral balance everywhere in a scene. Most man-made objects, large or small, mimic nature (and the human bilateral body); the "built environment" is also primarily symmetrical, employing mirror images.
- There is logic and repetition in natural space and in man-made space. For example, stars are not underground, it does not naturally rain inside buildings, houses are not customarily constructed using wavy and leaning walls. We expect a mountain scene to be different from an urban scene or an aquatic scene.
- There is geometry in physical space; the world seems to be constructed using Lego-like building blocks. We perceive circles,

rectangles, squares, and triangles (etc.) embedded in scenes. The universe seems to be constructed on a geometric matrix.

- Invariants, the environmental redundancies listed here, are true across timelines. Image-invariants were true during the caveman days, for centuries after the hunter-gathers, in the present moment, and they will continue to be invariant in the future.

- Although spatial locations and time frames vary, experiences repeat. There are only so many kinds of experience; for example: birth, death, the chronological growth sequence (aging), stages of cognitive development, family (group) gatherings, eating meals, going to the bathroom, navigating from domain to domain, and so on.

- Spatial and temporal scale is important, but there will always be variations in scale—everything in a domain will follow the same rules of scale. For example, we can use a microscope to perceive details in a scene or we can use a telescope (or a map) to get a broad overview. It is always possible to adjust our scopes to get ever closer or ever farther-away views of the physical world.

Interestingly, the design of the physical world is mirrored by the design of the human brain. As I mentioned earlier, the neocortex of the human brain has a redundant biological architecture—a similar neuronal design can be seen in the visual cortex, auditory cortex, motor cortex, etc.—everywhere in the neocortex, neurons are connected in a similar pattern and use a basic universal circuit. This implies that a similar brain-based software algorithm is being used to process the world. In other words, the mind evolves using the same neurological plan (blueprint) repeatedly to construct/represent reality.

More interesting, perhaps, is the supposition that *the way we think* also mirrors the way the neocortex (and the physical world) is designed. Structure dictates function. For example, neurons operate within gravity and have cellular designs that take gravity into consideration. Perception identifies a physical world that is also constructed under the constraints of gravity. Concepts (thoughts, reasoning, emotions), which are made from perceptions, are also built from within the constraints of gravity; that is why some thoughts are weighed down, pulled, centered, why some emotions are grave or light, and why we struggle to overcome unseen forces.

Once we see this connection between the invariant design of the physical universe and the resultant evolution of the brain and mind, the more examples surface. I cannot go into detail here (the subject is too vast), but I can give a few more examples of structure dictating function:

- The mind treats all ideas (thoughts) as objects. *The mind navigates the mental terrain using thought-landmarks, thought-pathways, and thought-scenes.*
- Everything in the universe is connected (embodied, nested). Neurons are all linked (they do not function on their own). In the same way, all our thoughts are connected, interconnected, and redundant. Just as there are physical networks, there are also mind-related networks.
- Behaviors (movement patterns) are made possible by parallel or serial firing of clusters of neurons. Likewise, *thinking* generates thoughts that are processed in parallel or are serially processed.
- Neurons have gaps between them (surrounding spaces that define their structure). Thoughts also have gaps. Everything is separated by these empty spaces. Meaning only arises because of the emptiness (the gaps). This sentence would make no sense without the spaces between words and letters.
- Our thoughts fall into two categories, as does the mind itself: Egocentric and Allocentric. The very essence of my Navigational Consciousness hypothesis is based on the connection between the mind and the structure of the physical universe.

The redundancies listed in this section are the structures/patterns that Helen Keller was born into, a world where patterns repeat and where the brain at birth is ready to recognize these redundant patterns—a world where thoughts are created in the image of the physical world. Helen Keller demonstrates that these patterns exist even in the absence of vision and hearing and can be detected and used by the rest of the senses.

Navigational Disability

I define the profession of Orientation and Mobility as *the art and science of navigation applied to people who have navigational disabilities.* This is a much broader definition than the profession usually employs when describing the practice. My definition also contains the term *navigational disability*, which is rarely used in the field. I coined the term *navigational disability* late in my career when I was justifying my work with children in special education who were not blind or visually impaired. This broad definition of Orientation and Mobility also contains the underlying assumption that purposeful movement (navigation) is fundamental to human evolution. Having gone down this long difficult journey into our cognitive universe, we now have the background to look at the concept of *navigational disability*.

When I was working with severely impaired children in special education, I realized that all of them—without exception and no matter what their special education label—had some degree of difficulty with navigation. The difficulties varied in degree and kind, but always it came down to problems navigating efficiently and safely through the environment. Why, I wondered, was the problem so ubiquitous? What was going on? Trying to answer that question was the portal through which I began to explore navigation and consciousness.

Here is the simple answer: If the brain and nervous system (the whole body) evolved to enable straight-ahead navigation, then any severe insult to the brain and nervous system would naturally affect navigational ability—you would *expect to find* navigational disabilities associated with severe impairments. Because of dual-process theory, we would also expect that a navigational disability would manifest two ways, Allocentrically and Egocentrically. That is, indeed, what we find, although nowhere will you find the distinction between Allocentric and Egocentric (as it is employed in dual-process theory) used in the blind rehabilitation or special education literature. What I am outlining/debating in this book is new to my profession.

Because the whole human body works in harmony to enable straight-ahead navigation, there is a robust adaptation system that adjusts to impairments. There is a constant and fluid adaptation to any insult that endangers navigation. Compensation methods abound. That is why we often cannot detect navigational disabilities—because the whole body has compensated. However, when impairments are severe (blindness, deafness) the body's compensation mechanisms can only provide partial and incomplete adjustments—navigational impairments become manifest the more severe the physical damage.

When we look at deaf children or blind children, we see two general kinds of severe navigational disability; blind kids have a severe Allocentric disability and deaf kids have a severe Egocentric disability. I introduced this difference between deaf children and blind children in my first book *Bugs Blindness and the Pursuit of Happiness* (2016). I will not go into detail here (the subject is complex) except to say that deaf kids live in a near total spatial world and blind kids live in a near total temporal world. The navigational strategy for teaching a deaf child is the opposite to the strategy needed when teaching a blind child. Obviously, a deaf-blind child is deficient in both Allocentric and Egocentric arenas; these kids require a blending of the strategies used with deaf children or with blind children.

With other children in special education (those who see and hear), the navigational disability is less obvious and less severe, but still present. Most often, we do not look for the navigational disability (or compensatory adjustments) and, therefore, fail to identify any problems with navigation. Almost always navigational disabilities are due to problems in either Egocentric processing *through failed attention* or Allocentric processing *through failed awareness*. I spent a lot of time teaching children in special education how to cross streets. *Almost always these kids were in danger because they did not know how to "pay attention, and/or "how to be aware."*

In my opinion, it is the responsibility of the Orientation and Mobility profession to embrace the concept of navigational disability and to offer practical solutions based on individual, developmentally-informed analysis of a child's impairments. I am suggesting that the profession of Orientation and Mobility reinvent itself around dual-process theory and navigational disability. This approach also assumes that O&M specialists would address the needs *of all children* with severe navigational disabilities regardless of the child's degree of vision.

The professionals in the field of occupational therapy are also in an excellent position to use this new perspective (Navigational Consciousness and Navigational Disability) to help children in special education—this also suggests a need to "blend" the two professions (OT and O&M) in some beneficial manner.[114]

The Long Cane and the Blind Child

Mobility specialists know that the long cane is a key tool to enable efficient navigation for blind travelers. There are professional debates about how long a cane should be, how to move the cane for maximum effectiveness, what alloy a cane should be made of to get maximum information up the shaft, what developmental age to introduce the cane, and what developmentally relevant lessons should be taught. However, the one thing everyone agrees on (in the developed nations) is that *a cane should be used* by a blind traveler, especially in unfamiliar or challenging environments. The long cane is a tool that enables independent movement—it frees the blind individual from constant monitoring by well-meaning caregivers.

There are short, thick support canes that are used for orthopedic purposes, but the long cane is constructed specifically for the blind to gather information from surfaces—from the uneven and textured ground. The cane also picks up drop-offs and detects obstacles in a path. The long cane is essentially an extension of the hand and fingers, transmitting information up the shaft. fMRI studies show that the cane (like any tool) is embodied, which simply means that the human brain incorporates the long cane as if the cane was an organic part of the arm, hand, and fingers. It is as if the hand grew a long finger that can explore floor surfaces.

Experienced blind travelers walk (flow calmly) behind the cane as if the cane were rhythmically whispering, "it is safe, it is safe, it is safe." The cane can easily tell a grassy surface from concrete or asphalt, pebbles from water, rugs from a hardwood floor, and so on. The floor (any surface) is a map that can be used for accurate location-based orientation. Because the cane subconsciously gathers ground-based information, a blind traveler can hold their head level with the ground (no longer worrying what the feet are doing) and can concentrate on auditory cues coming from the surrounding environment.

When a cane is tapped on a floor, the sound will vary depending on what the floor is made of and what is on and under the floor. Tapping on a floor will also cause an echo that will help determine the distance from walls and openings (for those who can hear). Helen Keller was exceptionally good at reading vibrational energy. I imagine she would have been able to detect the vibrations made as the cane contacted surfaces and to use these vibrational patterns for orientation.

After a short while, a blind traveler learns to trust the information that the cane provides. Vibrational patterns flow up the shaft of the cane and are incorporated and remembered subconsciously; eventually, the blind traveler begins to flow gracefully and with confidence through environments using the full-length cane. Many blind people in third world nations learn to use sticks of various kinds to aid their self-movement. A simple wooden stick works where a modern cane is lacking.

I am not sure why Helen Keller was not trained to use the long cane, especially after World War Two, when the field of Orientation and Mobility first appeared as a university-based discipline. Lions Clubs across the world championed the long cane as soon as they became aware of the tool. I am inclined to think that somewhere on the planet, at some moment in time, someone had shown Helen Keller a long cane. If that happened, nothing came of the introduction and there are no records.

A few months after I wrote the above paragraph, I watched a newsreel of Helen's trip to Israel after the Second World War had ended (late 1940s). She and Polly Thomson were visiting a village set up for blind people. The newsreel showed Helen and Polly walking toward the blindness community when a representative of the community rushed to greet them This representative held a cane in one hand and was holding the harness of a dog guide in the other hand. Because of this experience (and probably others), we can say for sure that Helen was aware that both canes and dog guides were tools used by blind people. In the book *Helen Keller, Sketch for a Portrait* (1956), author Van Wyck Brooks reports that in Scotland Helen occasionally "used a shepherd's crook to guide her." This makes sense because it is almost intuitive for a blind person to pick up a long stick and move it in front of the body to avoid hitting obstacles or falling in holes.

Daniel Kish even advocates placing an age-appropriate "soft stick" in an infant's hands as soon as the infant can grasp. According to Daniel, banging the stick about at random would eventually lead to a deliberate probing of objects and surfaces outside arms reach. Also, tactual feedback from the stick would set the child up for learning to eventually use echolocation for navigation (if the child could hear).

Therefore, the first tool a modern Anne Sullivan would have used when she arrived in Tuscumbia Alabama, would have been a full-length cane—one of Helen's first gifts from Anne Sullivan would have been a "navigation-stick."

Guide Dogs for the Deaf-Blind

It would not take Daniel Kish long to realize that Helen Keller loved dogs. Daniel knows that dogs are specially trained to be used with blind individuals. There are even programs that use dogs as navigational assistants for deaf-blind people. As an adult, Helen's own dogs followed on her daily walks and at times nudged her this way or that. What was lacking in her time were training institutions that taught the blind to use "technologies" like canes and dog guides.

The first dog guide school in the United States was *The Seeing Eye*, which was incorporated in Nashville, Tennessee on January 29, 1929, when Helen Keller was 49 years old. She was born too late to take advantage of dog training programs for the deaf-blind. I have a feeling that Daniel Kish would have prepared the young Helen for the possibility of eventually using a dog as a guide. Here is a quote from the web page for *Leader Dogs for the Blind* (located in Rochester, Michigan):

> In 1992, Leader Dogs for the Blind became the first organization to provide guide dogs specifically trained for clients who are both deaf and blind. Instruction is provided via American Sign Language, either tactile or visual, based on a client's range of vision.
>
> A guide dog working with a person who is deaf-blind must be extremely mature. Their training stresses partner awareness because they receive all commands from their handler via hand signals. Much attention is placed on traffic awareness and proper street crossings since these can be extreme safety issues for people who are deaf-blind.[115]

Because she loved dogs so much, had they been available, Helen would have used a trained guide dog to assist with her navigation.

Dogs are trained these days to be more than just guides for the blind or deaf-blind. They are also trained to assist physically impaired people, deaf individuals, and they are carefully trained to help people with mental and emotional traumas. Dogs are therapy assistants by nature; good for what mentally ails any of us. To have a dog friend is to have a lifelong faithful companion, something Helen Keller and Anne Sullivan (who also loved dogs) knew firsthand.

Training Perception

Daniel Kish is a psychologist and a special educator; he knows the importance of training perception, especially in blind kids. That is why he insists that freedom of movement comes before everything else. Movement generates sensations and perceptions, which further generates concepts (thoughts). Sophisticated brains are created through movement, through building a catalog of experiences that show, firsthand, how space is constructed. Watching Anne Sullivan work with Helen Keller, Daniel would perceive that Sullivan, through her teaching methods and homegrown philosophy, was developing Helen's perceptual skills. Sullivan was laying the perceptual foundation that would enable Helen Keller to later develop sophisticated concepts and eloquent language.

All animals are born ready to survive in a specific kind of environment. Fish, for example, are obviously born to swim and to breathe water. A bird is born to fly and breathe air. The human infant comes "factory-ready" to respond to a ground-based environment. A bird and a fish do not need to go to school to learn behaviors, like how to move to find food and shelter, how to mate and who to mate with, how to avoid predators, how to swim or how to fly, and so on. Most behaviors are innate for birds, fish, and most animals. The same is true to a great degree for human beings. It is just that many human behaviors are potential. For example, infants are born ready to learn a language. But the language they become proficient in depends upon what they are exposed to (what they experience); a French kid will learn to understand and speak French, while English kids will learn English.

A child who moves around a lot, guided by their own curiosity, will develop highly formed gross and fine motor skills, as well as acute perceptual abilities. A child whose movement is restricted will have atrophied muscles and weak, ineffective sensory systems.

Whether or not certain behaviors develop normally depends upon the circumstances surrounding a human life. A child will walk between ages one and two if that child gets food, shelter, love, and opportunity. Likewise, language will develop within a set time, socialization will grow in sophistication as a child matures, and physical developmental milestones will unfold as chronological age increases—provided the environment and social structure are encouraging and supportive. In other words, there is a very particular way that human behaviors manifest over time. These behaviors are predictable and reliable.

But what happens when a child is born blind (or deaf, or deaf-blind)? How does deaf-blindness affect behavioral development? How is language affected by impairments? How is navigation affected by impairments? How is socialization affected? The first thing to understand, if we are to begin to answer these complex questions, is the concept of *embodiment*, which I discussed earlier in different contexts.

The brain is part of the human body. If you dissect it out of the body and put it on a coffee table, it will die and so will the body it was once in. The brain cannot be dissected from a body because the brain is embodied—it is an inseparable part of the whole. Likewise, the body cannot be separated out of the domain it was designed to function in. The human body needs an earth to stand on, a sun to shine above, air to breathe, and gravity. If you put the body under water for too long it will die—we are not water creatures with gills, we are air creatures with lungs.

Whatever behavior a human being manifests, that behavior incorporates *all* the systems of the body simultaneously. The whole-body walks, for example, there is no time where some part of the body walks while some other part of the body declines to cooperate (except where severe physical impairments are manifest). Vision works synchronously with hearing, which works in harmony with proprioception, which works seamlessly with touch and with the olfactory and vestibular systems. Everything is networked and everything functions synchronously.

What this implies is that a sensory system, like vision, can be knocked out, but the rest of the body's systems still work together to enable behaviors—you can still walk (think, imagine, create) even if you are deaf, blind, or deaf and blind. The loss of a sensory system can dampen an organism's efficiency and accuracy, but overall (general) behaviors are not knocked out. However, the loss of a dominant sense, like vision and/or hearing, does affect efficiency and accuracy—developmental milestones are often delayed. What should a teacher do, then, to decrease the impact of sensory deprivation?

The answer an Orientation and Mobility specialist would offer is that, when impairments are present, *perception itself needs to be trained*. Perceptions arise through experience—through emersion in diverse environments and cultures. Through targeted perceptual training, the systems that enable behaviors can be maintained, even enhanced. Simply put, hearing, for example, can be trained to compensate for the loss of vision, and proprioception can be trained and enhanced to compensate for deaf-blindness.

Daniel would have shown Anne Sullivan how Orientation and Mobility training can address perceptual impairments and developmental delays. This is not as intuitive as allowing a child to play and explore. And it is not as intuitive or easy as training the remaining senses, such as experiencing and labeling different kinds of odors.

A further critical understanding is that children must be developmentally ready to learn new skills. You cannot teach a baby to read a book or play catch with a baseball; a baby's brain has not matured enough, nor have the baby's muscles and senses matured enough to enable complex tasks. However, with each passing year, a child becomes ready to add new skills. Just like learning to read and write print, learning to read and write braille is incremental; we must teach children's minds in stages, when they are ready to take in what we are offering—it takes about twelve years, for example, for a blind child to become highly proficient with braille. The same is true for teaching perceptual skills and for teaching the Orientation and Mobility curriculum—it takes about twelve years of incremental perceptual training to enable a blind child to become navigationally proficient. We can only develop what a child's brain is ready to learn. The reason we have twelve grade levels in our educational system (in the United States) is because each year presents the teacher with a more sophisticated child; each year more difficult skills can be introduced.

I do not have the space here to explore the complex field of perceptual training further. Entire professions are built around studying and training perception (occupational therapy and special education, for example). I will also leave my reverie at this point—Daniel, Helen, and Annie at Ivy Green—as we dive deeper into modern approaches to teaching Orientation and Mobility skills.

Training Dual-Cognition

As I spent Chapter Four explaining, the Ego and the Self are different. The Ego uses a system called *attention* to understand the world, while the Self uses a system called *awareness* to understand the surroundings (my hypothesis). Anatomically and physiologically, these two systems are mutually exclusive, as one system wanes, the other system emerges. This ebbing and flowing is the very essence of my version of dual-process theory. There are implications and responsibilities that arise from this understanding of human duality, not the least of which is that we need to train (educate) both attention *and* awareness.

Students need to learn (to know) when they are using one system or the other. Attention is very localized, a "tunnel-vision" perception, holding convergence and focus on a specific location in space. Awareness is a whole-body knowing, an absorption-process that requires movement to be activated and that is mostly operating below Egoic consciousness. Let me explain this better with an example.

Think of figures embedded in a scene. The Egoic attention-based perceptual system is about processing the figures that stand out in an environment. We can locate these figures and go directly to them. However, if we ignore the objects (the figures) in a domain, and simply flow around them as we navigate, then we are using the Allocentric awareness-based perceptual system. Human perception employs two systems for navigation, one that hunts for objects (figures, landmarks that attract or repel) and a second system that flows around objects.

Here is the key understanding: The more we concentrate on a figure, the more we lose the perception of the ground. The more we defocus and become aware of the ground (the scene), the less detail we can extract from the figures. This is a sliding scale perceptual design—there is a dynamic balance between object-perception (attention), and action-perception (awareness).

The two perceptual systems also oscillate at speeds that allow for the illusion of what we call *reality*. We do not feel that we are attending or being aware (that there are two systems oscillating) as we go about our daily tasks. The two systems seamlessly cooperate.

As a teacher, Anne Sullivan must have sensed the two mutually exclusive perceptual systems inherent in human design. Therefore, she unconsciously used two separate but equal approaches to Helen Keller's education. Knowledge acquisition was important (the Egoic curriculum; learning to read and write braille, for example), but so, also, was the experiential curriculum equally important—the education of the Self. Anne Sullivan intuitively understood the need for real-life experiences, for movement through various physical domains. Helen not only read about fruit trees (gained knowledge), but she also climbed the trees, felt the bark and leaves, and she picked and ate the fruit as it ripened—she moved through the branches, explored with her body, hands, and feet.

Anne Sullivan understood that Helen was not going to truly comprehend the environment unless Helen could experience her surroundings. Once Helen was exposed to an experience, she became curious and wanted more experiences. Experience is the food of the Allocentric mind, and it is the source of wisdom. American philosopher John Dewey articulated *the need for experience* in American education. In Daniel Kish's forthcoming book in this series, I show how Daniel's philosophy is in keeping with Dewey's theories. Both men saw freedom of movement and rich (tailored) experiences as the key to excellence in education. We are fortunate that Anne Sullivan intuitively agreed with Daniel Kish and John Dewey—her approach with Helen Keller essentially crafted Helen's sophisticated mind.

I told Daniel about my thought experiment, placing him in Tuscumbia Alabama face-to-face with Sullivan and Keller. Daniel said he was not an expert on Helen Keller, but he had a feeling that he shared with me, which I like:

> It is difficult to say what would happen if we took the Helen Keller of the 20th century and applied modern approaches to movement and navigation to her. How would Helen Keller emerge from our training? Doubtless she would emerge with different insights, not better or worse perhaps, but different. It seems that many of her insights came from the expertly strategic way she managed her social circumstances to establish and maintain her connection to the world. If she had access to some of our modern skills, it is hard to say how that might have altered her perspective and strategies. I know that if my eyes had not been removed as a baby, I would not have grown to become much like the Daniel Kish I am now. Likewise, if Helen Keller had somehow become independently mobile, I dare say she would not be the Helen Keller who we know to have graced history.[116]

Daniel is cautioning us to be careful with our modern strategies, our speculations, and our highly evolved technologies. We are altering perception (and cognition) as we apply our modern knowledge; we are altering how the future unfolds for the people we educate.

～

If Helen Keller were alive today (I am letting my imagination flow again), she would be doing yoga, Tai Chi, Qigong, meditation, breathing exercises, and she would probably be a vegetarian or a vegan (a Post-Modern profile). She would be carrying a cane or using her guide dog to assist independent travel. Helen would use a laptop computer with a refreshable braille display; she would have access to email, texts, social media, and search engines. Her technologies would automatically translate her braille or typed documents into speech for others to access. The spoken language of others would be translated, in real time, to her braille display. She might have written a lot more books had she lived in our era, because the task of authorship during her lifetime was arduous, labor intensive, and exceedingly difficult to edit.

If she wanted, Helen would have access to vibrational technologies, such as handheld sonar flashlights that would tell her where the walls were or where solid objects were located within the spaces around her. Sonar systems can also be placed in canes or in head-mounted systems. Helen might even have a service robot at her beck and call. She would have taken Orientation and Mobility lessons from preschool to college and learned how to understand and navigate through space. She would have had access to complex tactile maps that showed her spatial perspectives and relationships—therefore, she would have been able to peruse the spatial layouts of rooms, buildings, parks, cities, etc. She would have learned about landmarks, clues, beacons, and spatial zones that surround the body; she would know about reference locations, taking perspective, trailing walls and ridge lines using sonar vibrations, and much more. A modern Helen Keller would travel independently through buildings, along outdoor pathways, and on public transportation.

I would like to believe that Helen Keller would look upon this book, this esoteric perspective, with supportive interest. She would also trust science and allow modern researchers to probe her unique mind, although in several of her books she bemoans how often the scientists probed and prodded her tired body and her overworked mind. Helen was a trooper, however—she let most scientists do their research using her as a subject.

Daniel Kish is right that a modern Helen Keller might not have become the unique treasure that we have come to know and love; she might not have become a global mythology. The miracle and the miracle worker were a product of their times. Anyway, it is a moot point, medicine and technology bloomed shortly after Helen Keller died and her contributions came without high technologies and advanced spatial training. As we look over her life, despite all the hardships, Helen Keller lived a charmed existence. The gifts she gave the world still inspire us and still inform our own spiritual evolution.

Helen Keller's Views about Blindness

I had great difficulty reading Helen Keller's perspectives on blindness. I know she was trying to raise money on behalf of her employer the American Foundation for the Blind, so she had to portray blindness as a devastating, life-altering disaster, which, given the state of services and technology when she lived, was probably somewhat valid. Although this dire perspective was assuredly a product of the times, Helen's perspective flies in the face of current thought, especially the views of visionaries like Daniel Kish and his colleagues at *World Access for the Blind* who believe the term *disability* to be a last-generation paradigm.

In our era, there has been a backlash against the custodial views held in the previous century. While Helen Keller was fundraising for AFB, she was understandably caught up in this custodial perspective, which was typical of the industrial age. I am sure that she would not hold these views in the modern world today; she was too openminded and sophisticated to get stuck in an outdated mindset. Here is a typical perspective from one of her fundraising speeches:

> The seeing man goes about his business confident and self-dependent. He does his share of the work of the world in mine, in quarry, in factory, in counting-room, asking others no boon save the opportunity to do a man's part and receive the laborer's guerdon [reward].
>
> In an instant, accident blinds him. The day is blotted out. Night envelops all the visible world. The feet which once bore him to his task with firm and confident stride stumble and halt and fear the forward step. He is forced to a new habit of idleness, which like a canker consumes the mind and destroys its beautiful faculties.
>
> Memory confronts him with his lighted past. Amid the tangible ruins of his life as it promised to be, he gropes his pitiful way. You have met him on your busy thoroughfares, with faltering feet and outstretched hands, patiently dredging

the universal dark, holding out for sale his petty wares, or his cap for your pennies; and this was a man with ambitions and capabilities.[117]

I know that when my blind colleagues read that quote, with the images of a stumbling, groping, shadow of a man begging for pennies, they will cringe—as I did. Contrast the above description with a more modern take on blindness. This is a quote taken from the next book in this series about my friend and colleague Daniel Kish:

> As a young man, Daniel decided to stride through the sighted world with poise and confidence—to embrace his blindness. All his life he refused to be perceived as helpless or unfortunate. In the words of the legendary Batman, Daniel says "I don't do helpless."
>
> He encourages his blind students to engage the world of people and engage the environment on their own terms. "Don't be passive," he tells his students. "Move with grace and connect with the world. Establish your own relationship with the world around you. Do not wait for others to do that for you." Daniel exemplifies this engagement with the world. He stands erect and looks directly at you when he speaks.
>
> Louis Braille gave the blind the avenue to become *academically literate* and to share in the world's body of knowledge. Daniel's legacy is that he has articulated an avenue that allows the blind to become *environmentally literate* and, in his words, "to share in the riches of interaction, self-determination, vocation, and camaraderie that sighted people already enjoy."
>
> Daniel also does not condone the public anxiety about blindness as a dreadful, devastating loss. This fear of blindness is prevalent in all cultures; but it is rarely challenged. Daniel was a fearless, curious, insistent toddler who became a curious, persistent adult who then formed a non-profit agency with the motto *No Limits*. Not only that, but Daniel dares to suggest that blindness comes with blessings that sighted people fail to appreciate or receive. His personal hero, and this is no surprise, is the Frenchman Jacques Lusseyran [featured in Volume Three of this series]. For Daniel, blindness is not a dreadful, devastating loss; it is simply a different way to perceive the world.[118]

Daniel Kish and his colleagues regard blindness as another way to process the world, different from visual processing, but in many ways equal to or better than what the sighted are doing. I love Daniel's in-your-face approach because it is very much in the vein of Helen Keller's Warrior consciousness—there is a similar courage and conviction. Daniel navigates so well because he uses a host of modern strategies and technologies, which Helen Keller had no access to.

To be fair to Helen, she was often talking about *unnecessary blindness*; the kind of blindness caused by accidents or by lack of medical help for the poor. This is from an essay called "The World's Work," published in her book *Out of the Dark* (1913):

> To begin at the beginning, we have found that much blindness is unnecessary, that perhaps a third of it is the result of disease which can be averted by timely treatment. Then the instruction of parents and friends in the care of blind children needs to be carried to every corner of the country. We have before us a long campaign to teach parents that they must encourage sightless children to romp and play and grow strong as their seeing brothers and sisters do. Failure to understand this, and the natural inclination to shield and pamper defective children impose upon the schools the unnecessary burden of straightening crooked backs and correcting nervous habits, engendered by lack of intelligent discipline at home.[119]

Daniel Kish and his colleagues would strongly support the statement that we *must encourage sightless children to romp and play and grow strong as their seeing brothers and sisters do.* The education of parents is also something Daniel believes to be critical, although he knows that what is mostly needed is a paradigm shift across entire cultures. Current worldviews and perspectives must change if the lives of blind individuals are to improve. Parents are simply caught up in the mores and expectations of their cultures. We must reach more than just parents, friends, and teachers if true change is to occur.

Below is another quote written by Helen (*Teacher*, 1955), which Daniel and his colleagues would certainly support. She is speaking of Anne Sullivan and Annie's attitude about blindness. This is how we should remember Helen Keller's attitude about blindness (deafness, deaf-blindness, any "disability"):

Teacher did not manufacture life out of her limitations, she lived it out of her Powers. She did not suit her actions to my weaknesses. She coaxed my spiritual faculties up to them. She did not tolerate the sense-arrogant, their patronizing authority over the blind or other unfortunate groups or their almsgiving where discerning love was needed . . . As often as possible she swept the fumes of false pity from their minds and confronted them with the upward looking humanity, which they had denied the handicapped. To be a Sappho one must have the soul of Sappho. To be a veritable Mother of Minds, as Teacher was, one must marry an active ideal and have a womb that brings forth souls.

Helen's views above are quite modern, as if they had been written for the twenty-first century. Equality is demanded, not pity; Love is needed, not alms. Sappho was a Greek poet; her work is often compared to Homer, as if she were the feminine balance to Homer's masculine perspective. Sappho writes of love and family, not wars or valor; her voice is in the moment, in Soul-communication.

Out of the Dark (1913) is the best source I encountered for understanding Helen Keller's position on blindness. Her insights and suggestions are often very sophisticated and often progressive, despite her images of helplessness and despair.

The missing voice in this discussion is Anne Sullivan. For most of her life she stayed in the background, as the Teacher, the emotional support person, the personal assistant. Yet many believe, as I do, that Anne Sullivan's visual impairments were central to the whole mythology. Sullivan had ocular pain for a lifetime. Her vision was never clear, near perfect; it was always fluctuating, never completely dependable. In short, Anne Sullivan was severely disabled by her vision impairment. The public view was that Helen Keller was the disabled one, not her Teacher. Here is what Helen wrote about Annie's dilemma:

Annie was one of the sensitive spirits that feel shamed by blindness. It humiliates them like a stupid blunder or a deformed limb. They do not count on the compassionate understanding of others, and they shrink from the comments of those who watch their struggle against misfortune. Blindness is a blow to their freedom and dignity, especially when they have always been active and industrious.[120]

If you add shame and embarrassment to physical pain and emotional depression you get a recipe for sadness that must have hung over Anne Sullivan for her entire life. There were people who could see this mess of emotions who helped Annie, including Helen, Kate Keller, Polly Thomson, and, in her youth, Sophia Hopkins, John Hitz, Mark Twain, and Alexander Graham Bell (and many other close friends who were less famous).

Interestingly, Helen blamed a lack of appropriate education for Annie's dilemma. Sullivan's own education had failed her, according to Helen. There was no special education in Sullivan's youth, no mobility training, no reasoned approach to helping a severely impaired child to cope. Sullivan never learned to braille well, and that, Helen thought, was a tragedy. Anne Sullivan could also have used a teacher like Daniel Kish.

When I was considering how to honor my friend Daniel in his own book, the next subject in this series, I realized that comparing Daniel to Helen Keller—something that makes him cringe—was only a half truth. In many ways, Daniel is more like Anne Sullivan. As I said earlier, Daniel lives for short periods of time with the families of the children he is teaching. He travels all over the planet to get to those families—always at the invitation of parents. Therefore, Daniel mirrors the brilliance and focus of Helen Keller—they both had lifelong missions—but, also, he is very much like Anne Sullivan: dedicated, with a backbreaking work ethic. Daniel qualifies as both a miracle *and* a miracle worker. I look forward to completing the next volume in this series about the very remarkable Daniel Kish.

As I mentioned earlier, I compiled a second book to support this work, a timeline of Helen's life. I assumed in this volume that the reader knew about the Keller-Sullivan story. However, for readers who want a more detailed look at the two superstars who became legends in their own time and have become a global mythology, have a look at *Helen Keller: A Timeline of Her Life* (2021).

I am now sitting blurry-eyed before my trusty computer, before the sun is even up, coffee in hand, as I write these final words to you. It is April 3, 2021. A brutal pandemic-driven, politically-volatile year has thankfully ended. As Helen Keller would insist, we should now look ahead with hope, optimism, and trust to the future.

A deaf-blind girl from Alabama was driven to give speeches and write books, insisting that our actions be guided by optimism, trust, Faith, and, above all else, Love. Remember to honor Helen Keller's wishes as you go about your days. Let us go forward now and do the bidding of the saintly and feisty Miss Helen Keller, never forgetting the remarkable teacher who honors all teachers everywhere, the saintly and feisty Miss Anne Sullivan. Thank you for joining me on this long, but very satisfying ride; I wish you well.

You and I are comrades journeying hand in hand to the end. When the way is dark, and the shadows fall, we draw closer. ~ *Helen and Teacher*, Joseph Lash, 1980.

Introduction

1. There is a companion book to this volume called *Helen Keller: A Timeline of her Life.* My focus, as I wrote the companion book was—as in this book—the evolution of Helen Keller's mind. I used Helen's words as I reviewed her books and books about her. *Helen Keller: A Timeline of her Life* is an exploration of Helen's subjective consciousness as she matured, as she had life-enriching experiences, and as she gained knowledge through attending college and through her reading—all set within a historic context.

2. After I retired in 2010, I volunteered at the Millet Center (Saginaw, Michigan) for two additional years, hoping to keep alive a community-based education program, which I had developed to address navigational disabilities. I also continued to dialogue about my profession with my colleague Daniel Kish. I still identity as a mobility specialist even though my retirement has stretched into a second decade, and—as my books attest—I am still trying to be helpful, still trying to make contributions to the profession.

3. I also have a doctorate in optometry, and I worked with blind seniors a few years before I began to work with children. I am deeply grateful to the optometric profession. It was at the Illinois College of Optometry in Chicago where I became fascinated with the human vision system. I spent my career studying vision and I continue to build on that knowledge.

4. Love, as a cultural concept, is well accepted and supported in our collective consciousness. Loving-kindness is at the heart of our efforts to advance tolerance, compassion, caregiving, and morality within Western religion, philosophy, and politics. I wrote repeatedly in this book that Helen Keller had faith that "love was the answer." I saw examples in our literature, in sermons, in speeches, in songs, and in the common language of the masses, that, *of course, love is the answer.* That phrase—love is the answer—has become a well-grooved cultural meme. In other words, Helen's sentiments, convictions, and actions are in keeping with the core values of Western civilization. However, Love has not been universally victorious. The Devil is busy still, and his army ebbs and flows. We must continue, day in and day out, to side with Love against forces that *do not feel* love (that lack empathy). There are many people alive today who do not find Love to be a valuable guiding principle. The rest of us are marching arm-in-arm with Helen Keller.

5. Daniel does not work alone; he is part of a brain trust and he is surrounded by brilliant blind teachers like Brian Bushway and Juan Ruiz. Daniel is also part of a worldwide network of blind intellectuals and activists.

6. Daniel allowed me to make this comparison between him and Helen Keller (also Anne Sullivan), although he prefers to stand alone and not be compared to heroes from the past. I respect his feelings, but I also feel an obligation to history. What Daniel has demonstrated (active echolocation) is revolutionary.

Chapter One: Knights for the Blind

7. *Blind Rage: Letters to Helen Keller,* by Professor Georgina Kleege, 2006. If you have any kind of "disability," you end up under a judgmental microscope. I often come across highly intelligent individuals who feel resentful and reactionary toward the Normals who display unconscious (unexamined) cultural prejudices. Astutely articulate people like Georgina Kleege, Daniel Kish, and Helen Keller ultimately get in the face of such sight-based arrogance.

8. From a speech to the Twentieth Century Club, 1922.

9. *Out of the Dark*, by Helen Keller, 1913.
10. *Helen Keller's Journal* (entry for February 23, 1937), by Helen Keller, published in 1938.
11. *Helen Keller's Journal*, by Helen Keller, published in 1938.

Chapter Two: The Esoteric Helen Keller

12. *Helen Keller in Scotland*, by Helen Keller, 1933.
13. *Helen Keller in Scotland*, by Helen Keller, 1933. Copied from a letter Helen wrote to her friend Sir Nevile Wilkinson in September 1932.
14. *The World I Live In*, by Helen Keller, 1908.
15. *The Story of My Life*, by Helen Keller, 1903.
16. *The Story of My Life*, by Helen Keller, 1903.
17. *The Story of My Life*, by Helen Keller, 1903.
18. My books about the evolution of consciousness are buried deep within Amazon.com. With a few exceptions, neither my profession nor the neuroscience community is aware of these publications. I have a feeling that it will be through this book that my ideas will become known. I am in my late seventies as I write this, and I have no desire to hit the lecture circuit to promote my insights. My books will have to speak for me after I am gone.
19. *The Special Needs Vision Clinic of Mid-Michigan;* located at the Millet Learning Center in Bridgeport, Michigan.
20. *The Institute for Innovative Blind Navigation.* I was not able to sustain (direct) the Institute when my wife Katherine was battling cancer. The non-profit was eventually closed in 2010 after Kath passed. I was in shock for a full year after the center of love fell out of my universe; I had no energy to keep the Institute going.
21. *The World I Live In*, by Helen Keller, 1908.
22. *Western Esotericism: A Guide for the Perplexed*, by Wouter J. Hanegraaff, 2013.
23. Rudolf Steiner is also a main interest of mine. If ever there was a philosopher who preferred the company of fairies and elves, it was Steiner. In my opinion, Jung, Steiner, and James understood humanity's strange dual consciousness, they just gave the duality different names. All three of these seekers knew that our knowledge was incomplete; they could sense a mystery and each man came at the same puzzle differently.

24. I began writing this book before I became aware of the violent conspiracy theories that had appeared in the United States, fueled by an irresponsible right-wing media. The American free press was under attack. Intellectuals were also under attack, as were humanitarians. A whole crowd of conspiracy theory "believers" became activated, looking exactly like the crowds that brought Mussolini and Hitler to power. President Trump's supporters were using the same words I am using here—spirituality, Gnosticism, esotericism, for example—but they were twisting the meaning 180 degrees from what the words genuinely mean. Kindness is not the goal of this insanely ignorant group of people. I felt that I should make it clear that my perspectives are diametrically opposite this lunatic fringe. In the America I see around me today, hatefulness has found a voice, a political platform, and a sympathetic media outlet. Helen Keller would have fought this hatefulness with every ounce of her strength.

25. *Leaps of Faith: Science, Miracles, and the Search for Supernatural Consolation*, by Nicholas Humphrey, 1996.

26. *Leaps of Faith: Science, Miracles, and the Search for Supernatural Consolation*, by Nicholas Humphrey, 1996.

27. *The Story of My Life*, by Helen Keller, 1903.

28. *The Story of My Life*, by Helen Keller, 1903.

29. *The Story of My Life*, by Helen Keller, 1903.

30. *Light in My Darkness*, by Professor Ray Silverman, 1994. This quote is also found in Joseph Lash's biography Helen and Teacher.

31. *Helen Keller in Scotland*, by Helen Keller, 1933.

32. *The Open Door*, by Helen Keller, 1957.

Chapter Three: The Evolution of Helen Keller's Mind

33. The developmental theories of Susanne Cook-Greuter. See the online PDF "Nine Levels of Increasing Embrace In Ego Development: A Full-Spectrum Theory Of Vertical Growth And Meaning Making;" © 2013 Cook-Greuter.

34. Ken Wilber's Integral Institute. See the Integral+Life website https://integrallife.com/. Wilber is the author of over 40 books, most of which are about the evolution of human cognition. Wilber divides knowledge into four quadrants. If we consider the

definition of consciousness using Wilber's quadrants, we see why there is so much confusion and debate about what consciousness is—people are talking from within different knowledge quadrants.

35. Developmental philosopher Jean Gebser. See (online) "The Stages of Life According to Jean Gebser," at the American Institute for Learning and Human Development.

36. Infant and child mortality rates were assumed to be exceedingly high so that the average age is skewed. There may have been many seniors in the caveman days.

37. *Teacher*, by Helen Keller, 1955. Evidently, Helen's family and a few friends (notably William James) were upset with Helen's description of her early years before she got language.

38. "How Helen Keller Learned to Write," by Cynthia Ozick, published in *The New Yorker Magazine*, June 16, 1923.

39. *Light in My Darkness*, by Professor Ray Silverman, 1994.

40. I am not sure Anne Sullivan said this. It might have been editor Nella Braddy who made the comment in *Anne Sullivan Macy, The Story Behind Helen Keller*. It seems likely that Braddy was quoting Sullivan, but the context is not clear.

41. I copied this from *Anne Sullivan Macy, The Story Behind Helen Keller*, by Nella Braddy Henney, 1933. However, this probably was taken from one of Helen's political articles.

42. *Anne Sullivan Macy, The Story Behind Helen Keller*, by Nella Braddy Henney, 1933.

43. *Light in My Darkness*, by Professor Ray Silverman, 1994.

44. *Light in My Darkness*, by Professor Ray Silverman, 1994.

45. *Anne Sullivan Macy, The Story Behind Helen Keller*, by Nella Braddy Henney, 1933.

46. Online article: "New Church History Fun Facts: Helen Keller Letter about Swedenborg," www.newchurchhistory.org.

47. "How I Would Help the World," by Helen Keller, 1935.

48. *My Religion*, 1927.

49. "The World I Would Help," by Helen Keller, 1935.

50. *Arcana Coelestia* (Heavenly Mysteries), by Emmanuel Swedenborg, published in eight volumes, one volume per year, from 1749 to 1756.

51. *Catching the Light: The Entwined History of Light and Mind*, by Arthur Zajonc, 1993.

52. *Swedenborg's Garden of Theology: An Introduction to Emanuel Swedenborg's Published Theological Works*, by Jonathan S. Rose,

2010.

53. "How I Would Help the World," by Helen Keller, 1935.

54. "How I Would Help the World," by Helen Keller, 1935.

55. From a speech Helen gave at the New (Swedenborgian) Church in Glasgow, June 22, 1932.

56. *Helen Keller's Journal*, by Helen Keller, published in 1938.

57. United States Holocaust Museum website.

58. *Out of the Dark*, by Helen Keller, 1913.

59. From the American Foundation for the Blind Helen Keller Digital Archives.

60. Wikipedia: World War Two deaths.

61. From singer-songwriter Susan Werner's album *The Gospel Truth*.

62. *Out of the Dark*, by Helen Keller, 1913.

63. *Out of the Dark*, by Helen Keller, 1913.

64. *Helen Keller: Rebel Lives*, by John A. Davis, 2005.

65. "The Hand of the World," American Magazine, December 1912.

66. *The New York Call Magazine*, by Helen Keller, 1911.

67. *Teacher*, by Helen Keller, 1955.

68. *Out of the Dark*, by Helen Keller, 1913.

69. Helen might be critical of my assertion that higher education was a major factor in her cognitive transformation. In an interview with Barbara Bindley published in the *New York Tribune*, January 16, 1916, Helen complained that her education at Radcliffe "amounted to nothing." She said her education was about the dead past and it supported outdated morality. She was probably being overly dramatic (maybe not) because it was at Harvard where she met John Macy and Charles Copeland, both of whom developed her writing skills and influenced her politics. I also want to stress that there are other ways to remove a person from their familiar surroundings besides going off to college. War, for example, takes young men and women out of their Traditional mindsets. Encountering cultures unlike their own, meeting other young people who challenge their worldviews, witnessing unspeakable atrocities, having to kill others, and constantly fearing the end of their own life, all this effectively rewires the brains of young men sent to fight on foreign soil. Young men coming back from war zones are changed forever; they cannot easily assimilate back into Traditional mindsets. For more than a century (to give another example), there has been a steady migration into cities. The transition from rural, village,

small town life to energy-filled and diverse urban communities can also cause the breakdown of Traditional mindsets.

70. See the books of Nicholas Humphrey in the bibliography. Humphrey is professor emeritus from Cambridge University in England. He is a Nobel prize winning neuropsychologist who wrote extensively about the evolution of primate intelligence and consciousness.

71. *Helen Keller's Journal*, by Helen Keller, published in 1938.

72. There are also plenty of Penguins on the Democratic side of the aisle, so I am over-glorifying this division between parties. This is obviously my politics, my emotions, and my worldview overflowing into this book. I said at the beginning that I would not restrain my passion. It is very much in keeping with Helen Keller's style to confront evil face on, even knowing the complexity that surrounds any observation of human behavior. There is also a growing trend wherein women and minorities are going to Congress as Republicans. We have passed the point of generalizing about women and minorities—humanity is changing and evolving. I am just hopeful that the Allocentric epigenetics of women and people of color will transform governing bodies globally, that people with higher levels of cognitive and spiritual sophistication will take control of decision making.

73. I always feel uneasy (worried) when I glorify the feminine perspective. I do not intend to deny the humanitarian males who have strong feminine Souls, men who have evolved Allocentric minds and who share the intention to champion loving-kindness and empathy. I also know, of course, that the spiritual pathway holds women with various degrees of sophistication. There are many women, some gaining power, who are just as unevolved as the worst patriarchal males. However, I sense that there is something "reachable" even in the most autocratic females. The Y-chromosome (a metaphorical rendering) is not directing aggression in females.

74. The military leadership in the United States contains highly educated and intellectually sophisticated individuals who understand loving-kindness and empathy. It is a mistake to deny their expertise, kindness, and guidance. The world is still a hostile and dangerous place and we need the military, but like in any profession, we are best served by people who have sophisticated levels of consciousness.

75. "A Christmas Appeal, 1917." *To Love this Life: Quotations by Helen Keller*, 1976.

76. Helen also felt (had faith) that socialism and communism would be the social systems of the future—that faith is yet to be validated or justified. China and Russia followed a communistic path, the Western world did not. Helen had been heavily influenced by H. G. Wells' book *New Worlds for Old*, which advocated Socialism as a more humane and intellectually more sophisticated worldview than Capitalism. Helen's "knowing that Faith would prevail" in the future is still in question.

77. *Let Us Have Faith*, by Helen Keller, 1940.

78. *Helen Keller's Journal*, by Helen Keller, published in 1938.

79. "Try Democracy," *The Home Magazine*, April 1935. Copied from *To Love this Life: Quotations of Helen Keller*, 2000.

Chapter Four: Our Strange Duet

80. *The Phantom of the Opera*, by Andrew Lloyd Webber.

81. I often used my good friend and colleague Daniel Kish to explore these insights. Daniel was open to my worldview and he was a willing debater. In a way, my professional worldview was a blending of my ideas and Daniel's. I regard my writing—this book especially—as the means to alert my profession to this important hypothesis. I did not try to actively market this idea within my profession; I did not publish the theory in the O&M literature. The unfolding of these ideas slowly manifested over time. I am also in my senior years and have no energy for marketing and debating—this book and those that follow will make my case for fundamental change in the profession.

82. Anil K. Seth is a British professor of Cognitive and Computational Neuroscience at the University of Sussex. See his Ted Talk: *Your brain hallucinates your conscious reality.*

83. I have had many students who had cerebral palsies of various kinds. These were kids who had difficulty moving smoothly straight-ahead (many used motorized systems to compensate). However, these youngsters had normal dual-processing systems and many of them were quite intelligent.

84. My use of the terms *Ego* and *Self* mirror the findings of psychoanalyst

Carl Jung. Jung discovered this duality from his work with patients. As far as I known, Jung did not offer an anatomical and physiological derivation for this duality, as I have done.

85. "How Helen Keller Learned to Write," by Cynthia Ozick, published in *The New Yorker Magazine*, June 16/23. Charles Dickens referred to deaf-blindness as "a marble cell."

86. I could have used just about any philosopher to make my point here about duality being everywhere in the philosophical literature. In my book, *The Confusion Caused by Being Your Own Twin*, I gave numerous examples. Also, the comparison between Keller and Kierkegaard is not consistent. For example, Helen was a determined optimist who lived a protected and charmed life. Kierkegaard was a pessimist, there was so much death and pain in his short life that he saw constant suffering and no evidence for optimism. The quote by Nietzsche is typical of what I found as I explored Western literature—duality is discovered and explored repeatedly,

87. *Let Us Have Faith*, by Helen Keller, 1940.

88. *The Open Door,* by Helen Keller, 1957.

89. *Helen Kellers Journal*, by Helen Keller, 1938.

Chapter Five: A Wonderful Child

90. *Fact and Faith*, by J. B. S. Haldane, 1934.

91. Daniel Kish, personal correspondence, 2020.

92. See Howard Gardner's theory of multiple intelligences—varieties of intelligence. Howard's list is detailed later in this chapter.

93. Address to the American Association to Promote the Teaching of Speech to the Deaf, July 1894.

94. Daniel Kish, personal correspondence, 2020.

95. "Could Multiple Personality Disorder Explain Life, the Universe and Everything?" Bernardo Kastrup, Adam Crabtree, Edward F. Kelly, June 18, 2018.

96. National Institutes of Health, https://www.ncbi.nlm.nih.gov/pmc/articles/PMC6172100/.

97. "A Wonderful Child," an article by Job H. Williams, published by the *Hartford Courant*, Friday, February 20, 1891.

98. The Proceedings of the Working Group on Human Neuroplasticity and Education, October 2010.

99. *Against the Pollution of the I*, by Jacques Lusseyran 2006.

100. "Language processing in the occipital cortices of congenitally blind adults," by Marina Bedny.

101. A letter to Elmer Ambrose Sperry, February 27, 1930, as quoted in *To love this life: Quotations by Helen Keller*, 2000 AFB Press.

102. From the American Foundation for the Blind Helen Keller Archives.

103. Daniel Kish, personal correspondence, 2020.

104. *The Story of my Life*; with her letters (1887–1901), by Helen Keller, Annie Sullivan, and John Albert Macy, 1903.

105. "A Deaf-Mute Evolution: How a body may get on with only one sense," published by The Sun, New York, New York on July 11, 1887.

106. And that is all I am doing in this short section—wondering and pondering out loud. I am not unequivocally declaring that Helen Keller had any vision or any hearing; we do not know, and we will never know.

107. This fluctuating, unreliable vision is certainly what Anne Sullivan experienced her entire life. The amount of light affects perception. Anne's ability to see and perceive was determined by the lighting conditions. Sullivan also had photophobia which is extreme pain in the presence of bright light.

108. American Foundation for the Blind Helen Keller Digital Archives.

Chapter Six: Passing the Torch to the Visionaries

109. Interview with Brian Bushway (*World Access for the Blind*) in Culver City, California, 2019. Brian is a pioneer in the use of active echolocation. He was trained by Daniel Kish and then became an instructor for *World Access*. Brian is a delightful and gentle teacher, exceptionally articulate and knowledgeable. With years of teaching experience and after attaining his master's degree in blind rehabilitation (Orientation and Mobility), Brian became one of the foremost global experts in active echolocation.

110. *Knights for the Blind in the Battle against Darkness: Volume Two, Daniel Kish*; a book in process.

111. *Knights for the Blind in the Battle against Darkness: Volume Two, Daniel Kish*; a book in process. I have learned through experience that quoting "books in process" is a questionable undertaking. I

took this quote from my notes, from an exceedingly rough draft of Daniel's upcoming book. I often rewrite and revise such quotes when I write the new book.

112. A letter from Anne Sullivan to Sophia Hopkins, May 8, 1887.

113. Daniel Kish, personal correspondence, 2020.

114. I worked closely with both physical therapists and occupational therapists, often team-teaching community-based lessons. Navigational disabilities cut across all the professions and, therefore, offer opportunities for cooperative teaching.

115. Leader Dogs for the Blind is located at 1039 S. Rochester Rd. in Rochester Hills, Michigan, 48307–3115. The web address is https://www.leaderdog.org. Toll free phone number: 888–777–5332.

116. Daniel Kish, personal correspondence, 2020.

117. *Out of the Dark*, 1913. A speech to the New York Association for the Blind, January 15, 1907.

118. *Knights for the Blind in the Battle against Darkness: Volume Two, Daniel Kish*; a book in process. As I said previously, these quotes are from my notes. It could very well be that I alter these paragraphs in the final edition of the volume about Daniel Kish.

119. "The World's Work," published in *Out of the Dark*, 1913.

120. *Beyond the Miracle Worker*, by Kim Nielsen, 2009.

BIBLIOGRAPHY

More than at any other time, when I hold a beloved book in my hand my limitations fall from me, my spirit is free. ~ *Midstream*, 1929.

Adamson, Glenn, Fewer, Better Things: The Hidden Wisdom of Objects, Bloomsbury Publishing, 2018.

Armstrong, David, Stokoe, William, Wilcox, Sherman, *Gesture and the Nature of Language*, 1995.

Ball, Philip, "Quantum Darwinism, an Idea to Explain Objective Reality, Passes First Tests," Quanta Magazine (online), 2019.

Baron-Cohen, Simon,

- Tourette's Syndrome: The Facts (The Facts Series), with Mary M. Robertson, 1998.
- Autism and Asperger Syndrome (The Facts), 2008.
- The Essential Difference: Male And Female Brains And The Truth About Autism, 2009.
- Teaching Children with Autism to Mind-Read: A Practical Guide for Teachers and Parents, with Patricia Howlin and Julie A. Hadwin, 2010.
- The Science of Evil: On Empathy and the Origins of Cruelty, 2011.
- The Maladapted Mind: Classic Readings in Evolutionary Psychopathology, 2013.
- Understanding Other Minds: Perspectives from Developmental Social Neuroscience, with Michael Lombardo and Helen Tager-Flusberg, 2013,

- The Pattern Seekers, 2020.

Battro Antonio M., Stanislas Dehaene Wolf J. Singer (editors), The Proceedings of the Working Group on Human Neuroplasticity and Education, October 2010.

Blatt, Burton, "Friendly Letters on the Correspondence of Helen Keller, Anne Sullivan, and Alexander Graham Bell," *Exceptional Children*: Volume 51 issue: 5, page(s): 405–409, February 1, 1985.

Blaxall, Arthur William, *Helen Keller Under the Southern Cross*, January 1, 1952.

Blesser, Barry and Linda-Ruth Salter, *Spaces Speak, are you Listening? Experiencing Aural Architecture*, 2007.

Boole, George, *The Laws of Thought*, 1854.

Borglum, John Gutzon de la Mothe, "Eyes of the Soul," available on the American Foundation for the Blind Helen Keller Digital Archives.

Brooks, Van Wyck, *Helen Keller: Sketch for a Portrait*, 1965.

Chesterton, G. K., *What's Wrong with the World*, 1910.

Cohen, Sascha, "Helen Keller's Forgotten Radicalism," Time Magazine, June, 2015.

Cromwell, John, *Hitler's Pope*, 1999.

Cutsforth, Thomas D., *The Blind in School and Society, A Psychological Study*, 1933.

Dickens, Charles, *American Notes*, 1842.

Easton, Steward C., *Man and World in the Light of Anthroposophy*, by Steward C. Easton, 1975.

Edelman, Gerald M. and Mountcastle, Veron, The Mindful Brain: Cortical Organization and the Group-Selective Theory of Higher Brain Function, 1982.

Emerson, Ralph Waldo, "Swedenborg, or the Mystic," published in his book *Representative Men*, 1850.

Evans, Jonathan,
- In Two Minds: Dual Processes and Beyond, 2009.
- Thinking twice: Two Minds in one Brain, 2010.
- Thinking and Reasoning: A Very Short Introduction, 2017.
- "The Duality of Mind: Historical Perspective," an online summary of dual-process theory, with Keith Frankish.

Frankish, Keith, Mind and Supermind, 2007.

Freeberg, Ernest, *The Education of Laura Bridgman* 2001.

Hawkins, Jeff, *A Thousand Brains: A New Theory of Intelligence*, 2021.

Huth, John Edward, The Lost Art of Finding Our Way, 2013.

Garrett, Leslie, *Helen Keller: A Photographic Story of a Life*, 2004.

Genechten, Désirée Martina van, A Psychobiographical Study of Helen Keller, Faculty of Health Sciences, Nelson Mandela Metropolitan University, November 2009.

Ginsberg, Simona and Eva Jablonka, *The Evolution of the Sensitive Soul*, 2019.

Gitter, Elisabeth, *The Imprisoned Guest: Samuel Howe and Laura Bridgman, the Original Deaf-Blind Girl*, 2001.

Goodrick-Clarke, Nicholas, *The Western Esoteric Traditions: A Historical Introduction*, 2008.

Hawkins, Jeff and Sandra Blakeslee
- On Intelligence, 2004.
- A Thousand Brains, 2021.

Haldane, J.B.S., *Fact and Faith,* 1934.

Hanegraaff Wouter J., *Western Esotericism: A Guide for the Perplexed*, 2013.

Harrity, Richard and Ralph G. Martin, *The Three Lives of Helen Keller*, 1962.

Harry, Gerard, *Man's Miracle: The Story of Helen Keller and her European Sisters*, 1913.

Henney, Nella Braddy, *Anne Sullivan Macy: The Story Behind Helen Keller*, 1933.

Hong, Howard V. and Hong, Edna H., *The Essential Kierkegaard*, 1997.

Humphrey, Nicholas,
- "Consciousness Regained:" Chapters in the Development of Mind, Oxford University Press, 1983.
- *In a Dark Time*, (ed. with R. J. Lifton), Harvard University Press, 1984.
- *Leaps of Faith: Science, Miracles, and the Search for Supernatural Consolation*, 1996.
- *The Inner Eye: Social Intelligence in Evolution*, Faber & Faber, 1986; Oxford University Press 2002,
- *A History of the Mind*, Chatto & Windus 1992, Simon & Schuster, 1992.
- *Soul Searching: Human Nature and Supernatural Belief*, 1995.
- "How to Solve the Mind-Body Problem," Imprint Academic, 2000.
- *The Mind Made Flesh: Essays from the Frontiers of Evolution and Psychology*, Oxford University Press, 2002.

- *Seeing Red: A Study in Consciousness,* Belknap Press/Harvard University Press, 2006.
- *Soul Dust: The Magic of Consciousness,* Quercus Publishing, 2011, Princeton University Press, 2011

International Research Centre for Japanese Studies, "Helen Keller's Civil Diplomacy in Japan in 1937 and 1948." Japan Review; No. 27, pp. 201–220. National Institute for the Humanities, 2014.

James, Henry (senior), *Substance and Shadow, the Secret Life of Swedenborg,* 1863.

James, William,
- The Principles of Psychology, 1890.
- The Will to Believe, 1896.
- Talks to Teachers on Psychology, 1899.
- The Varieties of Religious Experience, 1902.
- "Laura Bridgman," Atlantic Monthly, Volume 93, 1904.
- The Letters of William James, Volumes one and two, 1920.

Keller, Helen
- **1901:** "I Must Speak: A Plea to the American Woman," is published in January 1901 in the *Ladies Home Journal.* Helen was 21 when this article appeared, a second-year student at Radcliffe.
- **1903:** *The Story of My Life* is Helen's autobiography (up to age 22). There is an abridged version credited to Helen, only 75 pages, and there is an unabridged version co-authored by John Macy, Anne Sullivan, and Helen that contains letters written by Sullivan, and a section about Helen's education—this collection was started by Sullivan and John Macy in 1901.
- **1903:** *Optimism,* Helen's second book, was written when she was in her last year at Radcliffe College, with the encouragement of her English professor Charles Copeland.
- **1905:** Essay "A Chat About the Hand," by Helen Keller, printed in Century Magazine.
- **1908:** *The World That I Live In* was written by Helen. Into this book (she says) she poured "everything that interested me at one of the happiest periods of my life."
- **1909:** "I must speak: A plea to the American woman," Ladies Home Journal, Volume 26, January 1909.
- **1910:** *The Song of the Stone Wall* is a long poem published as a book. I found this fascinating because for me it is a reflection on the vibrational universe that Helen lived within.

- **1911:** "Social Causes of Blindness;" published in the socialist daily *The New York Call*, February 15, 1911.
- **1911:** "The Unemployed;" published in the *Zeigler Magazine for the Blind*, 1911.
- **1912:** "The Hand of the World," an article for *American Magazine*, December 1912.
- **1912:** "How I Became a Socialist," published in the socialist daily paper *The New York Call*.
- **1913:** *Out of the Dark: Essays, Lectures, and Addresses on Physical and Social Vision.* This is a collection of early articles and speeches written by Keller. It was reissued in 1920.
- **1919:** *Deliverance* is a silent motion picture about Helen's life. It is a convoled, over-the-top symbol-heavy dramatization of Helen's mythical life. It was a flop at the box office and somewhat of an embarrassment for Helen, yet she never regretted her enjoyable experience in Hollywood.
- **1927:** *My Religion* is Helen Keller's attempt to explain her religion, Swedenborgianism.
- **1928:** "A Vision of Service." An address delivered May 14, 1928 at the Church of the Holy City, Washington, D.C. Available as a pamphlet in the Swedenborg School of Religion Library, in Newton, Massachusetts.
- **1929:** *Midstream, My later Life*, was written by Helen with a lot of help from Professor John Macy. The book is a look back at the first half of Helen's remarkable life.
- **1929:** *We Bereaved* is a short set of inspirational comments by Helen. *Peace at Eventide* is the same book printed in Great Britain; there are very minor differences.
- **1931:** *Double Blossoms: Helen Keller Anthology*, complied by Edna Porter.
- **1931:** The Underprivileged, published
- **1932:** "Put Your Husband in the Kitchen," August 1932 article in *The Atlantic*.
- **1933:** *Anne Sullivan Macy: The Story Behind Helen Keller.* This is the only in-depth biography of Anne Sullivan. It was written by a close friend of Helen and Annie, a professional editor by trade, Nella Braddy Henney.
- **1933:** *Helen Keller in Scotland: A Personal History Written By Herself*, as recorded by James Kerr Love.

- **1933:** "Three Days to See," an article in The Atlantic, January 1933.
- **1935:** "The World I Would Help," a long essay by Helen Keller about her spiritual process as influenced by Emanuel Swedenborg. With a modern introduction by Helen Keller scholar Ray Silverman.
- **1938:** *Helen Keller's Journal*, foreword by Augustus Muir. Helen wrote this after the death of Anne Sullivan.
- **1940:** *Let Us Have Faith*, by Helen Keller.
- **1944:** Comments to the U.S. House of Representatives Committee on Labor.
- **1951:** *Ladies Home Journal*, March 1951, "The World Through Three Senses."
- **1955:** *Teacher* is Helen Keller's personal reflection on her education and her relationship with the demanding and loving Anne Sullivan.
- **1957:** *The Open Door,* by Helen Keller.
- **1957:** *The Miracle Worker* was a 3-part stage play that was later made into a TV drama, and classic movie. When I watched this after reading all of the books listed here, I was amazed how accurate and powerful this play still is. The Miracle Worker is a play by William Gibson. It was based on Helen Keller's autobiography *The Story of My Life.*
- **1962:** *The Three Lives of Helen Keller* by Richard Harrity and Ralph Martin.
- **1967:** *Helen Keller, Her Socialist Years,* is another look at Helen's radical position on the attitudes of her generation; edited by Philip S. Foner.
- **1980:** *Helen and Teacher* by Joseph Lash was the first in-depth biography of Helen Keller. It is very well written and enjoyable,
- *1987:* An article called the *Cape Cod Campus.* This is a short article about Anne Sullivan's lifelong friend Sophia Hopkins. Many letters were exchanged between Sullivan, Keller, and Hopkins that are now a national historic treasure. *The Cape Cod Campus, Summer-Fall 1987.*
- **1994:** *Light in my Darkness* is a re-edited version of Helen's book *My Religion.* Ray Silverman, a Swedenborg scholar and expert on Helen Keller re-interpreted *Light in my Darkness.*
- **1998:** *Helen Keller, A Life*, by Dorothy Herrmann.
- **2000:** *To Love This Life: Quotations by Helen Keller,* AFB Press,

American Foundation for the Blind.
- **2004:** *The Radical Lives of Helen Keller*, written by Professor Kim Nielsen takes a hard look at Helen's lifelong passion for social justice. Nielsen is a Helen Keller scholar.
- **2005:** *Helen Keller: Rebel Lives*, by John Davis. Like *the Radical Lives of Helen Keller* this small book is a vivid look at Helen's social activism.
- **2006:** *Blind Rage: Letters to Helen Keller* is a form of novel, written as a series of letters to Helen Keller after she had died. The author is Georgina Kleege, a Berkeley professor of English who is blind herself. This is a feisty, fun book written by a woman who became a Helen Keller scholar.
- **2009:** *Beyond the Miracle Worker: The Remarkable Life of Anne Sullivan Macy*, by Kim Nielsen.
- **2016:** "Helen Keller: A life with dogs; From scrappy Scotties to dignified Great Danes to a famous Akita."
- There is a YouTube channel dedicated to Helen Keller. This is a wonderful archive of old photos and film clips.
- There are many children's books written about Helen Keller, but I did not use them in this narrative.
- Alabama History Notebook: A collection of Alabama symbols, maps, and photographs for students; Alabama Department of Archives and History, 624 Washington Avenue, Montgomery, AL 36130; www.archives.alabama.gov.

Kish, Daniel with Jo Hook, *Echolocation and FlashSonar*; American Printing House for the Blind, 2016.

Kleege. Georgina,
- Home for the Summer, 1989.
- Sight Unseen, 1999.
- Blind Rage, 2006.
- More Than Meets the Eye, 2018.

Kurzweil, Ray,
- The Age of Intelligent Machines, 1992.
- The Age of Spiritual Machines When Computers Exceed Human Intelligence, 2000.
- Fantastic Voyage: Live Long Enough to Live Forever, with Terry Grossman, 2004.
- The Singularity Is Near: When Humans Transcend Biology, 2006.
- How to Create a Mind? The Secret of Human Thought Revealed,

2013.

Lamphier, Peg A. and Welch, Rosanne, *Women in American History: A Social, Political, and Cultural Encyclopedia*, 2017.

Lash, Joseph, *Helen and Teacher, 1980.* This was the first in-depth biography of Helen Keller.

La Mettrie, Julien Offray de, *Man a Machine* (French: *L'homme Machine*), 1747.

Leblanc, Georgette, The Girl Who Found the Blue Bird: A Visit to Helen Keller, 1914.

Leiber, Justin, "Helen Keller as Cognitive Scientist," Philosophical Psychology, Volume 9, Issue 4, 1996.

Lusseyran, Jacques,
- Against the Pollution of the I: Selected Writings of Jacques Lusseyran, 2006.
- And There Was Light, 1963

Macy, John Albert
- The Story of My Life (1887–1901) and a supplementary account of her education, including passages from the reports and letters of her teacher Anne Sullivan, by John Macy, Helen Keller, and Anne Sullivan, 1903.
- Edgar Allan Poe, 1907.
- Child's Guide to Reading, 1909.
- A Guide to Reading for Young and Old, 1910.
- The Spirit of American Literature, 1912.
- Socialism in America, 1916
- Walter James Dodd: A Biographical Sketch, 1918.
- The Critical Game, 1922.
- Story of the World's Literature, 1925.
- Do You Know English Literature? A Book of Questions and Answers for Students and General Readers, 1930.
- American Writers on American Literature, 1931.
- About Women, 1932.

McDermott, Robert A., *The Essential Steiner: Basic Writings of Rudolf Steiner*, edited and introduced by Robert A. McDermott, 1984.

Menand, Louis, "Laura's World: What a deaf-blind girl taught the nineteenth century;" by Louis Menand in *The New Yorker Magazine*, June 25, 2001.

Nielsen, Kim, E.,
- The Radical Lives of Helen Keller, 2004.

- Helen Keller: Selected Writings, 2005.
- "Was Helen Keller Deaf? Blindness, Deafness, and Multiple Identities," Double Visions: Multidisciplinary Approaches to Women and Deafness, edited by Susan Burch and Brenda Brueggemann, 2006.
- "The Southern Ties of Helen Keller," Journal of Southern History, 2007.
- Beyond the Miracle Worker: The Remarkable Life of Anne Sullivan Macy, 2009.

Neumann, Erich, *The Origins and History of Consciousness*, by Erick Neumann, 1954.

O'Connor, M. R., *Wayfinding: The Science and Mystery of How Humans Navigate the World*, 2019.

Pike, Kenneth, *Language as Particle, Wave, and Field*, 1959.

Pollan, Michael, *How to Change Your Mind: What the new science of psychedelics teaches us about Consciousness, dying, addiction, depression, and transcendence* (2018).

Porter, Edna, *Double Blossoms: Helen Keller Anthology*, 1931.

Rajneesh, Bhagwan Shree (Osho),
- The Mustard Seed: A Living Explanation of Jesus from the Gospel According to Thomas, 1975.
- Philosophia Ultima, 1983.

Rose, Jonathan S., *Swedenborg's Garden of Theology: An Introduction to Emanuel Swedenborg's Published Theological Works*, 2010.

Saxe, John Godfrey, The poems of John Godfrey Saxe, 1872.

Shattuck, Roger,
- "Two Hearts that Beat as One," *New York Magazine* review of Joseph P Lash's book *The Story of Helen Keller and Anne Sullivan Macy*, June 30, 1980, with George V. Higgins.
- Restored Classic: *The Story of my Life*, edited by Roger Shattuck, with Dorothy Herrmann, 2003.

Sicherman, Barbara and Green, Carol Hurd, *Notable American Women: The Modern Period: a Biographical Dictionary*, 1980.

Sperry, Reverend Paul Andrew, "New Church History Fun Facts: Helen Keller Letter about Swedenborg." New Church history website: http://www.newchurchhistory.org/funfacts/index6ca3.html?p=534#more-534.

Steiner, Rudolf,
- *How to Know Higher Worlds*, by Rudolf Steiner, 1994.

- *Intuitive Thinking as a Spiritual Path: A Philosophy of Freedom,* by Rudolf Steiner, 1995.
- *Becoming the Archangel Michael's Companions: Rudolf Steiner's Challenge to the Younger Generation,* from the Collected works of Rudolf Steiner, 2007.

Stelson, Caren, *Sachiko: A Nagasaki Bomb Survivor's Story,* Lerner Publishing Group, 2016.

Strassman, Rick, *DMT: The Spirit Molecule: A Doctor's Revolutionary Research into the Biology of Near-Death and Mystical Experiences,* December 2000.

Sullivan, Anne, Teacher Whimsically Sketches Her Life and Philosophy, Calling Them 'Foolish Remarks of a Foolish Woman.' Available on the American Foundation for the Blind Helen Keller Digital Archives.

Sultan, Rosie, *Helen Keller in Love: A Novel,* 2012.

Swedenborg, Emanuel,
- Heaven and Hell, 1758.
- Arcana Cœlestia, 1756.

Takemae, Eiji, Ricketts Robert, and Swann, Sebastian, *Allied Occupation of Japan,* 2003.

Taylor, Eugene, Studia Swedenborgiana: "William James and Helen Keller;" Vol. 4, January 1981.

Tversky, Barbara, *Mind in Motion,* 2019.

Thomson, Jeanie, *The Myth of Water: Poems from the Life of Helen Keller,* 2016.

Versluis, Arthur, *Magic and Mysticism: An Introduction to Western Esotericism,* 2007.

Wehr, Gerhard, *Jung and Steiner: The Birth of a New Psychology,* 2002.

Wells, H. G., *New Worlds for Old,* Global Classics, 2019.

Werner, Marta L., "Helen Keller and Anne Sullivan: Writing Otherwise," an online article at: http://labos.ulg.ac.be/cipa/wp-content/uploads/sites/22/2015/07/86_werner.pdf

Wilson, Frank, *The Hand: How its Use Shapes the Brain,* 1988.

Winter, Bill, Helen Keller: A life with dogs; From scrappy Scotties to dignified Great Danes to a famous Akita, dogs always brought joy to Helen Keller, June 24, 2016. Available online at http://www.perkins.org/stories/helen-keller-a-life-with-dogs

Whitman, Walt, *Leaves of Grass,* 1855.

Woods, Katherine, *Helen Keller's Journal,* a book review from the New

York Times, June 5, 1938.

Zajonc, Arthur, *Catching the Light: The Entwined History of Light and Mind*, 1993.

Zeldin, Theodore, *An Intimate History of Humanity*, 1994.

The American Foundation for the Blind and Perkins School for the Blind have extensive online archival material about Helen Keller, which they continue to compile and clarify. I took advantage of both archives.

American Foundation for the Blind Helen Keller Archives

The Helen Keller Archive at the American Foundation for the Blind (AFB) is the world's largest repository of materials about and by Helen Keller. Materials include correspondence, speeches, press clippings, scrapbooks, photographs, photograph albums, architectural drawings, audio recordings, audio-visual materials and artifacts.

The collection contains detailed biographical information about Helen Keller (1880–1968), as well as a fascinating record of over 80 years of social and political change worldwide. Keller was a feminist, a suffragist, a social activist, and a pacifist, as well as a prolific writer and published author.

Her impact reached far beyond the United States. She traveled to 39 countries as an advocate and global goodwill ambassador and met and corresponded with many of the leading figures of her time, including nine U.S. presidents, and prominent social activists, philanthropists, industrialists, writers, artists, and actors. The collection contains information on all these subjects and individuals as well as the countless ordinary men, women, and children who corresponded with her.

Thanks to the enormous generosity of the National Endowment for the Humanities, this digital archive is being made accessible to blind, deaf, deafblind, sighted, and hearing audiences alike. Please note that additional accessibility features are being constantly added. ~ Copied from the AFB webpage

This collection contains 58,733 items comprising 186,820 images.

Perkins School for the Blind Nella Braddy Henney Archives

The Nella Braddy Henney Collection is comprised of correspondence, notes, photographs, articles, clippings, publications, and other materials related to Helen Keller, Anne Sullivan Macy, Polly Thomson, and Nella Braddy Henney. The correspondence spans the years of 1927 to 1969, and is to and from Helen Keller, Anne Sullivan Macy, Polly Thomson, and Nella Braddy Henney between themselves and others.

The notes, photographs, articles, clippings, publications and other materials relate to the lives of Helen Keller, Anne Sullivan Macy, Polly Thomson and Nella Braddy Henney, and are interspersed throughout the collection, as well as within their respective series.

The extensive correspondence collection contains letters, memos, and notes in relation to Braddy Henney's work for Helen Keller during Keller's lifetime, and on research for Braddy Henney's book, Anne Sullivan Macy: The story behind Helen Keller (1933). Keller's correspondence includes letters with others, such as Samuel Clemens (Mark Twain; copies), Perkins Directors Edward E. Allen and Gabriel Farrell, Charles F. F. Campbell, actress Katherine Cornell, and other notable people. These letters were forwarded to Nella Braddy Henney for use while working on her book.

Nella Braddy Henney's personal journal entries are included in this collection and supplement the correspondence. These journal entries span the years of 1938 and 1962.

The photograph collection includes portraits, publicity photographs with prominent individuals, materials related to film projects in Hollywood, advocacy for blinded veterans, many casual images from visits to Helen Keller's Arcan Ridge and Forest Hills homes, and trips to Martha's Vineyard with Eleanor Roosevelt. Many of the photographical items can be attributed to the work of Keith Henney. ~ Copied from the Perkin's website.

The American Antiquarian Society in Worcester, Massachusetts also has retained materials about Helen Keller and Anne Sullivan. The Perkins School has collaborated with The American Antiquarian Society to digitally combine their materials.

Newspaper Articles

Understandably, there are thousands of newspaper (media) reports about Helen Keller. I used a subscription to Newspapers.com, a genealogical resource, to track a few of these. The American Foundation for the Blind Helen Keller Digital Archives also contain an extensive list of newspaper links. I will list what I found below. I did not read all the references because there is considerable redundancy. If I did find a gem, I hand-typed what I found and included the quote in the book. I organized this section by publication date.

1887: "A Deaf-Mute Evolution: How a body may get on with only one sense." Published in *The Sun*, New York, New York, July 11, 1887 . . . a story about Laura Bridgman with comments about Helen Keller, age 7.

1888: "The Most Wonderful Child of the Age," published in *The Montgomery Advertiser* (Montgomery, Alabama) March 2, 1888. Observations of Job Williams while visiting Helen when she was learning to speak.

1888: "Helen Adams Keller; She is Blind, Deaf and Dumb and Rivals Laura Bridgeman," published in *The Burlington Weekly Free Press* (Burlington, Vermont), May 4, 1888.

1890: "A Blind, Deaf Mute Talks," published in *The Charlotte Democrat* (Charlotte, NC), June 6, 1890.

1891: "A Wonderful Child," published in the *Hartford Courant*, February 20, 1891.

1892: "A Modern Wonder: Helen Keller, The Phenomenal Blind and Deaf Mute," published in the *Lincoln Evening Call* (Lincoln, Nebraska), March 25, 1892.

1896: "Miss Helen Keller Admitted to Harvard," published in *The Kansas City Journal* (Kansas City, MO), October 25, 1896.

1900: "Helen Keller a Radcliffe Pupil: Blind, Deaf, and Dumb Girl Now Studying There," published in the *Asheville Citizen-Times* (Asheville, North Carolina), October 19, 1900. Original from the *New York Sun*.

1900: "Helen Keller begins attending Radcliffe College of Harvard at age 20." Published in the *Ashville, North Carolina Citizens-Times*, October 19, 1900.

1900: "Helen Keller Talks," published in *The Evening Star* (Washington,

DC), December 17, 1900.

1902: "How Helen Keller Writes," published in *The Free Press* (Southern Pines, NC), March 14, 1902.

1903: "A Human Document: Helen Keller's Story of Her Life," published by *The Inter Ocean* (Chicago, Illinois), March 23, 1903.

1903: "My Future as I See It," The Ladies' Home Journal, Vol. XX, No. 12, November.

1904: "Helen Keller, Most Wonderful of Girls, Graduates from College Next Week," published in The Evening World (New York, NY), June 25, 1904.

1904: "Wonders of the Fair "Seen" and Described By Miss Helen Keller," published in *The St. Louis Republic* (St. Louis, MO), October 23, 1904.

1912: "Helen Keller, Deaf-Blind Wonder Would Like to be Socialist Orator," published in *The Farmer and Mechanic* (Raleigh, NC), June 25, 1912.

1913: "Helen Keller's Glowing Speech: Opens Her Novel Lecture Tour at Tremont Temple," published in *The Boston Globe* (Boston, Massachusetts), March 23, 1913.

1913: "Thinks Drinking Is A Result of Poverty," published in *The South Bend News-Times* (South Bend, IN), December 22, 1913.

1914: "Helen Keller, Blind, Sees Great Light That Will Purify The World," published in *The Day Book* (Chicago, IL), March 18, 1914.

1915: "At Home With Helen Keller," published in *The Arizona Republican* (Phoenix, AZ), March 7, 1915.

1916: "Helen Keller Would Be I.W.W.'s Joan of Arc," published in *The New-York Tribune* (New York, NY), January 16, 1916.

1916: "Wonderful Helen Keller Lectures In Greenwood," published in *The Commonwealth* (Greenwood, MS), March 24, 1916.

1916: "Did Helen Keller Really Hear Caruso?" published in *The Richmond Times-Dispatch* (Richmond, VA), May 14, 1916.

1916: "Helen Keller Gives Interview to Newspaperwoman," published in the Quad-City Times (Davenport, Iowa), January 12, 1916.

1920: "Launch New Organization to Protect Civil Rights," published in *The Richmond Times-Dispatch* (Richmond, VA), January 20, 1920.

1921: "Oppose All Injustice Helen Kellers Creed," published in *The Minneapolis Star* (Minneapolis, Minnesota), August 31, 1921. Speaking out after World war One:

1926: Into the Light, by Helen Keller: "More of Anne Sullivan." *Boston*

Daily Globe (September 29, 1926).

1930: "Helen Keller, at Fifty, Looks Forward to Years of Further Good Deeds," published in the *Star-Gazette* (Elmira, New York), June 27, 1930. This article celebrates Helen's 50th birthday.

1932: "Helen Keller's Tutor Gets Degree." *New York Times* (February 16, 1932).

1933: "The Liberator of Helen Keller," by Wilson, P.A. *New York Times* (October 1, 1933).

1933: "Great Teacher, Great Pupil: How Anne Sullivan, Herself Almost Blind, Opened Up the World For Helen Keller," by Ross, M. *New York Herald Tribune.* (October 1, 1933).

1933: "The Other Self of Helen Keller: An Irish Immigrant's Daughter Who Taught a Blind Girl To *See*," by Copinger, Irene May, published in *The Baltimore Sun*, November 19, 1933.

1936: "Mrs. Macy is Dead," published in *The New York Times* on October 21, 1936.

1937: "U.S. Celebrates Helen Keller's *Tribute Year*: Period Until March 3 Marks the 50th Anniversary of Her Meeting with Teacher." Published in the *New York Herald Tribune* October 18, 1937.

1938: "Schools, Churches Honor Helen Keller." Published in *The Chicago Defender (National Edition)* March 12, 1938.

1938: "The Blind See: The Dumb Speak," published in *The Age* (Melbourne, Victoria, Australia), March 5, 1938.

1938: "The Beauty I have Seen," by Helen Keller, published in the *Weekly Magazine of The Sunday Star*, Washington, D.C. April 10, 1938.

1955: "Helen Keller In Her Life," by Cornell, K., published in *Newsday* June 24, 1955.

1955: "Helen Keller, America's First Lady of Courage, Marks 75th Birthday," by Grover Brinkman, published in the *Palladium* (Richmond, Indiana), June 27, 1955.

1966: "Awards to Honor Helen Keller's Teacher." Published in *The Washington Post, Times Herald* March 16, 1966.

1968: The September 1968 issue of *The New Outlook for the Blind* was devoted to Helen Keller; it contains a biographical sketch by M. Robert Barnett.

1968: "Helen Keller Dies at Country Estate," published in *The Greenville News* (Greenville, South Carolina), June 2, 1968.

1980: "How Much of 'Helen Keller was Anne Sullivan." by Whitman, A. published in *Newsday* May 25, 1980.

1980: "How the Miracle Worked: Helen and Teacher," by Evans, W. K. E. published in *The Washington Post* June 15, 1980.

1987: "Making Pilgrimage to Helen Keller's Alabama Home," published in the *St. Louis Post-Dispatch* (St. Louis, Missouri), June 7, 1987.

2003: "How Helen Keller Learned to Write," by Cynthia Ozick, published in *The New Yorker Magazine*, June 16/23.

2004: "Helen Keller: Brief life of a woman who found her own way: 1880–1968," published in Harvard Magazine by Roger Shattuck. In the July/August edition.

INDEX

My dreams, my career and mission, were moved along because I got support from a Lions Club, 11D-1 in Mid-Michigan. These dedicated men and women helped to create the Special Needs Vision Clinic located in Bridgeport, Michigan at the Millet Learning Center, where I worked for over 30 years with blind children. I dedicate this book especially to these Lions Club members and I thank them from the depths of my heart for their past and ongoing contributions and dedication.

The Special Needs Vision Clinic has operated at the Millet Learning Center since the 1980s under the leadership—for most of those years—of Dr. Dolores Kowalski, who is both a pediatric optometrist and a low vision specialist. Therefore, this book is also dedicated to Dr. Dolores Kowalski for her expertise and her leadership as director of the Special Needs Vision Clinic.

Knights for the Blind in the Battle against Darkness is also dedicated to Lions Club members across the world for the non-stop devotion they have poured forth since the founding of Lions International in 1917. This book honors the work of this great civic organization.

The title of this book—*Knights for the Blind in the Battle against Darkness*—is paraphrased from a line that Helen Keller used in a speech in 1925. She told the assembled members of Lions International that they were "Knights of the Blind in this Crusade Against Darkness." This poetic line is vintage Helen Keller with its call to spiritual battle. I left Helen's exact words alone to stand untouched in history; however, the title of this book was inspired by her eloquence.

I also dedicate this work to the profession of orientation and mobility (O&M). Although I was trained initially as an optometrist—and deeply value the contributions of that profession—I spent my entire career as an O&M specialist in Michigan. For over thirty years, I taught blind children how to move through the world gracefully and efficiently. The profession of Orientation and Mobility was a paradigm shift for the field of blind rehabilitation when it was established after World War Two.

I was part of the first wave of O&M specialists to teach in the public schools in the United States—I came out of the university steeped in the philosophy that blind people could be independent and could navigate on their own without help from the sighted population. This book, the first in a series, is a gift to my O&M colleagues. My hope is that our fascinating profession will continue to evolve.

To my former students: Not everyone can become globally famous, like Helen Keller, but every life is a miracle, and every life is to be honored. Be who you are—that is miracle enough. Remember what Helen Keller told us: we are on Earth to serve others. When you are busy serving others, your struggles diminish. I also dedicate this book:

To all those individuals who are blind, deaf, and deaf-blind.

To all those individuals who have vision and/or hearing impairments.

To all those going blind or deaf and looking for a mission in life, and for a mentor.

ACKNOWLEDGMENTS

My friend and colleague Daniel Kish dialogued with me hours on end until I could no longer remember which insights came from his mind and which thoughts were originally mine. Daniel inspired this book series, and he is the featured Knight for the Blind in Volume Two.

My friend Karen Horwath—the PianoPoet—edited Daniel's unpublished autobiography and helped with the crafting and editing of this book series. I am deeply grateful for Karen's insights, skills, and friendship. This is the fifth book Karen has helped me craft. It is wonderful to realize that Karen has read my books and understands my theories; she has added valuable insights to my thoughts as they evolved.

I worked in special education my whole career in parallel with my wife Katherine Louise (Jones) Baldwin's career. Kathy (1946–2007) was a school psychologist in the same system where I spent my career; she was my anchor and go-to person in all arenas of life; she was brilliant and emotionally powerful, a wonderful mother and soulmate.

Kathy's family was deeply important to me for my entire adult life. Kath's sister Susan (Jones) Elkins and her husband Bob Elkins were instrumental in the forming of my ideas and philosophy; they were both child development specialists and special education consultants. Sue and Bob's insights were especially astute and helpful as my ideas evolved over several decades. We raised our children in parallel and remain best friends to this day.

Kathy's two brothers, Morgan (Eileen) and Rick (Danielle), became the brothers I never had. We grew up alongside each other; they influenced my passions and helped shape my personality. The Jones family melted into my essence—I am deeply blessed by their love, and I love them deeply.

My family (especially my sisters Barbara, Peggy, and Suzanne) and my close friends are my emotional foundation, the reason I embrace life and creativity. My three kids, Noah (Mandy), Tyler (Agatha), and Anna (Brad) are successful adults with fascinating and challenging lives. My grandkids, Jared and Althea are delightful and brilliant. I am a proud grandfather. I love my family with all my heart. My books are enabled because my life has been filled with Love.

Author Bio

Doug Baldwin is a retired special education teacher from Michigan. He has a doctoral degree in Optometry and a master's degree in Blind Rehabilitation. He is also the founder of two non-profit agencies established to help children in special education, *The Special Needs Vision Clinic*, and *The Institute for Innovative Blind Navigation*. Dr. Baldwin is the author of four previous books about the evolution of human consciousness. His ideas are based on dual-process theory, the concept that evolution engineered duality into the anatomy and physiology of bilateral creatures. Dr. Baldwin worked as an Orientation and Mobility teacher for thirty years for the Saginaw Public School system in Michigan before retirement in 2010. He continues to write and is now working on a multi-volume set of biographies called *Knights for the Blind in the Battle against Darkness*.

~

The artist who created the front and back covers for this book series, Terry LeBarr, enjoys drawing what she calls Personalized Typography Art. She created the typography design for the cover of *Helen Keller: A Timeline of Her Life*, and she did this image for my author pages. Digital publishing does not allow for color, so this is a black and white version of the original artwork. Here is Terry's explanation of my personalized typography:

The D
DOUG: You love bread, soups, and cheese. Music is also a big part of your soul, so I put your guitar and Bodhran next to your favorite foods.

You enjoy duality and write about this in your books, so I drew opposites like rain and sun, Tortoise and Hare, Yin and Yang. The Tibetan bell represents your interest in Eastern religious ideas, especially Buddhism. The entire D represents Winter, which you love (or why would you live in Michigan!) Each letter in your name represents a different season. At the base of the staff, part of the D, is a partial view of a woman's face. She is Scottish as is your ethnicity; she is showing you an eye by lowering her sunglasses. The eye and sunglasses symbolize your profession.

The O

As you move onto the O, you come across ants, which refer to your first book *Bugs, Blindness and the Pursuit of Happiness*. If you look behind the ants, you see a shovel and a plant coming up from the pile of dirt (I was told you love plants). Notice that the O is black and white (duality again). I mixed in green, representing new growth. The tulips and rain are symbolic of Spring. The tortoise (representing the evolution of consciousness) is creeping along while the Rabbit (representing technology) is still hanging out at the D.

The U

U is the heart of your name, representing Summer, sunshine, and water. The purple in the top of the U represents the loyalty you have towards the sight-impaired and special education. The dolphin is symbolic of wisdom; its playfulness reminds us to enjoy living in the moment with friends and family. The staff of the letter says *family*; family adventure has been instilled in your kids and grandkids. Next to the word family is a Luckenbooth, a Scottish symbol of romance. It has two hearts entwined and a crown above representing love and loyalty.

The G

At the base of the G, you see a suitcase and backpack, representing your love of travel and adventure. The images are meant to bring back memories of when you and Kathy traveled around the world as young hippies, and later, when you traveled with your kids. G depicts Fall and all the glorious colors that trigger poignant thoughts of days gone by. G holds a refreshing chill, meant to be deeply breathed in and savored. And there are clear night skies filled with stars. You will find the books you wrote at the base of the G. You will see the thoughts still hanging around them every time you notice them. Maddie [from *A Martyr for Mandelbrot*] is there, camera in hand. She is wearing her blond wig this time (she felt it was the best choice with the hat). Last, but not least is your cat Napoleon (Nappy), a treasured gift left by your daughter Anna when she went off on her own youthful adventures.

Other Books by Doug Baldwin
Bugs, Blindness, and the Pursuit of Happiness, 2016
Consciousness: A New Slant on an Old Conundrum, 2017
The Confusion Caused by Being Your Own Twin, 2018
A Martyr for Mandelbrot; Inside the Minds of God, 2019

www.ingramcontent.com/pod-product-compliance
Lightning Source LLC
Chambersburg PA
CBHW031423270326
41930CB00007B/549